# Development and Crisis of the Welfare State

# Development and Crisis of the Welfare State

*Parties and Policies in Global Markets*

Evelyne Huber and
John D. Stephens

THE UNIVERSITY OF CHICAGO PRESS
CHICAGO AND LONDON

The University of Chicago Press, Chicago 60637
The University of Chicago Press, Ltd., London
© 2001 by The University of Chicago
All rights reserved. Published 2001
Printed in the United States of America

10 09 08 07 06 05 04          2 3 4 5
ISBN: 0-226-35646-9 (cloth)
ISBN: 0-226-35647-7 (paper)

Library of Congress Cataloging-in-Publication Data

Huber, Evelyne.
    Development and crisis of the welfare state : parties and policies in
    global markets / Evelyne Huber and John D. Stephens.
        p.  cm.
    Includes bibliographical references and index.
    ISBN 0-226-35646-9 (cloth : alk. paper)—ISBN 0-226-35647-7 (pbk. : alk. paper)
    1. Welfare state—Cross-cultural studies. 2. Political parties—Cross-cultural studies.
    3. International economic relations. I. Stephens, John D., Ph.D. II. Title.

    JC479 .H83   2001
    361.6′5—dc21

                                    00-012178

In memory of Merlin G. Pope, Jr.

# CONTENTS

◆

# TABLES

◆

# PREFACE

◆

Writing this book has been a very long, at times difficult, but more often immensely interesting and rewarding undertaking. One of the reasons it took so long was that the very dynamics we were trying to understand kept changing. When we began our research, the Nordic economies and welfare states were still doing comparatively well, only to enter into a phase of deep crisis almost immediately thereafter. In Germany, optimism about unification was still high, only to give way shortly afterward to major tensions between the social partners, the government, and the Bundesbank, which ended in a significant induced recession. The Maastricht criteria had not yet taken effect but were to weigh heavily on the governments' room for maneuver in fiscal and monetary policy for most of the 1990s. Now, as we finish the writing, the Nordic economies have undergone a remarkable recovery, and the Nordic welfare states have been partially reformed but have proven remarkably resilient. Germany continues to struggle with the effects of unification and the need for reform of its welfare state regime. The introduction of the European Monetary Union continues to be a significant constraint on political choices and leaves many questions about the adaptation of production regimes and welfare state regimes to the new conditions unanswered. Alas, these questions will have to be the subject of future research; the present book offers an analysis of development, crisis, and adaptation of welfare state and production regimes up to the end of the twentieth century.

Another reason this book has been so long in the making is our decision to combine quantitative analysis of the universe of welfare states in advanced industrial societies with in-depth comparative historical study of nine welfare states and the production regimes in which they are embedded. Collecting and analyzing the case study materials for these nine cases and the statistical data for our eighteen cases proved a formidable task. We were able to accomplish it only due to the crucial support from many individuals and institutions in many countries. Acknowledging the specific ways in which each of them helped us would turn this preface into a rather lengthy chapter, so we shall express thanks in a more parsimonious fashion.

Originally, this project received support from the Center for Urban Affairs and Policy Research at Northwestern University and the National Science Foundation (grant SES 9108716). We then received support for field research in Sweden from the Swedish-American Bicentennial Exchange Fund and for research in Germany from the German Academic Exchange Service. The Swedish Institute in Stockholm did an absolutely wonderful job arranging interviews for us, and the Swedish Institute for Social Research at Stockholm University provided a stimulating academic home for us in the spring of 1992. The University of Konstanz offered the same in the fall of 1991. We then had the opportunity to spend the spring semester of 1995 in residence at the Swedish Collegium for the Advanced Study in the Social Sciences (SCASSS) in Uppsala and the academic year 1998–99 at the School of Social Science of the Institute for Advanced Study (IAS) in Princeton, New Jersey. Both of these stays were enormously valuable not only because of the time they offered us to do additional research and writing, but also because of the interaction with colleagues from very different backgrounds interested in similar issues. Additional support was provided for John Stephens by the German Marshall Fund of the United States. Finally, the Departments of Political Science at both Northwestern University and the University of North Carolina generously provided us with research leaves to pursue this project.

Many colleagues generously gave of their time and advice to help us in our research. Some provided guidance to the relevant studies and primary information in their countries or subject areas of expertise, others offered statistical advice, and still others shared with us data that they had collected. Particularly helpful in these ways were Thomas Cusack, Roland Czada, Gøsta Esping-Andersen, Alexander Hicks, Olli Kangas, Walter Korpi, Gerhard Lehmbruch, Michael MacKuen, Deborah Mitchell, John Myles, Joakim Palme, George Rabinowitz, Charles Ragin, Duane Swank, Kees van Kersbergen, Bruce Western, and Hans Zetterberg. Over the years, we presented our work in progress, jointly and individually, at many conferences and seminars, where we received valuable feedback. Some of the most enjoyable and valuable such occasions were the conferences of Research Committee 19 of the International Sociological Association in Vuoranta, Finland, in Bremen, Germany, in Canberra, Australia, and in Oxford, England. Other very productive seminars were those at SCASSS, the IAS, the Trade Union Research

Institute in Stockholm, the Institute for Social Research in Oslo, the State and Capitalism Seminar at Harvard University, and the Departments of Political Science at Northwestern University and the University of North Carolina.

Some of these same colleagues helped us in yet another way, together with many others, by offering insightful comments on various drafts of our work. We acknowledge a few of the most important suggestions in the places in the text where we make use of them; here we want to acknowledge the many other helpful critiques and suggestions that were offered to improve the final product. We wish to express our gratitude to Francis Castles, Robert Erikson, Gosta Esping-Andersen, Mauro Guillén, Peter Hall, Markus Haverland, Alexander Hicks, Torben Iversen, Olli Kangas, John Keeler, Desmond King, Herbert Kitschelt, Walter Korpi, Hanspeter Kriesi, Miriam Laugesen, Michael Mann, Philip Manow, Gary Marks, Rudolph Meidner, Lars Mjøset, Jonathon Moses, John Myles, Klaus Offe, Ann Orloff, Joakim Palme, Paul Pierson, Charles Ragin, Bo Rothstein, Dietrich Rueschemeyer, Diane Sainsbury, Herman Schwartz, Robin Stryker, Duane Swank, Kees van Kersbergen, Juhana Vartiainen, and Michael Wallerstein. We feel truly fortunate to have so many generous colleagues. Where we succeed in making our case well, we gladly share the credit; where we fall short in our efforts, we accept sole responsibility.

We dedicate this book to the memory of Merlin G. Pope, Jr. (1943–1998), former fellow graduate student, friend, and colleague. After graduate school, Merlin devoted his great talents as a social scientist to a highly successful career in applied social science, helping organizations to turn ethnic and gender diversity from an obstacle into an asset and thus helping the outsiders in these organizations, women and minorities, to realize their potential and advance their careers. Merlin was also a very generous and warm-hearted person who shared his success with friends and the wider community. He was beloved by all whom he touched. He left the world a better place.

*Chapel Hill, May 1, 2000*

# CHAPTER ONE

◆

# Introduction

As the title indicates, this book is about the development of welfare states in advanced industrial democracies in the first three postwar decades and the crisis these welfare states have faced in the past twenty years. The reference to parties in the subtitle indicates the central element of our argument. Based on extensive quantitative and comparative historical analysis, we show that partisan politics was the single most important factor that shaped the development of welfare states through time and accounts for the variation in welfare state outcomes across countries. More specifically, the dominant political coloring of the incumbent government—social democratic, Christian democratic, or secular center and right—over the three or four decades after the war is the most important determinant of the kind of welfare state that a given country had in the early 1980s; its generosity, the structure of its transfer payments, and the type and volume of services it offered. Of course, partisan political incumbency was strongly related to social structural features, most importantly the strength of organized labor and religious cleavages. The "global markets" phrase in the subtitle indicates the context of the political struggle. We argue that a given country's position in international markets influenced the kind of social policy regime it developed. Generous social policy regimes have to be embedded in production regimes that generate high investment levels and high employment rates. This was the case for the generous welfare states of Northern Europe that are the focus of this book. These were always export-dependent economies, and the kind of welfare state they developed had to be compatible with international competitiveness in order to maintain high investment and employment. We further argue that political choice remains important though much more constrained by the new more internationalized economic environment.

In our analysis of the crisis of the welfare state in the last two decades, we found that retrenchment was pervasive: Almost all advanced industrial democracies cut entitlements in some programs in this period.

1

However, in all but two countries, these cuts in entitlements were quite modest; the basic contours of the system of social protection remained intact. We found that the immediate cause of welfare state retrenchment was a large and apparently permanent increase in unemployment. With more people dependent on welfare state transfers and fewer people paying taxes to support the welfare state, budget deficits ballooned and governments moved to control and then reduce deficits by cutting entitlements. In this era, the effects of the political coloring of governments declined substantially as conservative governments were reluctant to cut popular welfare state programs and leftist governments found it difficult to raise taxes in times of economic difficulty. We found little support for the view that the cutbacks were caused by increasingly sharp trade competition in the new global economy, though we did find that the deregulation of financial markets increasingly constrained the policy options of governments faced with unemployment problems.

Given the complexity of social phenomena, it is hardly surprising that we found that factors other than partisan governance also influenced the development of the welfare state in industrial democracies. The most important of these was the structure of decision making resulting from constitutional provisions. Constitutions that create many "veto points" in the policy process (e.g., with strong bicameralism, presidentialism, federalism, and referenda) slowed the pace of policy change, whereas constitutions with few or no veto points (e.g., those with unicameralism, a parliamentary system, a unitary system, and no referenda) allowed for rapid policy change. In the era of welfare state expansion, governing systems with many veto points and thus a dispersion of power, for example, the United States and Switzerland, retarded welfare state expansion, while those with few veto points, such as the United Kingdom and Denmark, allowed for rapid expansion. In the retrenchment period, we found that only in systems with few veto points and conservative government and an additional constitutional feature—single-member district plurality elections (United Kingdom and New Zealand)—was dramatic retrenchment possible. By contrast, the multiple veto points provided by the Swiss constitution allowed the left to block the welfare state retrenchment planned by the government.

We found a more modest relationship between women's labor force participation and welfare state expansion. More important, we found a strong interactive effect of women's labor force participation and social democratic governance on the development of one aspect of welfare states, the expansion of public social services. Indeed, we argue that though the Nordic social democratic welfare states do have generous transfer systems, it is public delivery of a wide range of social services that is their most distinctive aspect. This was a product of an interactive process linking social democratic government, increases in women's labor force participation, women's political mobilization, and public social service expansion. Rising women's labor force participation fed demands for social services that both enabled women to enter the labor force and provided employment for them. Where social democratic parties were in government, they responded to these demands. This, in turn, led to increased mobilization among women and to increased support among women for the maintenance and expansion of welfare state services. Thus, the dynamic was a path-dependent feedback process.

Many recent works of comparative historical social science have argued that political developments frequently unfold in a path-dependent fashion. We did find this to be very true of welfare state development, and we identify four mechanisms that account for this path dependence. However, we did not find that welfare state development fit the strongest version of the path dependence argument, a "critical junctures" argument, in which countries develop a trajectory and a set of supporting institutional arrangements early in the postwar period that then lock in later welfare state development. Rather, we found that existing power relations, public opinion, policy configurations, and institutional arrangements limit what any sitting government can do, but that the governments do have a measure of political choice and that a sequence of governments with a political coloring different from that which had been dominant in the past can move a social protection system onto a new path.

## Outline of the Argument

In chapter 2, we outline our theoretical and methodological approach. We build on power constellations theory presented in our previous work with Rueschemeyer (Rueschemeyer, Stephens, and Stephens 1992).[1] The first constellation is the class power balance, which was the focus of the power resources approach to the explanation of variations in welfare state development.[2] The second constellation is the structure of the state and of state-society relations, and the third is the complex of relations in the international economy and system of states. According to power resources theory, the balance of class power is the primary determinant of variations through time and across countries in welfare state effort, particularly the distributive outcomes effected by social policy. Quantitative studies have measured the balance of class power by proportion of votes going to parties of the left, by left participation in government, by union density, or some combination of these. We have argued (Stephens 1979b; Huber, Ragin, and Stephens 1993; Huber and Stephens 1993a) that it is left or Christian democratic presence in government that is crucial for social policy development, and we continue to make that argument here. Our theory makes two important modifications to power resources theory: it incorporates the impact of state structures and of mobilization of women. In addition, we make a number of minor modifications to our theory as previously presented in order to adapt it to explaining welfare state development.

Our goal is to explain the long-term patterns of welfare state development: An adequate analysis of the Golden Age should be able to account for the long-term change within a country and for differences across countries at the end of the Golden Age, and an analysis of the retrenchment era should be able to do the same for that period. We argue that analyses of short-term change in either comparative historical or quantitative studies can lead to quite misleading conclusions about long-term change. Arguing that the determinants of long-term change are distinctive implies that the processes we are examining have an important element of path dependence in them. We make this argument explicit and propose four different mechanisms that link long-term partisan government to long-term change in social policy: structural limitation, ideological hegemony, the policy ratchet effect, and regime legacies.

In chapter 3, we turn to a quantitative analysis of the development of the welfare state. Our methodological discussion leads us to analyze determinants of the level of welfare state effort rather than annual change in welfare state effort. We analyze the determinants of eight different variables that measure various dimensions of welfare state effort in a pooled time series analysis and then cross-check and extend our analysis examining fourteen additional dependent variables in a cross-sectional analysis. Both the pooled analysis and the cross-sectional analysis show very powerful partisan effects across the various indicators, and they also show the expected varying effects of social democracy and Christian democracy across the indicators.

An additional political variable whose impact on welfare state development we explore is state structure, specifically the concentration or dispersion of political power resulting from constitutional provisions. We show that high dispersion of power, or the availability of multiple veto points, has very strong effects on welfare state development, slowing welfare state expansion. In addition, we include a gender variable among causes of welfare state expansion, namely women's labor force participation. We show that higher levels of women's labor force participation have both a direct effect on welfare state expansion through demands for better welfare state services, and an indirect effect in interaction with supportive allies in government.

In chapter 4, we examine the interrelationship between welfare state and production regimes. Our quantitative analysis in the previous chapter indicates that there is strong empirical evidence for Esping-Andersen's (1990) view that Christian democratic and social democratic governance both led to generous welfare states but different types of welfare states (see also Stephens 1979b: 123–24). Thus, we take his "three worlds" as our point of departure. To underline the political origins and the basically progressive thrust of the Continental European type, especially the Northern European variant, we rename his conservative-corporatist category "Christian democratic welfare states." Following Castles and Mitchell (1993), we distinguish an Antipodean category of wage earner welfare states, which deliver "social protection by other means." Our case study materials make it clear that welfare states are embedded in particular types of production regimes; that is, in different patterns of relationships between enterprises, banks, labor, and the government, accompanied by different policy patterns. We devote the remainder of the chapter to an exploration of the fit between production regimes and welfare state regimes in the Golden Age.

In chapter 5, we turn to an examination of these empirical associations in a comparative historical analysis. Following our methodological discussion and the approach we used in *Capitalist Development and Democracy,* we include a large number of cases and examine their development over long periods based on secondary materials. We select half of the advanced industrial democracies for in-depth analysis (four Nordic countries, three Northern Continental European countries, and Australia and New Zealand) and collected and analyzed materials on five more. Because Sweden has been considered prototypical of the social democratic welfare state and because it would appear to be the most vulnerable to the pressures of "globalization" given the exceptionally high level of multinationalization of Swedish business, we select Sweden for more intensive analysis of historic welfare state development and for primary research on the retrenchment period.

In the comparative historical analysis, we analyze the political struggles over the introduction and expansion of various types of welfare state programs, looking both at the power distribution among actors and the impact of political institutions on the decision-making process. Consistent with our methodological approach, we examine not only the narrative sequence of events as would a historian, but we also compare the cases over long periods using the analytical comparative historical method and employing counterfactual thinking to explore possible alternative explanations of the case trajectories. We also examine the production regimes that prevailed in this period, with a special focus on relationships among labor market and political actors and government policies designed to promote growth and full employment. Our comparative historical analysis provides powerful confirmation for the pivotal role of partisan government and constitutional structures in explaining the long-term outcome of welfare state development in the Golden Age, and it also shows the important role of women's mobilization, particularly in explaining the service heaviness and "women friendliness" (Hernes 1987) or gender egalitarian character of the Nordic welfare states.

In chapter 6, we begin our examination of welfare state development in the era of retrenchment, from the 1980s on, through the lens of statistical analysis. We find that the predominant pattern is a slowdown of expansion and then a stagnation; and finally pervasive but generally modest or at least not system-transforming cuts in entitlements. Only in Britain and New Zealand can one see large reductions, true system shifts, in the systems of social protection. However, a consistent result is the decline of partisan political effects; the agenda is by and large either defense or retrenchment of the welfare state. Expansion is off the agenda, with the exception of public social services and gender-egalitarian legislation in Scandinavia up to the early 1990s.

Our comparative historical analysis of the era of retrenchment in chapter 7 shows that welfare state retrenchment was primarily driven by unemployment. Higher levels of unemployment meant that more people were drawing on welfare state benefits and fewer people were paying contributions, which caused severe fiscal stress. Everywhere governments attempted to reduce expenditures, and in many places they also increased contributions. Typically, serious cutbacks in entitlements and expenditures followed increases in unemployment, and the cuts were deepest where unemployment was highest and persisted at high levels for long periods of time. In this situation of severe fiscal stress, the left was prevented from pursuing welfare state expansion, and the right was prevented from cutting welfare state expenditures radically by strong popular support for welfare state entitlements, which together produced the reduction of the partisan incumbency effect on welfare state generosity that we saw in the quantitative analysis.

State structure again had an important effect. Just as the availability of multiple veto points had slowed down welfare state expansion, so it now slowed down welfare state retrenchment. The only two cases where a real shift of welfare state regimes was imposed, Britain and New Zealand, were countries with constitutions that produced very high power concentration and made it possible for governments with minority support to push through unpopular changes.

We found that the impact of globalization was most significant in Australia and New Zealand, because these countries had historically heavily protected their economies. They had provided social protection through high wages and benefits delivered through the arbitration system, the costs for which could largely be passed on by employers to domestic consumers. As these countries opened their economies, import competition resulted in substantial increases in unemployment and also put downward pressure on wages. Our other cases had been highly integrated into international trade for a long time, and globalization mainly affected their ability to stimulate productive investments through the low interest rates and preferential credits for industrial investors that had been enabled by controlled financial markets. In the European context, of course, one needs to separate analytically European integration from globalization; the former process clearly has had an even more restrictive impact on full employment policies than the latter, as most kinds of subsidies of production have become illegal and the process of monetary integration has imposed a highly deflationary policy regime.

In our concluding reflections on chances for generous welfare states to adapt successfully to the new economic environment of lower growth and increased international movements of capital compared to the Golden Age, we emphasize the importance of active to passive ratios, that is, ratios of active labor force participants paying contributions to nonworking people who are entitled to benefits. Based on our comparative examination of the Northern Continental European and the Scandinavian welfare states, we argue that the latter are in a better position to adapt to the new economic environment mainly because they invest more in human capital and have higher labor force participation rates, particularly among women. We conclude our analysis with a number of suggestions for welfare state adaptation, such as more emphasis on active rather than passive labor market policies, expansion of public child and elderly care to facilitate higher women's labor force participation, provision of social protection for part-time work, greater flexibility in hiring and firing for small and medium-sized enterprises, and partial funding of pensions and other social transfers to increase the fiscal robustness of the systems and increase the savings rate in the national economy.

## Methodological Contributions

In our own past work on macro societal change, we have argued for the necessity of bringing comparative historical and quantitative work into a dialogue with one another. In *Capitalist Development and Democracy* (Rueschemeyer, Stephens, and Stephens 1992), we began with the purpose of reconciling the apparently contradictory findings of the two research traditions, which had largely ignored each other. We accepted the findings of the quantitative tradition but sought to provide a better theoretical explanation supported by a systematic comparative historical analysis of the universe of cases in regions where democracy had a significant history in the twentieth century: Western Europe, North and South America, Central America and the Caribbean, and the Antipodes.

The first methodological contribution of the present book is to demonstrate the benefits of actually bringing quantitative and comparative historical analyses into a systematic dialogue with one another in the context of a single work. We start with theory based on previous studies, subject the hypotheses to statistical analysis, identify robust patterns of association, and then examine historical evidence to establish causal sequences that explain these patterns. We provide historical evidence that is consistent with the robust statistical results and thus are able to show that these correlations are not spurious but represent actual causal relationships supported by historical narrative. By the same token, we are able to explain weak or absent statistical correlations with the lack of historical evidence that these factors played a role in shaping welfare states. The previous studies from which our theory is derived, of course, include both quantitative and comparative historical studies. We also utilize the analytic comparative historical method, further buttressed by our quantitative results, and the posing of counterfactuals to strengthen the argument for one cause over another in cases where there are ambiguities in the historical materials.[3]

Our second methodological contribution is to demonstrate that in both comparative historical and quantitative work analyses of short-term change and short-run events can be misleading indicators of the causes of long-term change (see chapter 2, 35–38; chapter 3, 57–62; chapter 5, 196–200; and chapter 8, 322–23). In the case of comparative historical work, we extend the arguments made in *Capitalist Development and Democracy* (32 ff.). To take the extreme, a single case study analyzing developments over a short period of time will privilege actors' choices and play down the structural constraints that limit the options of some actors and enable others because these constraints are constant within the case and over the period examined. As we expand the number of cases and widen the time horizon, we introduce more variability in structural constraints. For example, several studies have noted the lack of employer and conservative party opposition to much of social democratic social policy and even nominal support for a number of important initiatives in the Golden Age in Sweden and even more so Norway. But if one expands the comparative case frame and the time frame, one finds that such behavior on the part of these forces was limited to the period in which the social democratic parties and the associated labor movements were near hegemonic and their social policy initiatives in particular enjoyed broad popular support. Thus, the implication, indeed in some of these studies the explicit assertion, that the welfare state would have been little different in the absence of social democratic governance does not appear plausible. Bringing our quantitative analysis to bear on this question further underlines our point: We show very strong relationships between social democratic governance and a wide variety of indicators of the Nordic-style universalistic and comprehensive welfare state. The argument made in these studies implies that these relationships are spurious, which clearly strains credulity.

We argue that quantitative analyses that analyze short-run change, such as analyses of annual change in indicators of welfare state effort, are also subject to these same drawbacks. In addition, we contend that a number of specific properties of the quantitative analyses of short-term change, such as the assumption of uniform leads and lags and the sensitivity of the expenditure and revenue data to economic cycles, will lead to extremely misleading conclusions if extrapolated to long-term change (chapter 3, 74–78). For instance, we show that regressions with short-term change measures of dependent and independent variables are dominated by economic cycle variables that systematically depress political effects. If we extrapolate the political effects found in these regressions over longer periods, these extrapolated effects are much, much smaller than the effects we find in regressions with long-term measures, and they are unable to explain the increasing divergence of welfare states over time.

### Theoretical Contributions

This book supports, amends, enriches, and specifies the power resources school in welfare state studies and the categorization of welfare states into different types. It supports the power resources school by providing systematic statistical and comparative historical evidence for the importance of the strength of labor movements and affiliated parties in building generous, universalistic, and redistributive welfare states. It also supports a previously suggested amendment to the class-based version of the power resources school that claims that mobilization through multi-class parties based on religious appeals leads to generous welfare states, albeit of a less redistributive nature (van Kersbergen 1995). It further elaborates this amendment by suggesting that religion-based mobilization is more likely to produce a generous welfare state if it is in competition with class-based mobilization. It amends and enriches the power resources school by incorporating gender as a basis for mobilization. It shows that greater participation by women in the labor force facilitates women's mobilization and the effective pursuit of demands for better welfare state services. It further shows that these demands are translated into policy most effectively where gender-based is supported by class-based mobilization, that is, where women find allies in social democratic governments.

We specify the power resources approach in that we emphasize the importance of the long-term partisan composition of government in explaining variations across countries and through time. Countries with strong left parties and strong unions but with infrequent periods of left government, such as Australia and New Zealand from 1950 to 1972, did not develop generous welfare states. This long-term relationship between left government and social policy development has a strong element of path dependence. In order to give the reader a preview of our argument, let us briefly outline how we see the operation of one mechanism, the policy ratchet effect, which specifies how this path dependence operates. In the period of welfare state expansion, it was rare for secular conservative parties to roll back welfare state reforms instituted by social democratic or Christian democratic parties. Indeed they generally accepted each new reform after it had been instituted. The reason for the change in posture of the conservative parties was that the reforms were popular with the mass public. The new center of gravity of the policy agenda became defined by the innovations introduced by the progressive forces in society.

Our analysis led us to attribute secondary roles to two other hypothesized specifications of the path-dependent operation of the balance of power resources. The first is the social democratic corporatism thesis advanced by Hicks (1999) and Swank (1999, forthcoming). In this view, strong and centralized unions and strong social democratic parties laid the ground for the development of tripartite bargaining between highly centralized unions and employers federations on broad ranges of social and economic policy relatively early in the postwar period, and these social democratic corporatist institutions put the countries on a track that led to the development of the social democratic welfare state. Once on this track, changes in the composition of government mattered little. As we point out above, this is a "critical junctures" argument, a very strong version of path dependence. While we do not dismiss the role of tripartism in policy innovation, we found that major social policy initiatives never emerged from corporatist bargains during periods of government by the secular center and right.

An alternative path-dependent specification is the argument that the strong social democratic labor movements developed ideological hegemony in society and so thoroughly dominated public opinion formation on social policy that the only way for a bourgeois coalition to win elections was to adopt social democratic policies. This is our ideological hegemony mechanism and we do find instances of bourgeois governments passing policy that had been put on the agenda by labor, such as the Norwegian supplementary pension plan in the mid-1960s. However, we do not find cases of sustained innovation with the social democratic labor movement being able to define the agenda and force policy choices on a series of consecutive bourgeois governments.

Our study demonstrates the usefulness of treating welfare states as distinctive types. It modifies Esping-Andersen's (1990) typology by adding the category of wage earner welfare states and by reconceptualizing his conservative-corporatist as a Christian democratic type, based on its political underpinnings, parallel to the social democratic and liberal type. It enriches the typology by putting more emphasis on the public provision of welfare state services and on gender-egalitarian policies as distinctive features of the social democratic welfare state.

In this book we side with those in the political-institutional school of welfare state studies who emphasize the importance of state structure rather than that of state bureaucrats as autonomous agents. We offer a transparent measure of state structure and show that it has a very consistent and strong effect on welfare state expansion. Moreover, we show that state structure is relevant not only for welfare state expansion but also for retrenchment. Dispersion of political power offers veto points that slow down the construction of generous welfare states, but these same veto points also slow down welfare state retrenchment. Thus, we also make a contribution to the theoretical debate about retrenchment.

An additional theoretical contribution is our insistence on the connection between welfare state and production regimes. We build on previous studies of the link between labor market institutions and welfare states, and we add a strong emphasis on institutions and policies responsible for stimulating productive investments and industrial adaptation. We argue that patterns of relationships among enterprises, banks, labor, and the government that favor the provision of capital to enterprises on preferential terms, that provide for training and retraining of a highly qualified labor force, that support efforts in R&D, and that facilitate wage restraint are the essential infrastructure on which generous welfare states can be built and sustained. They enable countries to occupy a high-skill-high-wage position in the international economy and thus to provide a high social wage along with a high money wage.

Our emphasis on production regimes establishes a clear connection to the impact of the international economy on the construction and maintenance of welfare states. Whereas we are skeptical about the view that high trade integration per se generates generous welfare states, as some studies have suggested based on statistical correlations, we do agree that the impact of the international economy on welfare states has been substantial, and therefore we argue that the relationship to the international economy has to be integrated systematically into the study of welfare states. Our theoretical contribution is to insist that the impact of the international economy has to be seen in both its economic and its political dimensions. For instance, we would formulate the relationship between high trade integration and generous welfare states as follows. High dependence on export competitiveness requires some mechanism for keeping wage costs under control, and where labor is strong this mechanism needs to produce policies that compensate labor in some way for wage restraint. Welfare state benefits financed out of general revenue rather than through payroll taxes are one possible compensation. Thus, strong labor movements have been able to turn support for international competitiveness into welfare state entitlements.

Since the 1980s, different dimensions of globalization have weakened both the economic and the political bases of generous welfare states. The deregulation of international capital flows and of national capital markets, which are integral elements of the phenomenon of globalization, have had a significant impact on production regimes. Most importantly, they have eroded some of the traditional institutions and policies that allowed countries to keep interest rates below world market rates and to provide investment capital on preferential terms to business enterprises, and thus they have contributed to lower investment rates. Insofar as high investment rates were an essential component of full employment–generous welfare state policy configurations, globalization has made the maintenance of this configuration more difficult. Another dimension of globalization, the internationalization of production, has altered the political power balances underpinning generous welfare states. The growth in transnational production networks has made capital exit easier and thus given capital more leverage vis-à-vis both labor and governments.

Finally, we would like to draw out the implications of our findings for theories of the state. Since power constellation theory—and also power resources theory—represents an alternative to pluralist and orthodox Marxist theories of the state, our empirical support for these theories also provides support for the validity of their alternative views of the state. Our arguments and evidence contradict the pluralist view of state policy as a result of the free interplay of different interests on a level playing field, without systematic advantages for some interests, i.e., capital, over others. They also contradict the orthodox Marxist view of state policy as a result of capitalist interests alone. Rather, they suggest that state policy is a result of power relations in society, mediated by political institutions. Power relations in society in turn are shaped by the constellation of capital interests on the one hand and the constellation of popular organizations, specifically the organization of subordinate classes and the subordinate gender, on the other hand, and by the political articulation of these organizations. Variations in these power relations over time and across countries account for variations in state policy, particularly the distributive impact of state policy. Capitalist interests have a systematic advantage as they depend much less on organization for their articulation than popular interests. This advantage has been aggravated by globalization, as capital has become increasingly multinational, whereas government and popular organizations have remained largely confined to the national level.

◆

## CHAPTER TWO

# Theoretical Framework and Methodological Approach

In this chapter, we briefly present the main theoretical approaches to the explanation of welfare state development in advanced capitalist democracies and then elaborate our own theory, based on our previous works on the development of democracy and on social reform in developed capitalist democracies and the developing countries of Latin America and the Caribbean. We conclude with a discussion of the methodological strategy of the research. We set as our theoretical task the goal of explaining long-term change within countries and the patterns of outcomes across countries. The period under study can be conveniently divided into the period of expansion beginning with the end of World War II and ending when the country in question hits a serious unemployment crisis that occurs between the late 1970s and the late 1980s depending on the country, and the period of retrenchment from that point to the present. Thus, concretely, to meet our criterion of theoretical adequacy, a theory must provide clear hypotheses about the direction of change and the patterns across countries within these periods. To meet our criteria of empirical adequacy, a theory must be empirically corroborated by the quantitative or comparative historical evidence, and it cannot be contradicted by either one.

## Theoretical Framework

### *Review of Main Theories*

The debate of the past quarter century about determinants of welfare state development has been carried out between proponents of three different theoretical approaches, the "logic of industrialism," "state-centric," and "political class struggle" approaches. More recently, feminist scholars have made important contributions to the debate, moving from early critiques of the welfare state as reinforcing patriarchy to more nuanced assessments of the differential effects of different welfare state regimes on the status of women and of the role of women as actors in welfare state development. We begin with a brief exposition of the three theoretical schools and the feminist contributions, as well as several other hypotheses about welfare state expansion and retrenchment that do not lend themselves to easy classification.

According to the "logic of industrialism" explanation, both the growth of the welfare state and cross-national differences in "welfare state effort" are by-products of economic development and its demographic and social organizational consequences (Wilensky 1975; Pampel and Williamson 1989). Those insisting on a "state-centric" approach have focused on the policy-making role of bureaucrats, who are assumed to be relatively autonomous from social forces, on the capacity of the state apparatus to implement welfare state programs, on the effects of state structure (e.g., federalism), and on the influence of past policy on new social policy initiatives (Heclo 1974; Orloff 1993a; Weir, Orloff, and Skocpol 1988; Skocpol 1988). Finally, the proponents of a "political class struggle" or "power resources" approach identify the distribution of organizational power between labor organizations and left parties on the one hand and center and right-wing political forces on the other hand as primary determinants of differences in the size and distributive impact of the welfare state across countries and over time (Stephens 1979b; Korpi 1983; Korpi 1989; Esping-Andersen 1985, 1990; Hicks and Swank 1984).

There are three other lines of argument in the literature about the expansion of and cross-national differences in the aggregate size of welfare states that cannot really be classified as theoretical schools, as they focus on one particular causal dynamic and are compatible to various degrees with the logic of industrialism and the power resources approach. The first holds that economic openness causes domestic vulnerability to external fluctuations and thus provides the incentive for the establishment of social safety nets for those affected by such external trends or cycles (Cameron 1978; Katzenstein 1985). Since smaller countries tend to be more open to international trade than larger ones, they are more likely to develop comprehensive systems of social protection as compensation for the victims of industrial adjustment. Recent contributions to the retrenchment literature turn this thesis on its head as they argue that increasing openness of financial as well as goods markets leads to cuts in the generosity of social policy, particularly in the most advanced welfare states (see chapters 6 and 7).

The second line of argument focuses on the institutional underpinnings of generous welfare states and holds that corporatist institutions are conducive to welfare state expansion. Corporatist institutions are understood as institutionalized consultation and bargaining between the state and encompassing and centralized representative organizations of labor and capital. One view sees corporatism also as a response to external economic vulnerability and thus as more likely to occur in small than in large countries (Katzenstein 1985); another view sees corporatism as a result of the strength of labor and the need of both employers and the government to come to accommodations with the labor movement, which enables the latter to extract concessions in social policy in exchange for wage restraint (Stephens 1979b; Western 1991). Yet a third view sees corporatism as an outcome of Christian democratic and social democratic governmental power (Wilensky forthcoming).

A third line of argument is that the strength of political Catholicism has led to the development of generous welfare states, though, until recently, there was no attempt to set this in a clear theoretical frame. Stephens (1979b: 100, 123–24) argues that political Catholicism leads to welfare states almost as generous but less redistributive than those developed under social democratic auspices. Wilensky (1981) presents cross-national data showing that Christian democratic cabinet share is the most important determinant of his measure of social spending. Based on a variety of indicators of welfare state patterns, Esping-Andersen (1990) argues for the existence of a distinctive type of "conservative" though generous welfare state regimes created largely by European Continental Christian democratic parties. Van Kersbergen (1995) provides a quantitative and an in-depth case study analysis and a power resources interpretation for the development of the Christian democratic welfare state.[1]

The contributions to the welfare state literature from a feminist perspective have mostly focused on the consequences of the welfare state for women's material position and for gender relations more broadly. From an early critique of the welfare state as reinforcing patriarchy (women's subordination to men), feminist scholars have turned their attention to variations across countries, across programs, and over time in the effect of welfare states on the status of women.[2] Recently, a number of interesting studies have investigated the extent to which the welfare state typologies developed in the mainstream literature correspond to clusters of welfare states with similar gender implications (e.g., see Lewis 1992; Hobson 1994; Sainsbury 1999b; Orloff 1997). Until the early 1990s, studies that have looked at gender and specifically women's political actions as causal factors in the development of welfare states were studies of the early formation of welfare state programs and typically focused on one or two cases in isolation rather than being systematically comparative (e.g., Jenson 1986; Koven and Michel 1993; Pedersen 1993; Skocpol 1992; Lewis 1994). Comparative studies of the role of women as active promoters of gender interests in shaping welfare states in the post–World War II era were rare, Ruggie's (1984) study of Sweden and Britain being a notable exception. Since the mid-1990s, there has been a proliferation of work on the role of women's movements in shaping the welfare state (e.g., see Bergquist 1998; Hill and Tigges 1995; Hobson and Lindholm 1997; Jenson and Mahon 1993; Lewis 1994; Lewis and Åström 1992; O'Connor, Orloff, and Shaver 1999; Sörensen 1999; and Stetson and Mazur 1995). Virtually all of these studies confirm that women, acting as independent women's movements, within established political parties, particularly leftist parties, and within state agencies, have been important actors promoting what Hernes (1987) calls women-friendly policies but that they were successful only when they had allies.

## *Our Theoretical Framework*

The theoretical framework that guides our analysis in what follows is an extension of our framework developed in our earlier work on social reform (Stephens 1979b; Stephens 1980; Stephens and Stephens 1982, 1986; Huber, Ragin, and Stephens 1993) and democracy (Rueschemeyer, Stephens, and Stephens 1992; Huber, Rueschemeyer, and Stephens 1997). For the purposes of the analysis of welfare states here, though we draw on some elements from all of the theoretical schools reviewed above, our approach is most closely related to the class struggle–power resource mobilization school and the feminist critique.[3] At the core of our theory is the class-analytic frame of the power resources theory: The struggle over welfare states is a struggle over distribution, and thus the organizational power of those standing to benefit from redistribution, the working and lower middle classes, is crucial. It matters, of course, how this organizational power is politically articulated, and political parties perform the crucial mediating role.

Our conceptualization of class is based on Elster's (1985: 330–31) definition of a class as "a group of people who by virtue of what they possess are compelled to engage in the same activities if they want to make the best use of their endowments." Endowments include tangible property, intangible skills and more subtle cultural traits, and the activities are related to the process of production. To delineate the class structure we add Weber's (1968) and Giddens's (1973) boundary criteria of mobility closure and interaction closure.[4] On the basis of this conceptualization, we distinguish the following classes in advanced industrial societies in the second half of the twentieth century: the bourgeoisie proper (owners of capital who employ large numbers of workers), the petty bourgeoisie (owners of small and medium enterprises), the upper middle class of professionals and managerial employees, the lower middle class of nonmanual employees, the working class of manual employees, and the farmers. In order for classes to become collective actors in modern democratic polities, there need to be organizations that articulate class interests and mobilize members into political action. This holds true for all social classes, though not necessarily to the same extent. The bourgeoisie clearly occupies a privileged position and has multiple avenues of access to influence political outcomes,[5] but at least where it confronts a well-organized working class, it will also resort to forming official employers' organizations and supporting one or more political parties to represent its interests. For the upper middle class, professional organizations are central for the representation of specific interests of class segments, and political parties for more general interests. In our study, professional organizations play an important role as pressure groups for both welfare state benefits and the protection of professional interests of welfare state service providers. For the lower middle class and the working class, unions and affiliated parties and auxiliary organizations are the key actors articulating and defending collective interests. In the case of farmers, farmers' organizations and again political parties play this role. In systems with proportional representation, there frequently are specific parties representing the interests of different classes, but even in two- and three-party systems where there is necessarily a greater degree of aggregation of interests, parties differ in their orientation toward the defense of lower middle class and working-class interests.

Our conceptualization of classes here excludes people without connection to the process of production. In the early post–World War II period these were mostly married women, and our discussion of gender and women's mobilization includes them as objects of welfare state policy and as actors in shaping the welfare state. Since the late 1970s, the group of long-term unemployed, mostly people with low skills, has grown and has come to constitute what is referred to as an underclass. This group has become an important target of welfare state policy, particularly of different versions of workfare. However, precisely because it lacks skills and connection to the process of production, it also lacks organization and power and thus is acted upon rather than being an actor in shaping the welfare state.

Class interests are not the only interests, of course, that can be the basis for collective action and political mobilization. Religious and ethnic divisions are relevant insofar as they form the basis for organizations that may reinforce but more typically divide the constituency of class-based organizations. Unions in ethnically or religiously divided societies tend to be weaker and more fragmented than in homogeneous societies. The same is true for working-class parties, as parties based on religious appeals compete with them for working-class support. Catholicism as a basis for organization and political action, in the form of Christian democratic parties and Catholic labor unions, in fact has played a very important role in shaping welfare states. Given the cross-class base of support of Christian democratic parties, and their political project of social integration, class compromise, and political mediation (van Kersbergen 1995: 28), their programs tend to cater to the interests of workers to some extent, but in a more fragmented and clientelistic than universalistic way. Their middle- and upper-class base makes them reluctant to impose high taxes to finance generous social policies. Their belief in the principle of subsidiarity, that is, the principle that the smallest social unit capable of taking care of its members should do so (family, congregation, local community, and the state only as a last resort or ultimate guarantor), leads them to decentralize and fragment responsibility for social programs (van Kersbergen 1995). Competition with strong working-class parties, though, pushes Christian democratic parties to support more generous, interventionist, and universalistic social policies than they would advocate on their own, or than secular center and right-wing parties would be prepared to support.

Gender has become an important basis for organization in advanced industrial democracies, particularly in the last three decades. The expansion of women's labor force participation has been an important factor favoring women's mobilization. Women's movements have become important advocates of women's political, economic, and social rights on their own, and they have been particularly effective where they managed to work with and through political parties. Just as for class-based organizations, it matters very much how women's organizations articulate with other organizations, most prominently political parties. Ultimately, to achieve lasting change in the status of women, legislation is a necessary (though not sufficient) condition, and in the established democracies of advanced industrial societies political parties are the key agents of legislation.[6] We argue that women's interests have been served best where women were highly mobilized, primarily in the social democratic party–affiliated women's movements but also through autonomous women's organizations, and where these social democratic parties were in power and thus in a position to pass gender-egalitarian legislation (Huber and Stephens 2000a; also see Stetson and Mazur 1995 and O'Connor, Orloff, and Shaver 1999).

Since political parties play crucial roles in welfare state development, not only is the nature of individual parties important, but so are the dynamics in the party system as a whole. The coalitions that the proponents of generous welfare state policies can build, as well as the nature of the opposition, are important. Fragmented oppositions leave more room for welfare state expansion and are less effective advocates of retrenchment (Castles 1978). Competition between left and centrist parties pushes centrist parties to adopt more generous welfare state legislation, particularly if the centrist parties compete for working-class support, as in the case of Christian democratic parties.

It is the role we attribute to political parties that makes our argument about working-class organization distinctive from other versions of the power resources approach. In this approach, differences among welfare states and changes in welfare states through time are seen as products of differences in and changes in working-class organization. In the quantitative studies, working-class organization is often measured as a combination of some of the following: votes for left parties, left seats in parliament, left shares in cabinet, union density, and union centralization (e.g., Korpi 1989; Palme 1990; Garrett 1998). In our past work, we have attempted to decompose such indices into their component items. It appears to us important to know, for instance, whether left presence in the government is crucial for policy development, or whether left sentiments in society and strong union organization are sufficient. In our previous quantitative analyses, we have consistently found that the long-run partisan character of government is a much better predictor of welfare state generosity than left votes, left seats, or union organization (Stephens 1979b; Huber, Ragin, and Stephens 1993). In our more recent work, we also have shown that the differences between Christian democratic, social democratic, and liberal welfare states are best predicted by which of these three party families (or combinations thereof) are in the government of a given country *over the long run* (Huber, Ragin, and Stephens 1993; Huber and Stephens 2000a). Fully developing our argument requires that we develop our view of preference formation, which we undertake at the end of this section.

As reviewed above, one variant of the state-centric theoretical framework in comparative welfare state studies postulates a strong role for state bureaucrats in social policy innovation, ascribing to them responsibility for the design of major programs and for getting these designs accepted by governments (e.g., see Heclo 1974; Orloff 1993b; Weir, Orloff, and Skocpol 1988). There is no question that the actual text of much social policy legislation was written by bureaucrats. Nevertheless, we are quite skeptical about the power of this theory in explaining long-term change within countries and the patterning of policy across countries for several reasons. First, the theory presents no hypothesis as to the direction in which bureaucrats should push policy. While the general assumption of most of these authors is that it will be in an expansive direction, treasury and finance department bureaucrats have often been found to be profoundly conservative in their policy orientations (Weir and Skocpol 1985; Cronin 1991; Schwartz 1994a). Second, structural conditions (the class power balance, partisan composition of the government, and state structures) profoundly limit the range of policies that bureaucrats are able to suggest. And as Stryker (1989) shows, when bureaucrats consistently suggest policies that are outside the parameters set by structural conditions, they are ignored and, if they persist, they may lose their positions.

The strength of the recent literature on state feminism or the influence of "femocrats" is precisely that it recognizes these limitations (Stetson and Mazur 1995; O'Connor, Orloff, and Shaver 1999). First, in advanced industrial democracies the femocrats have been overwhelmingly progressive, so this literature presents a clear hypothesis about the direction of change in which the femocrats will push legislation if they have influence. Second, these authors argue that the femocrats' effectiveness is dependent on the strength of the women's movement within and outside of the social democratic party and the presence of the social democrats in government. Thus, the independent influence attributed to the femocrats is significant but modest. In sum, while we do not in principle reject the idea that bureaucrats may have some independent influence over state policy, we argue that variations in the policy-making activity of bureaucrats cannot account for the long-term changes in social policy and the very large differences in policy and policy outcomes across countries documented in chapters 3 and 4.[7]

A second line of argument in the state-centric approach to welfare state development emphasizes the influence of policy legacies on subsequent legislation. While no serious student of social policy development can deny that current policies are almost always in part a positive or negative reaction to past policies, the literature on welfare state expansion is not completely clear on the direction in which past policies are likely to influence future developments. The one definite hypothesis is that policies create political constituencies for their defense, the beneficiaries of the policies, and thus we should expect resistance to cutbacks. For the politics of retrenchment this is an important and powerful hypothesis (Pierson 1996). For the period of expansion the hypothesis mainly states that organizational forms of welfare states have a certain inertia. For instance, after World War II the groups that had held privileged positions in the previously existing fragmented pension and health programs pushed for a reestablishment of these programs and opposed the plans for unified social insurance in Germany and the Netherlands. However, in both countries plans for unified social insurance came close to being adopted, and had the social democratic forces that were supporting these plans held political power, they would have become the new organizational form (chapter 5). Thus, the policy legacies argument has to be supplemented with a power constellation hypothesis to account for the outcome. This is confirmed if we look at subsequent developments in which rules and benefits under the different programs became increasingly uniform, as a result of strong pressures from the union movement and the social democratic parties. Later in this chapter, we suggest an additional hypothesis that includes policy legacies in an explanation of the patterns observed in the analyses in chapters 3 and 4. Our solution admits an independent effect of policy but links it to the development of particular policy regimes that themselves are political creations. Thus, the effect of policy legacies is interactive with partisan regime and helps explain why welfare state types tend to get more distinctive through time, at least up to the end of the period of expansion.

We agree with the third line of argument in the state-centric literature, the impact of state structure on social policy development. The observation that constitutional features such as strong federalism have a retarding effect on social policy is commonplace in this literature. Our own thinking was influenced by Immergut (1992), who argues that the existence of "veto points" in the policy process (e.g., second chambers, presidency, etc.) will slow social policy expansion. In this view, comprehensive welfare state legislation necessarily affects the interests of a wide variety of groups, some in positive and some in negative ways. The more opportunities that political institutions offer to those whose interests are affected negatively for mobilizing opposition, extracting concessions, or blocking the legislation altogether, the less likely it is for comprehensive programs to be implemented. Conversely, the more that political institutions concentrate power, the higher are the chances that narrow parliamentary majorities can bring about major policy innovations. A similar logic holds for welfare state cutbacks; a dispersion of political power enables potential losers to mobilize opposition and effectively resist cuts, whereas a concentration of political power enables governments to implement cutbacks despite widespread political opposition.[8]

The international economy is relevant for understanding welfare state formation and retrenchment both directly and via its impact on the production regimes in which welfare states are embedded. We adopt the basic distinction between flexibly coordinated and uncoordinated, deregulated, or liberal market economies developed by Soskice (1991) and apply these labels to production regimes, that is, economies with specific patterns of relations between enterprises, financial institutions, labor, and the government, and specific constellations of labor market and economic policies.[9] Essentially, in coordinated production regimes relationships among economic actors and between them and political actors are built on a basis of mutual cooperation, typically with a high degree of institutionalization, whereas in liberal production regimes they are based on arms-length, market-determined transactions. Coordinated production regimes are characterized by higher degrees of organization on the part of capital and labor, by higher contract coverage, and by some degree of coordination of wage setting. Coordination of wage setting is essential for those coordinated market economies to function successfully under conditions of openness to trade, conditions under which these production regimes and corresponding welfare states were constructed. Our central argument, which we develop in chapter 4, is that there must be a mutually enabling fit between essential aspects of welfare state programs and the production regimes in which they are embedded. Therefore, as international economic conditions change, national production regimes are affected and in turn may stimulate adaptations of welfare state regimes. For instance, the internationalization of financial markets and European integration have made it much more difficult for governments to promote investment through interest rate manipulation or tax subsidies, which in turn may stimulate a search for new models of funded social security schemes designed to increase national savings.

The international economy influences welfare state formation and retrenchment both in structural and conjunctural respects. International expansion provides positive growth impulses and shapes positive perceptions of economic room of maneuver in the welfare state area, based on expected tax revenue. International shocks and regional crises shape opposite perceptions. Structurally, successful integration into competitive

world markets allows for higher money wages and social wages, but initial integration after periods of relative closure leads to dislocations and
declines in tax revenue and thus leaves less room for welfare state expenditure. As noted above, some authors have proposed that a high degree
of integration into world markets, or economic openness, causes the
emergence of domestic coping mechanisms in the form of corporatist
arrangements and generous welfare state programs (Cameron 1978;
Katzenstein 1985). In our view, openness is a necessary but not sufficient
condition for the development of tripartite corporatist bargains; corporatist arrangements emerge only when unions are strong and the social
democratic party is a frequent participant in government either alone or
in coalition with other parties (Stephens 1979b: 121–22).[10]

The retrenchment literature hypothesizes the opposite effect of increasing openness to financial as well as trade flows. In the neoliberal
view, increased openness exposes generous welfare states to trade competition and permits capital to move to the lowest-cost producer and thus
produces pressure for generous welfare states to cut entitlements in order to cut wage costs. Since the literature on corporatism, particularly
Katzenstein's (1985) contribution, made it abundantly clear that the corporatist countries were among the most open in the world in terms of
trade barriers and trade flows and competed quite effectively under these
conditions, the neoliberal view on trade liberalization would appear to be
implausible. On the other hand, from our power constellation perspective, it is plausible to hypothesize that financial liberalization and increased financial flows might cause retrenchment because immobile labor will be weakened vis-à-vis capital as capital becomes increasingly
mobile. The details of our view on this matter emerge in the process of
our analysis of retrenchment in chapters 6 and 7.

Adopting a class analytic frame as the core of our explanatory theory
does not mean that we claim to be able to read off individuals' or classes'
political behavior from their class (or gender) position. As we argued in
*Capitalist Development and Democracy* (Rueschemeyer, Stephens, and
Stephens 1992: 53), "[C]lasses may indeed have *objective* interests, but in
historical reality class interests are inevitably subject to *social construction*" [italics in original]. Only organization leads to the formation and
expression of collective interests, and this expression may take different
forms for groups in similar locations due to particular historical constellations. For instance, different segments of the working class may find
their interests articulated at different points in time and in different countries through social democratic, anarchist, communist, Christian democratic, personalistic populist, or even conservative parties, depending on

the cleavage structure of the society and the pattern of political mobilization. Part of this variation in interest articulation is structurally determined, and part of it is historically and ideologically determined. Let us begin with structural determination if only because it is the less controversial of the two.

A good example of the structural determination of the articulation of class interests is the literature on centralized bargaining. A central theme in this literature, commonplace since Olson (1982), but dating at least back to Headey (1970; also see Stephens 1979b: 122 ff.) is that since centralized trade union movements de facto represent the whole working class, they are much more likely to enter into agreements that trade wage restraint for lower levels of unemployment and social policy innovation, while in decentralized movements, unions represent only their narrow constituency of members and are unlikely to sacrifice their members' wage gains in the interests of a broader collectivity. As we have pointed out, this difference in interest articulation between centralized and decentralized unions goes far beyond wage bargaining. Let us quote at length from our contrast of Sweden and the U.K., as this passage takes us seamlessly into our next, and more controversial, point (Stephens 1979b: 142):

> Centralisation also affects the degree and character of politicisation of trade unions. Centralised trade union movements are more likely to take a more leftist class-wide perspective rather than a narrow group-interest view. They are more likely to become and remain committed to political action. And they have the resources to translate this leftist politicised orientation into action. The well-known differences between craft and industrial unions are only a special case of this general principle. To exaggerate the differences between Britain and Sweden a little, let us compare the point of view of the officials at the centres of power in the two movements, the local official in Britain and the head of LO. To best further the interests of his constituency, which is the whole working class, the Swedish leader will contribute to the financing of the Social Democratic Party and of Social Democratic newspapers. He will promote a policy of wage solidarity and will be willing to consider wage policy as one part of a total package to promote the interests of the working class. For the British local official, none of this will be done if he attempts to promote his constituents' interests in the most rational way. The immediate returns he would get for setting up a newspaper or even contributing to the Labour Party would not justify the outlay. A solidaristic wage policy makes no sense from the point of view of the British official whether he is in an unprofitable or profitable firm. In one

case his members will be without a job and in the other, they will end up
with lower wages. And in the case of the official in a craft union, the
pressure towards narrow group egoism is even greater. From the point
of view of the general secretary of the TUC, supporting newspapers and
the like may be rational, but he lacks the power and the resources to
carry out this policy.

A central argument in the quoted passage is that union leaders will
not only articulate interests in different ways, they will spend different
amounts of resources on broader political agendas and opinion formation. In fact, the Swedish LO (Landsorganisationen, manual workers'
central union organization) did do this and the British TUC (Trades
Union Congress, central union organization) did not, and this is perhaps
most apparent in the support given to the development of the socialist
daily press in the two countries, with the result that, in the 1970s, 20 percent of the press in Sweden was Social Democratic (much of it LO owned
or subsidized), while there was no real party press in the U.K., though
some dailies did support Labour at election time. Moreover, as we show
in another work (Stephens 1979a), the devotion of resources to mobilization and opinion formation arguably did have quite significant effects
on the levels of class consciousness and leftist voting in the two countries.

That resources devoted to changing public opinion are in fact effective
is not very controversial in social science. Nor are other implications of
our analysis: (1) that labor movements that are more successful in promoting an agenda of consciousness transformation are likely to be more
electorally successful, (2) that, if they are more electorally successful,
they are more likely to influence state policy and transform the policy regime in a social democratic direction, and (3) that, if they are more electorally successful, they will be more powerful vis-à-vis capital than labor
movements that are less electorally successful. This underlines the causal
connection of ideology and social consciousness to the central hypothesis of our analysis and that of power resource theorists: The power relations between labor and capital vary greatly across advanced industrial
democracies, due to the level of organization and centralization of the
union movement and the incumbency of parties of the left and to concentration, organization, and exit possibilities of capital, and these differences in power relations are highly consequential for the policy regime
and its distributive consequences. Our point here—a point that will receive substantial empirical support in chapters 3 and 5—is that the
greater the dominance of social democratic ideology within the labor

movement and in the social consciousness of wage and salary earners, the greater the power of labor vis-à-vis capital and the more redistributive the policy outcomes.

The same general argument about the social construction of collective interests applies to gender interests. From conservatives to communists, a wide variety of political tendencies have claimed to represent women's interests, and many have attracted support from women and active participation in affiliated women's organizations. Among feminists, there are two distinctive positions that are reflected in different approaches to welfare state policy toward women. Feminists who are generally referred to as "equity feminists" advocate gender equality in terms of equal access to social and professional positions for women and for men, which entails a sharing of power and responsibility in the household. Realizing this agenda requires social policies like the provision of affordable child care, parental leave, and comparable worth pay scales. Equity feminism reflects the interests of working women and is typically promoted by women's organizations allied with social democratic parties. Hobson (1998) argues that institutions shape the social construction and articulation of gender interests, and she shows how the dual-breadwinner family model became hegemonic in the Swedish Social Democratic Party and in Swedish social policy, so that no political party could challenge women's rights to daycare or parental leave, or defend a housewives' pension any longer by the end of the 1970s.

Feminists who are generally referred to as "difference feminists" start from the fact that in most societies women do perform different roles and thus have different needs from men. They advocate social policies that reward private care-giving activities, such as pension rights on the basis of years spent raising children or subsidies for mothers who stay home and take care of small children. Difference feminism reflects the interests of women who identify primarily as care givers, regardless of their employment status, and it is typically promoted by independent women's movements. In practice, the dividing line between equity and difference feminism is often blurred, as many women's movements promote an expansion of women's rights both as workers and as care givers. Sainsbury (1996) calls the first approach to social policy the individual or "shared roles" model, and the second the "separate gender" model, distinguishing them both from the traditional male breadwinner model that neither provides nor rewards care-giving activities. In either case, the social consciousness of women and social policy outcomes are heavily influenced by the extent of female labor force participation, the strength of women's organizations, and the political allies available to women's organizations.

Feminists have argued forcefully against conservative claims to represent "true" women's interests by promoting the traditional family. They have pointed out that the conservative as well as religious glorifications of women as mothers and centers of the private sphere are ultimately highly confining and imply the subordination of women to men. For women to have the opportunity to fully develop all their capacities, no different from men, they need to be able to occupy positions as equals in the private and the public spheres, and they need to be able to have economic independence from men. If we accept the value of gender equality, we can say that women should have the same access to the labor market as men and, in Orloff's (1993b) terminology, the same capacity to form and maintain autonomous households. Indeed, we shall show that where women have been more mobilized and allied with political parties that support gender equality, more progress has been made toward women's equality in the labor market, social services that make it possible to combine working lives with family responsibilities, and generous social safety nets for single parents. Thus, parallel to the argument about class interests and class power, we can say that greater power resources mobilization by feminist women results in policies that redistribute power and material resources between genders.

Our claim that class (gender) interests are socially constructed and that changes in class (gender) power relations operate in part through changes in the consciousness—the changing preferences—of the population provides us with the key link in our argument that it is the long-term pattern of partisan government that is critical for welfare state development. We identify four mechanisms through which the pattern of long-term government changes the preferences of actors, changes the universe of actors (and thereby the distribution of preferences), and/or changes the expectations of actors and thus affects social policy: the policy ratchet effect, structural limitation, regime legacies, and ideological hegemony.[11]

Perhaps the most important way in which the long-run pattern of partisan government affects policy is what we call the ratchet effect on social policy. Until the era of retrenchment, it was rare for secular conservative parties to roll back welfare state reforms instituted by social democratic or Christian democratic parties. Indeed they generally accepted each new reform after it had been instituted, and the new center of gravity of the policy agenda became defined by the innovations proposed by the progressive forces in society. The reason for the change in posture of the conservative parties was that the reforms were popular with the mass public, especially the broad-based policies in the areas of pensions, education, and health care, which constitute the overwhelming majority of social expenditure in all the countries under study here. The support for policies quickly broadened once citizens enjoyed the benefits of the new policies, and thus the mass opposition to cutbacks in the policies was much broader than the mass support for their introduction.[12] Thus, the new policy regime fundamentally transforms the preferences of the population.

Our policy ratchet argument is a variant of the policy legacies argument. Recently, Pierson (1996) has argued that policy legacies are distinctively important in the current era of retrenchment with much the same logic we employ here: most welfare state policy, particularly the expensive broad entitlements mentioned above, are popular, and thus even conservative parties are reluctant to cut them. If we are correct about the importance of the policy ratchet in preventing rollbacks in the era of expansion, then what is distinctive about the current period is less the strong effect of policy legacies than the weakening of the effect of partisan government due to the constraining effect of economic difficulties on social democratic and Christian democratic governments.

By "structural limitation," we mean that the policy options are limited by the constellation of power in a country in a given period. A whole range of policy alternatives is ruled out by power relations within the society; thus certain policy alternatives that societal actors might otherwise find attractive will not even be considered by them. Organized labor in the United States in the late 1990s would not even consider putting on the agenda policies enacted in Sweden in the 1960s. Swedish business in the 1960s, faced with a very powerful, united, and centralized labor movement and a social democratic party with a near hegemonic grip on state power, ruled out a huge range of policy alternatives that might appear attractive to employers in other political contexts. Thus, changes in the power balance in society change preferences, or at least preferences that get expressed in the policy-making process based on the expectation that they might be realized. Power balances shape these expectations. If it is highly probable that a given party will be returned to power time after time, societal actors will adjust the expectations about the feasibility of given policy alternatives.[13]

In chapter 4, we argue that the largely politically created welfare state regimes are associated with different production regimes, distinctive patterns of organizing labor markets and the productive process and the financing of investment (also see Ebbinghaus and Manow 1998). At each point in their development, the future possibilities for the development of the welfare state–production regimes are determined by what happened previously. Thus, similar to our policy legacies effect, the existing regime affects the distribution of preferences as each actor takes the current situation as a given, or at least the new starting point, which forecloses some opportunities and opens others. Moreover, past developments weaken or even eliminate some actors and strengthen and create others. For example, the strong and centralized union movements and the political influence of the left in Northern Europe and Scandinavia predisposed employers, unions, and politicians to pursue a high-wage, high–social wage path, and this path, once chosen, progressively eliminated low-wage sectors and thus eliminated one source of opposition, low-wage employers, to the further pursuit of this path. Thus, regime legacies also affect the universe of actors and thereby the distribution of preferences.

Actors' intentions and desires are not self-generating but are products of social and political struggles over decades and even centuries. The "ideological hegemony" that a movement or social class may enjoy is partly a product of the three foregoing mechanisms, which all shape preferences. But the distribution of preferences, or what might be termed social consciousness in a class analytic frame of reference, cannot be read off existing policy arrangements, societal power balances, and production regimes on a one-to-one basis. They are also in part the historic creation of past struggles. Given the dearth of good comparative and especially long-term historical evidence on the policy attitudes and political ideologies of mass publics, this is a much more difficult question to investigate than the previous ones. Yet, to the extent that progressive social and political movements can change political consciousness, they are very likely to have effects on the posture of centrist and conservative parties and thus to move the political center of gravity in society. This then is partly an effect of partisan politics. Moreover, to the extent that progressive social and political movements are strengthened by having allies in government (through laws facilitating organization and the access of movement organizations to the media and so on), these are, in part, effects of partisan government also. However, we do want to limit our claim of how large an effect ideological hegemony can have on social policy in *the absence of partisan government*. In the short run, a conservative government coming to power after a long period of government by the left may have to implement the policy agenda worked out by the labor movement, but it is impossible for a movement out of government to force its policy agenda on a government over a sustained period of time.

Our argument about the importance of long-run patterns of the partisan composition of government implies that welfare state development is path dependent. "Path dependence" is a term that covers many social and historical processes, so it is necessary for us to specify how we conceive the path dependence of social policy development in the post–World War II period. Here we have to treat the expansion and retrenchment periods somewhat differently. For the expansion period, we reject the strongest version of path dependence, a critical junctures interpretation, such as that applied by Lipset and Rokkan (1967) to the development of European party systems and Collier and Collier (1992) to labor incorporation in Latin America, in which events at critical junctures lock in future developments. Based on pooled time series statistical analyses, both Hicks (1999) and Swank (forthcoming) have argued that political and institutional arrangements developed in the first decade and a half after World War II put countries on a track that determined later welfare state development. More specifically, early social democratic political dominance along with centralized and strong employer and union organization led to the development of social corporatism, which then locked in later development. Subsequent periods in government by left or Christian democratic parties had little influence on the outcomes.

The polar opposite interpretation with regard to party politics would be that partisan government effects are uniform over the expansion period. That is, for example, a four-year period of social democratic or Christian democratic government had an equal effect on welfare state generosity and the configuration of policy whether it occurred in the late 1940s, 1950s, 1960s, or 1970s. In this case, the effect of left or Christian democratic government is a constant cause in Stinchcombe's (1968) terms whereas, in the critical juncture interpretation, the effect of (early) social democratic government is a historic cause as it contributed to the crystallization of social corporatism that led to the welfare state outcome. In this view of uniform historic effects, the social processes are only weakly path dependent or perhaps only apparently path dependent. To the extent that countries follow a path that reproduces and deepens welfare state patterns, it is because the underlying social forces that produce political outcomes—union strength, party organization, religious sentiments, etc.—reproduce themselves.

Our view is between these two polar types.[14] Welfare state developments were not locked in by the early 1960s; later periods of government did matter and sustained changes in the pattern of partisan government could have substantial effects on welfare state regimes. On the other hand, our four mechanisms, particularly the ratchet effect and regime legacies, do imply more path dependency than the uniform effects theory hypothesizes. As each policy is put into place it transforms the distribution of preferences; as the regime increasingly entrenches itself, it transforms the universe of actors. The economic and political costs of moving to another regime become greater, and conversely the returns of staying on the same track become greater.[15] Moreover, the implication of our argument is that early years of party governance matter more, particularly if one party family is dominant over a relatively long period of time. Long duration of government by one party family (or by the same coalition) also matters in another way, regardless of the time period in which it occurs. Repeated victories by a given party or coalition are likely to affect the expectations of societal actors and these actors in turn are likely to adjust their "realistic" preferences accordingly.

The preceding paragraphs all concern the period of welfare state expansion that ended, depending on the country, between the late 1970s and the late 1980s. At that point the economic crisis profoundly affected the politics of social policy. Partisan effects declined because, while the right was still constrained by the popularity of existing policies, fiscal constraints now tied the hands of the left. The same theoretical framework still helps to explain changes in the welfare state, but external and internal economic constraints loom larger. Power constellations continued to matter over the medium and longer run, but to a significantly smaller extent. Dispersion of power through the constitutional structure remained important, but as pointed out repeatedly, it now worked in the opposite direction, in favor of more generous welfare states, by slowing down retrenchment. Going beyond this, specifying the role of globalization, demographic change, and the growth of the service economy, would take us to the explanation of retrenchment that we develop inductively from the case studies and quantitative data in chapters 6 and 7.[16]

## Methodological Approach

We will test and substantiate our arguments through both cross-national quantitative and comparative historical analyses, engaging the two methods in a dialogue. The combination of these two methods allows us to achieve generalizability and to establish causality through tracing links between events and actors' behavior in the historical narrative. We select nine cases for our comparative historical analysis, half of the countries included in our quantitative analysis, or half of the universe of advanced industrial democracies with more than one million people that have been

democracies since World War II. It is important to have a large number
of cases for analysis, in order to have variation in all the hypothesized
causal factors, because it is quite clear that the choice of focus can
influence the theoretical conclusions of a study (see below). For example,
a one-country case study holds the broad class power distribution, the
structure of political institutions, and the level of economic development
more or less constant, unless it covers a very long period of time. Naturally, with the structural and institutional framework fixed, the role of
specific actors, including state bureaucrats and actors in civil society, is
what varies most over time and attracts the attention of the researcher.
Accordingly, researchers are likely to attribute more causal importance
to the preferences and strategies of these actors than warranted, or at
least they lose sight of the way in which the constraints of the larger
power distribution and the institutional context shape the preferences
and strategies of these actors to begin with. The inclusion of cases that
vary substantially along structural and institutional dimensions allows
the researcher to identify the impact of these dimensions on the nature of
welfare states.

Our case selection for the quantitative analysis was governed by the
desire to include the universe of advanced industrial countries[17] large
enough to have some degree of autonomy in economic and social policy,
and democratic for a long enough period of time for domestic power distributions and institutions to have shaped economic and social policies
and their outcomes. The quantitative analysis of these cases establishes a
set of interrelationships that form the parameters within which we then
place the causal historical narrative uncovered in the comparative historical analysis of the cases.

When we began this study in 1989, we conceived of it as a study of the
development of welfare state regimes in the postwar period. Had this remained our goal, a compelling case could have been made that our cases
should have been a sample of countries selected to represent the total
variation in welfare state regimes. This criterion would have dictated the
selection of two liberal welfare states and at least one Southern European
Christian democratic welfare state, and fewer countries in Scandinavia,
Northern Europe, and Australasia. After the onset of the Scandinavian
crisis in the early 1990s, however, our interest shifted to the impact of
globalization on retrenchment, and this heavily influenced our final case
selection. The conventional neoliberal wisdom holds that globalization is
particularly detrimental to the most generous welfare states because
these welfare states interfere extensively with market mechanisms and

globalization strengthens markets against states, and because intensifying competition forces a lowering of wage costs and most forms of taxation and thus makes generous social programs unaffordable. Accordingly, we chose nine cases that had achieved a very high degree of social protection but through different types of welfare state regimes; four through social democratic (Sweden, Norway, Finland, and Denmark), three through Christian democratic (Austria, Germany, and the Netherlands), and two through wage earner welfare state regimes (Australia and New Zealand). The analysis of these nine cases sheds light on the ability of governments to adjust welfare state and production regimes to the new international economic environment while maintaining high standards of protection.

We feel confident that the bias in the selection of cases of regimes does not affect our analysis of the development and retrenchment of welfare states in the chapters that follow because our case knowledge extends well beyond the nine cases covered in chapters 5 and 7. First, in addition to the cases covered here, we collected and analyzed case materials and wrote historical sketches of the development of the welfare state in Italy, Switzerland, and France. Second, our initial analysis of retrenchment (Stephens, Huber, and Ray 1999) included case materials on France and the United Kingdom written by our coauthor, Leonard Ray. Third, we covered the historical development of the British and American welfare states in a previous work (Stephens 1979b). Finally, the participation of one of the two coauthors in the Max Planck Institute project on "The Adjustment of National Employment and Social Policy to Economic Internationalization" organized by Fritz Scharpf and Vivien Schmidt allowed us to cross-check our conclusions on the cases covered in this book with the case studies also in that project (Sweden, Denmark, Austria, Germany, Netherlands, Australia, and New Zealand) and to add materials on cases we do not cover here (Belgium, France, Switzerland, and Italy) to support our generalizations about variations across all regime types.[18] We draw on the case materials for these other countries in the conclusions of chapters 5 and 7 and in chapter 6.

We select Sweden for in-depth analysis and, for the period of retrenchment, for primary research. We do this for two reasons. Since Sweden has been seen as the prototype of the generous social democratic welfare state, special attention to its historic development is called for. For the period of retrenchment, the prototypical status alone might be enough to designate the country for more intensive analysis and primary research. In addition, the structure of Swedish business with its highly multinationalized firms that long ago had outgrown Swedish borders and become European or even worldwide concerns argues that Sweden should be particularly vulnerable to pressures brought on by the increased globalization of the economies of all advanced capitalist countries in the past few decades.

In this book, our interest is in long-term change, that is, in the causes of the differences in social policy patterns and their distributive outcomes at the close of the Golden Age of postwar capitalism and in the causes of the changes in this pattern from that point to the present. This interest has a profound affect on how we carry out our comparative historical and quantitative analyses and how they inform one another. We agree with King, Keohane, and Verba (1994) that the only valid test of the causal effect of one social factor on another would be the social science counterpart of a fully controlled scientific experiment, that is, varying the experimental (independent variable) while all other factors are held constant and then examining the change in the dependent variable. As King, Keohane, and Verba make clear, conceptually this means we must rerun history, varying the experimental factor and holding other factors constant. Thus, causal inference in social science involves a counterfactual (the rerun version of history) that cannot be verified. Our central argument in the first half of this book is that the long-term pattern of partisan governance is the single most important determinant of the social policy differences across countries.[19] The counterfactual then involves imagining the outcome in a given country had another political configuration prevailed over a long period of time. The counterfactual has to have some realism given the historical circumstance of the country. That is, it does not make sense to ask whether the Australian welfare state would have been different if Christian democracy and not the secular right had been in power for the period 1950 to 1972, but it does make sense to ask if the Australian welfare state would have been different if the Labor Party had been in power for the 1950–72 period or if the secular right and the Labor Party had alternated in terms in government in this period.

Since it is impossible to rerun history, how can we find evidence that our favored counterfactual and not some other one is correct? We identify three sources of evidence.[20] First, there is the evidence from the quantitative analyses. For instance, if we assert the Norwegian welfare state would have been different in 1980 had bourgeois coalitions been predominant up to that point, we can point out that if Norway's welfare state were the same in the case of bourgeois predominance, it would have been an extreme statistical outlier in our data analysis. Second, we can cite comparative case evidence, applying Mill's method of difference or Przeworski and Teune's (1970) most similar systems design. We can do this by comparing country experiences; for instance, by comparing Norway to Australia and New Zealand, countries with labor parties that garnered high percentages in elections and with high levels of union density like Norway, but in which secular right coalitions formed most governments before 1980. Or we can compare periods, preferably long periods, of government by parties of a given color within a country. For example, we could compare social policy development in Australia under Labor in 1941–49 and 1983–96 with Australia under Liberal-led coalitions in 1950–72. Finally, we can refer to the historical narrative examining which parties and interest groups influenced legislative developments.

Relegating historical narrative to only one of three sources of relevant evidence is directly connected to our interest in long-term change. Our interest in long-term change affects not only our comparative historical methodology but also our quantitative approach in related but distinctive ways. There are traditions of studying short-term change in both of these research methodologies, and in both cases we contend not only that a simple cumulation of the causes of short-term change will result in a misleading picture of long-term change, but also that the very fact that it results in this misleading picture of long-term change questions its picture of short-term change. In other words, as we point out in *Capitalist Development and Democracy,* it is not our intention to counterpose the determinants of the longue durée to those of short-term events.[21] Rather, we contend that only by putting the short-term events in longer historical and broader comparative perspective can we understand the determinants of the short-term events and how they cumulate in a path-dependent fashion to lead to a given outcome. Here we refer back to four mechanisms (structural limitation, ideological hegemony, the policy ratchet effect, and regime legacies) to show how an analysis of short-term policy changes can give a misleading picture of the determinants of long-term *and* short-term outcomes that would lead the researcher to underestimate partisan effects.

As in *Capitalist Development and Democracy* (32 ff.), we take the historian or historical sociologist examining short-term policy change, for example the immediate post–World War II "harvest time" legislation in Sweden (see chapter 5) or New Deal legislation in the United States, as our point of departure. In this type of research, the actions and intentions of various actors are examined in detail and the outcome is attributed to the clashes and cooperation of these actors, thus privileging agency and process and neglecting all four factors mentioned above. In terms of "structural limitation," such research ignores the fact that a whole range of alternatives are ruled out by, to take one example, power relations within the society. Thus, the decision of the Swedish Conservative Party and the employers federation to support the basic parameters of the harvest time reforms has to be understood in the context of their facing a Social Democratic Party that had been in office for over a decade, a leftist electoral bloc with increasingly large absolute majorities in the electorate in successive elections, and a strong and increasingly well organized trade union movement.[22] Their support for the social policy reforms is relevant but hardly conclusive evidence for the hypothesis that there were no partisan effects. The relevant counterfactual in this case would be what would have happened in Sweden if the bourgeois bloc had been in power in the 1932–48 period. To examine this question in a comparative historical vein, we should both increase the time period and/or add cases such that the structural variables, the social and governmental power of the labor movement, vary. Did Swedish Conservatives and employers have the same positions before the rise of Social Democracy to governmental power? Did employers and conservative parties in other countries that did not face such strong labor movements have similar pro–social policy positions? The quantitative evidence can be brought to bear here also, as we pointed out above. If a historical study, or rather a number of studies that might be thought to form a school of thought, deny partisan effects, how can the proponents of this school explain the powerful statistical evidence that we present in chapters 3 and 4 that show very strong associations between partisanship and welfare state outcomes?

By privileging process and actors' intentions and actions, the historical case study also denies any role for ideological hegemony and the policy ratchet effect. Thus, when we find that the Swedish bourgeois parties did not dismantle the welfare state during their period in office in 1976–82, one has to ask if those parties and their voters had been influenced by the powerful social democratic labor movement's cumulative effect on the social consciousness, or more narrowly stated policy preferences, of the Swedish citizenry and by the fact that they had lived under and many had benefited from the existing policy regime. Finally, the short-term historical case study will also not recognize the regime legacies effect because, over the short run, regime legacies will not vary. Thus, returning to our example above, the absence of low-wage employers in Northern Europe will not be recognized as a product of past union strength and left influence.

Let us end by summarizing the implications of this discussion for the conduct of comparative historical and quantitative analyses. In the case of comparative historical analyses, the analyst should attempt to lengthen the time period examined and increase the range of cases in order to reveal how structural factors, which are more likely to vary across a wider variety of social settings, have an impact on the phenomena to be explained. In the case of quantitative analyses, our attention should be on long-term changes within countries and broad differences across countries, not on changes from year to year or even changes over a relatively small number of years. This position has clear implications for an appropriate approach to measurements, namely that one should use levels rather than yearly change data. Even change data for short-term intervals, such as five-year intervals, fail to capture the full range of effects. We shall expand on this further in our discussion of approaches to quantitative analysis in the next chapter.

◆

## CHAPTER THREE

# The Development of Welfare States: Quantitative Evidence

This chapter presents a variety of quantitative analyses of the development of welfare states and their different policy configurations from the end of World War II to the mid-1980s. Depending on the country, the expansion phase of the welfare state ended between the late 1970s and early 1990s; thus we select the median date, 1985, as the end data point in our pooled cross-sections and time series analyses. In the pooled analyses on eight different dependent variables, we examine the determinants of welfare state expansion and of specific welfare state characteristics that our theoretical framework postulates as crucial, as well as the determinants that have been emphasized by other authors. In order to tap outcomes of welfare states on which data are available only for a few time points, we analyze cross-sectional data on inequality, redistribution, poverty, and decommodification, a measure of transfer generosity.

To preview our main findings briefly, we can point to the very consistent and strong effects of political incumbency of social democratic and Christian democratic parties on different measures of welfare state effort. They both promote generous welfare states, but the characteristics of these welfare states are different. Christian democratic parties rely on social insurance and generous transfers to keep people out of poverty, whereas social democratic parties provide a wide variety of social services in addition and emphasize maximal labor force participation of the working-age population. Both types of welfare states are effective in keeping people out of poverty and are highly redistributive, though the social democratic welfare state is clearly more so. Equally stable results emerge for constitutional structure; political institutions that disperse power reduce welfare state effort. Women's labor force participation has strong effects on the expansion of welfare state services, both directly and in interaction with social democratic incumbency. The level of affluence of a society facilitates welfare state expansion. The proportion of people over sixty-five is associated with higher welfare state expenditure, but not with the generosity of pension benefits per aged person, suggesting that this association demonstrates a need effect rather than the political influence of a pressure group.

## Hypotheses

### *Dimensions of the Welfare State*

The welfare state literature has come a long way, from early studies with a single indicator of welfare state effort, mostly some version of an expenditure measure, to more recent studies based on a variety of indicators, including entitlements and outcomes (e.g. see Korpi 1989; Esping-Andersen 1990; Mitchell 1991; Korpi and Palme 1998). Early work was also plagued by the fact that the existing hypotheses in the literature suggested more variables than there were cases in cross-national studies of advanced capitalist democracies, thus rendering it impossible to test the extant theories comprehensively. More recent works that pooled data points over time and across cases appear to have solved this problem (e.g. see Hicks and Misra 1993; Huber, Ragin, and Stephens 1993; Korpi 1989). Unfortunately, direct measures of social rights, such as replacement rates or qualifying conditions in social insurance, and outcome measures, such as income inequality or poverty rates, are available at too few time points to make time series analysis feasible.[1] Nevertheless, the expenditure and employment data available in annual time series do measure the total commitment of the society to the public provision of income support and social services and, once need variables such as the size of the client population are controlled for, do provide one with good measures of welfare state generosity. Moreover, unlike previous studies that focus on one or two expenditure variables, we employ eight expenditure and employment measures as dependent variables. Following up on our previous work (Huber, Ragin, and Stephens 1993; Huber and Stephens 1993a, 2000a), we argue that these variables measure distinct dimensions of the welfare state; thus our independent variables, particularly the political variables, should affect the different dependent variables to different degrees. Moreover, using a number of different dependent variables also provides us with an additional test of the robustness of our analysis.

Though the use of a large number of dependent variables in the pooled analysis makes this study an advance over previous analyses of pooled data on expenditure or employment, one still is ultimately most interested in social rights and outcomes. Fortunately, we can cross-check and extend the findings of our pooled analysis by examining the relationship of our most important independent variables to the social rights and outcome variables in a cross-sectional analysis.

### Class Power, Religion, and Political Power Distributions

Our central hypothesis, built on previous studies of welfare state expansion (Stephens 1979b; Castles 1982; Schmidt 1982; Korpi 1983; Esping-Andersen 1990; Huber, Ragin, and Stephens 1993) and on the theoretical framework developed in the last chapter, is that incumbency of political parties based on the organizational power of the working and lower middle classes, results in generous and redistributive welfare states. A strong union–social democratic party alliance is the most consistent political promoter of not only a generous welfare state, but one with a strong universalistic, citizenship-based, solidaristic, redistributive, and service-oriented character (Castles 1982; Myles 1984; Korpi 1989; Palme 1990; Huber, Ragin, and Stephens 1993; Korpi and Palme 1998; Huber and Stephens 2000a). In Catholic or religiously mixed societies, where Christian democratic parties manage to attract a significant working- and lower-middle-class base, these parties are also major promoters of welfare state expansion, but the welfare state assumes different characteristics (Stephens 1979b). Entitlements are heavily based on the insurance principle and thus on employment, not on citizenship; they are different for different groups, not universalistic and solidaristic; they are more concerned with preservation of the accustomed standard of living of the beneficiaries than with redistribution per se; and they emphasize transfers more than public social services (Esping-Andersen 1990; van Kersbergen 1995). These characteristics are largely due to the need of Christian democratic parties as multiclass parties to mediate the diverse interests of their social base and due to the centrality of integration and mediation in the Christian democratic political project (van Kersbergen 1995: 28). Nevertheless, despite the absence of an egalitarian motivation, some of these Christian democratic welfare states have ended up being quite redistributive and effective in maintaining low poverty rates. Certainly, competition with strong social democratic challengers, such as in Germany, was a major incentive for Christian democratic governments to promote generous and redistributive welfare state programs, but our data indicate that these welfare state commitments are not due solely to social democratic influence in these countries.

There are good theoretical reasons for expecting social democracy and Christian democracy to differ in regard to the funding and delivery of public goods and services. First, two elements of Christian democratic social thought lead to less emphasis on the public sector as provider of social services (van Kersbergen 1995). According to the principle of subsidiarity, that is, the reliance on the smallest possible group that can perform a given social function, the state is called upon to perform only those functions that cannot be performed by the family or various voluntary communities, in particular the church and church-related organizations. In addition, given the strong emphasis on the traditional family and the male breadwinner–housewife ideal, Christian democracy is reluctant to promote increased women's labor force participation and thus public services that might facilitate it, such as day care. Second, by contrast, the Scandinavian experience suggests that the social democratic ideology of equality has increasingly been extended from its traditional domain of class relations to gender relations.[2] Third, since most social services are provided as citizenship rights while most transfer benefits are conditional on previous employment and income, one would expect social democracy, which has traditionally emphasized citizenship as a criterion for social benefits, to promote the expansion of social services. Fourth, as Garrett (1998) and Boix (1998) argue, part of the social democratic agenda, especially recently, has been to promote competitiveness by investing in human capital. This can be most clearly seen in the social democratic emphasis on active labor market policy, job training, and expansion of higher education (Janoski 1990; King 1995). Fifth, based on OECD data, Esping-Andersen (1996b) has argued that the Scandinavian welfare states are distinctive in terms of the high levels of transfers to youth as compared to the aged. With the exception of health care, services (e.g., education, day care, job training) are arguably even more skewed toward younger citizens. Finally, social democracy has promoted state *delivery* (as opposed to simply state funding) of social services and goods because it has believed that only through public provision could it ensure that all citizens had equal access to benefits of equal value.

On the basis of these considerations, then, we would expect incumbency of social democratic parties to effect an expansion of publicly provided welfare state services. These services are publicly provided because the commitment to citizenship rights entails a commitment to equal access and equal quality of these services for all citizens. We hypothesize that the association of governance by Christian democratic parties with expansion of publicly funded social services will be less than that of social democracy, though they also have a commitment to providing for the welfare of all citizens. Thus, core social services such as health and education will be publicly funded, but those services in which the family can be seen as an alternative provider will receive less generous funding in Christian democratic welfare states because of the Christian democrats' commitment to the principle of subsidiarity and to the preservation of the traditional male breadwinner–female care giver family. Subsidiarity also leads to a diminished role for the state as deliverer of social services; thus, we expect little or no association between Christian democratic governance and the public provision of welfare state services. The contrast between Christian democratic and social democratic welfare states in the health sector is instructive here: All of the social democratic welfare states instituted national health services, while only Italy (in 1978) among the Christian democratic welfare states did so. The rest instituted systems of national health insurance in which the private provision of health services retained an important role. This can be seen in the contrast between the public share of health expenditure (88 percent in social democratic welfare states, 77 percent in Christian democratic ones) and the public share of health care employment (88 percent in social democratic welfare states, but only 46 percent in Christian democratic ones).[3]

Our hypotheses, then, specifically state that incumbency of left-wing parties is associated with (1) overall expansion of the public economy, driven by the public provision of social services, (2) the decommodifying effect of welfare state provisions (i.e., their quality with regard to an individual's ability to maintain his or her standard of living when not participating in the labor market), and (3) redistributive effects, as indicated by the posttax, posttransfer income distribution and the redistributive effect of direct taxes and transfers. In contrast, incumbency of left-wing parties should be less associated with transfer payments. Incumbency of Christian democratic parties should be associated with these factors in a different pattern. It should be associated (1) primarily with direct transfer payments; (2) moderately with overall expansion of the public economy and taxation, but clearly less so than social democracy; (3) moderately with decommodification but clearly less so than social democracy; and (4) not with redistribution. In terms of our specific measures, then, we expect social democracy to be more strongly associated with the broad measures of expenditures and revenue, and Christian democracy with the narrow, heavily transfer-based, expenditure measures. Social democracy should have a strong positive effect on public-sector employment, whereas Christian democracy should not. Both political tendencies should be positively associated with decommodification and negatively with poverty rates, but the association should be stronger for social democracy, and only social democracy should be negatively associated with measures of inequality.

Since we emphasize the organizational power of working and lower middle classes underlying the strength of different parties, we expect measures of the strength of labor movements, such as union density, political unity, and centralization, to have a strong positive effect on welfare state expansion and on the redistributive character of social policy. We expect the same of measures of corporatism, conceptualized as a pattern of interest representation in which the state and peak associations of labor and capital engage in tripartite negotiations on major economic and social policies. Some authors have argued that corporatism itself is a result of working-class power mobilization (Stephens 1979b; Korpi 1983; Western 1991), whereas others have claimed that it is a result of the openness and thus vulnerability of the economy (Katzenstein 1985). Which side one takes in this dispute depends to a large extent on the importance one attributes to labor's substantive participation in major decisions as a key element of corporatism (Lehmbruch 1984: 65–66). Labor strength is obviously an integral element of the conceptualization of corporatism for those authors who see labor's role in shaping key national policies through corporatist negotiations as central to the very essence of corporatism. Thus, Switzerland, one of the two paradigmatic cases analyzed by Katzenstein, is not highly corporatist in their and our view, despite the presence of "an ideology of social partnership . . . ; a relatively centralized and concentrated system of interest groups; and a voluntary and informal coordination of conflicting objectives through continuous political bargaining among interest groups, state bureaucracies, and political parties" (Katzenstein 1984: 27). Labor in Switzerland is comparatively weak and, as Kriesi (1980) has shown, it is often marginalized from informal negotiations about important decisions. Empirically, previous studies have shown high correlations between corporatism and the strength of social democratic parties and labor movements (Hicks and Swank 1992), and the same correlations appear in our data. Western (1991) tested the alternative explanations of corporatism with openness and left power, and he came to the conclusion that left power was decisive and openness did not matter.

### State Structures

In our discussion of state-centric theories in the last chapter, we underlined the difficulty in carrying out quantitative tests of hypotheses on two of the core variables of this literature: the effect of past policy legacies and the autonomous policy-making role of bureaucrats. However, we argued that a third line of thinking, that concerning the effect of state structures, offered a very promising hypothesis explaining the long-term development of welfare states. Our second major hypothesis is that constitutional provisions can create "veto points" in the policy-making process that impede social reform. The development of our measure was heavily influenced by two comparative historical studies (Immergut 1992 and Maioni 1998)[4] that provide interesting systematic analyses of the effects of constitutional structure on social policy formation (also see Weir, Orloff, and Skocpol 1988: 16 ff. for reference to some of these factors). In a comparative study of health insurance in Switzerland, France, and Sweden, Immergut argues that political institutions decisively shaped the ability of different groups to activate power resources and influence the making of health insurance policies. She emphasizes the importance of centralization and insulation of executive power from parliamentary and electoral pressures as a precondition for the implementation of reforms that significantly modify the status quo. Where power is dispersed in representative institutions, relatively small interest groups are able to block reform legislation, a situation that greatly favors maintenance of the status quo and allows at most incremental reforms. The perception of such opportunities for veto, in turn, induces interest groups to be more intransigent in the pursuit of their demands (Immergut 1992). The Swedish system, with an executive assured of parliamentary support delivered by disciplined parties, represents one polar case in her analysis; the Swiss system, with a collegial multiparty executive, changing parliamentary majorities, and above all the institution of the popular referendum,[5] represents the other.

Maioni, in her study of health insurance politics in the United States and Canada, shows that the lobbying power of the medical association was weaker in Canada because of the existence of parliamentary government. She argues that parliamentary government encourages party discipline, which means that entire parties need to be influenced. In contrast, in the American presidential system parties have remained weak political organizations and individual members of Congress can be lobbied because they depend primarily on their own fund-raising capacities and have few incentives to put party directives above the interests of their wealthy supporters. Thus, as does Immergut's work, Maioni's study demonstrates that the availability of more points of access to political decision making, or of more veto points, results in less comprehensive and generous welfare state legislation.

These two studies provide several strong leads for the development of a more general conceptualization of a key attribute of states: constitutional structures favorable or inimical to reform. It is our hypothesis that those features of constitutions that make it difficult to reach and implement decisions based on narrow majorities—and that conversely let minority interests obstruct legislation—will impede far-reaching reforms in social policy, especially reforms that might benefit the underprivileged majority. Thus, we hypothesize that aspects of constitutional structure that disperse political power and offer multiple points of influence on the making and implementation of policy are inimical to welfare state expansion and will be negatively associated with our various measures of welfare state effort. These aspects include federalism, presidential government, strong bicameralism, and provisions for referenda.[6]

### *Policy Legacies*

We argued in the last chapter that policies once instituted become the new reference point for battles about the welfare state (what we called the ratchet effect) and that policy regimes create their supporting clienteles and can weaken or even eliminate actors opposed to them. Thus, past generosity in policies should be related to present generosity in policies independent of other causal factors.

Flora and Alber (1981) and Esping-Andersen (1990) have argued that the legacies of late nineteenth-century political regimes have long-term effects on welfare state development. They contend that the efforts of absolutist regimes to co-opt the growing working class along Bismarckian lines affected later welfare state development. Such welfare state policies introduced by absolutist regimes were corporatist and segmented; that is, they treated different occupational groups differently and thus reproduced inequalities created by the labor market. State employees in middle and higher ranks were treated best; white-collar workers were treated better than blue-collar workers; and among the blue-collar workers the most strategically located and the best organized, such as miners and metalworkers, were treated preferentially. Once such differential schemes were established, it became exceedingly difficult to unify them and equalize benefits. Rather, later welfare state expansion tended to build on existing programs. Two cases in point are the German and the French experiences after World War II, where plans to establish a unified and comprehensive social insurance system failed due to the resistance of groups privileged under the old system (Hockerts 1980; Galant 1955).

Accordingly, policy legacies of absolutist regimes should be associated with higher expenditure but lower levels of redistribution. Our operationalization of "authoritarian legacies" is discussed below.

## Women's Labor Force Participation

In most advanced industrial democracies, the integration of women into paid work outside the home has increased significantly in the post–World War II period. However, this increase took place with widely varying speed, so that differences in the rate of women's labor force participation among countries have increased also. Increasing women's labor force participation can be expected to generate demands for a greater public role in care giving and thus pressures for an expansion of welfare state services. Where such demands and pressures are supported and reinforced by powerful political allies, they are likely to result in policies that facilitate the combination of paid work and family care obligations, such as the provision of public day care and elderly care and parental leave insurance. Expansion of welfare state services in turn has a positive feedback effect in that it enables more women to enter the labor force and creates demand for labor in these services, a demand that is predominantly met by women. Where welfare state services are publicly provided, this leads to an increase of the female public-sector labor force. Increased female labor force participation, particularly in the typically well-organized public sector, increases the level of organization of women through unionization and thus the potential for women's political mobilization.

This process of economic and social mobilization of women also leads to increased political mobilization of women, in existing parties, in women's organizations, in new social movements, and so on. The combined effect of mobilization and of the expansion of the public sector also makes women stronger supporters of the welfare state and the public sector in general and of the political left, reversing the traditional direction of the gender gap. Accordingly, we would expect the mutual reinforcement between women's labor force participation and public welfare state employment to be particularly strong in countries where social democratic incumbency facilitated the comparatively early (beginning in the 1970s) implementation of policies supportive of women's labor force participation (see chapter 5 for a comparative historical sketch). Thus, we would expect a positive effect of an interaction between women's labor force participation and social democratic rule on the expansion of public social services. However, even in countries where social democracy has been weaker and either Christian democratic or secular center and right-wing parties stronger, we would still expect a positive effect of women's labor force participation on the expansion of public social services because working women's demands for public care facilities provided an incentive for political actors to win women's votes on the basis of support for public social services.

## *The International Economy*

The international economy figures prominently in the political debate about the sustainability of the welfare state. The neoliberal argument claims that international economic competition tends to make economies with generous welfare states uncompetitive, particularly those based heavily on financing through payroll taxes, and thus leads to retrenchment of welfare state expenditures. We disagree strongly with this view and shall discuss it at length in chapter 7. The scholarly debate is much more nuanced, distinguishing between the impact of the international economy on the welfare state in different phases. Some authors claim that economic openness implies vulnerability to external economic shocks and thus stimulates the buildup of a generous social safety net to protect citizens from such shocks (Cameron 1978). As discussed above, Katzenstein (1984, 1985) claims that economic openness leads to corporatism, and corporatism functions as an intervening variable in creating a generous social safety net. We are skeptical about the openness argument, both with regard to its presumed direct effect on welfare state expansion and its indirect effect via corporatism, because decisions about welfare state expansion are politically mediated rather than automatic reactions to needs for social protection, and the labor movement has to be strong and influential for informal tripartite bargaining arrangements to deserve the label "corporatism" and result in welfare state expansion. Nevertheless, we include a measure of openness in our analysis.

A second line of argument runs directly contrary to Katzenstein's as it holds that globalization, defined as the increased flow of goods, capital, people, and information across borders, has led to an ascendancy of the market and a general retrenchment of the state, including in the area of welfare state provision. The general view is that globalization accelerated very rapidly from the 1980s on, and in this periodization it clearly coincides with the era of welfare state retrenchment. Again, we are looking for a political mediation of such economic effects, and our case studies suggest that the growth of investment abroad by major corporations in fact gave these corporations more leverage domestically vis-à-vis labor as well as governments. Assuming that business preferences in general are for lower taxes and welfare state expenditures, we could expect at least a dampening effect on welfare state expansion. A significant acceleration of globalization did occur in the 1980s, so our major discussion of this phenomenon and its impact will come in chapters 6 and 7, but we do include a measure for direct foreign investment flowing out of the country in our analysis here in order to tap a possible earlier effect.

## Logic of Industrialism and Pluralism

Though the theoretical debate has often been phrased in terms of "politics versus logic of industrialism," accepting the importance of constitutional structures and the distribution of political power does not require rejection of the proposition that economic and social variables also have an impact on welfare state formation. It is theoretically plausible that rising affluence of a society facilitates an expansion of welfare state expenditures. However, the empirical research contains apparently contradictory findings. Most cross-sectional studies of affluent countries do not show any effect of GDP per capita on welfare state expenditure, while cross-sectional studies of a broader group of countries and studies that pool cross-sectional and time series data on affluent countries do. This difference is almost certainly due to the restricted range of variation in cross-sectional studies of affluent countries. We expect results in line with previous analyses of pooled data.

As Myles (1984) has made clear, the view of politics and of the state held by proponents of the logic of industrialism school (e.g., Wilensky 1975) is essentially pluralist. Economic change creates new needs for social protection, those needs get articulated and channeled into the political process, and they are met through the expansion of the welfare state. Pampel and Williamson (1989) make their pluralist view explicit, as they argue that people over 65 are an important welfare state clientele and act as a pressure group to promote their interests in public pensions and health care, and that therefore the higher the proportion of people over 65 in a society is, the stronger their influence is and the more generous the welfare state is expected to be. In addition, they argue that the level of voter turnout is an indicator of mobilization of a society and thus predicts levels of welfare state spending. Now, it is quite obvious that, once pension and health care programs are instituted, a higher percentage of elderly people in the population should cause increased expenditures, a phenomenon we would call a demographic or need effect. The proportion of elderly people in the population would seem to be at best a proximate measure for their influence as a pressure group; at least one would want to have some indication of their degree of organization. At any rate, it is empirically difficult to separate out the pressure group from the need effect in quantitative analyses.

## *Other Causes*

The level of unemployment also influences public expenditures in several ways, depending on the programs in place. Higher unemployment causes higher expenditures for unemployment compensation; where early pension programs for unemployed people exist, it causes an increase in pension expenditures; and where governments pursue active labor market policies, it raises the costs of such policies. Thus, we also expect unemployment to be related to our expenditure measures. Inflation is also conventionally included in quantitative studies of welfare state development. The rationale is that in countries with progressive taxation systems inflation pushes households into higher tax brackets, which lets government revenue grow and thus makes it easier to expand welfare state expenditures. Military expenditure is hypothesized to have a positive relation to the size of the total public sector, but to be negatively related to transfer payments and social benefit expenditure due to a "guns for butter" trade-off (Russet 1970; Wilensky 1975: 74–80). We have included a final variable, strike activity, which is frequently used to represent a political view put forward by Piven and Cloward (1972). This view holds that direct protest activity is the most effective means for lower classes to maintain mobilization and successfully pressure the state for concessions, such as welfare state benefits.

## Operationalizations

### *Basic Measures of Dependent and Independent Variables*

In choosing our dependent variables for the pooled cross-sections and time series analysis, we strive for variability in order to tap overall welfare state effort, emphasis on transfer payments, the extent of public financing of and of public provision of social services, and the generosity of benefits for individuals (see table 3.1).[7] In the cross-sectional analysis we use a number of additional measures to again tap the extent of public provision of social services and the generosity of benefits, along with measures of support for mothers combining paid work and child rearing, the redistributive effect of taxes and transfers, poverty levels for various groups, and inequality. First, we use the most commonly employed expenditure measure, the ILO measure of social security benefits, which includes transfer payments and many but not all in-kind welfare benefits (e.g., medical care but not housing, day care, or education). Second, we use a somewhat narrower measure, OECD's measure of transfer payments, also computed as a percentage of GDP. Third, at the other end of the spectrum, we use total revenue and total expenditure of all levels of government, a measure of the size of the total public sector. All measures are expressed as a percentage of GDP.

We use two measures in our pooled cross-sections and time series analysis to gauge the importance of public financing and one measure to gauge the importance of public delivery of social services. The measure for public delivery is an employment measure, total civilian government employment as a percentage of the working age population; it was compiled by the Welfare State Exit Entry Project (WEEP) at the Wissenschaftszentrum Berlin (see Cusack 1991). An even better measure is public employment in health, education, and welfare, but that measure is available only in a cross-sectional WEEP data set for the early 1980s on employment structure in fifteen countries (see Cusack and Rein 1991) and a pooled data set on employment structure for nine countries at three points in time, roughly 1975, 1980, and 1985 (see Cusack, Notermans, and Rein 1989).[8] These data enable us to evaluate the validity of our other measure, total civilian government employment as a percentage of the working-age population and to cross-check the results of the pooled analyses with those of analyses based on these other two data sets. Although civilian government employment includes civilian employment in non–welfare state sectors (e.g., police, judiciary, infrastructure), its high correlation with public employment in health, education, and welfare as a percentage of the working-age population in the WEEP data (.95 in the cross-sectional data on 15 countries and .93 in the pooled data on 9 countries) indicates that virtually all of its variation across countries and through time is accounted for by welfare state employment. Given its high correlation with this measure, civilian government employment is an extremely good proxy for welfare state employment. One of the two measures for public financing of social services is total civilian nontransfer government expenditure as a percentage of GDP. This measure is conceptually different from civilian government employment as it includes government spending on social welfare that is not delivered by the government. Like our employment measure in the pooled data, it has the

**Table 3.1**    Variables

*Dependent variables, pooled analysis*
Government revenue as a percentage of GDP (HRS,[a] OECD[b])
Government expenditure as a percentage of GDP (HRS, OECD)
Social security benefit expenditure as a percentage of GDP (HRS, ILO[c])
Social security transfers as a percentage of GDP (HRS, OECD)
Civilian non transfer expenditure as a percentage of GDP (HRS, OECD)
Civilian government employment as a percentage of the working-age population (HRS,
    WEEP[d])
Public health expenditure as a percentage of total health expenditure (HRS, OECD)
Pension spending as a percentage of GDP divided by the proportion of the population
    over 65 years of age (HRS, ILO)

*Dependent variables, cross-sectional analysis*
Support for mothers' employment (Gornick, Meyers, and Ross, 1997)
Spending on the nonaged (OECD)
Public health, education, and welfare employment as a percentage of the working age
    population (WEEP). Canadian figure provided by John Myles on the basis of Statistics
    Canada data.
Decommodification in unemployment insurance programs (Esping-Andersen 1990: 50)
Decommodification in sickness pay programs (Esping-Andersen 1990: 50)
Decommodification in pension insurance programs (Esping-Andersen 1990: 50)
Decommodification index (Esping-Andersen 1990: 52)
Poverty—single mothers: percentage of single mothers with disposable incomes below
    50% of the average disposable (posttax and posttransfer) household income[e]
Poverty—aged: percentage of households in which the household head is over 65 with dis-
    posable incomes below 50% of the average disposable household income[e]
Poverty—age 25–59: percentage of households in which the household head is between
    24 and 60 with disposable incomes below 50% of the average disposable household in-
    come[e]
Inequality—aged: Gini index for disposable household income among the aged[e]
Redistribution: percentage reduction in the Gini index for pretax and pretransfer income
    caused by taxes and transfers (Mitchell 1991)[e]
Inequality: Gini index for disposable household income[e]

drawback that it includes expenditure for the provision of non–welfare state goods and services. However, there is little question that welfare state expenditure dominates this indicator; health and education expenditure alone forms the bulk of governmental nontransfer civilian expenditure. The second measure we employ to tap the extent of public financing of social services is the percentage of total health spending that is accounted for by the public sector. To measure the generosity of pensions, we divide total pension spending as a percentage of GDP by the proportion of the population over 65. As Pampel and Williamson (1989: 78)

**Table 3.1** *(continued)*

*Independent variables*

Left cabinet: scored 1 for each year when the left is in government alone; scored as the fraction of the left's seats in parliament of all governing parties' seats for coalition governments, 1946 to date (HRS)

Christian democratic cabinet: religious parties' government share, coded as for left cabinet (HRS)

Union density: union membership as a percentage of total wage and salary earners (HRS, Ebbinghaus and Visser 1992)

Corporatism (Lehmbruch 1984)

Constitutional structure: veto points created by constitutional provisions (HRS)

Female labor force participation: Percentage of women age 15 to 64 in the labor force (HRS, OECD)

Left*female: left government centered on its mean multiplied by female labor force participation centered on its mean

Voter turnout: voter turnout as a percentage of the adult population (HRS)

Aged population: percentage of the population over 65 years old (HRS, OECD)

Strikes: working days lost per 1,000 workers (HRS, ILO)

Authoritarian legacy: political regime in the late nineteenth century (HRS)

GDP per capita: gross domestic product per capita in constant US dollars (HRS, PWT[f])

CPI: percent increase in the consumer price index (HRS, OECD)

Unemployment: percentage of total labor force unemployed (HRS, OECD)

Military Spending: military spending as a percentage of GDP (HRS)

Outward foreign direct investment as a percentage of GDP[g]

Openness: imports + exports as a percentage of GDP (HRS, OECD)

[a]Data from the Huber, Ragin, and Stephens (1997) data set.

[b]Original data source is OECD.

[c]Original data source is International Labour Office.

[d]Data from the Welfare State Exit Entry Project, Science Center—Berlin.

[e]From Luxembourg Income Surveys. The calculations were done by David Bradley with household adjustments and other definitions such that the figures are consistent with those in Mitchell 1991, Atkinson et al. 1995, and those periodically updated at the LIS web site, http://lissy.ceps.lu.

[f]Original data source is the Penn World Tables, http://pwt.econ.upenn. edu/.

[g]1962–85 provided by Duane Swank (see Swank 1998), originally coded from IMF, *Balance of Payments Statistics,* various years. Data for 1960–61 coded by the authors from the same source.

point out, this is mathematically equivalent to the ratio of pension expenditure per aged person to GDP per capita (pension expenditure/aged population)/(GDP/population) and thus yields a quasi replacement rate. The values for our dependent variables at selected dates are listed in tables A.1 through A.8.

For our cross-national analysis, we collected data for 1980 or as close to that date as possible. We included a number of direct measures of welfare state entitlements, beginning with Esping-Andersen's (1990: 49–54) decommodification measures. He conceptualizes decommodification as the capacity, conferred by welfare state benefits, to maintain one's standard of living while separated from the labor market due to old age, sickness, or unemployment. The decommodification indices for pensions, sickness benefits, and unemployment are composed of five variables measuring the replacement rates, qualifying conditions, duration of benefits, and take-up rates. The overall decommodification index is a composite of the three separate indices, and it captures the generosity of pension, sickness, and unemployment benefits for workers at two different levels of income. From a gender perspective, the extent to which the welfare state entitles mothers to support in the pursuit of gainful employment is important. We use an index constructed by Gornick, Meyers, and Ross (1997, 1998) for public policies that support employment for mothers with children under three. The index aggregates 8 indicators pertaining to generosity and protection of maternity leave, paternity benefits, tax relief for child care, and the availability of public child care.

In the cross-sectional analysis we also use a number of measures of the impact of the welfare state on poverty and inequality. These measures are all based on Luxembourg Income Survey (LIS) data (the values for the countries are shown in table 4.4).[9] One of the poverty measures, the poverty rate among single mothers, indicates a welfare state commitment to supporting women's autonomy (Hobson 1990). The measure of poverty among the aged indicates the strength of the social safety net for the retired population, and the measure of poverty among the population aged twenty-five to fifty-nine the strength of the social safety net for the working-age population. The first two of the three measures we use to tap the distributive outcomes of the welfare state are Gini indices for the post-tax, posttransfer income distribution, one among the population at large, the other one among the aged. Of course, we are fully aware that the degree of inequality in the final income distribution is heavily shaped not only by the tax and transfer system but also by the primary income distribution and thus by the production regime. Levels of employment and unemployment and wage levels are very important, and those in turn are heavily influenced by the strength and structure of unions and by macro-economic policies. We devote an entire chapter to an exploration of the relationship between welfare state regimes and production regimes. Nevertheless, theoretically it is clear that class-based mobilization and the balance of political power should be determinants of the final distribution of income in a society, their effect being mediated in part through the production regime and in part through the welfare state. Our final measure of redistribution directly assesses the redistributive effect of the tax and transfer system; it calculates the percent reduction in the Gini index from before to after taxes and transfers.

Our final measure of welfare state characteristics is the proportion of total welfare state spending that goes to the nonaged, based on the OECD measure of spending on human capital. It indicates the active, or labor-mobilizing, as opposed to passive orientation of the welfare state. The spending on the aged is mostly passive, for income support and health care, whereas the spending on the nonaged has a strong component of training, retraining, relocation, and child care, with the purpose of integrating people into the labor force.

Turning now to the independent variables, we coded the political variables, left-party government share and Christian democratic party government share, as "1" for each year that these parties were in government alone, and as a fraction of their seats in parliament of all governing parties' seats for coalition governments. The full party data contained in our data set includes percentage of votes and percentage of parliamentary seats of parties categorized according to seven different political tendencies. We adopted Castles and Mair's (1984) left-center-right classification with some modifications and additions, and then subdivided the center and right parties into three categories: secular, Catholic, and other Christian (Protestant and mixed). We examined all of these variables in the analysis; the two listed in table 3.1 proved to be the most powerful predictors of welfare state effort. We expected cabinet share variables to be more powerful predictors of welfare state effort than the percentage of votes or seats, because cabinet share measures direct influence on policy. From the previous theoretical literature and empirical studies and our own comparative historical studies, a case could be made for either Christian democratic or centrist party power as the more important variable in determining welfare state effort. We experimented with various combinations of center, right, and Christian democratic parties and subgroupings of them (e.g., centrist Christian democracy, rightist secular). Our empirical analyses revealed that the findings for Christian democracy (right and center, Catholic and Protestant) were stronger and more robust; thus we report these results.

Our measure of constitutional structure is an additive index of federalism (none, weak, strong), presidentialism (absent, present), bicameralism (absent, weak, strong), and the use of popular referenda as a normal element of the political process (absent, present). Thus, a high score indicates high dispersion of political power and the presence of multiple veto points in the political process.[10]

Following Wilensky (1990), Hill and Tigges (1995), and Norris (1987), we measured female labor force participation by the size of the female labor force as a percentage of the female population aged fifteen to sixty-four. From our explanation above, it is clear that we expect both a direct effect on social service expansion of women's labor force participation via changing attitudes of women (and men) toward the value of welfare state policies in general and social services in particular, and an indirect effect via a process of social and political mobilization of women in existing unions and parties, in women's organizations, and in other new social movements.[11]

One drawback of employing female labor force participation as an independent variable is that it is, in turn, in part determined by the expansion of welfare state service employment since women very disproportionately occupy these jobs (Esping-Andersen 1990). Thus, in the case of the regression on civilian government employment the direction of causality between the independent variable and the dependent variable might not necessarily be clear. However, our choice of cumulative average measures for this and most other independent variables (see our discussion below) greatly reduces the probability that reverse causality would be present.

Our discussion of the relationship of women's political mobilization to the development of public social services suggests that there should be an interaction effect between social democratic governance and women's mobilization, with the combination of them leading to particularly high levels of public social services. Accordingly, we include an interaction term. A simple multiplicative term proved to be collinear with social democratic governance. To eliminate the collinearity, we centered both female labor force participation and social democratic governance on their respective mean values and then multiplied the two variables to create the interactive variable (left*female in the tables that follow).

The operationalization of the other independent variables listed in table 3.1 follows convention, as established by previous studies of the welfare state and of comparative political economy. For union density, we use union membership as a percentage of total wage and salary earners (Ebbinghaus and Visser 1992), and for corporatism we use Lehmbruch's (1984) index, which bases its categorizations on the degree of integration of organized labor into the policy-making process. We make one change in Lehmbruch's coding, moving the Netherlands from the category of "strong corporatism" to "medium corporatism" based on our analysis of the Dutch case (see chapters 4 and 5). We measure openness as the sum of imports and exports as a percentage of GDP, and the importance of direct investment abroad by total investment made by nationals overseas as a percentage of GDP. To measure authoritarian legacies, we developed a measure of regime forms in the late nineteenth century, based on our work on democracy (Rueschemeyer, Stephens, and Stephens 1992: chap. 4). The countries are divided into three categories: full democracies, parliamentary governments without full working-class suffrage, and "neoabsolutist" governments in which the principle of cabinet responsibility to the parliamentary majority had not yet been established. The operationalizations of gross domestic product per capita in thousands of constant U.S. dollars, voter turnout, percentage of the total labor force unemployed, military spending as a percentage of GDP, working days lost through strikes per 1,000 workers, percent increase in the consumer price index, and percent of the population over sixty-five are self-explanatory.

Sixteen of the eighteen large advanced industrial countries that have been democracies since World War II are included in the analysis. New Zealand and Ireland are excluded due to missing data for some of the variables. The dates chosen (1960–85) were governed by data availability for the dependent variables.

### Levels versus Change

Most of the pooled time series analyses of the development of the welfare state to date have measured the dependent variable as the level of expenditure rather than change from year to year or over somewhat longer time periods. In the last chapter, we argued that there were important theoretical and methodological reasons to focus on long-term development and not processes over the very short term. In our view, those arguments alone are sufficient grounds to choose the level of expenditure, employment, etc. as the dependent variables in our statistical analysis and not annual change in expenditure or employment. In addition, there are several properties of the data used here that further strengthen the case for the choice of level rather than change measures. First, the annual changes in the expenditure measures are strongly determined by economic cycles. Let us remember that we are not interested in expenditure per se, of course, but rather in underlying entitlements, which are a major determinant of expenditure. With controls for the size of some of the more important target populations (the aged and unemployed), one would hope that the remaining variation was primarily due to variations in entitlements. Business cycles confuse the picture for the expenditure data because they affect not only the numerator (e.g., expenditure goes up in recessions because of the increase in unemployment and down in booms because of the fall of unemployment) but also, and more importantly, the denominator (e.g., GDP falls in recessions and increases in booms). All of these effects are even greater given a greater level of social expenditure. For example, due to the deep recession, total government expenditure in Sweden skyrocketed from 59 percent of GDP in 1990 to 71 percent in 1994, despite cuts in entitlements.

Second, though data on advanced industrial democracies (collected principally by the OECD) are vastly more accurate than those available for less developed countries, they nonetheless contain errors, and these errors are greatly exaggerated when one moves from levels to annual change with the same set of data. Since the coefficients for the independent variables are typically much lower in analyses of change data, as we show later in this chapter, it is easy to get a significant coefficient (or a falsely insignificant one) as a result of data error.[12]

Third, some important social policy programs, most notably pensions but also most other programs in which entitlements are based on the duration and/or level of contributions, mature over a long period of time. Thus, expenditure will gradually climb without any additional legislation by the sitting government. For example, not only the level of expenditure in 1980 but also the change from 1979 to 1980 will be determined in part by legislation that may have been passed decades before. Depending on how they are constructed, direct measures of entitlements may also be subject to the maturation effect. For instance, the SCIP data on pension entitlements measure the replacement rate in a given year as the replacement rate received by a "newly retired worker," not the one that will be received under existing legislation by a worker entering the workforce when she or he retires (Palme 1990). This measure will increase as workers with more contribution years retire until the system is fully mature, that is, until the cohort that first contributes the required maximum number of years actually retires.

This maturation effect makes a mockery of the assumption in any analysis of short-term change, particularly annual change, of uniform leads and lags—that a given independent variable affects the dependent variable with a constant time lag across cases and through time. In addition to programs that mature through time, many, many programs are phased in over time, and the phase-in period varies greatly across programs and across countries. Of course, more realistic models can be developed by using moving averages, experimenting with various lags, and so on. Moreover, though it involves a sacrifice of degrees of freedom, moving from annual data to changes over a four- or five-year period considerably relaxes the assumptions of how uniform the time lags must be. These broader intervals also greatly smooth out the business cycle and thus reduce the effect of business cycle variables on the dependent variables. However, even these broader intervals suffer from the other drawbacks pointed out in this chapter and the previous chapter. Ultimately, they suffer from the fact that the lags are variable, unknown, and often of long duration.

With all of these factors considered, the choice of the level as the measurement of the dependent variable becomes inescapable. This has the additional advantage of making our quantitative analysis more comparable with previous studies, most of which measure the dependent variable as a level. However, these benefits are purchased at a cost. First, the assumption of independence of the observations, always problematic in pooled data, is yet more questionable when dependent variables are measured as levels, since it is at least plausible to claim that changes from one year to the next are at least partly independent while it is clear that the levels of expenditure or employment are not. Moreover, since the independent variables must also be measured in a corresponding fashion (as levels, cumulative indicators, or cumulative averages—see below) the consecutive measurements of the independent variables are necessarily correlated to one another and the independent variables are also more highly intercorrelated than they are if they are measured as change variables. Thus, multicollinearity is a larger problem in the levels data than in the change data. By the same token, these measurement decisions introduce a time trend into many of the variables, increasing the probability of spurious correlation.

A solution to this problem might appear to be to measure the dependent variable as a level and then include a lagged dependent variable in the equation, as suggested by Beck and Katz (1996). Conceptually (though not mathematically), this turns the analysis into an analysis of annual change; since once one controls for the level in the previous year, the remaining unexplained variation is the change from the previous year to the current year. Thus, an analysis with a lagged dependent variable will have all the drawbacks of annual change analysis listed above. Moreover, it has the additional drawback that the lagged dependent variable inappropriately drives the equation. That is, the correlation between the dependent variable and the lagged dependent variable is so high that almost nothing else matters.[13] While our ratchet effect hypothesis implies that the level of expenditure, for instance, is directly causally connected to the level of expenditure at time $t - 1$, most scholars in the field would agree that the high correlation between the two variables is a result of the fact that both share a variety of causes including policy legacies, etc., but also political, demographic, historical, and economic causes. Thus, a large part if not most of the extremely high coefficient for the lagged dependent variable is spurious.[14] This problem is further aggravated by the fact that measurement errors in the dependent variable within a country between years are certainly correlated, though it cannot be stated with any precision how large a bias this is. Our argument can be illustrated graphically in the following way:

where X is a vector of independent variables and y is the dependent variable. We contend that the very strong correlation between $y_{t-1}$ and $y_t$ is produced primarily by the fact that $X_{t-1}$ and $X_t$ are very strongly correlated and only secondarily by the more modest causal effect of $y_{t-1}$ on $y_t$. In these data, the coefficient for the lagged dependent variable is .92 or higher, and few other variables have substantively meaningful effects on the dependent variable when the lagged dependent variable is included. Our comparative historical analysis does not support the argument that policy ratchet effect and other policy legacy effects are anything near that large; thus we contend that an equation without the dependent variable lagged one year is a better estimation of the causal dynamics than an equation with it since, though the true coefficient for policy legacies is not 0, it is a lot closer to 0 than to .9. However, since we hypothesize that it is not 0, we also include an alternative specification in which we lag the dependent variable by five years. While this specification is still vulnerable to the spuriousness outlined above, it will allow us to get some estimation of the importance of policy legacies and provide a further test of the robustness of our main results.

The operationalizations of the dependent variables used in the pooled analysis are listed in table 3.1 and their values for selected dates are listed in tables A.1 through A.8 in the appendix to the book. Having decided on the level as the appropriate measure for the dependent variables, we are faced with the task of specifying the appropriate measures for the independent variables. In the case of the political cabinet share variables, it is clear that one would not hypothesize that it was only the partisan cabinet share the year before or the average of the previous few years that should determine the level of expenditure or employment in a given year, but rather the cumulative cabinet share over a long period of time. Thus, we measure the Christian democratic and social democratic cabinet share by the cumulative cabinet shares from the first year for which we have data (1945) to the year of the observation in question, that is, for example for Australia 1960, the cumulative share from 1945 to 1960. This cumulative measure captures the effects of long-term incumbency of a given political tendency.

A similar logic applies to the other variables that measure long-term political inputs. For example, in the case of strikes, again it does not make sense to hypothesize that it was only the level of strikes in the previous year or few years but rather the long-term level of militancy that should determine the level of the dependent variable. Thus, we measured the strike rate as the cumulative average of the level of strikes from the first year for which we have data (1950) to the year of the observation in question. The same logic applied to the following variables, which similarly were measured by the cumulative average of the value from the first year for which data were available (in parenthesis) to the year of the observation: voter turnout (1946), female labor force participation (1956), and union density (1946).[15]

The aged proportion of the population is a special case, since, as we pointed out above, there are two distinct hypotheses about its effects on the dependent variables. First, like unemployment, it has been hypothesized to push up spending because it increases the number of recipients of transfers. To test this hypothesis, it is appropriately measured as the aged proportion of the population in the year in question. It has also been argued that the aged act as a political lobby group, in which case it should be measured as a cumulative average (from 1946, the first year in our data set) as in the case of the other political variables. The development of both measures posed no problem, but, not surprisingly, they are so highly correlated that they create a multicollinearity problem, which we discuss in the next section.

The consumer price index measures change in a given year. Since it was not plausible to hypothesize that the dependent variables were affected only by inflation in the year of the observation, we also measured inflation as a cumulative average of the consumer price index (beginning in 1950), though for quite different reasons than in the case of the political variables that are measured in the same fashion.

Both the constitutional structure and authoritarian legacies variables are conceptually invariant through time, thus they pose no operationalization problem. By contrast, the degree of corporatism, that is, tripartite policy making by government, labor, and employers, does vary through time, though only marginally in this time period (1960–85) in most of our cases. However, the index we employ here, Lehmbruch's (1984) measure, gives only a snapshot at one point in time, the early 1980s.[16] An alternative to using this index is to use bargaining centralization as a proxy for tripartite policy making and develop a measure from the Golden, Lange, and Wallerstein (1999) data set, which contains data for this whole time period. In our assessment the loss of validity and reliability in the use of the single time point was less than the loss in using the proxy, because of the limited time variability in tripartism and misclassification of some cases when the bargaining centralization proxy was used. Moreover, since conceptually tripartism, like the other political variables, should be measured as a cumulative average variable, the annual variations in tripartism would be smoothed out resulting in a very high correlation with Lehmbruch's single–time point measure.

The remaining control variables—unemployment, military spending, per capita income, trade openness, and outward direct foreign investment—are operationalized by the level in the year of the observation. In the literature, unemployment has been hypothesized to push up spending primarily because it pushes up the number of recipients of transfers; thus it is appropriately measured as the level of unemployment in the year in question rather than by the long-term historical level of unemployment. Openness and outward DFI can be regarded similarly as driving up need by displacing workers. The level of military spending has been hypothesized to create a straight trade-off between military and social spending, so it too is best operationalized by the level of spending in the year of the observation rather than by average historic levels. Finally, GDP per capita measures the strength of the resource base of the society.

## Analytic Techniques

### Multicollinearity

As we pointed out in our first analysis of these data (Huber, Ragin, and Stephens 1993), the cluster of variables composed of left cabinet, trade openness, union density, and corporatism, all elements of what Czada (1988) calls the "size complex," creates multicollinearity in these data. In addition, the aged proportion of the population and the cumulative version of the same variable are so highly correlated (.93) that they create multicollinearity problems. As a first step, we chose to eliminate one of the two aged variables. Since deletion of the level variable reduced the multicollinearity problem with the size complex variables, we deleted this variable. Clearly, since we no longer control for the increased need created by an aging population, the cumulative average variable cannot be interpreted as measuring the effect of the political mobilization of the elderly but rather is measuring both the automatic effect on the dependent variable caused by an increasing client population and the political effect. We discuss this problem more extensively in the results section below.

With regard to the "size complex," we followed the same procedure we followed in the 1993 analysis. Our aim was to increase the tolerance levels to one at which we no longer observed the inflated regression coefficients and instability of the coefficients across equations for different time periods. Our bases for elimination rested on both statistical criteria and other empirical evidence. Statistical criteria were the level of tolerance of the variable, the strength of the correlation of the variable in question with the other candidates for elimination, and how its elimination from the analysis affected the tolerance levels of the remaining variables. In addition, we favored retention of variables for which there was strong comparative historical evidence that the variable in question (and not the alternative highly correlated variable) was directly related to the dependent variable.

The first decision was straightforward. The high correlation between left cabinet and union density (.84) made it impossible to include both variables in the analysis. Since comparative historical evidence indicates that its effect on social welfare legislation operates largely through left cabinet, we dropped the unionization variable from the analysis. This still left us with unacceptable tolerance levels and instability of coefficients. Statistically, the next candidate for elimination was corporatism because it had the lowest tolerance level of the remaining variables and its elimination substantially increased the tolerance levels of left cabinet, Christian democratic cabinet, and openness, and it reduced the instability of left cabinet. Moreover, as just discussed, the corporatism measure suffers from greater measurement error than the other two measures because the degree of corporatist bargaining varies somewhat through time within countries but the measure does not. From the point of view of the theoretical and comparative historical literatures, however, the elimination of corporatism was less desirable because most of the discussions of the effect of openness on public expenditure argue that openness operates through corporatist bargains (which compensate labor's wage restraint with an expanded social wage). Nevertheless, because elimination of openness left us with more serious multicollinearity than elimination of corporatism, we chose the latter course of action. However, in order to test whether corporatism yielded better predictions than left government, we reran our equations replacing left government with corporatism and compared the results. We did the same with union density and left government.

### *Estimation Technique*

In his thorough review of pooled time series analysis, Hicks (1994: 172) notes that "errors for regression equations estimated from pooled data using OLS [ordinary least squares regression] procedures tend to (1) be temporally autoregressive, (2) cross-sectionally heteroskedastic, and (3) cross-sectionally correlated, as well as (4) conceal unit and period effects, and (5) reflect some causal heterogeneity across space, time, or both." He points out that the Parks model as revised by Kmenta most thoroughly deals with these errors. For this reason, it became state of the art to use the Parks model in analyses of pooled time series data on welfare state development and comparative political economy.

Hicks notes in passing that the Parks model underestimates standard errors and overestimates $t$ statistics as the number of units $(N)$ approaches the number of time points $(T)$. (The Parks model requires that $T$ be larger than $N$.) Unfortunately, as Beck and Katz (1995) have recently shown by means of Monte Carlo simulations, the underestimation of the standard errors and overestimation of the $t$ statistics is quite severe unless $T$ is very much larger than $N$. Complete data for the dependent and independent variables included in most pooled time series analyses of OECD countries are not typically available before 1960 or after 1995 and the number of units (countries) is generally between 15 and 19. According to Beck and Katz's estimate even in the very best of cases ($N = 15$ and $T = 35$) the Parks method yields $t$ statistics that are inflated by almost 50% and in the more typical case ($N = 16$ to 18 and $T = 20$ to 30), the inflation of the $t$ statistic is on the order of 200 to 300% or even more (Beck and Katz 1995: 640).

We follow Beck and Katz's (1995) recommended procedure using panel corrected standard errors (PCSEs), corrections for first-order autoregressiveness, and imposition of a common rho for all cross-sections. This procedure is implemented in version 8.0 of the Shazam econometrics program.[17] Since the regressions in tables 3.2 to 3.4 are GLS regressions, there is no conventional $R^2$. Two alternative measures of goodness of fit, the Buse 1973 $R^2$ and the Buse raw moment $R^2$, are calculated by the Shazam program. Given the sensitivity of these GLS "pseudo $R^2$s" to the assumptions made in order to calculate them, some analysts consider the OLS $R^2$ to be a better indicator of goodness of fit. We report the OLS $R^2$. In all regressions, the raw moment Buse was quite similar to the OLS while the Buse 1973 was substantially lower. With the exception of openness, our hypotheses are directional, so we conduct a one-tailed $t$ test for significance levels. For openness, we report the two-tailed test.

As we indicated above, our measurement decisions introduce a time trend into the data, making it likely that the time series for individual variables are integrated and the independent and dependent variables are cointegrated. Indeed, as Durr (1992: 215) observes, "policy outcomes . . . are virtually by definition integrated," and our policy ratchet hypothesis argues as much. Dickey-Fuller tests indicated that this was the case. In the case of our independent variables the existence of time trends are most obvious in the cases of GDP per capita and aged proportion of the population and, to a lesser extent, female labor force participation, but the partisan government variables also exhibit a strong trend in countries in which one bloc dominates government over a long period of time. This makes spurious correlation a problem. To deal with this problem, the researcher can opt for several different solutions, the first of which, differencing the series, we have already rejected as inappropriate for the purposes of analyzing long-term change. The second solution is to lag the dependent variable, and we do include a specification with the dependent variable lagged five years. The third is to include a time trend variable in the equation in order to detrend the data, which we also do. The time variable proved to be collinear with GDP per capita, and GDP per capita flipped to strongly negative in the presence of the time variable, which made no theoretical sense. Therefore, we ran separate regressions with GDP per capita and with the time variable.

The nature of the macro phenomena we are studying offers us important advantages in our attempt to move from (possibly spurious) association to cause not open to most economists and political scientists dealing with cointegrated time series.[18] Their dependent variables, say economic growth or presidential popularity, are the products of the actions of thousands or even millions of actors; firms, consumer, voters, etc. Even where the independent variable is macrosocietal, say aggregate demand or economic prosperity, the intervening variables are these multitudes of agents' actions. Thus, it is impossible to trace the causal chain from aggregate demand to economic growth, for instance. In this study, we have a universe of eighteen cases and we do comparative historical research on nine of them. The actors are macrosocietal—governments, parties, employers associations, unions—and policy making consists of discrete acts of government. Though these acts are large in number, there are only a limited number of them that have major impacts on expenditure, and it is possible to trace the historical sequence in order to strengthen the case for one hypothesized causal chain over another. Moreover, we can employ the comparative method of comparing close cases to strengthen the case for one causal claim over another.[19]

As we mentioned above, we also ran regressions with corporatism in place of left government as independent variables, with time in place of GDP per capita and with the dependent variable lagged five years. We ran further regressions to address the problem of the feedback effect between women's labor force participation and civilian government employment and thus also social expenditure, dropping women's labor force participation and the interaction term. Since including all of these specifications in the chapter would greatly increase the number of tables, we present all of the specifications for one dependent variable, the ILO measure of social security benefits expenditure. We chose this measure because it is the most commonly used measure of welfare state effort in past quantitative analyses. We want to underline that it is not our intention to privilege this dependent variable over the others. Each measures different aspects of the welfare state and none can be used as a replacement for the others. For the other dependent variables, we present two specifications and highlight the key aspects of the results of the regressions not shown here in discussions in the text and refer the interested reader to our web site for the full presentation of the results of these analyses.[20]

For our cross-sectional analysis, where we have data for 13 to 18 cases only, depending on the measurement, we present first simple correlations between our three political master variables and indicators focusing on more qualitative aspects of the welfare state and on poverty and redistribution. We regressed the three political variables on these indicators, with stepwise deletion of the least significant of them, until only significant effects were left. We present only the coefficients for the independent variables that reached a significance level of .10 for a one-tailed test; we set the level so low because of the small number of cases.

## Results

### *Pooled Cross-Sections and Time Series Analyses*

Table 3.2 (pp. 68–69) displays the results of the regressions on social security benefit expenditure. Our preferred specification (column 1) strongly supports our hypotheses on the significant and strong effects of social democratic and Christian democratic government, constitutional structure, female labor force participation, and the left*female interaction term. Percent aged, per capita GDP, and unemployment are also highly significant. With the time controls substituted for per capita GDP, left government falls just below significance and female labor force participation is also insignificant (column 2). The political effect of social democracy is still exhibited in the interaction term. As one can see from the specifications in columns 3 and 4, social democracy exhibits significant effects if female labor force participation and the interaction term are removed from the equation.

In the regression in column 5, we deal with the time trend in the data and attempt to estimate the policy legacies effect by entering the dependent variable lagged five years. The main political effects of interest; social democracy, Christian democracy, constitutional structure and left*female interaction term remain significant and only somewhat diminished in strength when compared with equation 1. For example, one additional year of Christian democratic government is associated with a 0.277% increase in social expenditure rather than 0.377%. The coefficient for the lagged dependent variable indicates that a 1% higher level of social expenditure will result in 0.2% increase in expenditure five years later. Examining all eight equations with dependent variables lagged five years (not shown), one finds that this is the bottom of the range. The unstandardized coefficient for the lagged dependent variable varied from .20 to .47. While this is considerably lower than the .92 to .97 with the one-year lag, the lagged dependent variable was still the most important variable in five of the eight equations. Based on our case studies, this would appear to be too high an estimate for the policy legacies effect and thus is probably inflated for the reason explained in the previous section. Thus, we prefer the specifications in columns 1 and 2.

To compare the explanatory power of corporatism and left cabinet, one can compare the specifications in columns 4 and 6. Given the different metrics for the two independent variables, the most convenient way to compare them is to examine the significance levels of the unstandardized coefficients and the size of the standardized coefficients. Left cabinet appears as the unambiguously better predictor of social security benefit expenditure, as it does in the case of six of our other dependent variables (not shown). Only in the case of public share of total health expenditure does corporatism yield a better prediction.

Tables 3.3 through 3.5 (pp. 72–73, 75, 76) display the results for the other seven dependent variables in our pooled time series analyses. For

**Table 3.2**  Regressions on Social Security Benefits

|  | 1 | | 2 | | 3 | | 4 | | 5 | | 6 | |
|---|---|---|---|---|---|---|---|---|---|---|---|---|
|  | b | β | b | β | b | β | b | β | b | β | b | β |
| Left cabinet | .179** | .24 | .128 | .17 | .183* | .24 | .284*** | .38 | .110* | .16 |  |  |
| Christian democratic cabinet | .377*** | .49 | .246**** | .32 | .149 | .20 | .281*** | .37 | .277*** | .39 | .171* | .22 |
| Constitutional structure | -1.071*** | -.31 | -.808**** | -.23 | -.403 | -.12 | -.529 | -.15 | -.924*** | -.27 | -.755* | -.22 |
| Female labor force participation | .109** | .16 | .044 | .06 |  |  |  |  | .025 | .04 |  |  |
| Left*female | .018*** | .19 | .016** | .17 |  |  |  |  | .019*** | .22 |  |  |
| Voter turnout | -.076 | -.12 | -.051 | -.08 | -.010 | -.06 | -.780 | -.13 | -.059 | -.10 | -.037 | -.06 |
| % aged | .689*** | .22 | .795*** | .25 | .418 | .11 | .990 | .31 | .436** | .14 | 1.394*** | .44 |
| Strikes | -.071 | -.18 | -.062 | -.16 | -.026 | -.07 | -.028 | -.06 | -.110 | -.32 | -.041 | -.11 |
| Authoritarian legacy | -.666 | -.09 | -.198 | -.03 | .464 | .06 | .217 | .01 | -.610 | -.09 | .508 | .07 |
| GDP per capita | .419*** | .17 | .177 | .05 |  |  | .284* | .12 | .296* | .11 | .518*** | .21 |
| Consumer price index | .318 | .08 |  |  | .419 | .11 | .620* | .16 | .436 | .11 | .724** | .19 |
| Unemployment | .479*** | .23 | .360*** | .17 | .354*** | .17 | .449*** | .21 | .495*** | .25 | .492*** | .23 |

**Table 3.2** (continued)

| | 1 | | 2 | | 3 | | 4 | | 5 | | 6 | |
|---|---|---|---|---|---|---|---|---|---|---|---|---|
| | b | $\beta$ | b | $\beta$ | b | $\beta$ | b | $\beta$ | b | $\beta$ | b | $\beta$ |
| Military spending | .123 | .03 | .175 | .05 | .177 | .04 | .055 | .02 | .182 | .04 | .059 | .02 |
| Foreign direct investment out | -.173 | -.02 | -.205 | -.02 | -.155 | -.01 | -.119 | -.01 | -.145 | -.01 | -.134 | -.01 |
| Trade openness | .003 | .01 | .002 | .01 | -.004 | -.02 | -.001 | -.01 | -.001 | .00 | .007 | .00 |
| Year | | | .237*** | .29 | .226*** | .27 | | | | | | |
| Corporatism | | | | | | | | | | | .530 | .12 |
| Benefits lagged five years | | | | | | | | | .200** | .18 | | |
| Constant | 1.944 | | -10.656 | | -446.4*** | | 1.048 | | 6.86 | | -8.251 | |
| Common $\rho$ | .87 | | .90 | | .95 | | .92 | | .78 | | .91 | |
| OLS adjusted $R^2$ | .89 | | .89 | | .84 | | .84 | | .92 | | .84 | |
| N | 416 | | 416 | | 416 | | 416 | | 336 | | 416 | |

b unstandardized coefficient

$\beta$ standardized coefficient

Significance level: *** = .001, ** = .01, * = .05 (one-tailed test, except for openness)

each dependent variable, we present regressions with the more theoretically meaningful measure of economic affluence, GDP per capita, as an
independent variable, followed by the specification that controls for the
time trend, thus presenting a more conservative estimate of the size of
some of the effects. These are the same specifications as in columns 1 and
2 of table 3.2. The partisan government and constitutional structure variables show by far the strongest effects on the dependent variables. One
or both of the partisan government coefficients were significant, and in
most cases highly so, in all of the regressions on the dependent variables
save the ones on public share of health expenditure. In the latter regressions, the positive and significant effects of left government are counteracted by the negative effects of the left*female interaction term, which
would have been significant with a two-tailed significance test. Similarly,
the constitutional structure variable has a highly significant negative effect
on seven of our eight dependent variables (including social security benefits expenditure). The only nonpolitical variable that rivals these three
variables in consistency and significance of effects is the need variable
unemployment, which has a highly significant strong positive effect on six
of the dependent variables, predictably the five variables in which expenditure as a percent of GDP was part of the calculation of the dependent variable, along with civilian government employment. Even in the
case of pension spending, unemployment appears to push up spending,
which is probably a result of the policy of many countries, particularly
Continental European ones, to permit people to retire early in periods of
high unemployment. The next most consistently significant variable is the
interaction term between left incumbency and female labor force participation, which is significant in both regressions on four of the variables.

The differences in the pattern between social democracy and Christian
democracy confirm our expectations. To assess the effects of social democracy, one has to consider both the left cabinet variable and left*female interaction term. Either or both of these variables are strongly associated with the broader measures of welfare state effort and size of the
public sector (total revenue and expenditure, nontransfer spending, public employment), and with generosity of entitlements (pension generosity). One of the two also has a significant but more modest effect on social security benefits and transfers. As we mentioned above, the two
variables essentially cancelled each other out in the regression on public
share of health spending. The lack of any significant effects of social democracy on this dependent variable is confirmed by the regressions in
which female labor force participation and the interaction term were excluded (not shown). In those equations, the coefficient for social democ-

racy was not significant in the detrended regression and was significant but modest in the equation with per capita income.

Christian democracy, in contrast, which is most strongly associated with the narrower measures of transfers and social security benefits and with pension generosity, also has strong effects on total revenue and expenditures but a weakly significant one in one regression on nontransfer expenditures only, and none in the other regression and in those on public employment and public share of health expenditures. Just looking at the significance levels and coefficients of these two variables, one might argue that there is no difference between the effects of social democracy and Christian democracy on total revenue and, if anything, Christian democracy is more strongly related to expenditure. However, one has to keep in mind that social democracy has an additional effect via the interaction with female labor force participation, an effect that is highly significant in three of the four regressions, as it is in the regressions on social security benefit expenditure. The regressions without women's labor force participation and the interaction term are helpful in this regard (see table 3.2 for social security expenditure, not shown for the other dependent variables). With this alternative specification, the coefficients for social democracy are significantly larger than the coefficient for Christian democracy in the regression on total revenue and insignificantly different from the coefficients for Christian democracy in the regressions on total expenditure and social security benefit expenditure.

Constitutional structure, our measure of the availability of veto points in the political institutions of a country, has the predicted effect of depressing welfare state effort very significantly on the broad and narrow expenditure and the employment measures, as well as on the public share of health expenditures. The only dependent variable on which it shows no effect is pension generosity. Female labor force participation alone has a highly significant effect only on public employment.[21] As we hypothesized, it is in combination with a supportive left-wing government that working women are best able to effect an expansion of public social services and thus the welfare state more broadly. This hypothesis is supported by the significant effects of the interaction term between female labor force participation and left government in both regressions on public employment, revenue, social security benefits, and transfer expenditure.

Of the other political variables that we included because they have been used in previous studies, only the percent aged proved to have consistent effects, though these effects were significant in the regressions on social security benefits, transfers, government employment, and total

**Table 3.3**   Regressions on Government Revenue, Expenditure, and Transfers

| | Government Revenue as a Percentage of GDP | | | | Government Expenditure as a Percentage of GDP | | | | Social Security Transfers as a Percentage of GDP | | | |
|---|---|---|---|---|---|---|---|---|---|---|---|---|
| | b | β | b | β | b | β | b | β | b | β | b | β |
| Left cabinet | .464*** | .43 | .365*** | .34 | .419*** | .33 | .271* | .21 | .038 | .06 | .011 | .02 |
| Christian democratic cabinet | .494*** | .45 | .293** | .27 | .616*** | .47 | .347*** | .26 | .436*** | .72 | .341*** | .56 |
| Constitutional structure | −1.799*** | −.36 | −1.432*** | −.28 | −1.882*** | −.32 | −1.536*** | −.26 | −.970*** | −.35 | −.787*** | −.28 |
| Female labor force participation | .086 | .09 | −.024 | −.02 | .089 | .08 | −.062 | −.05 | .035 | .07 | −.010 | .02 |
| Left*female | .022*** | .16 | .020** | .15 | .021** | .14 | .016* | .10 | .008** | .11 | .007* | .09 |
| Voter turnout | −.118 | −.13 | −.074 | −.08 | −.076 | −.07 | .017 | .02 | −.083 | −.17 | −.059 | −.12 |
| % aged | .400 | .09 | .522 | .11 | .712* | .13 | .778* | .14 | .609*** | .24 | .645*** | .26 |
| Strikes | −.089 | −.16 | −.091 | −.16 | −.035 | −.05 | −.044 | −.07 | −.100 | −.33 | −.093 | −.30 |
| Authoritarian legacy | −1.658 | −.16 | −.971 | −.09 | −.886 | −.07 | .367 | .03 | −1.232 | −.22 | −.856 | −.15 |
| GDP per capita | .677*** | .19 | | | .576** | .14 | | | .288** | .15 | | |
| Year | | | .411*** | .34 | | | .507*** | .36 | | | .181*** | .27 |

Table 3.3    (continued)

| | Government Revenue as a Percentage of GDP | | | | Government Expenditure as a Percentage of GDP | | | | Social Security Transfers as a Percentage of GDP | | | |
|---|---|---|---|---|---|---|---|---|---|---|---|---|
| | b | β | b | β | b | β | b | β | b | β | b | β |
| Consumer price index | .630* | .11 | .338 | .06 | .959** | .15 | .559 | .09 | .359* | .12 | .191 | .12 |
| Unemployment | .141 | .05 | −.061 | −.02 | .814*** | .23 | .558*** | .16 | .453*** | .27 | .360*** | .27 |
| Military spending | .523** | .09 | .585** | .10 | 1.072*** | .16 | 1.285*** | .19 | .053 | .02 | .126 | .04 |
| Foreign direct investment out | −.166 | −.01 | −.217 | −.01 | −.335 | −.02 | −.424* | −.02 | −.103 | −.01 | −.132 | −.02 |
| Trade openness | .016 | .05 | .011 | .03 | −.001 | .00 | −.015 | −.04 | −.016 | −.08 | −.018 | −.08 |
| Constant | 26.759*** | | 6.183 | | 14.871* | | −14.861 | | 8.496* | | −1.428* | |
| Common $\rho$ | .88 | | .91 | | .90 | | .93 | | .85 | | .88 | |
| OLS adjusted $R^2$ | .87 | | .87 | | .89 | | .90 | | .89 | | .88 | |

b unstandardized coefficient

β standardized coefficient

Significance level: *** = .001, ** = .01, * = .05 (one-tailed test, except for openness)

N = 416 (16 countries; 26 years, 1960–85)

expenditure only. In no case do voter turnout, authoritarian legacies, and militancy in strike behavior have the significant positive effects as hypothesized. In fact, if one applies a two-tailed nondirectional test, all three have significant negative effects in several regressions.

Turning to the economic variables, clearly the most consistent and significant effect is that of unemployment. As we mentioned, unemployment has a highly significant positive effect on total expenditure, social security benefits, transfers, and nontransfer spending, as well as on civilian government employment and pension generosity. In the regressions in which it is included, GDP per capita shows the next most consistent effects in line with the hypotheses, with highly significant positive effects on revenue, social security benefits, and civilian government employment and weaker significant effects on total expenditure, transfers, nontransfer spending, and public share of health expenditures. However, these results have to be taken with some caution since the variable is so strongly correlated to the time trend that all of these positive effects flip to negative if both variables are included in the equations (results not shown). The data offer at best weak support for the predictions regarding the effects of the consumer price index, with significant positive effects on total revenue and expenditure and on transfers, but only in the regressions that were not detrended, and on public employment.

Military spending shows a highly significant positive effect on total expenditure and a moderately significant positive effect on total revenue as hypothesized, but it does not have the predicted significant negative effects on the other dependent variables. Finally, the two measures of the influence of the global economy are insignificant in all but one regression. The only significant effect is the negative effect of the outflow of direct foreign investment on transfer spending, offering weak support for the hypothesis.

As we mentioned, in the regressions with the dependent variable lagged five years, the lagged dependent variable was the single most important determinant of the dependent variable in five of the eight regressions (see table 3.2 for social security benefit expenditure, others not shown). The coefficients for at least two of the three government variables (including the interaction term) were significant at the .01 level or higher in all equations except the regression on public share of health expenditure. While the coefficients were not as large as those shown in tables 3.2 through 3.4, they were substantively meaningful (see table 3.2 for social security benefit expenditure). For instance, the estimated change in revenue per year of left government was 0.177 (compared to 0.464 in table 3.2); in civilian government employment, it was 0.124

**Table 3.4**    Regressions on Civilian Nontransfer Spending and Public Employment

| | Civilian Nontransfer Spending as a Percentage of GDP | | | | Civilian Government Employment | | | |
|---|---|---|---|---|---|---|---|---|
| | b | $\beta$ | b | $\beta$ | b | $\beta$ | b | $\beta$ |
| Left cabinet | .334*** | .40 | .227* | .27 | .158*** | .33 | .147*** | .31 |
| Christian democratic cabinet | .190* | .22 | .017 | .02 | −.043 | −.09 | −.033 | −.07 |
| Constitutional structure | −1.151*** | −.29 | −.995*** | −.25 | −.499** | −.22 | −.357 | −.16 |
| Female labor force participation | .057 | .08 | −.035 | −.05 | .145*** | .34 | .224*** | .52 |
| Left*female | .014* | .14 | .012 | .12 | .018*** | .31 | .017*** | .28 |
| Voter turnout | .014 | .02 | .065 | .09 | .014 | .04 | .086* | .22 |
| % aged | .039 | .01 | .068 | .02 | .341** | .17 | .189 | .09 |
| Strikes | .040 | .09 | .026 | .06 | .005 | .02 | .001 | .00 |
| Authoritarian legacy | .301 | .04 | .951 | .12 | −1.014 | −.22 | −1.786 | −.39 |
| GDP per capita | .445** | .16 | | | .273*** | .18 | | |
| Year | | | .350*** | .38 | | | .082** | .15 |
| Consumer price index | .506 | .12 | .168 | .04 | .264** | .11 | .223** | .09 |
| Unemployment | .387*** | .16 | .238*** | .10 | .068** | .05 | .020** | .02 |
| Military spending | .034 | .01 | .155 | .04 | .050 | .02 | .000 | .00 |
| Foreign direct investment out | −.273 | −.02 | −.341* | −.03 | −.025 | .00 | −.009 | .00 |
| Trade openness | .017 | .06 | .012 | .04 | −.006 | −.04 | −.005 | −.03 |
| Constant | 6.261 | | −12.376 | | −4.764 | | −14.070*** | |
| Common $\rho$ | .90 | | .91 | | .97 | | .99 | |
| OLS Adjusted $R^2$ | .83 | | .85 | | .90 | | .90 | |

b unstandardized coefficient
$\beta$ standardized coefficient
Significance level: *** = .001, ** = .01, * = .05 (one-tailed test, except for openness)
$N$ = 416 (16 countries; 26 years, 1960–85)

(compared to 0.158 in table 3.4). In the case of Christian democracy, the estimated change in transfers per year of government was 0.233 (compared to 0.436 in table 3.3); in pension effort, it was 0.094 (compared to 0.147 in table 3.5).

In our two replications of the analysis presented here using (a) annual change as the dependent variable and (b) using level as the dependent variable but including the lagged level as an independent variable, the independent variables were measured so that they would conceptually be the best determinant of change over the period in question. For example, the political variables, such as cabinet share and strikes, were measured by cabinet composition and strike levels in the previous year while the need variables, such as unemployment and percentage aged were

**Table 3.5**  Regressions on Public Share of Health Expenditure and Pension Generosity

| | Public as Percentage of Total Health Expenditure | | | | Pension Spending as a Percentage of GDP Divided by Percentage of Population over 65 | | | |
|---|---|---|---|---|---|---|---|---|
| | b | β | b | β | b | β | b | β |
| Left cabinet | .469** | .26 | .364* | .20 | .076*** | .36 | .049* | .24 |
| Christian democratic cabinet | .301 | .17 | .054 | .17 | .147*** | .70 | .101** | .48 |
| Constitutional structure | −5.189*** | −.63 | −4.659*** | −.56 | −.002 | .00 | .012 | .01 |
| Female labor force participation | .250* | .16 | .122 | .08 | .019 | .11 | −.005 | −.03 |
| Left*female | −.043 | −.19 | −.042 | −.19 | .004* | .14 | .003 | .12 |
| Voter turnout | .087 | .06 | .133 | .08 | −.027 | −.16 | −.016 | −.09 |
| % aged | 1.222 | .16 | 1.364 | .18 | −.011 | −.01 | −.007 | −.01 |
| Strikes | −.012 | −.01 | −.015 | −.02 | −.006 | −.06 | −.008 | −.08 |
| Authoritarian legacy | .782 | .05 | 1.347 | .08 | −.071 | −.04 | .160 | .08 |
| GDP per capita | 1.182** | .20 | | | .062 | .09 | | |
| Year | | | .551*** | .28 | | | .071*** | .31 |
| Consumer price index | −1.629 | −.18 | −2.067 | −.23 | .130 | .12 | .046 | .04 |
| Unemployment | .214 | .04 | −.024 | .00 | .068** | .12 | .045* | .08 |
| Military spending | −.576 | −.06 | −.490 | −.05 | .016 | .01 | .036 | .03 |
| Foreign direct investment out | −.356 | −.01 | −.370 | −.01 | .001 | .00 | −.017 | −.01 |
| Trade openness | −.026 | −.04 | −.020 | −.03 | .000 | .00 | −.001 | −.01 |
| Constant | 41.400 | | 17.888 | | 2.759 | | −1.09 | |
| Common ρ | .91 | | .91 | | .92 | | .93 | |
| OLS Adjusted R² | .70 | | .71 | | .72 | | .72 | |

b unstandardized coefficient

β standardized coefficient

Significance level: *** = .001, ** = .01, * = .05 (one-tailed test, except for openness)

N = 416 (16 countries; 26 years, 1960–85)

measured by the change in unemployment levels and percentage aged from the previous year to the present. It is useful here to cite a few of the findings for some of our key political variables in order to support our argument that these analyses are completely incapable of accounting for the patterns of long-term welfare state development.

In the last chapter, we stated that the goal of our quantitative and comparative historical analyses was to account for long-term change and for the pattern of variation across countries. Thus, our analyses in this chapter and in chapter 5 should account for the pattern across countries shown in chapter 4 and the change over the first two periods shown in tables A.1 through A.8. One can see, for example, that total revenue was much higher in the social democratic welfare states in 1980 than in the other types and that it increased much more rapidly from the first date for which we have data to that date (table 4.1 and table A.1). The social democratic welfare states are high on our measures of left cabinet, female labor force participation, and the left*female interaction term, and low on the measure of constitutional structure. The regression in table 3.3 indicates that these account for the total revenue figures seen in the tables in chapter 4 and the appendix. Let us take the left cabinet variable and give more precise estimates for the average increase in total revenue for the four social democratic countries for the period 1960–80. In this period, total revenue increased an average of 19.1% and the average number of years of left government on our index was 13.0 years. Taking the metric coefficient for left cabinet in table 3.3 (0.464), which gives the estimated change in revenue per year of left government, the effect of thirteen years of government is estimated to be a 6.03% increase in revenue, almost a third of the total increase. Were we to follow the same procedure with female labor force participation and the left*female interaction term, we would find that well over half of the change was accounted for by the three variables.

Now let us turn to the annual change data and make the same calculations. The coefficient for left cabinet (which is not significant) indicates an annual increase in revenue of only 0.058. Thus, the estimated change in revenue in the social democratic welfare states over the period 1960–80 caused by left government is only 0.75%. The only statistically significant coefficients in the regressions are the economic cycle variables. Thus, the results of this regression give us no clue whatsoever as to why total revenue increased so strongly over this period. The results with level and the lagged dependent variable are even more dismal: There the *total* increase in revenue over the whole period caused by left cabinet is estimated to be only 0.46%. Thus, we conclude that the change data and the lagged dependent variable specification do a poor job of accounting for the pattern of long-term change and variation across countries of interest to us in this book.

## Cross-Sectional Analyses

The correlations and regressions in the cross-sectional analysis of indicators of social rights, poverty, redistribution, and other welfare state indicators not available in time series further support our hypotheses and elucidate the effects of our three political master variables (table 3.6, pp. 80–81). Social democracy shows strong positive correlations with public employment in health, education, and welfare, three of the four indicators of decommodification (which measure transfer generosity), and labor-mobilizing policies (support for mothers' employment, spending on the nonaged, and spending on active labor market policies), and redistribution through the tax and transfer system; it shows strong negative correlations with poverty and inequality among all groups. Christian democracy in contrast shows moderate positive correlations only with indicators of decommodification and moderate negative correlations with public employment, spending on active labor market policies, and poverty among single mothers. Constitutional structure shows moderate to strong correlations with all indicators except for decommodification through unemployment insurance, and all the correlations are signed in the direction predicted by our hypotheses.

The regressions again confirm the importance of social democracy, which showed significant effects as predicted on all the dependent variables save decommodification through unemployment insurance and support for mothers' employment. Christian democracy shows significant negative effects on public employment in health, education, and welfare and on poverty among single mothers and adults, and positive ones on overall decommodification and decommodification through sickness insurance. The absence of significant effects of Christian democracy on labor-mobilizing policies (support for mothers' employment, spending on the nonaged, and spending on active labor market policies) and on inequality and redistribution through the tax and transfer system is also consistent with our hypotheses. The absence of a significant effect on decommodification through pensions and on poverty among the aged, though, is surprising. Constitutional structure shows significant negative effects on support for mothers' employment and redistribution through the tax and transfer system, and positive ones on poverty and inequality among the aged, all in line with our expectations.

The weak effects of the political variables on decommodification in unemployment insurance programs run contrary to our hypotheses. This does not appear to be an artifact of how Esping-Andersen constructed his measure. Using the biennial OECD data for gross replacement rates in unemployment insurance shown in the appendix (tables A.9 and A.10), we found no significant positive effects for social democracy or Christian democracy for the period 1961–85. Similarly, in his analysis of the SCIP social rights data on unemployment insurance, Carroll (1999) found no political effects on net replacement rates.

## Conclusion

Our pooled cross-sections and time series and our cross-sectional analyses have firmly supported the primacy given to political variables, both indicators of partisan mobilization and of state structure, in our theoretical framework. We chose incumbency of left-wing parties as our main indicator of mobilization of the working and lower middle classes since it is so highly correlated with other indicators of class-based mobilization, such as union density and corporatism, that we could only enter one of these indicators in the regressions. Left-wing parties are committed to values of equality and solidarity, and they have used governmental power to correct market outcomes and move their societies closer to these values. Left cabinet incumbency in practice means mostly social democratic incumbency, as communist parties rarely participated in government in advanced industrial democracies after World War II. The results of our analyses confirmed that social democratic incumbency led to the construction of large welfare states, with generous entitlements, a heavy emphasis on public provision of social services, on labor mobilization, and on redistribution through the tax and transfer system. It is in the provision of public social services and in the emphasis on redistribution that the social democratic welfare state differs most from the other kind of large welfare state, built under Christian democratic incumbency.

Christian democracy has been the second strongest political force attracting working- and lower-middle-class votes, along with votes from the middle and upper middle classes, competing with left-wing parties on the basis of religious appeals. Christian democratic parties with their more heterogeneous class base are primarily committed to the values of conciliation and mediation of interests, not equality. Their adherence to the principle of subsidiarity restricts the expansion of the public sector in social services. Our results confirmed that Christian democratic incumbency led to the construction of large welfare states also, with generous entitlements to transfers mainly, but a reluctance to provide public social

**Table 3.6**   Cross-Sectional Data Circa 1980

| | Correlations | | | Regressions | | | | | | | | |
|---|---|---|---|---|---|---|---|---|---|---|---|---|
| | Left Cabinet | Christian Democratic Cabinet | Veto Points in Constitution | Left Cabinet | | Christian Democratic Cabinet | | Veto Points in Constitution | | $R^2$ | $N$ |
| | | | | b | β | b | β | b | β | | |
| Support for mothers' employment | .52 | −.04 | −.59 | | | | | −6.40 | −.59 | .29 | 13 |
| Spending on nonaged | .57 | .05 | −.33 | .21 | .57 | | | | | .28 | 17 |
| Public HEW employment | .77 | −.46 | −.49 | .37 | .71 | −.18 | −.34 | | | .66 | 16 |
| Decommodification—Unemployment | .23 | .26 | .07 | | | | | | | | 18 |
| Decommodification—Sickpay | .73 | .23 | −.31 | .33 | .77 | .13 | .32 | | | .59 | 18 |
| Decommodification—Pensions | .72 | .05 | −.49 | .26 | .72 | | | | | .49 | 18 |
| Decommodification index | .72 | .18 | −.37 | .61 | .75 | .22 | .28 | | | .54 | 18 |

**Table 3.6**  (continued)

| | Correlations | | | Regressions | | | | | | | | |
|---|---|---|---|---|---|---|---|---|---|---|---|---|
| | Left Cabinet | Christian Democratic Cabinet | Veto Points in Constitution | Left Cabinet | | Christian Democratic Cabinet | | Veto Points in Constitution | | $R^2$ | $N$ |
| | | | | b | β | b | β | b | β | | |
| Active labor market policy | .68 | −.23 | −.22 | 1.19 | .68 | | | | | .43 | 18 |
| Poverty—single mothers | −.63 | −.27 | .51 | −1.01 | −.71 | −.56 | −.41 | | | .49 | 16 |
| Poverty—aged | −.55 | −.03 | .69 | −.17 | −.29 | | | 1.62 | .55 | .47 | 16 |
| Poverty—age 25–59 | −.80 | −.08 | .26 | −.26 | −.85 | −.08 | −.24 | | | .65 | 16 |
| Posttax and Posttransfer Inequality—Aged | −.76 | .08 | .67 | .00 | −.57 | | | .01 | .40 | .65 | 16 |
| Redistribution | .68 | .01 | −.61 | .43 | .50 | | | −1.59 | −.38 | .50 | 15 |
| Posttax and Posttransfer Inequality | −.81 | .07 | .40 | −.004 | −.81 | | | | | .63 | 16 |

Regressions include independent variables that reach the significance level of .1 or better (one-tailed test).

services and an emphasis on mobilization of labor into the workforce. As we shall see in our comparative historical analysis, Christian democratic welfare states have been passive in character, a characteristic that has become highly visible and problematic in the period of rising unemployment since the late 1970s. Christian democratic incumbency is also associated with low poverty rates, which is not surprising in the light of the commitment to generous transfers, but not with redistribution and low degrees of inequality.[22]

Our theoretical framework also attributes great importance to state structure, as institutions strongly shape decision-making processes and thus influence outcomes. Our analyses showed very clearly that power dispersion through political institutions is a serious obstacle to constructing generous welfare states. The availability of multiple veto points makes it possible for a variety of special interest groups to mobilize and torpedo major pieces of legislation, thus depressing every kind of welfare state expenditure as well as public employment. Accordingly, it also prevents redistribution and the lowering of poverty rates.

Our hypotheses regarding the effect of women's labor force participation were also supported by our results. The interaction effect between female labor force participation and left incumbency had significant positive effects on public employment, revenue, social security benefits, transfer expenditure, and (in one of the equations) on total expenditure and on nontransfer expenditure. Female labor force participation by itself had significant positive effects on public employment and, in one of the regressions, on social security spending and public health expenditure. We can interpret these results by pointing out that working women make demands on the state for better health, education, and welfare services, regardless of the institutional and political context, and that they are more successful in getting their demands met where their numerical strength is greater and particularly where political allies control the government. They make these demands because, once they enter the labor force, they need relief from the traditional female care-giving responsibilities for children, the elderly, and the sick (see, e.g., Wilensky 1990). Our results also suggest that working women pressure for an expansion of public delivery of these social services. This might be explained by the fact that women fill these social service jobs disproportionately and that, with the exception of countries where union contract coverage is very extensive, working conditions in the public social service sector tend to be better than in the private social service sector.[23]

Of all the other political variables we included, only the percentage of the population that is over sixty-five years old had consistent and significant effects in the direction predicted by the hypotheses in the literature. As we pointed out, there are two ways in which to conceptualize this variable. One way is to see it as a need variable like unemployment, which automatically pushes up expenditures in any existing pension and health care programs. The other way is to see it as a political input variable, assuming that elderly people mobilize in defense of their interests and that the more elderly people there are the stronger their influence is, in good pluralist fashion. Our results here clearly deny support to the latter conceptualization, as they show no effect on pension generosity, the only dependent variable that is not affected by an automatic increase in the client population.[24] The three other highly significant effects, on social security benefits, transfer spending, and public employment, by contrast, can all be interpreted as escalation of expenditure and public social service employment in response to rising need under existing legislation.

Unemployment functioned clearly as a need variable, as it had the predicted effect of driving up welfare state expenditures. It also had the effects of expanding public employment and raising pension generosity, two effects that may seem unexpected. These effects can easily be interpreted in the context of case knowledge. In some countries, rising unemployment was countered by shifting redundant workers into disability schemes or early pensions. This of course drove up pension expenditure, which is captured in the numerator of our measure of pension generosity, but not the population over sixty-five, which is the denominator. In other countries, unemployment was countered by active labor market policies, that is, public assistance for retraining and relocation, or the provision of temporary public employment, all policies that expand employment in the public sector.

The positive effects of GDP per capita, our measure for the level of affluence of a society, on the whole range of revenue, employment, and expenditure measures supported the hypotheses of the logic of industrialization school. It is certainly plausible that a stronger resource base makes it easier to construct a comprehensive and generous social safety net and to provide a variety of social services. The impact of this variable, of course, would be even starker if we included countries outside the exclusive club of advanced industrial democracies in our analysis.

The results of our analyses show only a weak impact of the international economy on any indicators of welfare state expansion. Trade openness shows no significant effects at all, and outflow of foreign direct investment shows only one. In the case of openness, few quantitative studies other than Cameron's (1978) have found more than marginally significant and substantively unimportant effects of this variable once other factors such as social democratic governance and corporatism were controlled for.[25] It is important to point out that we not only found no significant positive but also no significant negative effects of trade openness. This supports our contention that generous welfare states are indeed viable in the context of highly open economies. As we pointed out in our discussion of the "size complex," openness is highly correlated with corporatism, union density, and left party strength. Our results, though, support our hypothesis that openness per se does not lead to welfare state expansion, but that the relationship is politically mediated and the crucial causal relationship is the one between left incumbency and welfare state effort. The absence of significant effects of outflow of foreign direct investment, save on transfer spending, is also not surprising. As we pointed out, in most of our countries there was a dramatic acceleration of investment abroad by major corporations in the mid-1980s, in connection with the renewed vigor of European integration, and it was only in that context that the problem of outflow of investment funds became linked in the political debate to the continued viability of the welfare state. Accordingly, we would expect to see stronger effects in our analysis of the phase of welfare state retrenchment.

The one big surprise to emerge from our cross-sectional data analysis is the weak effect of the political variables on decommodification in unemployment insurance programs. From the point of view of the power resources literature, one might expect political effects, particularly the effect of social democracy, to be strongest on this variable of all of the variables analyzed in this chapter. Together, the duration of unemployment insurance and the replacement rate appear to be among the most important determinants of the reservation wage and thus a hot point of struggle between capital and labor. Fear of unemployment empowers capital vis-à-vis labor, thus removing that fear shifts the balance of power toward labor. By contrast, the replacement rate in pensions would be relevant to capital only in the severest labor shortages, when employers might be willing to take on aged workers. Even sick pay replacement rates would not appear to be as central to the power balance between the labor market adversaries. We return to this anomaly in chapter 5.

# CHAPTER FOUR

◆

# Welfare State and Production Regimes

In the last chapter, we conducted what Ragin (1987) refers to as a "variable-oriented" analysis demonstrating the centrality of partisan governance in predicting the values of cases on a number of indicators of welfare state effort and outcomes. As Ragin points out, such analyses obscure the identity of particular cases and thus also how the characteristics under consideration may, or may not, occur in distinct clusters. To prepare the ground for our comparative historical analysis in chapter 5, this chapter moves to an examination of the country profiles on welfare state characteristics and an investigation of cohesion of the countries into distinct groupings of "welfare state regimes." We also examine the characteristics of their labor markets and broader production regimes, attempting to link these regimes to their countries' welfare state characteristics, thus linking the welfare state regimes literature to the parallel literature on the "varieties of capitalism."

Since the publication of Esping-Andersen's *Three Worlds of Welfare Capitalism* (1990), the dominant approach to the study of welfare states in advanced capitalist democracies has come to use the lens of a typology of three or four types of "welfare state regimes." Esping-Andersen and Kolberg (1992) argue that welfare state regimes are interrelated with different labor market institutions and policies, and the literature on corporatism also posited a link between corporatism and generous social policy. While the corporatism literature had focused mainly on institutionalized interaction between the government, labor, and employers, the more recent literature on "varieties of capitalism" has focused investigators' attention on the nature of relations among enterprises as well as between enterprises and financial institutions and between them and the government (Albert 1991; Soskice 1991, 1999; Hollingsworth, Schmitter, and Streeck 1994; Hall 1999). Only recently have there been attempts to examine the relationship between these varieties of capitalism or production regimes and welfare state regimes (Ebbinghaus and Manow 1998; Kitschelt et al. 1999b; Huber and Stephens 2000a). In this chapter, we extend our earlier effort on this idea and attempt to link the study of welfare state regimes more systematically to the study of production regimes.

While we build on Soskice's work, we do not limit "production regime" to the microrelationships among firms, employees, financial institutions, etc. We conceptualize production regimes in a parallel manner to welfare state regimes, to denote a configuration of institutions and policies. In the case of production regimes, the relevant institutions are private and public enterprises (industrial and financial), associations of capital interests (business associations and employer organizations) and labor, labor market institutions, and governmental agencies involved in economic policy making, as well as the patterns of interaction among all of them; the relevant policies are labor market policy, macroeconomic policy, trade policy, industrial policy, and financial regulation. Whereas our conceptualization of production regimes is broad, we do not attempt to investigate all their characteristics in an exhaustive way. Rather, we concentrate on institutions and policies that shape wages, employment, and investment levels. These institutions constitute "national frameworks of incentives and constraints" (Soskice 1994) that shape the behavior of actors and are relatively impervious to short-run political manipulation. We continue to apply the terminology that Soskice uses for different types of market economies—coordinated and uncoordinated/deregulated/liberal—to our wider concept of production regimes.

Building on the multivariate analysis in the previous chapter, we begin by fleshing out the welfare state regime typology introduced in chapter 1. We then briefly discuss the interrelationship between these welfare state regimes and production regimes. In the second section, we examine the data on poverty and inequality analyzed in chapter 3 in order to dissect the relationship between these outcome measures and the different welfare state regime types. We also briefly examine the relationship of the welfare state–production regimes with conventional indicators of economic performance—growth, unemployment, and inflation.

## Welfare State and Production Regimes

In his work on social policy regimes, Esping-Andersen goes beyond previous work, which classified welfare states along a single dimension of generosity. Esping-Andersen argues that (1) welfare states vary along multiple dimensions and (2) they cluster around three distinct regimes. While subsequent work on the welfare state has disputed aspects of Esping-Andersen's argument such as the number and types of regimes, the classification of various countries, and the degree to which countries cluster into the three (or four) distinct groups, his typology has proved to be a useful explanatory device. We adopt Esping-Andersen's typology, with a few modifications. First, following Castles and Mitchell (1993), we distinguish an Antipodean type of "wage earner welfare states." Since our typology is based on the regime configuration circa 1980, before the beginning of the era of retrenchment, it is important to distinguish this group from the liberal welfare states that do exist in the other Anglo-Saxon countries (table 4.1), as their systems of social protection were quite different at this point in time. Second, we label Esping-Andersen's conservative-corporativistic group "Christian democratic." This labeling is consistent with the "liberal" and "social democratic" labels in that it underlines the main political force behind the creation of these welfare states, Christian democratic, secular center and right, and social democratic parties, respectively. More important, the label gets away from the misleading implication of Esping-Andersen's work that the "conservative" welfare states of Continental Europe reinforce inequalities created in the market and thus preserve the stratification system. Though there is no question that Christian democratic welfare states preserve gender stratification, they are quite redistributive across income groups, though not as redistributive as social democratic welfare states, as we shall see below.

It is important to point out here that, despite the labels we have given them, the categories are developed on the basis of particular welfare state characteristics, *not* on the basis of the political predominance of particular parties in the countries in question. The names of the categories are political, but these refer to the type of welfare state that these political tendencies prefer. We chose these names for convenience in the place of alternatives that would have been clumsier. As the discussion below will show, we could have called the social democratic welfare state a "universalistic, comprehensive, citizenship-based, income security, gender-egalitarian, labor-mobilizing welfare state," the Christian democratic welfare state a "fragmented, employment-based, comprehensive, transfer-heavy, male breadwinner, passive welfare state," the liberal welfare state a "residual, partial, needs-based, service-poor welfare state," and the wage earner welfare state a "male breadwinner system of social protection based on wages and benefits delivered through the arbitration systems backed up by a residual, income-tested, service-poor social policy regime."

We leave it as an open question how clearly countries clustered into the four distinct types.[1] We do contend that within a given country, different aspects of the welfare state "fit" together and "fit" with different aspects of the production regimes, in particular their labor market

**Table 4.1**  Welfare State Regimes Circa 1980

| | (1) Left Cabinet Years | (2) Christian Democratic Cabinet Years | (3) Social Security Expenditure | (4) Transfer Payments | (5) Total Taxes | (6) Public HEW Employment | (7) Health Expenditure Percentage Public | (8) Health Employment Percentage Public | (9) Pension Expenditure Percentage Public | (10) Spending on Nonaged | (11) Decommodification Index | (12) Support for Mothers' Employment |
|---|---|---|---|---|---|---|---|---|---|---|---|---|
| *Social democratic welfare states* | | | | | | | | | | | | |
| Sweden | 30 | 0 | 31 | 18 | 56 | 20 | 92 | 92 | 86 | 12.7 | 39 | 62 |
| Norway | 28 | 1 | 20 | 14 | 53 | 15 | 98 | 88 | 82 | 8.5 | 38 | 43 |
| Denmark | 25 | 0 | 26 | 17 | 52 | 18 | 85 | 85 | 71 | 11.5 | 38 | 64 |
| Finland | 14 | 0 | 17 | 9 | 36 | 9 | 79 | | 69 | 10.5 | 29 | 66 |
| Mean | 24.3 | 0.3 | 23.6 | 14.5 | 49.4 | 15.5 | 88.5 | 88.3 | 77.0 | 10.8 | 36.2 | 58.8 |
| *Christian democratic welfare states* | | | | | | | | | | | | |
| Austria | 20 | 15 | 21 | 19 | 46 | 4 | 69 | | 68 | 4.1 | 31 | |
| Belgium | 14 | 19 | 21 | 21 | 43 | 6 | 82 | 31 | 60 | 10.2 | 32 | 59 |
| Netherlands | 8 | 22 | 27 | 26 | 53 | 4 | 76 | | 69 | 12.6 | 32 | 34 |
| Germany | 11 | 16 | 23 | 17 | 45 | 4 | 79 | 34 | 70 | 8.0 | 28 | 36 |
| France | 3 | 4 | 25 | 19 | 45 | 7 | 79 | | 68 | 7.5 | 28 | 53 |
| Italy | 3 | 30 | 20 | 14 | 33 | 5 | 84 | | 72 | 3.4 | 24 | 36 |
| Switzerland | 9 | 10 | 13 | 13 | 33 | 5 | 68 | | 71 | | 30 | |
| Mean | 9.6 | 16.4 | 21.6 | 18.4 | 42.4 | 5.0 | 76.7 | 32.5 | 68.3 | 7.6 | 29.3 | 43.6 |

**Table 4.1** *(continued)*

| | (1) | (2) | (3) | (4) | (5) | (6) | (7) | (8) | (9) | (10) | (11) | (12) |
|---|---|---|---|---|---|---|---|---|---|---|---|---|
| | Left Cabinet Years | Christian Democratic Cabinet Years | Social Security Expenditure | Transfer Payments | Total Taxes | Public HEW Employment | Health Expenditure Percentage Public | Health Employment Percentage Public | Pension Expenditure Percentage Public | Spending on Nonaged | Decommodification Index | Support for Mothers' Employment |
| *Liberal welfare states* | | | | | | | | | | | | |
| Canada | 0 | 0 | 13 | 10 | 36 | 7 | 75 | 79 | 58 | 5.7 | 22 | 35 |
| Ireland | 3 | 0 | 19 | 13 | 39 | | 92 | | 55 | 6.8 | 23 | |
| U.K. | 16 | 0 | 17 | 12 | 40 | 8 | 90 | 95 | 67 | 9.2 | 23 | 22 |
| U.S.A. | 0 | 0 | 12 | 11 | 31 | 5 | 42 | 23 | 61 | 4.5 | 14 | 14 |
| Mean | 4.7 | 0.0 | 15.2 | 11.5 | 36.5 | 6.7 | 74.8 | 65.7 | 60.3 | 6.6 | 20.6 | 23.7 |
| *Wage earner welfare states* | | | | | | | | | | | | |
| Australia | 7 | 0 | 11 | 8 | 31 | 7 | 62 | 59 | 59 | 2.8 | 13 | 22 |
| New Zealand | 10 | 0 | 16 | 10 | | | 84 | | 88 | 3.1 | 17 | |
| *Japan* | 0 | 0 | 10 | 10 | 28 | 3 | 71 | | 54 | 2.4 | 27 | |
| Grand mean | 11.1 | 6.5 | 19.1 | 14.5 | 41.1 | 7.9 | 78.2 | 65.1 | 68.2 | 7.3 | 27.2 | 42.0 |

Data sources and definitions (1–7, 10–12), see table 3.1; (8) Public health employment as percentage of total health employment, WEEP; Canadian figures, Statistics Canada; (9) Public pension spending as a percentage of total pension spending, Esping-Andersen 1990: 85.

components. This "fit," however, was (and is) not a one-to-one correspondence between a whole configuration of welfare state and production regimes. Rather, an essentially similar set of interenterprise and em-
ployer-labor-government relationships can be the framework within
which different—but not just any—welfare state regimes emerge; conversely, the same welfare state regime is compatible with different—but
not any—labor market institutions and policies. The groups themselves
varied in their homogeneity, with the social democratic group being the
most homogeneous and the Christian democratic being the most heterogeneous, particularly if one includes production regimes into the analysis. Accordingly, we have divided the Christian democratic group into
three subgroups.

The data in table 4.1 outline the basic differences between the policy
configurations in the different types of welfare states. All data are for
1980 or the closest available year and thus represent a cut in time before
the recent era of retrenchment. The first two columns document, in con-
junction with the implicit absent category—years of secular center and
right cabinet—the differences in the political underpinnings of the
groups. The Nordic countries were distinctive in terms of their years of
social democratic governance. Of these countries, Finland was the lowest
on this indicator and was also lowest on all of the indicators of welfare
state generosity. As we discuss in the next chapter, in the mid-1960s Finland experienced a "system shift" marked by the coming to power of a social democratic–led government including the communists and by the
unification of unions and the development of a corporatist social pact
with the employers. In the subsequent two and one-half decades, Finland
caught up with her Nordic neighbors in terms of welfare state generosity
(Stephens 1996; Huber and Stephens 1998). For instance, between 1980
and 1990, Finland moved from last to first among the Nordic countries on
Esping-Andersen's decommodification index (column 11).[2]

Liberal welfare states were characterized by the absence of Christian
democratic government and, with the exception of Britain, little or no
influence of social democracy in government. The British Labour Party
was in office relatively frequently before 1980, and this is reflected in the
indicators of social policy, where it appears as more generous than other
liberal countries, especially in the area of health care, one of the key elements of the policy initiatives of the first postwar Labour government
(see columns 7 and 8 of table 4.1).[3] Keep in mind that the figures in tables
4.1–4.3 cover years quite early in the first Thatcher government and thus
do not indicate the effects of her cutbacks.

The wage earner welfare states were characterized by strong labor

parties, which nonetheless were narrowly defeated in most elections between 1945 and 1980, and by strong unions (see table 4.2). As we will see
in the next chapter, earlier in the century interventive labor courts
awarded Antipodean workers many wage and nonwage benefits that
elsewhere were products of welfare state legislation. The postwar political situation reinforced the tendency of the Antipodean labor movements to rely on "social protection by other means," that is, through
highly regulated labor markets (Castles 1985).

Since the Christian democratic welfare states were the most heterogeneous, we have broken them down into three subgroups that will play
some role in our subsequent discussion. The first group contains the lone
country of Austria. It is the only Christian democratic welfare state in
which social democracy was more influential than Christian democracy.
Its production regime, particularly relations among capital, labor, and
the government, its macroeconomic policy, and to a lesser extent its labor market policies were closer to the social democratic model than to
the Christian democratic (Huber and Stephens 1998). In the comparative political economy literature, it is often classified with Sweden as
the most corporatist political economy among the advanced industrial
democracies. In the next group, Belgium, Netherlands, and Germany, social democracy was influential but not as influential as Christian democracy. Along with Austria, these countries also were more generous than
the other three Christian democratic countries on most of the welfare
state indicators in table 4.1. These countries also shared—to different
degrees—production regime characteristics with the Nordic economies,
which set them off from the other three countries in the Christian democratic group. As one can see from table 4.1, both the Christian democratic and social democratic welfare states were much more generous
than the other groups in terms of their social expenditure (columns 3,
4, and 7). Indeed, it would appear that the Christian democratic welfare
states actually provided more generous transfer payments than the social
democratic welfare states. While it is true that they spent more on transfers and they were transfer heavy as compared to the service-heavy social democratic welfare states (Huber, Ragin, and Stephens 1993; Huber
and Stephens 2000a), the transfer spending figures in table 4.1 for Christian democratic welfare states were high in part because the target
populations were large. Unemployment was high, thus expenditure on
unemployment compensation was correspondingly high and, in addition,
many of these countries dealt with unemployment problems by putting
workers on early pensions or disability payments.

Esping-Andersen's decommodification index (column 11) is a better indicator of the generosity of transfer entitlements than the transfer expenditure figure. It is a composite measure of the characteristics of three income transfer programs (pensions, sick pay, and unemployment compensation), the components of which are various measures of qualifying conditions and benefit duration and income replacements for two categories of workers, a "standard production worker" and those qualifying for only minimum benefits (Esping-Andersen 1990: 49, 54). One can see from the index that social democratic welfare state transfer systems were more generous than the Christian democratic ones.

While not all of the data on which this index is based, the Social Citizenship Indicators Project at the University of Stockholm, are yet public, it is apparent from what is available and from the OECD unemployment replacement rate data (tables A.9 and A.10) that a principal reason for the difference between the social democratic and Christian democratic welfare states on the decommodification index is that income replacement rates among those with minimum qualifying conditions were much better in the former (Palme 1990; Kangas 1991; Carroll 1999). Palme's data on minimum and standard pensions for this period show that minimum replacement rates in the Nordic countries were considerably higher than in all other countries except Austria and the Netherlands, which achieve parity with the Nordic countries (Palme 1990). Indeed, the Christian democratic countries as a group, even with Austria and the Netherlands included, actually come out worse than the liberal welfare states on this measure. The reason for this is obvious: All of the social democratic countries had a basic flat-rate pension that went to all citizens when they reached retirement age, an earnings-related pension dependent on years of work and income, and a supplement for all those with low or no earnings-related pensions. Most of the Continental countries lacked the citizenship pension or its equivalent. By contrast, income replacement rates of the "standard production worker" were only slightly higher in the social democratic countries than in Christian democratic countries, and in both groups they were considerably higher than in the liberal welfare states. In the case of unemployment insurance, the OECD figures in appendix tables A.9 and A.10 show a similar pattern; there was a much larger difference between the Christian democratic and social democratic welfare states in replacement rates for the low-income workers than for workers with the average wage.

It was not, however, in the structure of transfers that the social democratic welfare states and Christian democratic welfare states differed most. As we showed in the last chapter, the most distinctive feature of the social democratic welfare state was the public funding *and* delivery of social services. While in all welfare states the government was the primary provider of education, only in the social democratic welfare states did the government provide a broad range of social services. One can see the dramatic differences in this regard from the figures for public health, education, and welfare employment as a percent of the working-age population in column 6 of table 4.1. In the case of health care, it is clear from a comparison of the figures in columns 7 and 8 that other welfare states picked up the tab for health but were not the primary deliverers of it. Outside of the Nordic countries, only three other countries—the U.K., New Zealand, and, from 1978, Italy—had national health services, and in two of these (U.K. and New Zealand), they were products of social democratic governments.[4]

It is apparent from the very great differences in public social service employment (column 6) that the social democratic welfare states were virtually alone in providing a wide range of services outside of education and, together with the U.K., New Zealand, and Italy, health care. The expansion of such programs as day care, elderly care, job training programs, temporary employment programs in the public services, and after-school programs, along with improvement of maternal and parental leave programs, were the main areas of welfare state innovation in the Nordic countries in the 1970s and 1980s. The differences in the level of public social services are the reason why taxation levels in social democratic welfare states were significantly higher than in the Christian democratic welfare states, averaging close to 49 percent of GDP compared to 42 percent in the latter group (table 4.1, column 5) despite the fact that transfer payments were actually lower on the average in the social democratic welfare states.

Two distinctive features of the social service intensiveness of the social democratic welfare states are worth underlining. First, they were gender egalitarian and have promoted the expansion of women's labor force participation, which we examine below. This is reflected in column 12 of table 4.1, which measures the extent to which a wide range of social provisions facilitate mothers with young children entering the labor force. Second, they were aimed at the nonaged, as can be seen from the OECD figures on spending on the nonaged as a percentage of GDP in column 10.[5] In both cases, these distinctive features involve investment in human capital and in the mobilization of labor.

Table 4.2 (pp. 96–97) outlines some of the parameters of labor market institutions corresponding to the welfare state types. As is well known, union organization was very high in the social democratic countries (column 1). While union density was lower in the Christian democratic countries, coverage of union contracts was quite high due to agreements between employers and unions which extended union agreements to non-unionized workers or due to government legislation which achieved the same end (column 2).

Centralized bargaining and corporatism have also been associated with social democratic governance and have often been seen as being one and the same. But as we pointed out in the last chapter, they are distinct but closely associated phenomena. Corporatism refers to a tripartite bargaining process over a range of social and economic policy issues, not simply to wage bargaining between employer and union federations. To our knowledge, the only attempt directly to categorize countries by the level of corporatist (tripartite) policy making is that of Lehmbruch (1984). Lehmbruch's ranking of countries on his scale of corporatism is based on the degree of trade union participation in public policy formation. According to Lehmbruch (1984: 66), "[s]trong corporatism is characterized by the effective participation of labor unions (and organized business) in policy formation and implementation across those interdependent policy areas that are of central importance for the management of the economy." In column 3, we present Lehmbruch's classifications with one adjustment: we have coded the Netherlands as 3 rather than 4 based on our understanding of the role of Dutch unions in economic policy making (see chapter 5). Iversen's (1998) index of bargaining centralization is presented in column 4. As one can see, corporatism and bargaining centralization are strongly associated with each other, and both are strongly associated with welfare state regime type. Note that the scores in the table for bargaining centralization are for 1976–80 and thus include the three years of the Social Contract under the Labour government in Britain. Iversen codes the U.K. as .36 during this period and .12 during the remaining years between 1973 and 1995. With this lower score, the liberal welfare states, like the social democratic welfare states, exhibit a great degree of homogeneity in their degree of bargaining centralization. Among the Christian democratic welfare states, one again observes a division between the northern tier and France and Italy, with the northern group being closer to the social democratic welfare states.

Columns 5 and 6 show two different measures of literacy skills of the less skilled derived from the recent OECD–Statistics Canada study (OECD/HRDC 2000). Column 5 is the average percentage of the adult population in the lowest of five categories of literacy skills on the three tests in the OECD/HRDC study: prose, document, and quantitative. Column 6 is the average score on the test of the fifth percentile. This is the first study that presents comparable measures of actual skills of the adult population based on the testing of random samples of working-age adults on a battery of tasks designed to be as strictly comparable as possible given the differences in language and culture. These data are the best available indicators of the actual skill level at the low end of the distribution. The data show clearly that the liberal welfare states have larger unskilled populations. While there is some heterogeneity among the Christian democratic welfare states, they exhibit higher average skill levels while the social democratic welfare states show the highest skill levels. This is not primarily a product of high levels of formal education, as the authors of the study observe (OECD/HRDC 2000: 24). For instance, 59% of Swedes who had not completed secondary school scored at level 3 or higher on the document test compared to 17% of Americans with that level of education (OECD/HRDC 2000: 135). We contend that the skill levels of those at the lower end of the skill distribution are in large part a product of the whole environment they grow up in. When the environmental conditions of the lower-status families are more similar to the mean—i.e., when there is more social equality—they are more likely to acquire skills similar to the mean. In fact, for the thirteen countries for which we have data on inequality and literacy, the correlations between inequality and literacy scores of the lowest 5% and the percent with low literacy are both very high, −.77 and .81 respectively.[6] Low levels of inequality did not appear to depress the literacy skill levels of the highly skilled. For instance, the ninety-fifth percentile in egalitarian Sweden scored higher than the same percentile in the inegalitarian United States (OECD/HRDC 2000: 135–36).

As a result of the differences in union organization, bargaining centralization, union contract coverage, and, arguably, literacy skills among the less skilled, wage dispersion was much greater in the liberal welfare states than in the social democratic welfare states, again with the Christian democratic welfare states falling in between, but in this case clearly closer to the social democratic group (column 7). In fact, other than in Austria, wage dispersion in the northern-tier countries was remarkably similar to that in the Nordic countries, which is surprising given the absence of explicit Nordic-type wage compression policies on the part of the unions in these countries.[7]

By contrast, the social democratic welfare states were very different from the Christian democratic welfare states, including the northern tier, in their levels of active labor market policy effort, their levels of women's labor force participation, and, as a result, in the levels of total labor force

**Table 4.2**  Production Regimes: Labor Market Indicators Circa 1980

| | (1) Union Density Percentage | (2) Union Coverage Percentage | (3) Corporatism Index | (4) Bargaining Centralization | (5) Low Literacy Percentage | (6) Literacy Score 5th percentile | (7) Wage Dispersion† | (8) Active Labor Market Policy Effort | (9) Female Labor Force Participation |
|---|---|---|---|---|---|---|---|---|---|
| *Social democratic welfare states* | | | | | | | | | |
| Sweden | 81 | 83 | 4 | .58 | 7 | 216 | 2.0 | 75 | 74 |
| Norway | 54 | 75 | 4 | .63 | 8 | 207 | 2.0 | 26 | 62 |
| Denmark | 67 | | 3 | .59 | 8 | 213 | 2.1 | 20 | 71 |
| Finland | 67 | 95 | 3 | .45 | 11 | 195 | 2.5 | 18 | 70 |
| Mean | 67 | 84 | 3.5 | .56 | 8.5 | 208 | 2.2 | 35 | 69 |
| *Christian democratic welfare states* | | | | | | | | | |
| Austria | 53 | 71 | 4 | .44 | | | 3.5 | 8 | 49 |
| Belgium | 57 | 90 | 3 | .27 | 17 | 161 | 2.4 | 10 | 47 |
| Netherlands | 32 | 60 | 3 | .35 | 10 | 202 | 2.5 | 10 | 35 |
| Germany | 35 | 76 | 3 | .34 | 10 | 208 | 2.7 | 10 | 51 |
| France | 15 | 92 | * | .10 | | | 3.3 | 7 | 54 |
| Italy | 38 | | 2 | .22 | | | 2.6 | 4 | 39 |
| Switzerland | 30 | | 3 | | 17 | 150 | 2.7 | 23 | 54 |
| Mean | 37 | 78 | 3.0 | .29 | 13.5 | 180 | 2.8 | 10 | 47 |

**Table 4.2** *(continued)*

| | (1) Union Density Percentage | (2) Union Coverage Percentage | (3) Corporatism Index | (4) Bargaining Centralization | (5) Low Literacy Percentage | (6) Literacy Score 5th percentile | (7) Wage Dispersion† | (8) Active Labor Market Policy Effort | (9) Female Labor Force Participation |
|---|---|---|---|---|---|---|---|---|---|
| *Liberal welfare states* | | | | | | | | | |
| Canada | 29 | 38 | 1 | .07 | 17 | 145 | 4.0 | 6 | 57 |
| Ireland | 44 | | 3 | | 24 | 151 | | 9 | 36 |
| U.K. | 48 | 47 | 2 | .27 | 23 | 145 | 2.8 | 6 | 58 |
| U.S.A. | 21 | 18 | 1 | .07 | 22 | 133 | 4.8 | 4 | 60 |
| Mean | 36 | 34 | 1.8 | .14 | 21.5 | 144 | 3.9 | 6 | 53 |
| *Wage earner welfare states* | | | | | | | | | |
| Australia | 44 | 80 | 1 | .57 | 17 | 146 | 2.8 | 5 | 53 |
| New Zealand | 40 | 67 | 1 | | 20 | 157 | 2.9 | 20 | 45 |
| *Japan* | 21 | 21 | * | .23 | | 173 | 3.0 | 6 | 54 |
| Grand mean | 43.1 | 65.2 | 2.6 | .35 | 15.1 | 173 | 2.9 | 14.8 | 53.8 |

* concertation without labor

† mid-eighties data for Belgium, Netherlands, and New Zealand, 1991 for Switzerland

Data sources and definitions: (1, 9) see table 3.1; (2) union contract coverage as a percentage of total wage and salary earners (Traxler 1994); (3) Lehmbruch 1984; (4) Iversen 1998; (5, 6) OECD/HRDC 2000; (7): 90–10 ratio, the wages of a full-time employee at the 90th percentile of the wage distribution as a multiple of one at the 10th percentile, OECD 1996a; (8) active labor market spending as percentage of GDP divided by the percentage of the labor force unemployed. Calculated according to Nickell 1997 by David Bradley.

participation of the working-age population. As we will show in the next chapter, the high level of women's labor force participation is both a result and a cause of the Nordic welfare state–labor market pattern. As of 1960, the Nordic countries were not distinctive in the level of public social service employment and, with the exception of Finland, in the level of women's labor force participation. By the mid-1960s, vigorous growth in all of the economies of northern Continental Europe (Austria, Switzerland, Germany, France, and the Benelux countries) and Scandinavia had produced high rates of male labor force participation and very low unemployment among males. Unlike the northern Continental countries, due in part to the influence of the strong union movements, the Scandinavian countries limited recruitment of non-Nordic foreign labor, which provided greater job opportunities for women in the private sector.

This growth of women's labor force participation stimulated demands by women for the expansion of day care and other social services, which, along with social democratic governance, helped fuel the growth of public social service sector employment. These public social service jobs were filled very disproportionately by women, so this in turn stimulated a further expansion of women's labor force participation. As a consequence, by the mid-1970s, all four Nordic countries were already characterized both by high levels of women's labor force participation and of public health, education, and welfare employment. This feedback cycle between left/union strength, women's labor force participation, and public service employment continued into the late 1980s when the employment crisis hit Sweden, Finland, and, to a lesser extent, Norway. Indeed, as we will document in the next chapter, one of the main areas of welfare state innovation in all four Nordic countries was in the area of gender relations, particularly policies enabling women to enter the labor force, not only through services such as day care, but also through transfers, such as paid parental leave.

The Continental Christian democratic welfare states followed a quite different trajectory. The labor migration issue was handled differently as foreign labor was imported in large numbers, arguably due to a combination of Christian democratic emphasis on the traditional male breadwinner family and weaker union influence on labor recruitment policies. Moreover, in these countries, union contracts cover a large proportion of the labor force, which prevented the expansion of a low-wage service sector, a source of employment for women in liberal welfare states (Esping-Andersen 1990, 1999). As a result women's labor force participation was the lowest in the Continental Christian democratic welfare states of the four welfare state types, despite the fact that social policy was more "working mother friendly" in the Christian democratic welfare states (compare column 9 of table 4.2 with column 12 of table 4.1).

As a result of these labor market configurations, then, both social democratic and Christian democratic welfare states did not produce the dualist labor markets with a low-wage-low-skill sector, largely though not entirely in private services, a characteristic of the liberal welfare states.[8] This "fits" with the generous welfare states of these countries and with an overall "high road" economic strategy, based on high-quality-high-wage manufacturing for export, and thus with the type of production regime these countries have.

Soskice (1991, 1999) contends that different production regimes were critically shaped by employer organization and by relationships between companies and financial institutions. In his view, employer organization takes three distinctive forms: coordination at the industry or subindustry level in Germany and in most northern European economies (industry-coordinated market economies); coordination among groups of companies across industries in Japan and Korea (group-coordinated market economies); or absence of coordination in the deregulated systems of the Anglo-American countries (uncoordinated market economies). France was a distinct variant, which Hancke and Soskice (1996) call a "state-business-elite coordinated market economy." In coordinated economies, employers are able to organize collectively in training their labor force, sharing technology, providing export-marketing services and advice for R and D and for product innovation, setting product standards, and bargaining with employees. The capacity for collective action on the part of employers shapes stable patterns of economic governance encompassing a country's financial system, its vocational training, and its system of industrial relations.

A central characteristic of the flexibly coordinated systems is the generalized acceptance by all major actors of the imperative of successful competition in open world markets. Successful competition in turn requires a high skill level of the labor force and the ability of unions to deliver wage restraint to the extent needed to preserve an internationally competitive position. In the industry-coordinated market economies of central and northern Europe, initial labor skills were effectively organized in companies or with strong company and union involvement in public schools. Unions were organized mainly along industrial lines and played an important cooperative role in organizing working conditions within companies and in setting wage levels for the economy as a whole.

Banks and industries were closely linked, providing industries with preferential sources of long-term credit, or the state played a major role in bank ownership and performed a similar role in preferential credit provision for industry. In uncoordinated or liberal market economies, in contrast to both types of coordinated economy, training for lower-level workers was not undertaken by private business and was generally ineffective. Private sector trade unions were viewed as impediments in employer decision making, had little role in coordinating their activities, and were weak. Bank-industry ties were weak and industries had to rely on competitive markets to raise capital.

Column 1 of table 4.3 (p. 102) measures various aspects of market coordination in the period 1960–73 based on indicators developed by Hicks and Kenworthy (1998). The items in the index are business confederation power, "long term, voice based relationships between firms and their investors," "long term, voice based relationships between purchaser and supplier firms," and "alliances among competing firms for research and development, training, production, standard setting, etc." The liberal wage earner welfare states were distinctive in their lack of coordination. The social democratic welfare states are all relatively highly coordinated but not as high as Japan or Germany. The Christian democratic welfare states were more heterogeneous but all appear as more coordinated than the liberal welfare states, and those in the northern tier, with the exception of the Netherlands, were similar to the Nordic countries.

While Soskice's analysis focuses heavily on factors underpinning competitiveness in manufacturing, these institutional frameworks can be seen as national and economywide (see Kitschelt et al. 1999b). With this extension, one can distinguish a Nordic and Austrian pattern in which there was economywide bargaining and a large state role in economic management from the Continental pattern in which bargaining was generally carried on at the industry level and the state's role was more muted.[9] In the social democratic welfare states and northern tier of Christian democratic welfare states, the combination of strong unions and dependence on competitive exports due to high trade openness (table 4.3, column 5) necessitated a policy of wage restraint, and the centralization of unions, employers' organizations, and the bargaining process made such a policy possible, with the partial exception of the Netherlands. The unions' "side payment" for wage restraint, at least up to the mid-1970s, was full employment and the development of the generous welfare state described above.

A full description of the Golden Age production regime would involve an outline of government monetary, fiscal, and industrial policy. Because the Continental European group was again heterogeneous along this line, we leave that task to the next chapter for that group and do so as well for the cohesive but rather unique political economies of the Antipodes. The liberal political economies were passive in industrial policy and focused on Keynesian demand-side management. Thus, they generally ran budget deficits across economic cycles (see table 4.3, column 4). In the case of the social democratic welfare states and Austria, it is worth sketching the policies here if only to dispel the common myth that they were demand-side, deficit-spending models.

Though the policy goals of all four Nordic countries were broadly similar, their specific production regimes vary more than their welfare state regimes. One can identify a general Nordic type that fits none of the countries perfectly.[10] They have small, open economies and thus are dependent on having competitive export sectors. Those sectors have traditionally been based on the countries' raw materials and have been closely linked to financial interests. The economies are characterized by strong industrial complexes that are both backward and forward integrated. Their human capital bases were strong, and this, combined with rising capital intensity, became increasingly important for international competitiveness as the countries moved beyond the export of raw and semi-processed materials. The combination of high labor and employer organization and centralization and bargaining centralization has made the pursuit of wage restraint possible. For the trade-off of wage restraint for full employment and welfare state expansion, cooperation of the sitting governments was necessary, and from a union point of view this was facilitated by the frequent government position of the social democratic parties, which are closely allied to the blue-collar union central organization in all four countries.

Given these underpinnings in the power balance in society, the domestic economic structure, and the international economy, it is not surprising that the goals of economic policy were full employment and rapid economic growth based on rapid technological change. In these countries (again Denmark partly excepted), fiscal and monetary policies were moderately countercyclical and backed up by occasional devaluations. Austria and Finland were partial exceptions in that the Austrian currency was pegged informally to the German mark already in the 1960s, and Finnish fiscal and monetary policies tended to be procyclical. The core of the long-term growth and employment policy, however—and this cannot be overemphasized—was a combination of supply-side and tax

**Table 4.3**    Production Regimes: Institutional Configurations and Macro Policy
                 Indicators, 1960–72

|  | (1)<br>Coordination<br>Index | (2)<br>Central<br>Bank<br>Independence | (3)<br>Degree of<br>Liberalization of<br>Capital Controls | (4)<br>Average<br>Budget<br>Surplus | (5)<br><br>Trade<br>Openness |
|---|---|---|---|---|---|
| *Social democratic welfare states* | | | | | |
| Sweden | 0.75 | 0.27 | 2.4 | 2.8 | 46.0 |
| Norway | 0.75 | 0.14 | 1.5 | 3.4 | 82.0 |
| Denmark | 0.63 | 0.47 | 3.0 | 1.8 | 60.0 |
| Finland | 0.75 | 0.27 | 1.0 | 2.3 | 45.0 |
| Mean | 0.72 | 0.29 | 2.0 | 2.6 | 58.3 |
| *Christian democratic welfare states* | | | | | |
| Austria | 0.75 | 0.58 | 2.2 | 0.0 | 53.0 |
| Belgium | 0.63 | 0.19 | 3.0 | −3.0 | 77.0 |
| Netherlands | 0.25 | 0.42 | 3.0 | −0.4 | 92.0 |
| Germany | 0.88 | 0.66 | 4.0 | 0.4 | 40.0 |
| France | 0.29 | 0.28 | 2.9 | −0.3 | 27.0 |
| Italy | 0.75 | 0.22 | 2.9 | −3.5 | 31.0 |
| Switzerland | 0.63 | 0.68 | 3.9 | 4.6 | 61.0 |
| Mean | 0.59 | 0.43 | 3.1 | −0.3 | 54.4 |

policies that themselves largely affected the supply side. Key among the
supply-side policies were an active labor market policy—though in Austria only from the 1970s on—regional policies, and support for selected
industries. Tax policies heavily favored reinvestment of profits over
distribution and industrial investors over consumers. Interest rates
were kept low through credit rationing, state supply of cheap credit,
and public sector surpluses. These policies were predicated on state controls of financial markets both externally (see column 3 of table 4.3) and
internally. In addition, fiscal policy was generally austere; these countries
usually ran budget surpluses (see column 4 of table 4.3). The demand side
of the growth-employment models in these small countries was only in
part internally generated; it was to a large part a result of demand for exports created by the vigorous postwar growth in the core advanced capitalist economies of North America and Europe.

    As we pointed out above, adding characteristics of the production re-
gime, even if restricted to labor market institutions and policies, to the
analysis challenges the assumption that countries follow clear patterns

**Table 4.3**    *(continued)*

|  | (1) Coordination Index | (2) Central Bank Independence | (3) Degree of Liberalization of Capital Controls | (4) Average Budget Surplus | (5) Trade Openness |
|---|---|---|---|---|---|
| *Liberal welfare states* | | | | | |
| Canada | 0.13 | 0.46 | 3.8 | −1.5 | 40.0 |
| Ireland | 0.13 | 0.39 | 2.0 | −4.3 | 78.0 |
| U.K. | 0.13 | 0.31 | 1.9 | −2.1 | 41.0 |
| U.S.A. | 0.13 | 0.51 | 3.7 | −1.9 | 10.0 |
| Mean | 0.13 | 0.42 | 2.8 | −2.5 | 42.3 |
| *Wage earner welfare states* | | | | | |
| Australia | 0.13 | 0.31 | 2.3 | 1.3 | 30.0 |
| New Zealand | 0.13 | 0.27 | 1.5 | na | 46.0 |
| *Japan* | 0.95 | 0.16 | 2.0 | 1.4 | 20.0 |
| Grand mean | 0.49 | 0.37 | 2.6 | 0.1 | 48.8 |

Data sources and definitions: (1) see Hicks and Kenworthy 1998; (2) Cukierman et al. 1992; (3) Quinn and Inclan 1997; (4, 5) Huber, Ragin, and Stephens 1997 from OECD.

and form neat clusters. This is true for overall patterns of welfare state and production regimes, and even more so if we break the regimes down into specific institutions and policies. So, for instance, while most of the Christian democratic welfare states of Continental Europe were coordinated market economies, Soskice points out that the Netherlands and Italy only partly fit this designation and France had a state-led production regime. Or, Denmark had different bank-firm and interfirm relations and relied much more on small to medium firms for export than did the other Nordic countries, yet it developed a social democratic welfare state regime. The Danish adaptation has been to rely much more on general taxation, above all income taxes and value-added taxes, rather than employer payroll taxes to finance its welfare state, arguably because of the labor cost burden on small employers that the latter would entail. Moreover, once we include policy and instruments of macroeconomic management as elements of our production regime typology, the Christian democratic group shows a high degree of heterogeneity as one can see from the figures on budget surpluses and central bank independence policies in table 4.3.

Rather than abandoning the typology of welfare states and production regimes altogether, though, our solution is to treat the types as ideal types to which countries more or less conform. Moreover, we would contend that within each country, certain—though not all—aspects of the welfare state and production regimes do "fit" each other in a mutually supportive or enabling way. Specifically, wage levels and benefit levels have to fit, and labor market and social policies have to be in accordance so as not to create perverse incentives. When this does occur, it is perceived as a deficiency, and governments generally make efforts to correct imbalances and restore the fit between labor market and social policies. These efforts do not automatically lead to a new fit or "equilibrium," of course, but situations of discord between welfare state and production regimes are unstable. In addition, the type of production for the world market has to fit with the qualification of the labor force and with wage and benefit levels. Business-labor-government coordination in R and D, training, and wage setting makes it possible to engage in high-quality production and thus to sustain high wages and a high social wage. Thus, statically, the fit is mutually supportive or enabling; dynamically and historically, the policies and practices making up the overall regime were initiated and adjusted to fit, and on the margin transform, the existing regime (see chapter 5).[11]

Our focus of interest in this book is the development of the welfare state. We do not aspire to fully account for the factors influencing the development of the production regime. The remarks in the last paragraph should not be taken to imply that partisan government is anywhere near as influential in shaping the production regime as it was in shaping the welfare state regime. The strong association between partisan government and production regimes is primarily due to common causes several steps back in the historical causal chain. We outline some of the antecedents to the social democratic production regime at the beginning of the next chapter. Suffice it to say here that the key link is the strength of union organization, which has been variously linked to the size of the domestic economy, economic openness, employer organization and centralization, union centralization, size of the dependent labor force, late and rapid industrialization, and concentration in the domestic economy, and that these same factors and union organization itself have been hypothesized to have shaped the various aspects of the production regime (Ingham 1974; Cameron 1978; Stephens 1979b; Katzenstein 1985; Hall 1986; Swenson 1991; Visser 1991; Wallerstein 1991; Western 1991, 1997; Crouch 1993; Hicks 1999). We would, however, insist that the development of the welfare state and production regimes should be seen as mutually enabling, and above all that coordinated market economies with their high skill emphasis and relative wage equality enable generous welfare state regimes and generous welfare states make it less likely for low-wage firms to survive.

## The Performance of Regimes

The combined welfare state regimes and production regimes, particularly the latter's labor market aspects, resulted in very large differences in the distributive outcomes in the three groups of welfare states, as one can see from table 4.4 (p. 109). The differences in income distribution after direct taxes and transfer payments between the social democratic welfare states and the northern tier of Christian democratic welfare states and the other countries were particularly striking (column 1). These differences were in part a result of the wage bargaining system outlined above and shown in table 4.2, columns 2 and 4, and in part the result of the redistribution effected by direct taxes and transfers (table 4.4, column 2). While the figures in column 2 (the percent reduction in inequality after direct taxes are levied and transfers are paid) overstate the redistributive effect of taxes and transfers,[12] neither they nor the figures in column 1 include the distributive effect of free or subsidized public goods and services that would increase equality in all welfare states (Saunders 1991), but particularly in the social democratic welfare states. The regressions in table 3.5 indicate that one should attribute the distributive difference between the northern and southern Christian democratic welfare states to the greater influence of social democracy in the former.

Columns 4 through 6 of table 4.4 document differences in poverty levels in countries with different welfare state regimes. Poverty is defined as less than 50 percent of median income in the country in question. Again, it is clear that the social democratic welfare states did very well in combating poverty and the liberal welfare states very poorly. One also observes a marked difference between the northern and southern Christian democratic welfare states. The data for Australia are perhaps surprising given Castles's (1985) argument regarding the effectiveness of the Antipodean system of social protection by other means. While the aged fared well and would probably have done even better once the very high level of home ownership among the aged was taken into account, as Castles points out, it is clear that there were holes in the safety net and that it primarily employed male breadwinners. The holes can be seen most strikingly in the figures on single mothers in poverty.

Without embarking on a detailed primary analysis of the LIS data, it is difficult to pinpoint with precision which policies were most responsible for the pre- and posttax and pre- and posttransfer reduction in inequality and the cross-national variations in disposable income inequality. Cross-national differences in disposable income inequality were in part a product of variations in market income inequality and these in turn were in large part a product of wage dispersion and unemployment levels. From tables 4.2 and A.12, one can see that part of the reason for egalitarian outcomes in the social democratic welfare states and the northern tier of Christian democratic welfare states is that, in the early 1980s, these countries had compressed wage differentials or low unemployment or both.

As to the redistribution effected by taxes and transfers, on the basis of Korpi and Palme's (1998) analysis, one can say with some confidence what the impact is of various types of overall policy configurations on cross-national differences in the reduction in inequality. They demonstrate that the systems that combine "basic security" (usually transfers with flat-rate benefits) and "income security" (transfers with earnings-related benefits) have the greatest redistributive impact. The Nordic pension systems, which combined a flat-rate citizenship pension and an earnings-related supplement, are good examples of this type, and Korpi and Palme point out that most other programs and thus the Nordic welfare states as a whole had this structure. What is surprising, so surprising that Korpi and Palme (1998) term it the "paradox of redistribution," is that these welfare states were much more redistributive than systems that rely on heavily "targeted" benefits, benefits for which there was an income or means test. While the use of targeted benefits is common among the liberal welfare states, it is the Antipodean wage earner welfare states that carried this principle the furthest. Most transfers in these countries, including public pensions, were designed to exclude upper-income groups.

In contrast to the social democratic welfare states, entitlements in the Christian democratic welfare states were largely employment based and earnings related. They generally lacked the basic security tier; the task of meeting the needs of those outside the labor market fell to means-tested benefits. Perhaps even more surprising than Korpi and Palme's paradox is the fact that the northern Christian democratic welfare states with their great reliance on employment-based, earnings-related benefits were more egalitarian in their impact than the liberal welfare states with their greater reliance on programs targeted to the needy. That this is true can be readily seen from table 4.4. Part of the explanation, following Korpi and Palme's logic, is that the northern Christian democratic welfare states were simply much larger: though their benefit structures were less egalitarian, they more than made up for it in greater expenditure. In addition, where benefits were generous, they tended to squeeze out private alternatives as can be seen from column 9 of table 4.1 (see Kangas and Palme 1993; Stephens 1995). As Kangas and Palme show in their analysis of LIS data on the income of aged, these private alternatives were *invariably much more inegalitarian* than the most inegalitarian of public pension systems (the Finnish).[13]

As to the policy measures that were most effective in combating poverty, we can give more precise answers, particularly with regard to the two groups most vulnerable to poverty, the aged and single mothers. Palme's (1990) data on minimum pensions for the early 1980s make it abundantly clear that the level of minimum pensions were the main factor that accounts for the international differences in poverty levels among the aged. The income replacement rates for this group were highest (around 50 percent) in the Nordic countries and the Netherlands and Austria, which were also among those with the lowest levels of poverty among the aged.

As for single mothers, a complex of labor market characteristics and transfer payments would appear to explain the pattern across welfare state regimes as well as outliers within the types.[14] The employment levels among single mothers and thus policies supporting mothers' employment are certainly very important, but low levels of wage dispersion, which indicate the absence of subpoverty full-time work, certainly contributed to the comparatively very low levels of poverty among single mothers in the Nordic countries. What is surprising, given the low overall level of women's labor force participation in Christian democratic welfare states, is that labor force participation among lone mothers in these countries was higher than in the liberal welfare states and only a bit lower than in the social democratic welfare states. This almost certainly was due to the stronger supportive policies for mothers' employment in Christian democratic welfare states (table 4.1, column 12). The intermediate levels of wage dispersion in the Christian democratic welfare states should also have contributed to the intermediate levels of poverty among single mothers.

In terms of transfer payments, family (child) allowances were clearly of great importance, especially for low-income families, since they were flat rate or means tested and never income related. On the average, family allowances were higher in Christian democratic welfare states than in social democratic welfare states, with liberal welfare states again ranking on the bottom (Wennemo 1994). Social assistance and unemployment compensation, especially for low-paid workers, reinforced the overall pattern as the Nordic welfare states provided the most generous transfers followed by Christian democratic welfare states and then the liberal welfare states.

The level of poverty among single mothers in Australia is striking but fully expected as Australia ranked near the bottom of every dimension mentioned (support for mothers, employment of single mothers, family allowances, unemployment replacement rates) save two: wage dispersion, where it was moderately low, and social assistance, where it was among the most generous. Again this demonstrates the weakness of the Antipodean system of social protection for those without full-time employment.

In the single mothers poverty data, one sees two outliers from the regime types, the United Kingdom and, to a lesser extent, Norway. The figures for Britain were strikingly different from the rest of the liberal group.[15] Certainly a large part of the explanation here is that family allowances were the fourth most generous of the eighteen countries examined here. Again it is important to remember that the British data are for 1979 and thus before the Thatcher reforms. We will see that, unfortunately for British single mothers, Britain's poverty figures become more typically liberal in the next decade and a half. Norway's figure for poverty among single mothers was high relative to the other Nordic countries. At that time, Norway also ranked lowest among Nordic countries on support for mothers' employment and labor force participation among single mothers. Fortunately for Norwegian single mothers, Norway became more typically social democratic in the next decade and a half.

For the working-age population, the combination of labor market characteristics and transfers most relevant to reducing poverty is only slightly different than in the case of single mothers. With regard to the labor market, unemployment and wage dispersion would appear to be the most important characteristics. With regard to transfers, unemployment compensation would appear to be the most important, followed by social assistance and family allowances. In this period (1979–87), unemployment was very low in the social democratic countries, followed by the Christian democratic countries and liberal countries, though there was a good deal of variation in each group (see table A.11). Wage dispersion followed the same pattern as did unemployment compensation and social assistance, while the Christian democratic countries ranked the highest on family allowances. Thus, these labor market patterns and transfers arguably account for the variations in poverty among the working-age population as well. Only one country was markedly deviant from the regime pattern on this poverty figure, the United Kingdom, which, compared to

**Table 4.4**    Welfare State Outcomes

|  | (1) | (2) | (3) | (4) | (5) | (6) |
|---|---|---|---|---|---|---|
|  |  | Redistri-bution | Posttax |  |  |  |
|  |  | Resulting | Post- | % of Group in Poverty | | |
|  | Year of | Posttax | from | transfer | | | |
|  | LIS | Post- | Taxes and | Gini— |  |  | Single |
|  | Survey | transfer Gini | Transfers | Aged | 25–59 | Aged | Mothers |
| *Social democratic welfare states* | | | | | | |
| Sweden | 1981 | .20 | 52 | .16 | 4.8 | 0.3 | 7.7 |
| Norway | 1979 | .22 | 40 | .26 | 3.7 | 4.7 | 12.1 |
| Denmark | 1987 | .26 | 36 | .24 | 4.8 | 9.2 | 4.5 |
| Finland | 1987 | .21 | 38 | .22 | 3.0 | 3.0 | 4.8 |
| Mean |  | .22 | 41.4 | .22 | 4.1 | 4.3 | 7.3 |
| *Christian democratic welfare states* | | | | | | |
| Austria | 1987 | .23 |  | .25 | 2.3 | 6.0 | 13.3 |
| Belgium | 1985 | .23 | 46 | .23 | 4.4 | 6.0 | 14.2 |
| Netherlands | 1983 | .28 | 38 | .27 | 6.7 | 3.9 | 6.6 |
| Germany | 1981 | .25 | 38 | .29 | 4.2 | 10.0 | 6.0 |
| France | 1984 | .33 | 34 | .37 | 15.9 | 18.9 | 22.8 |
| Italy | 1986 | .31 | 28 | .30 | 10.5 | 8.3 | 17.5 |
| Switzerland | 1982 | .32 | 21 | .37 | 6.1 | 15.2 | 22.4 |
| Mean |  | .28 | 34.2 | .30 | 7.1 | 9.8 | 14.7 |
| *Liberal welfare states* | | | | | | |
| Canada | 1981 | .29 | 24 | .31 | 10.3 | 9.3 | 42.0 |
| Ireland | 1987 | .33 | 35 | .32 | 10.9 | 4.9 | 15.4 |
| U.K. | 1979 | .27 | 33 | .26 | 5.5 | 4.8 | 10.8 |
| U.S.A. | 1979 | .31 | 26 | .34 | 11.9 | 21.8 | 42.3 |
| Mean |  | .30 | 29.4 | .31 | 9.7 | 10.2 | 27.6 |
| *Wage earner welfare states* | | | | | | |
| Australia | 1981 | .29 | 29 | .29 | 9.3 | 5.3 | 44.8 |
| Grand mean |  | .27 | 34.4 | .28 | 7.1 | 8.2 | 17.9 |

Data sources and definitions: see table 3.1.

the other liberal countries, had low levels of wage dispersion and very generous family allowances.

Table A.11 outlines the economic performance of the countries under study. Here it is impossible to embark on even a brief summary of the vast literature on the comparative economic performance of advanced industrial societies. We will analyze the experience of nine countries in the next chapter. However, we do want to draw out a few simple points regarding the relationship between welfare state–production regimes and performance in growth and unemployment here. First, as table A.11 indicates, it is difficult to maintain that the generous social democratic and Christian democratic welfare states have been a clear drag on economic growth or unemployment levels. In fact, in the Golden Age, they clearly outperformed the liberal welfare states, whereas there is no obvious pattern since then. A more complex argument might be made in which it is claimed that generous social policy and high taxes produced micro level disincentives that were a drag on growth, but then the associated production regimes provided incentives that more than made up for the disincentives.[16] In any case, there is no clear evidence from the postwar record of advanced industrial democracies that the same regime cannot simultaneously and successfully promote growth and redistribution.

Second, both the social democratic and Christian democratic welfare states were built in economies very open to trade (see table 4.3, column 5) and, especially in the social democratic welfare states, they were built around the interest of the export sector workers, whose unions were the dominant force within their respective union movements. These workers and unions had and have strong interests in the competitiveness of the export economies of their countries. As the discussion of the welfare state and production regimes of the European core, especially the social democratic welfare states and the northern tier of Christian democratic welfare states, should have made clear, these countries "chose" a high-road niche in the world economy based on highly skilled and educated labor, cooperative production, and capital-intensive production techniques, which was compatible with both high wages and generous social benefits, at least up to 1980. Whether this situation still prevails will be a central topic of chapters 6 through 8.

## Conclusion

In the first section of this chapter we argued that it is heuristically useful to view the political economies of advanced industrial societies as falling into one of four types of welfare state and production regimes. Indeed, the cross-national data we have presented on the welfare state and production regimes and their outcomes support the view that it is not only heuristically useful, but that there is also empirical evidence that the distinct types exist even if they do not cluster as cleanly as sometimes implied. Moreover, the welfare state regime types are clearly rooted in different political constellations as the labels social democratic, Christian democratic, and liberal imply, though other structural and historical causal factors such as the timing of industrialization, size of the domestic economy, export dependence, export specialization, economic concentration, historic legacies of employer organization, and the effects of World War II would have to be brought in to provide even a relatively parsimonious account of the origins of production regimes and thus the overall welfare state–production regime complex.

The social democratic welfare state regimes were characterized by (1) predominance of universalistic entitlements, (2) comprehensiveness of social policy regimes in the sense that programs existed in all major program areas, (3) dominance of citizenship based entitlements, (4) high income replacement rates in transfer programs, (5) emphasis on high levels of publicly delivered social services, (6) gender egalitarianism, and (7) policies aimed at labor force training and mobilization. The associated production regime was a nationally coordinated market economy with strong unions, high levels of union contract coverage, centralized wage bargaining, peak level corporatist tripartitist policy making, high levels of wage compression, high levels of female labor force participation, and a strong state role in the economy. Denmark deviated from the coordinated market economy pattern insofar as bank industry and interfirm linkages were weaker, industry less concentrated, and the central bank more independent.

The Christian democratic welfare states were characterized by (1) fragmentation of entitlements with different groups enjoying different entitlements,[17] (2) predominance of employment-based entitlements, (3) emphasis on transfers, (4) moderate to high income replacement rates in transfer programs, (5) private or "third sector" delivery of publicly funded services, (6) reinforcement of the male breadwinner family pattern, and (7) passive labor market policy. The associated production regime was a sectorally coordinated market economy with moderately strong unions, high levels of union contract coverage, sectoral wage bargaining, moderate role for labor in corporatist bargaining, low levels of female labor force participation, and a modest state role in the economy. Netherlands, France, and Italy deviated somewhat from the coordinated market economy pattern in different ways.

The liberal welfare state was characterized by (1) partial program coverage, (2) a significant role for income or needs testing, (3) moderate to low replacement rates in transfer programs, (4) few publicly delivered services outside of education and few publicly funded services outside of health and education, (6) passive family policy, and (6) passive labor market policy. The associated production regime was a liberal or uncoordinated market economy with weak to moderately strong unions, low levels of union contract coverage, decentralized wage bargaining, no corporatist policy bargaining, moderately high levels of female labor force participation, and very little state intervention in the economy.

The parameters of the wage earner welfare states of Australia and New Zealand will fully emerge only in the next chapter. Suffice it here to provide a parallel description in advance. The wage earner welfare state was a male breadwinner system of social protection based on wages and benefits delivered through the arbitration system. The formal welfare state played a backup role and was characterized by (1) partial program coverage due, in part, to the social protection delivered through the wage-setting system, (2) a significant role for income testing but with relatively high income limits, (3) moderate to low replacement rates in transfer programs, (4) few publicly delivered services outside of education and few publicly funded services outside of health and education, (5) reinforcement of the male breadwinner family pattern, and (6) passive labor market policy. The associated production regime was a liberal market economy with important modifications as the arbitration system rather than markets determined wages and many social benefits and the state provided substantial protection to domestic producers and periodically intervened with active industrial policy.

The data on outcomes provided very strong evidence that these regime types were associated with, and arguably causally related to, quite different distributive outcomes and levels of poverty. Students of the comparative social policy of advanced industrial societies will not be very surprised that the social democratic and liberal welfare states exhibited the opposite outcomes. What may be more surprising to at least some of these scholars, given the conventional characterization of the Christian democratic welfare states as "conservative" and "reinforcing market outcomes" is how redistributive they were. In fact, the four countries that we have referred to as the "northern tier"—Austria, Germany, Netherlands, and Belgium—were quite similar to their Nordic neighbors in these outcomes as well as in many aspects of their welfare state and production regimes. These distributive outcomes can be attributed in part to the influence of social democracy in these countries and in part directly to the production regime, which delivered low levels of wage dispersion and was predicated on a high-wage, high–labor productivity competitive niche in the world economy. In the next chapter, we shall investigate the historical development of these welfare state regimes and flesh out their connection to the production regimes for our nine focus cases.

# CHAPTER FIVE

◆

# The Development of Welfare States and Production Regimes in the Golden Age: A Comparative Historical Analysis

In this chapter, we examine the development of welfare state regimes and production regimes in nine countries focusing on the period 1945–73, the "Golden Age" of postwar capitalism. Our primary interest is in the development of the welfare state regime, so we focus on social policy development. However, as we explained in the last chapter, the development of the welfare state cannot be understood in isolation from the development of the interlocking production regimes, particularly labor market policies. Thus, we also sketch the development of production regimes and their interface with social policy developments, emphasizing institutions and policies shaping the labor market and investment levels.

Our case selection is guided by our theoretical and normative interest in the most generous welfare states. Thus, rather than choosing a sample of cases representative of different regime types, we focus on those cases in which labor movements and social democratic parties have had a significant influence on the development of the overall regime. Moreover, our goal is to sketch a new type of generous welfare state regime that is compatible with the new economic and political circumstances of the 1990s and 2000s not just in the traditional homeland of social democracy in Scandinavia but also in a broad range of other advanced capitalist countries. The most likely additional cases for this are those in which social democracy and labor have been influential and in which social protection is well developed and the production regimes bear some similarity to the Nordic production regimes. Austria, with a Christian democratic welfare state regime but a production regime very similar to the Nordic regimes, is an obvious choice. The Netherlands, with the most generous system of social protection on the Continent, also had to be included. If the developments of the past and models for the future were and are to be generalizable outside the smaller economies, then Germany with its coordinated market economy, high-wage labor market, and

113

relatively generous welfare state also had to be included. The comparison of these three northern Continental countries to the Nordic countries also allows us to identify the distinctive factors that have influenced the development of the two welfare state types.

Finally, we include Australia and New Zealand for somewhat different reasons. First, as we pointed out in the last chapter, based on Castles's (1985, 1996) work, these two countries developed extensive and effective systems of "social protection by other means." However, in sharp contrast to the northern European welfare states, which were developed under conditions of stiff international competition, the generous regimes of social protection were developed in, and were predicated on, primary product exports and a protected manufacturing sector. Thus, as we will show in chapter 7, they were vulnerable to the opening up of the economy to international competition in a way that the northern European welfare states were not. Establishing this is pivotal to our contention that the key parameters of social democratic welfare state regimes are not incompatible with the increased economic internationalization and intensified competitive pressure of the present era.

Second, Australia and New Zealand are important points of comparison and contrast to the Nordic countries for our contention that it is social democratic governance that is the key to the development of generous welfare states in non-Catholic countries. Both Australia and New Zealand had very strong labor movements; the labor parties garnered as large a proportion of the vote as in the Nordic countries, and labor was in power in the late 1930s and 1940s. However, labor was excluded from power for most or all of the period from 1950 to 1972, narrowly losing a number of elections. As a result, these two countries fell from a position of being welfare state leaders in 1950 to welfare state laggards in 1972.

Among the four Nordic cases, we devote the most attention to developments in Sweden. Space constraints make it impossible for us to flesh out historical details for the four Nordic cases, much less all nine countries. Sweden was selected for detailed analysis in part because it is frequently singled out as the paradigmatic example of the achievements (and limitations) of social democracy. In addition, Sweden was a leader in social and economic developments, and actors in the other three countries frequently attempted to emulate (or avoid) Swedish policies. Finally, the historical and contemporary structure of business in Sweden, characterized by highly internationalized, export-oriented, privately owned large firms, makes it more relevant for the future of social democracy elsewhere in the advanced capitalist world, where governments and labor movements are likely to have to deal with such business structures.

The following narrative and analytical comparisons are oriented by our theoretical framework and the results of our quantitative analyses. We identify causal patterns of welfare state development by tracing the impact of incumbency of different political parties, of women's mobilization, of constitutional structures, of policy legacies, and of production regimes. We also look for evidence that would support competing theoretical views, such as the role of corporatist institutions, of independent organizations of old people, or of autonomous bureaucrats. Our goal is to establish agency by analyzing welfare state policies promoted or opposed by different political parties and by collective actors, most prominently organized labor, business associations, women's movements, and professional organizations, and the process by which certain policies but not others are implemented. By linking the behavior of specific actors and the impact of specific political institutions to policy outcomes we are able to show causality and to eliminate competing explanations of the outcomes.

In addition, in the individual case studies and even more so in the cross-case comparisons in the conclusion of the chapter, we employ the comparative method to strengthen our counterfactual claims. We have already mentioned the use of the comparison of the Nordic countries and the Antipodes to strengthen the left government hypothesis and the comparison of the Nordic countries and northern Continental European countries to support the contrasting outcomes of Christian democratic and social democratic government. Closer pair comparisons, for example, of Finland, the Nordic laggard, with the other three Nordic countries, or of federal and bicameral Australia with unitary New Zealand, offer support for other hypotheses outlined in chapters 2 and 3.

## Paths to the Nordic Welfare State

### *The Nordic Model: Antecedents*

In the literature on social democracy, one source of social democratic strength is almost undisputed: a strong union movement, one not divided by ideology or confession and with a high portion of the labor force organized, results in higher levels of support for leftist parties and, in turn, leftist parties once in government facilitate union organization. Union organization has been linked directly or indirectly (via industrial concentration and/or centralized employers organizations) to the size of the domestic economy (Wallerstein 1989, 1991; Stephens 1979b, 1991; Visser 1991; Swenson 1991). In European countries with Catholic majorities or strong Catholic minorities, Catholic parties have competed with social democrats for workers' votes and Catholic unions for workers' loyalty in the workplace, thus weakening social democratic parties and splitting the union movement. Ethnic and linguistic homogeneity is also associated with high degrees of union organization (Stephens 1979b; Visser 1991). Conditions in Scandinavia have thus been very favorable for social democracy and their affiliated unions: The economies of all four Nordic countries are small; all are religiously homogenous and Protestant; and only Finland is linguistically divided.

As we noted in the last chapter, corporatist arrangements are crucial for the successful functioning of small countries with strong union movements in export markets. There are different accounts of the social origins of corporatism. Stephens (1979b) and Czada (1988) contend that strong and centralized unions and social democratic governance are prerequisites for strong corporatism and link these in turn to economic concentration and a small domestic market (also see Korpi 1983; Western 1991). Katzenstein (1985) contends that economic openness is a precondition for the development of corporatism. Wallerstein (n.d.) contends that high dependence on nonagricultural exports encourages union centralization, which in turn is a precondition for corporatist tripartite bargaining. All of these characteristics are shared by Norway, Sweden, and Finland. Denmark's primary exports have been processed agricultural goods. Wallerstein (n.d.) argues that this has contributed to the lower degree of centralization of Danish unions. It is also one root of the contrasting growth policy pursued in Denmark as compared to the other three countries.

The political right is deeply divided in all Nordic countries. Katzenstein (1985) has argued that a divided right encourages the development of corporatism, and Castles (1978) has linked the presence of a divided right to the success of Nordic social democracy. Both authors see divisions on the right as opening up the possibility of center-left coalitions, which result in the inclusion of labor in the policy-making process. As Rokkan (1970) points out, the Protestant smallholding countries of Scandinavia produced agrarian parties that further divided an already divided bourgeois bloc. This facilitated the formation of the red-green (i.e., worker-farmer) alliances that brought social democracy in the region to power. It also made possible an autonomous agrarian contribution to welfare state development, a distinctive feature of the Nordic cases.

As Rokkan (1970) and Katzenstein (1985) point out, these structural-historical splits in the bourgeois bloc led to the development of proportional representation, which in turn sustained the divided right. These small states also tended to produce weak or no bicameralism and weak or no federalism. The reader will recognize these as features of constitutional structure that we identified as facilitating reform, as they facilitate the development of disciplined parties and provide few openings for special interest groups to intervene and block reforms based on narrow political majorities.

## *Sweden*

Turning from the Nordic commonalities to the distinctive features of each country, we can begin by characterizing the singular features of Sweden. Perhaps the most distinctive feature of Sweden is the character of business. While Sweden shares with Finland and Norway a high degree of concentration in the secondary sector and concentration on nonagricultural exports, it differs in that industry, particularly export industry, has been dominated by a small number of privately owned, internationalized, oligopolistic firms since the very onset of industrialization. More quickly than the other two countries, Sweden turned from export of raw materials and semiprocessed goods from the forest industry and mining to export of capital goods and finished consumer products.

As we pointed out above, the common features of all four countries' economies fostered high degrees of employer and union centralization and union organization. In the Swedish case, the character of the business sector encouraged the development of aggressive policies on the part of the employers' association (SAF) aimed first at defeating the nascent union movement and then, when this failed, at limiting its political influence and, finally, when this failed, at preserving private ownership and employers' prerogatives in the workplace and private sector direction of the overall investment process.[1]

### SOCIAL POLICY DEVELOPMENT

Before the system's first turning point of the 1930s, when the red-green compromises laid the first foundations for the postwar model in the Nordic countries, one feature of Nordic social policy development became apparent in Sweden: the strong role of farming interests.[2] Farming interests did not initiate social policy development. It was the rising labor movement and the Bismarckian conservative and liberal reaction to it that played that role. Rather, once the issue was on the agenda (in this case, pensions), the political representatives of farmers pressed to ensure that the reforms did not benefit wage earners alone but that their constituency was covered, thus pressing for universal coverage. Thus the farming interests did make a contribution to the early development of universalism. In addition, they pressed for tax financing rather than contributory financing, thus lightening the contribution of their constituency to the financing of the reform. Otherwise the alignments in Sweden were hardly unusual: Liberal reformers initiated social legislation supported by Social Democrats, who nevertheless criticized the reforms as not sufficiently generous, and, belatedly, by a (declining) Bismarckian wing of the Conservatives.

The 1930s were a watershed but more for the political alignments and labor market compromises that laid the basis for the postwar model than for the innovations in social and economic policy. In 1933, the "cow trade" was consummated in which the Social Democrats agreed to agricultural price supports in exchange for agrarian support for their employment programs. Much international attention has been devoted to the modest Keynesian stimulative policy of the Social Democratic government. Though this policy was important for its break with economic orthodoxy, which prescribed procyclical policy, the stimulative package made at best a modest contribution to the reduction of unemployment that did occur. More important for our purposes, the policy did not prefigure postwar employment and growth policy in which the supply side was more important than the demand side. The employment policy did, however, prefigure a distinctive feature of unemployment policy and economic policy, active measures to get workers back to work rather than passive unemployment cash support. As Åmark (1998: 8) points out, this policy, already labeled "the work policy" in Social Democratic rhetoric was more "commodifying" than "decommodifying."

The social policy positions and alignments that dominated politics until the supplementary pension reform of the late 1950s, including the Social Democratic "harvest time" of immediate postwar reforms, did emerge in this period. Here we cannot go into the details of the development of even the major legislative initiatives and must generalize at the risk of oversimplification. With regard to transfers, the agrarians followed their previous pattern: They were not the policy initiators, but once a policy was initiated they sought to ensure that its structure was favorable to their primary constituency, family farmers. In the case of transfers, this generally meant the Agrarian Party favored flat-rate, universalistic, tax-financed benefits—in a word, citizenship entitlements. Thus, we agree with Baldwin (1990) that the Agrarians made a critical contribution to the development of Nordic social policy and that this contribution has incorrectly been attributed to social democracy by other scholars.

However, as the data in the last chapter indicate, it is incorrect to characterize Nordic social transfer systems at the end of the Golden Age as "flat rate, universalistic, and tax financed," since an earnings-related tier with a high income replacement rate and generous qualifying conditions are also essential characteristics of these systems.

The position of the Social Democrats and LO, the allied central organization of blue-collar trade unions, on the major transfer programs was more complex. The Social Democratic social minister, Gustav Möller, favored uniform, flat-rate benefits and thus shared common ground with the agrarians. Others favored combining citizenship benefits with income-tested benefits either because they saw it as more just to concentrate benefits on the needy or because the savings would allow additional reforms in other areas. The common ground was that social policy should offer all citizens sufficient financial support to keep them out of poverty *as a right*—a decisive break with the poor law tradition in which only the "deserving poor" were supported. This emphasis was clearly articulated by Möller, then Social Democratic party spokesman for social policy, at least as early as 1928 (Åmark 1998: 7–8). In part because of the coalition with the Agrarians and in part because the Social Democrats did not want to be upstaged by their bourgeois opponents, the flat-rate-for-all line won out in the case of most of the "harvest time" reforms, not only in the case of pensions but also child allowances. Thus the wide to universal benefits side of the Swedish welfare state pattern was firmly established by the end of the 1940s.

In addition to the two aforementioned positions on transfers, a segment of the labor movement—LO and above all the unions in the higher-paid manufacturing unions—favored earnings-related benefits. Many analysts have mistakenly assumed that this emerged on the Social Democratic agenda first with the supplementary pension struggle as part of the party's effort to appeal to white-collar workers. In fact, this first emerged in a dispute between the Social Democrats and their Agrarian coalition partners on cost-of-living areas for pensions in the 1930s in which LO and the Social Democrats favored higher benefits for urban dwellers. It then emerged in the debate on sick pay during the harvest time reforms. The then existing voluntary, but state-subsidized, sick pay funds provided earnings-related benefits. The initial postwar legislation provided for flat-rate benefits but was postponed twice and never implemented, in part because LO favored earnings-related benefits, which the 1955 law eventually provided for. Finally, as we will see below, it was LO that took the initiative on the issue of supplementary earnings-related pensions (ATP). While this is generally conceded, it is often forgotten that LO's position favoring earnings-related pensions had already emerged in the late 1940s.

We return to the ATP issue below but it is worth underlining why LO supported earnings-related benefits, as it is of some importance for the future of the Nordic welfare states. Any flat-rate scheme could not, by its nature, provide a very high income replacement rate for an average production worker not to mention a well-paid skilled worker. Were such a scheme to provide a high flat income replacement of, for example, 90 percent of an average production worker's wage in the case of sickness, injury, unemployment, or retirement, it would actually result in raised remuneration for lower-paid workers thus creating highly perverse work disincentives. Thus, an earnings-related scheme was necessary.

In the case of pensions, LO believed that it could never achieve equality with white-collar workers through negotiations. In LO's view, only a statutory, obligatory system would cover the needs of all workers. A variety of historical and comparative evidence indicates that LO was correct.[3] First, at that point in time, fewer manual than nonmanual workers were covered by supplementary schemes and their replacement rates were lower (Classon 1986: 30–40). Moreover, even the proposal of the employers' federation(SAF) for voluntary negotiated pensions was opposed in internal discussion by textile and clothing employers who contended they could not afford it, which casts some doubt on whether a generous scheme could have emerged from negotiations (Söderpalm 1980). The fact that when they did turn to negotiations for the third tier of pensions in the 1970s, the benefits negotiated by LO (the STP scheme) were markedly inferior to those in the scheme (ITP) negotiated by the white-collar central organization, TCO, supports the view that blue-collar workers would have difficulty in reaching parity (in relation to work income of course) with white-collar workers via negotiations (Von Nordheim Nielsen 1991; Ståhlberg 1990: 114). The comparative evidence also supports this contention: Blue-collar workers outside large capital-intensive enterprises and the public sector rarely receive adequate retirement pensions through negotiations. Finally, the comparative evidence surveyed in chapter 4, above all the analysis of income of the aged by Kangas and Palme (1993; also see Palme 1990), supports the contention that all alternatives to legislated schemes are considerably more inegalitarian. The evidence and arguments cited here pertain to pensions but should, we contend, apply with equal force to other transfer payments. Throughout the postwar period, LO frequently resorted to legislation to extend coverage to, increase benefit levels of, or reduce waiting days of blue-collar workers to make their entitlements similar to those already achieved by white-collar workers through negotiations. At least beginning with the equality debate of the late 1960s, LO argued for these increased entitlements less from a point of view of the material deprivation of blue-collar workers than from the principle of equality: manual workers ought not to be treated differently.

To return to the topic of party and interest group alignments on transfers in the pre-ATP period, the Liberals continued their interwar posture of supporting social legislation. It has been argued that the big change came on the part of the Conservatives, to whom Baldwin (1990) attributes a leading role in the development of citizenship pensions. In the interwar period, the antistatist wing of the Conservatives had gained ground vis-à-vis the Bismarckians; thus, the support for the more generous pension line as well as social policy innovations in 1946–47 that emerged from the government's harvest time package was a significant change. However, it is also noteworthy that the Conservatives opposed obligatory sickness insurance throughout this period (Elmér 1960: 125). Moreover, the party, while supporting a given policy initiative, frequently expressed concern over the cost of the entire range of policy initiatives under consideration.

Officially, SAF followed a similar line. That is, in its official comments on legislation under consideration by parliamentary commissions (remiss statements), SAF frequently supported the specific policy while expressing concern over the cost of social welfare policies as a whole. On the basis of research in SAF archives opened to researchers decades later, Söderpalm and Swenson argue that SAF's remiss statements were partly strategic but disagree almost completely on SAF's preferred solution. Söderpalm contends that SAF preferred no legislation whatsoever. On the most general level, by this time, in the spirit of the Saltsjöbaden agreement (see below), SAF and LO had agreed on the desirability of, and cooperated in the promotion of, productivity growth. However, according to Söderpalm (1980: 82), the employers preferred that this productivity growth be taken out in the form of wage increases or price decreases. Social legislation made a flexible adaptation to production demands difficult.[4] This discrepancy between SAF's public posture and private preference is a good example of the disincentives created by Swedish political institutions for minority interests to actively lobby for their position. As Immergut (1992) points out in her study of health care policy, since they have no possibility of blocking legislation, there is no reason to expend political capital in opposing it.

Though Immergut notes that this behavior of interest groups is based

on Social Democratic political dominance as well as Swedish political institutions, she appears to underestimate the former. SAF critiques and attacks on the Social Democrats' social policy were intense when it looked
as if the party was vulnerable, e.g., in the lead-up to the 1948 election on
the planning issue, but also on socializing medicine, after the 1956 election, which produced a bourgeois majority in the second chamber. On a
more general level, as Söderpalm (1980: 121) notes, cooperation between
the government and industry was greatest in times of stable Social Democratic rule, Söderpalm's immediate case in point being the contrast between the early 1960s and the ATP struggle. This fits Korpi's thesis that
the historic compromise (corporatism, etc.) was rooted in the labor
movement's achieving a stable government position ("separating political and economic power"). This would appear to be a powerful explanation of SAF's aggressive behavior in periods in which the Social Democrats appear vulnerable (1932–36, 1946–48, 1956–60, 1976 on) and its
cooperative stance in other periods.

In contrast to Söderpalm, Swenson (1999, forthcoming) contends that
the SAF archives reveal that employers actually welcomed many of the
Social Democrats' postwar reforms, among others the basic pension reform, the health care and sick pay reform, and the active labor market
policy. Swedish employers were faced with severe labor shortages after
the war and stiff foreign competition, which made wage restraint in the
export sector a necessity. Failing to convince the government to allow
greater importation of labor, SAF sought other ways of checking competitive bidding of employers for labor. On the wage bargaining front,
this led to support for centralized bargaining and the solidaristic wage
policy. With regard to social benefits, legislated benefits would impose
equal costs on all employers, thus also taking benefits out of wage competition. Thus, according to Swenson, SAF either supported the reforms
in the legislative process or accepted them after the fact.

Since we have not examined the SAF archives, we cannot mediate this
debate. Our hypothesis on the importance of Social Democratic governance in shaping Swedish welfare state outcomes does not require us to
challenge the assertions made in the previous paragraph. It does, however, require us to challenge Swenson's (1999: 7) explicit assertion that
the correlations between labor political power and welfare state outcomes shown in many quantitative studies are spurious, and his implicit
contention that the Swedish welfare state would have been no different
without the Social Democrats in power for long periods of time. Since our
challenge is based on counterfactual reasoning, we defer this discussion
until the conclusion of this chapter.

The foregoing discussion considered only transfer payments and thus exaggerates the consensus around the full range of social policy reforms contained in the 1944 LO–Social Democratic program, known as the "Postwar Program of the Labor Movement," not to speak of the economic policies contained in that document. Two points provoked heated dispute. First, while supporting the concept of national health insurance with universal coverage, the bourgeois parties united in opposition to the Social Democrats' plan to introduce a national health service along British lines. As a result the Social Democrats shelved this plan in the context of their general retreat from the more radical features of the Postwar Program, beginning with the 1948 election campaign. Second, the bourgeois parties, particularly the Conservatives, were stridently opposed to the tax policies proposed by the government, not only opposing tax increases but also favoring tax reductions. Since they favored a reduction of taxes, it is fair to ask how they planned to pay for the social reforms. This question could be repeated in the case of many subsequent elections in which the Conservatives promised to preserve existing social reforms while cutting taxes.

In favoring tax cuts, the party was reflecting, and probably partly shaping, the opinions of its voters. In response to a public opinion poll in September 1948, Conservative voters, when queried about "which two of the following political tasks do you think are the most important for your party to work for," 41 percent responded "lower taxes" while any of four social reforms listed garnered only 18 percent of votes (Stephens 1976: 225).[5] The voters of the Agrarian Party and Liberals showed a similar pattern while supporters of the two left parties showed the opposite pattern, strong support for the reforms and weaker support for less taxes. In fact, the dominant issues in the years leading up to the 1948 election were taxes, economic management, and the Social Democrats' plans for increasing state intervention in the economy (Hadenius, Wieslander, and Molin 1991: 75–77, 183 ff.). The bourgeois parties, had they won the 1948 election, would have had to violate their own election promises and their voters' wishes not to prioritize tax cuts over an increased pace of social reforms.

In sum, we can say that, at the end of the first phase of postwar Swedish social policy development (before the ATP struggle—circa 1955), the Swedish welfare state already displayed some of the characteristic features of the Nordic institutional model. It provided for citizenship benefits and it was comprehensive, covering all core transfer and service programs. However, though some benefits, notably sick pay, were earnings related, replacement rates for even these programs were not high.

Moreover, though the transfer programs other than unemployment were state administered, the service side of the welfare state had yet to be developed and a key service, health care, was still provided by private deliverers.

The passage of ATP marks the beginning of the second phase of Swedish welfare state development. Unlike the immediate postwar reforms, the positions of the parties and interest groups on this issue were highly polarized. As we pointed out, LO was the driving force behind this legislation. LO and the Social Democrats favored compulsory, earnings-related, fully indexed, public pensions with a large public pension fund. SAF, the Conservatives, and the Liberals favored voluntary pensions negotiated by the labor market partners. They were particularly adamant in their opposition to the formation of large pension funds under public control.[6] Consistent with their previous line, the Agrarians favored large increases in basic pensions along with state subsidies to voluntary supplementary pensions.

Our emphasis on the origins of ATP in LO's concerns is not meant to indicate that the ATP struggle was not part of a new strategy on the part of the Social Democrats to woo the rapidly growing strata of white-collar workers and that this entailed abandoning the farmer-worker alliance. Rather, we want to emphasize that the LO support for earnings-related benefits was based on their perception of the material interests of their members. One can see the strategic element in LO–Social Democratic strategy in such concessions to TCO (the white-collar union central organization) such as cutting the contribution period for full benefits to thirty years and making pensions dependent on the fifteen best earning years. In the short run, this was only partially successful as TCO split on the issue in the 1957 referendum and in the run-up to the 1958 election. But after ATP was passed by the narrowest of margins (on the basis of an abstention by a single Liberal member of parliament), TCO increasingly came on board and the 1960 election campaign, which was still partly fought on the pension issue, resulted in a big victory for the Social Democrats in large part due to a breakthrough into the middle class.

This struggle marked a turning point in Swedish welfare state development in several ways. First, it firmly established the earnings-related/high–replacement rate principle, and in the next two decades a principal area of reform of transfer systems was increasing replacement rates. Second, it marked the beginning of the "wage earner alliance" strategy of the Social Democrats. Third, the outcome of the pension struggle convinced the middle parties (the Liberals and the Agrarian—

now Center—Party) that it was politically suicidal to appear to be opposed to social policy expansion. Thus, not only did they not oppose new Social Democratic initiatives, they often "overbid" the Social Democrats on selected policies during election campaigns. Fourth, in retrospect, it marked the beginning of the service welfare state, though this appears to be merely temporally coincident with the ATP outcome rather than a result of it. One big step in this direction was the "Seven Crown Reform" of 1969, which essentially resulted in the introduction of a national health service, this time with the support of the middle parties, in contrast to their posture of two decades earlier. Health care is only one in a broad range of social services in which the state entered, as public health, education, and welfare employment greatly increased in the two decades following 1960, as we saw from the data presented in chapters 3 and 4. Finally, the inevitable result of this vigorous expansion of the welfare state was an extremely high tax burden (see table 4.1). Income taxes were high and very progressive, reaching an 83 percent marginal rate in the highest brackets, and indirect taxes were also among the highest in the advanced capitalist world.

To complete the story of the creation of the social democratic welfare state, one must add a third—a feminist, or gender relations—stage to this chronology of Swedish welfare state development, though this stage accompanied the second phase rather than replaced it. As we pointed out in chapters 3 and 4, this stage is also the phase of expansion of social services mentioned in the previous paragraph. Consistent with the data analysis and discussion in these chapters, this third stage can be dated as beginning roughly in 1960, at which point the Nordic welfare states were not distinctive in terms of the size of public social service employment or, other than in Finland, in the level of women's labor force participation. Indeed, in the late 1940s and early 1950s, labor force participation of married women in Norway and Sweden was among the lowest in Europe (Leira 1993). The quantitative analysis showed that rising women's labor force participation and social democratic government were associated with an expansion of public funding and delivery of social services. In addition, the combination of social democratic government and high levels of women's labor force participation was conducive to high levels of social service employment.

Here, based on recent literature on the role of women's movements in shaping the Swedish welfare state (e.g., see Bergqvist 1998; Hobson and Lindholm 1997; Hinnfors 1992, 1999; Jenson and Mahon 1993; Leira 1993; Lewis and Åström 1992; Sörensen 1999) and our own comparative historical research, we can elaborate on the dynamics of these processes for the most thoroughly researched case of the effect of women's movements on social policy. With some modification, similar processes occurred in the other Nordic countries. Unlike the northern Continental countries (which welcomed "guest workers"), due in part to the influence of the strong union movements, Sweden limited recruitment of non-Nordic foreign labor, which provided greater job opportunities for women in the private sector (Jenson and Mahon 1993: 87). The entry of women into the labor force helped stimulate the "sex role debate," in which feminists argued for equal access to the labor market for women, a higher value to be put on caring work, and a more equal division of labor in the household (Dahlström 1967). This debate about gender equality had an important impact on Social Democratic ideology and resulted in the incorporation of gender equality as a goal in the LO–Social Democratic common "Increased Equality" program of 1969 (LO-SAP 1969). This goal manifested itself in an explicit commitment among Social Democrats to a dual-earner household model, and government policy began to promote this goal, beginning with the transition to separate taxation in 1971 (Lewis 1992; Lewis and Åström 1992).[7] The growth of women's labor force participation stimulated demands by women for the expansion of day care and other social services, which, along with Social Democratic governance, helped fuel the expansion of the public social service sector. These public social service jobs were filled very disproportionately by women, so this in turn stimulated a further expansion of women's labor force participation.

As a consequence, by the mid-1970s, all four Nordic countries were already characterized both by high levels of women's labor force participation and by high levels of public health, education, and welfare employment. This feedback cycle between left-union strength, women's labor force participation, women's mobilization, and public service employment continued to the late 1980s, when the employment crisis hit Sweden, Finland, and, to a lesser extent, Norway. Indeed, it is fair to say that the main area of welfare state innovation in all four Nordic countries in the 1970s and 1980s was in policies enabling women to enter the labor force, not only through services such as day care, but also through transfers, such as increased duration of and replacement rates for maternity leave, parental leave for fathers, and sick pay for parents with ill children.[8]

Politically, one result of this was a change in the political alignments of women. In the early postwar period, Nordic women displayed a greater tendency to vote for the right than men, though not to the degree of women in Catholic Europe. By the mid-1970s, this gender gap had disappeared (Stephens 1976). By the early 1990s, the reverse gender gap had emerged in Scandinavia, with women being more likely to vote for the parties of the left and more likely to support expansion of the welfare state than men (Oskarson 1992; Valen 1992; Svallfors 1992).

### THE DEVELOPMENT OF ECONOMIC POLICY AND THE PRODUCTION REGIME

To outline the development of the economic policy underpinning the Swedish production regime in the Golden Age, we have to return briefly to the 1930s for the institutional foundation of later policy.[9] After the re-election of the Social Democrats in 1936 for a second term, SAF abandoned its attempt to defeat the labor movement and entered into negotiations with LO, resulting in the Saltsjöbaden agreement of 1938. Korpi (1983: 47–48) characterizes the long-term effects of this "historic compromise" as an agreement by both parties to cooperate in creating economic growth—the labor movement would receive greater influence over the results of production—and employers would retain the right to control the productive process and the direction of investment. The cooperative arrangement paved the way for labor peace and later for the centralization of collective bargaining at the national level: in other words, to the development of corporatism in Sweden.[10]

The Postwar Program contained elements of more ambitious planning that would have moved Sweden closer to the more statist direction of investment characteristic of Norway and Finland. Such a move was cut short by the Social Democratic retreat in the postwar "planning debate." The difference in outcome, we contend, was certainly due partly to the differences in the character of national capital in the three countries. As a result the Swedish version of the Nordic supply-side model focused on labor supply, influencing investment only indirectly.

The contours of this policy emerged in the famous Rehn-Meidner model, named for the two LO economists who developed it (Meidner and Öhman 1972; Pontusson 1992b: 57–96). The model called for LO to demand equal pay for equal work across the economy, the so-called solidaristic wage policy. This wage policy would force labor-intensive, low-productivity enterprises to rationalize or go out of business. The displaced labor would then be moved to high-productivity sectors through the active labor market policy. Wages in high-productivity, often export-oriented, sectors would be restrained to facilitate international competition.

The active labor market policy, by reducing structural unemployment, would further facilitate wage restraint and thus reduce the trade-off between unemployment and inflation, moving the Phillips curve down and to the left.

Restrictive economic policy should be pursued in order to facilitate wage restraint. In the face of restrictive macroeconomic policy, full employment would be achieved through the active labor market policy and other selective measures and loans at low interest rates from public savings such as pension funds. State controls in currency and credit markets facilitated macroeconomic adjustment and low real interest rates. Acceptable distributive outcomes for labor were achieved by tight fiscal policy, which dampened domestic demand and thus profit levels[11] and by expansion of transfer payments and free or subsidized public goods and services. Given modest profit levels, levels of business investment adequate for economic growth were to be achieved through the low-interest-rate loans from public savings. The tax regime also heavily favored investment over distribution of profits. The most celebrated feature of the corporate taxation was the countercylical investment funds established in 1955, in which firms could deposit 46 percent of their profits tax free and could later draw on them during economic downturns or after a five-year waiting period (Pontusson 1992b: 69 ff.).

Note that the role of the funds was to increase the volume of investment, not to influence where it was invested. Contrary to the fears of business, the pension funds developed in the same way: Initially, they were invested in the housing market, but even when the so-called fourth supplementary pension fund was instituted for investment in the stock market, it was invested passively. As it was originally envisioned, the "active industrial policy" initiated in the late 1970s would attempt to steer the direction of investment, but as it developed it did not play this role (Pontusson 1992b: 127–60; Benner 1997: 109–29). Nonetheless, judged from the standpoint of producing moderate profits and high levels of reinvestment, which were social democracy's goals, the policies have to be judged to be relatively successful, as one can see from table 5.1.

Table 5.1 suggests that investment promotion policies in Sweden and in the other Nordic countries and Austria were highly effective in promoting domestic investment. The investment performance of our cases becomes even more impressive if one takes into account the comparatively low levels of profits as indicated by the operating surplus as a percentage of national income in these countries.[12] To gauge the propensity to invest at a given level of profits we have calculated the ratio of gross fixed capital formation to operating surplus. As table 5.1 demonstrates,

**Table 5.1** Investment, Profits, and Reinvestment Ratios

| | Gross Fixed Capital Formation as Percentage of GDP | | | Operating Surplus as Percentage of National Income | | | Ratio of Gross Fixed Capital Formation to Net Operating Surplus | | |
|---|---|---|---|---|---|---|---|---|---|
| | 1960– 1973 | 1974– 1979 | 1980– 1989 | 1960– 1973 | 1974– 1979 | 1980– 1989 | 1960– 1973 | 1974– 1979 | 1980– 1989 |
| *Social democratic welfare states* | | | | | | | | | |
| Sweden | 23 | 21 | 19 | 21 | 15 | 17 | 1.12 | 1.39 | 1.14 |
| Norway | 28 | 33 | 25 | 27 | 20 | 27 | 1.08 | 1.72 | .94 |
| Denmark | 24 | 22 | 17 | 30 | 24 | 24 | .81 | .91 | .73 |
| Finland | 25 | 27 | 24 | 32 | 24 | 22 | .80 | 1.13 | 1.11 |
| Mean | 25.3 | 25.7 | 21.3 | 27.5 | 20.9 | 22.5 | .95 | 1.29 | .98 |
| *Christian democratic welfare states* | | | | | | | | | |
| Austria | 27 | 26 | 24 | 30 | 23 | 24 | .89 | 1.13 | 1.01 |
| Belgium | 22 | 22 | 18 | 34 | 25 | 29 | .65 | .89 | .63 |
| Netherlands | 24 | 21 | 20 | 32 | 25 | 29 | .75 | .82 | .68 |
| Germany | 25 | 21 | 21 | 30 | 23 | 23 | .85 | .90 | .89 |
| France | 24 | 24 | 20 | 32 | 25 | 24 | .74 | .96 | .87 |
| Italy | 25 | 24 | 21 | 41 | 38 | 40 | .60 | .64 | .52 |
| Switzerland | 28 | 23 | 25 | 31 | 25 | 23 | .92 | .90 | 1.08 |
| Mean | 24.8 | 23.0 | 21.3 | 32.9 | 26.4 | 27.4 | .77 | .89 | .81 |
| *Liberal welfare states* | | | | | | | | | |
| Canada | 22 | 24 | 21 | 26 | 25 | 26 | .84 | .93 | .83 |
| Ireland | 20 | 26 | 20 | 31 | 29 | 33 | .68 | .90 | .64 |
| U.K. | 18 | 19 | 17 | 21 | 18 | 20 | .84 | 1.10 | .86 |
| U.S.A. | 18 | 19 | 17 | 25 | 22 | 21 | .72 | .86 | .81 |
| Mean | 19.4 | 21.9 | 18.8 | 25.7 | 23.5 | 25.0 | .77 | 1.01 | .79 |
| *Australia* | 25 | 24 | 23 | 31 | 24 | 27 | .81 | .99 | .88 |
| *Japan* | 33 | 32 | 30 | 43 | 31 | 28 | .73 | .98 | 1.06 |
| Grand mean | 24.1 | 23.9 | 21.3 | 30.4 | 24.6 | 25.7 | .81 | 1.01 | .86 |

Data source: Duane Swank from OECD.

Sweden, Norway, and Finland, along with Austria, were consistently among the top performers in this reinvestment ratio.[13]

As we mentioned above, the demand side to this essentially supply-side model was taken care of in part by growth in demand for Swedish export products in the rapidly growing capitalist core economies. The growth of the economy was, of course, essential for the expansion of the welfare state that occurred in this period. An expanding pie made it easier to expand the welfare state share. At least as important was the pattern of employment production that was generated by the welfare state and production regime. Low levels of unemployment and high levels of labor force participation meant that high proportions of the total population were working and thus supporting the welfare state with taxes and contributions and lower proportions (in relative terms) were entirely dependent on it. Thus, the same level of entitlements in Sweden and elsewhere in Scandinavia was much less costly than it would have been had these countries had the labor force participation rates of the Continental European countries, not to mention the unemployment levels that some of them suffered beginning in the mid-1970s.

The production regime and the welfare state regime established by the mid-1950s in Sweden provided clear "incentives and constraints," in Soskice's apt terminology. The universalistic welfare state and the unions' wage policy constrained Swedish business not to compete on the basis of wage costs, as it saddled them with relatively high wage costs compared to their international competitors. Thus, the system constrained employers to raise labor productivity in their efforts to keep relative unit labor costs in line. The Rehn-Meidner model also provided incentives for employers. The most obvious is the active labor market policy's publicly funded labor training and worker relocation policy. The model was also predicated on the notion that workers did not enjoy job security in a specific firm; employers should be allowed to shed labor in order to reap the benefits of productivity enhancements. As a result, Swedish employers had much more flexibility in adjusting workforce size than did employers in many countries in Continental Europe due to legislation, as well as in Britain and even the United States in sectors in which unions were strong. The cheap credit policies and the channeling of credit to businesses also had obvious appeal to employers.

Our overview is not meant to indicate that employers were simply on the receiving end of policies developed by the unions and the Social Democratic–led government. As Swenson (1999, forthcoming) points out, export-oriented employers, who dominated SAF, supported the basic parameters of the wage policy because it promised to control wage inflation transmitted from the sheltered sector. And though they were concerned about the total costs of the social policy reforms, the universalistic feature of the policy took the "social wage" out of wage competition also. We have seen that employers did oppose the Social Democratic supplementary pension plan, though primarily due to fears that the government might use the public pension funds called for by the legislation to steer investment. With regard to the (social) wage cost issue, more telling here were the internal divisions in SAF as the clothing and textile employers opposed even SAF's own proposal for voluntarily negotiated supplementary pensions as they contended that they could not afford it (Söderpalm 1980). Thus, while a universalistic and generous welfare state might not have been the first choice of employers, due to the structure of Swedish business, it was an acceptable alternative.

Moreover, the policy pattern determined by the interplay of the unions, Social Democratic government, and employers further accentuated a central historical characteristic of Swedish industrial structure, the dominance of a small number of privately owned, internationalized and internationally competitive, oligopolistic firms. This should be obvious from our discussion of the solidaristic wage policy and universalistic social policy. These provided a hostile environment for small, generally low-productivity, low-wage firms and a highly favorable one for large high-productivity firms. The countercyclical investment fund policy had a similar effect. This policy had the effect of locking investment into existing profitable enterprises thus further accentuating the characteristic feature of Swedish business structure.

### Norway

Though, as we saw above, the Norwegian welfare state pattern is closest to the Swedish, its historical path to that end point is somewhat different.[14] That difference in historical trajectory and the differences in the production regime are due to differences in the social and economic structure. Norway lacked the internationalized, large-scale haute bourgeoisie that characterized Sweden. Relatedly, the unions in the large industrial establishments, especially in the export-oriented sector, were less dominant in LO and yet less dominant in the Social Democratic party. The peripheral "small folk" of fishermen, small farmers, primary sector workers, and workers in small work units carried more weight in the Norwegian party than in its Swedish sister party (Rokkan 1967).

As in Sweden, the advent of Labor to a stable governing position during the depression was accompanied by and in part based on a similar agreement with the Agrarian Party and followed by a union-employers compromise between the Norwegian LO and the employers' federation, NAF. When the Labor party took office in 1935, the Norwegian welfare state was underdeveloped in comparative terms. In terms of average coverage in four insurance schemes, Norway ranked second to last among twelve western European countries, followed only by Finland. By 1940, it ranked among the leaders (Flora and Alber 1981). This would appear to indicate that Labor took the leading role in welfare state development, and while this is not inaccurate, the social legislation was also supported not only by the Agrarian Party but also by most of the rest of the bourgeois opposition.

Postwar development followed this same pattern. During the war, LO published a program calling for a comprehensive, coordinated, and universalistic social security scheme, but also declared that implementation of the scheme was dependent on full employment and economic growth. This document prefigured the 1945 "Joint Program" signed by all of the major parties. Reform work over the next two decades followed this early consensus. To be sure, there were differences among the parties but this was a matter of emphasis. For example, as in the Swedish case, the Agrarians pressed for the early introduction of citizenship pensions and elimination of income testing while the Labor Party, though in principle favoring these changes, prioritized the introduction of other reforms such as sickness insurance.

As in Sweden, the demand for earnings-related pensions originated in LO's ambitions to achieve pension rights for wage earners equal to those of white-collar workers and civil servants and not in Labor's ambition to gain political support from the middle class (Åmark 1998: 20; West Pedersen 1990: 140). LO had hoped to solve the question through negotiation, in part because, in the late 1950s, the bitter pension struggle in Sweden made it appear that the legislative path would be risky and in part because LO hoped to attract members by excluding the unorganized from the pension system, something that the employers were unwilling to go along with. A negotiated solution would have excluded farmers, fishermen, and other self-employed persons, as well as low-paid white-collar workers, which is why the Agrarian Party demanded legislation. The Labor Party switched to this position, and LO supported the change in tactics. The outcome of the Swedish supplementary pension struggle strengthened the consensual nature of the reform. The remaining bourgeois parties were determined not to be divided and politically defeated as in Sweden and thus supported statutory supplementary pensions. The Conservatives and NAF opposed large pension funds under government control while NAF opposed high replacement rates because of their economic costs. At a point when relative consensus had been achieved, the bourgeois parties won the 1965 elections and were in a position to pass their version of the bill. It provided for a larger increase in basic pensions (a concession to farmers), a lower replacement rate in the earnings-related scheme (45 percent rather than 50 percent) and much smaller pension funds than the Labor-LO proposal (both concessions to NAF and the Conservatives).

In accounting for relative consensus around an extensive program of welfare policy, certainly one explanation is the hegemonic weakness of Norwegian capital.[15] The hegemonic, and economic, weakness of Norwegian capital is yet more important in accounting for the trajectory of economic policy as compared to Sweden. At a time when the idea of economic planning was under intense attack by SAF and the bourgeois parties in Sweden, the bourgeois parties accepted state leadership in economic planning in Norway. In large part, this reflected the objective reality that it would be difficult for Norwegian business to mobilize the capital necessary for an ambitious program of industrialization and structural transformation and in part their weaker ability to oppose such a program had they wanted to. The Norwegian model was characterized by direct intervention of the state through active industrial policy, low interest rates and channeling of credit to industry facilitated by extensive state ownership of industry and of banks, and tripartite wage bargaining in which the state (unlike in Sweden) played an active and not just facilitative role. The credit policies of the government were sufficiently important for the growth and employment policies that Mjøset (1986: 121) has characterized the Norwegian model as "credit socialism."

Active labor market policy was less central to the Norwegian model. One reason for this was the possibility of direct intervention to support employment in declining areas. Thus, Norwegian policy has always had a strong regional policy element to it, by sharp contrast to the Rehn-Meidner model, which hastened the decline of peripheral regions to such an extent that it stimulated policies in the 1970s to counteract these effects. Norwegian policy in this area also reflects the greater political clout of the periphery in Norwegian politics in general and, as noted above, within the Labor Party in particular. As a result, the industrial policies and the industries created by them face greater microefficiency problems than in the Swedish case.

This configuration also helps explain why Norwegian policy is less post–Fordist family, less profeminist than in the other Nordic cases. While, as a result of 1993 reforms, maternity leave is second in generosity only to Sweden, Norway lags far behind the other Nordic countries in public day care provisions and other policies that facilitate women's entry into the workforce (Leira 1993; Sörensen 1999; also see table 4.1 herein). Women's labor force participation, though high by international standards, was considerably lower than the other Nordic countries until the late 1980s and remains lower than Denmark and Sweden despite the fact that unemployment rates have been the lowest in the four countries in the 1990s (see table 5.2, pp. 136–37). The lower level of development of active labor market policy and day care provisions and related policies have certainly contributed to this outcome. These have in turn been linked to ideological-attitudinal differences: the greater influence of Christian confessional forces (Leira 1993), influence of the more traditionally familistic periphery in the base of the Labor Party (Von Nordheim Nielsen 1989: 33), and weakness and divisions in women's organizations (Sörensen 1999). We would contend that the character of Norwegian capital has contributed indirectly to the outcome by making possible the strong regional policy and thus protection of peripheral employment and by weakening the push to active labor market policy.

### Finland

Finland deviates from the Nordic pattern in a number of ways that have affected the development of its welfare state and production regime. It lagged far behind in level of economic development as of the end of the war: for example, in 1950, 46 percent of the economically active population was involved in agriculture, a figure more similar to those of Hungary (54 percent) and Poland (57 percent) than of the other Nordic countries, where agriculture accounted for no more than 26 percent of the labor force in that year (Alestalo 1986: 26). As a result of the Finnish Civil War, the left was divided between Social Democratic and Communist Parties of approximately equal strength. In the initial postwar decades, the union movement was similarly divided and the Social Democrats suffered from internal splits. As a result the Agrarian Party, which was situated in the middle of the political spectrum, was in a position to exert a major influence on legislative outcomes. Finnish constitutional provisions indirectly reinforced the influence of the Agrarians. One third of members of parliament could table bills to the next session, thus increasing the effective size of the parliamentary majority needed to pass a bill and making the centrist Agrarians an essential part of most political coalitions. In addition, the Finnish system is semipresidential and the long presidency of Agrarian Urho Kekkonen certainly increased the party's influence.

Finnish economic and political development to the mid-1980s can be divided into two distinct phases (Alestalo and Uusitalo 1986; Andersson, Kosonen, and Vartiainen 1993).[16] The first phase stretches from the late 1940s to the mid-1960s. Politically, this period is characterized by a divided left and split unions and Agrarian dominance. Economically, it is a period of state-led industrialization based on export of wood and wood products. If anything, the state was more involved in the industrialization process than in Norway, with the state not only promoting and subsidizing industrial diversification but also directly owning and creating new industrial concerns. As in Norway and Sweden, the state used low interest rates and channeling of credit to industrial users to spur industrial transformation. In order to create public savings the model was fiscally very conservative, running consistent surpluses. Unlike labor in Norway and Sweden, labor in Finland was largely excluded from the planning process in this period; it is a case of what Lehmbruch (1984) calls "concertation without labor," bearing similarities to Japan and East Asian NICs (Vartiainen 1997).

In part because of the exclusion of labor, Finnish macroeconomic policies were procyclical. With competitiveness of the export sector as practically the sole goal, the government reacted with contractionary policies in recessions. As profits in the export sector increased during expansionary periods, workers moved to capture a share of the profits through strikes. Along with low interest rates that stimulated the economy, this eventually led to inflation and an erosion of competitiveness; the government responded with devaluation. Thus, in contrast to the other Nordic countries, Finnish development is characterized by frequent devaluations and high strike rates.

In this first period, Finland was a clear laggard among the Nordic countries with respect to welfare state development. With the pressure of backwardness and its sensitive international situation, national energy was focused on economic development. Even during the center-left popular front government of the immediate postwar years, which included the Communists, few social policy innovations were passed, in sharp contrast to similar governments in Italy and France or the Social Democratic governments in Sweden, Norway, or Britain in this period. The dominance of the Agrarians and the weakness of the left also help explain this laggard position. It is significant that the one important piece of legislation passed in this period, the basic pension act of 1956, followed Agrarian preferences not only in that it provided for citizenship pensions (combined with an income-tested supplement) but also because pensions were prioritized over reforms of greater interest to organized labor and the Social Democrats.

Nonetheless, enduring political alignments on social legislation did

**Table 5.2** Labor Force Participation by Gender

| | Female Labor Force, Percentage of Females 15–64 | | | | | Male Labor Force, Percentage of Males 15–64 | | | | |
|---|---|---|---|---|---|---|---|---|---|---|
| | 1960 | 1973 | 1980 | 1990 | 1994 | 1960 | 1973 | 1980 | 1990 | 1994 |
| *Social democratic welfare states* | | | | | | | | | | |
| Sweden | 50 | 63 | 74 | 80 | 74 | 99 | 88 | 88 | 84 | 78 |
| Norway | 36 | 51 | 62 | 71 | 71 | 89 | 86 | 88 | 85 | 82 |
| Denmark | 44 | 62 | 71 | 78 | 74 | 99 | 90 | 89 | 90 | 84 |
| Finland | 66 | 64 | 70 | 73 | 70 | 91 | 80 | 83 | 81 | 77 |
| Mean | 49.0 | 60.0 | 69.3 | 75.5 | 72.2 | 94.5 | 86.1 | 87.0 | 84.7 | 80.3 |
| *Christian democratic welfare states* | | | | | | | | | | |
| Austria | 52 | 48 | 49 | 55 | 62 | 93 | 90 | 82 | 80 | 81 |
| Belgium | 36 | 41 | 47 | 52 | 56 | 83 | 83 | 79 | 73 | 72 |
| Netherlands | 26 | 29 | 35 | 53 | 57 | 95 | 85 | 79 | 80 | 79 |
| Germany | 49 | 50 | 51 | 57 | 62 | 94 | 90 | 86 | 80 | 81 |
| France | 47 | 50 | 54 | 58 | 60 | 95 | 85 | 82 | 75 | 74 |
| Italy | 40 | 34 | 40 | 46 | 43 | 95 | 85 | 83 | 80 | 74 |
| Switzerland | 51 | 54 | 54 | 60 | 67 | 100 | 100 | 94 | 96 | 97 |
| Mean | 43.0 | 43.7 | 47.2 | 54.4 | 58.2 | 93.7 | 88.3 | 83.5 | 80.6 | 79.6 |

**Table 5.2** *(continued)*

| | Female Labor Force, Percentage of Females 15–64 | | | | | Male Labor Force, Percentage of Males 15–64 | | | | |
|---|---|---|---|---|---|---|---|---|---|---|
| | 1960 | 1973 | 1980 | 1990 | 1994 | 1960 | 1973 | 1980 | 1990 | 1994 |
| *Liberal welfare states* | | | | | | | | | | |
| Canada | 32 | 47 | 61 | 75 | 68 | 91 | 86 | 86 | 84 | 83 |
| Ireland | 35 | 34 | 36 | 39 | 47 | 99 | 91 | 88 | 82 | 79 |
| U.K. | 46 | 53 | 58 | 65 | 66 | 99 | 93 | 90 | 86 | 84 |
| U.S.A. | 43 | 51 | 60 | 69 | 71 | 91 | 85 | 85 | 85 | 85 |
| Mean | 38.9 | 46.3 | 53.8 | 62.1 | 63.0 | 94.9 | 88.8 | 87.3 | 84.4 | 82.7 |
| *Wage earner welfare states* | | | | | | | | | | |
| Australia | 34 | 48 | 53 | 63 | 63 | 97 | 91 | 88 | 86 | 85 |
| New Zealand | 31 | 39 | 45 | 63 | 65 | 94 | 89 | 86 | 83 | 84 |
| *Japan* | 60 | 54 | 55 | 60 | 62 | 92 | 90 | 89 | 88 | 91 |
| Grand mean | 43.2 | 48.5 | 54.2 | 62.1 | 63.2 | 94.3 | 88.2 | 85.8 | 83.2 | 81.6 |

Data source: Huber, Ragin, and Stephens 1997 from OECD.

emerge in this period. On transfers, the Agrarians followed the pattern of their Nordic sister parties favoring universal entitlements and adequate minimums. As in Sweden, their position was reactive not proactive; once activity on a piece of social legislation was initiated, they intervened to shape the final legislation in the interests of their family farming constituency as far as possible (Kangas 1991: 155). The differences in the parties of the left reflected their constituencies. With a social and economic structure most like Norway's, the peripheral element of the left vote fell to the Communists, who also garnered a portion of the industrial wage earner vote, the bulk of which accrued to the Social Democrats. As a result, the Social Democrats generally supported high replacement rates, while the Communists supported both high replacement rates and universal entitlements and adequate minimums. The Conservatives generally acted as "brakemen" on welfare state development (Alestalo and Uusitalo 1986).

The mid-1960s mark a system shift in the Finnish welfare state and production regime strongly in the direction of the Swedish and Norwegian regimes. The 1966 election resulted in a left majority in parliament and ushered in a period of Social Democratic rule in cooperation with the Communists and/or Agrarians. In the same period, divisions in the trade union movement were overcome and union membership began to increase from about 40 percent of the labor force in the mid-1960s to twice that figure two decades later. As a result, the Finnish regime moved from concertation without labor to tripartite corporatism with the agreement on the comprehensive incomes policy in 1968, the first of its kind in Finland, symbolically marking the transition. In this same period, economic policy shifted to an emphasis on diversification of large industrial firms, both state and private; manufacturing exports; and increasing exports to Sweden and the Soviet Union, the latter of which accounted for 19.4 percent of Finnish exports by 1980 (Andersson, Kosonen, and Vartiainen 1993: 10). In the following two decades, Finland also continued its impressive growth record, effectively catching up with its Nordic neighbors (see table A.11). The figures in table 5.1 demonstrate that this transition in the Finnish production regime was accompanied by a parallel transition from one of the lowest reinvestment ratios during the Golden Age to one of the highest in the following two decades.

The social policy outcome followed a similar pattern: Enabled by the new affluence, the center-left political alignment carried out a series of social reforms over two decades, extending into the period of slowdown or retrenchment in the other three Nordic countries, in which the Finnish welfare state caught up with its neighbors. The political alignments, as outlined above, are similar with similar results, as we saw in the previous chapters. There are, of course, many nuances, some idiosyncratic and some due to the differing strength of the political coalitions at different times and to the relative lateness of Finnish development. In addition, social legislation in Finland was much more frequently the subject of *explicit* corporatist deals in which the unions traded wage restraint for social policy concessions, though even there it was primarily to modify and improve existing programs rather than institute new ones (Alestalo and Uusitalo 1986: 258–60).

One of these systematic differences is worth mentioning: Despite the fact that the Finnish production regime, along with the Norwegian, is the most statist in Scandinavia, the welfare state regime is the least statist. The development of pension legislation illustrates why this was so (Kangas 1988; Salminen 1993). The development of the basic pension plan was dominated by the Agrarians and involved the founding of the National Pension Institute to administer the plan and the folding of previous pension funds into the new national plan. Since these funds had been developed via contributions from employers and employees, the Social Democrats, the trade unions, and employers felt with some justification that this amounted to a massive subsidy from wage earners and employers to the rural population. In addition, the Pension Institute was dominated by Agrarians, including the chief officer, who was a former chairman of the party. Thus, the Social Democrats and trade unions viewed with considerable suspicion proposals by the Agrarians to have supplementary pensions administered by the institute. In the wake of the defeat of Swedish bourgeois parties and SAF in the ATP struggle, SAF advised its Finnish counterpart not to oppose compulsory legislated supplementary pensions and to focus its efforts on avoiding state pension funds and maintaining private pension funds that could be drawn on as a source of risk capital. This laid the basis for a common front against the Agrarian Party for statutory, compulsory, earnings-related pensions with private administration. Similarly, the first week of sick pay, passed in 1970, is statutory and compulsory but is an employer mandate and thus avoids state administration and is not part of the state budget. Government employment follows this pattern; though above the European average, it is well below the level in other Nordic countries (see table 4.1).

With regard to income-related benefits, we underline once more for the case of Finland that the main pressure group for statutory earnings-related benefits was the industrial workers unions. As in Sweden, it was their assessment that all nonstatutory alternatives would leave them with benefits inferior to those of other groups.

As of 1960, Finland had by far the highest women's labor force participation rate among all advanced industrial democracies, with two thirds of women in the age group 15–64 working (table 5.2). By 1980 this rate had increased to over 70 percent and was comparable to that of Denmark and just slightly below that of Sweden. Moreover, Finland had the highest full-time women's labor force participation rate, with only 10 percent of women working part-time (Gornick 1999: 220–21). Perhaps surprisingly, given the persistence of a large agrarian sector well into the post–World War II period, Finland also had the highest proportion of women college students among advanced industrial democracies as of 1960, and remained the fifth highest in 1981 (Norris 1987: 86). Early in the post–World War II period women rose into leadership positions in the left-wing parties, followed by women in the center parties (Lovenduski 1986: 152–53). This combination of high women's labor force participation, education, and participation as leaders in political parties accounts for Finland's leading position in the mid-1960s in terms of women's representation in parliament, with 15 percent of members of parliament being women. Finland retained the leadership position into the 1980s, with 31 percent of members of parliament being women in 1984 (Lovenduski 1986: 152–53).

The high levels of women's mobilization and political representation, in combination with Social Democratic incumbency, translated into a leadership role in gender-egalitarian social policy development as well. In 1975 Finland already had the longest paid maternity leave (thirty-five weeks), though at a comparatively low replacement rate, and by 1985 maternity leave had been extended to fifty-two weeks at an 80 percent replacement rate, more generous than Sweden with a 70 percent replacement rate for the same duration (Gauthier 1996: 174). Both mothers and fathers enjoyed longer leaves in the early 1980s than their counterparts in Sweden and Denmark (Sainsbury 1999b: 183–84). By the 1990s, Finland along with Sweden and Denmark had developed the best care facilities for the elderly and for children.

### Denmark

Danish industrial structure and economy differ from those of the other Nordic countries, which goes far in explaining why the Danish welfare state and production regimes, specifically the employment and growth policies, are different. Denmark's only natural resource is fertile soil, thus agricultural products, above all processed foods from the dairy and animal husbandry branches, dominated exports until the 1960s. Though

Denmark like the rest of Scandinavia lacked Junker-style large estates, landholding was more differentiated, creating a division of political interests in the countryside. In sharp contrast to, above all, Sweden, industry was traditionally small scale and craft oriented. Even after the "second industrial revolution" beginning in the late 1950s, small-scale manufacturing dominated the new niche-oriented manufacturing export industries. Moreover, Denmark lacked the finance-industry linkages achieved via the concentrated industrial-financial conglomerates in Sweden or via the state in Norway and Finland.

As a consequence, agrarian interests were stronger and the left weaker in Denmark than in Sweden or Norway. Moreover, agrarian interests were split into two parties, the Liberals and Radicals, representing in large part the divide between large and small farming. The Liberals' stance on social and economic policy was closer to the Conservatives while the Radicals were similar to, if a bit more reformist than, their sister agrarian parties in the other Scandinavian societies. As a result of the industrial structure, craft unions carried more weight in the Danish LO and there was a separate union for unskilled workers within LO. Thus, the union movement was more decentralized, more diverse in its interests, and not dominated by the industrial unions in the export sector as in the other Nordic countries. The net result of this economic and industrial structure for Social Democracy was that not only was it weaker than in Norway and Sweden, the interests of its political base were more diverse.[17]

Given the Social Democrats' weakness and need for bourgeois coalition partners, it is not surprising that their postwar statist planning initiative went nowhere (Esping-Andersen 1985: 206). But neither did a more modest Swedish-style supply-side policy encouraging industrial development and structural rationalization emerge. The petty bourgeois character of both the rural and urban sectors and the lack of finance-industry ties militated against it as did the character of the union movement. In Sweden, such a policy was based on the hegemony of export-oriented manufacturers among the employers and industrial unions in the export sector and on a high degree of centralization on both sides, all of which were lacking in Denmark. In sharp contrast to the other Nordic countries, Danish financial markets were strongly integrated with international credit markets in the Golden Age and thus interest rates were higher than in the other countries (Mjøset 1986). With no long-term supply-side policies, government efforts to combat unemployment were predominantly short-term Keynesian demand management measures that fueled inflation thus threatening the balance of payments and consequently leading to contractionary measures, the "stop-go" cycle familiar to students of British political economy (Esping-Andersen 1985: 207).[18]

These same economic and political characteristics strongly influenced the social policy outcome. Except for short periods, the Social Democrats could not dispense with the coalition with the agrarian Radicals. Up to 1967, when the coalition broke up and the Radicals moved to the right, the Radicals were the most important partner for the Social Democrats in shaping the Danish welfare state. As in Sweden, the Social Democrats were the driving force behind the expansion of the welfare state, and the Radicals pushed for the interests of their small-farming base, which lay in universalistic, flat-rate, tax-financed benefits (Petersen 1998: 148–49). In another parallel, the Social Democrats were divided in the early post–World War II period on the question of a universalistic pension, with a strong current of opinion holding that funds were needed more urgently for other social policy reforms. However, by 1952 the party had adopted a universal pension as a central goal, and by 1956 combined pressure from the Social Democrats and the Radicals resulted in legislation that introduced a universal pension with a combination of flat-rate and earnings-related benefits, the latter declining with rising incomes (Petersen 1998: 83, 139–40, 147–48). Just a few years later, though, rising incomes led to a loss of these earnings-related benefits even for blue-collar workers, and the pension issue was on the table again. In 1960, the unions asked for a supplementary pension scheme in collective negotiations but employers refused. Instead, the Social Democratic–Radical government spearheaded legislation for a labor market supplementary pension that increased with years of work but not income, for all wage and salary earners (except for civil servants), to be paid by employer (two-thirds) and employee (one-third) contributions and invested through a central fund; this legislation passed in 1964. This scheme was viewed by the government as a step toward a more encompassing and earnings-related one, following the Swedish model, but that model was strongly opposed by employers and bourgeois parties because of employer contributions and the collective pension fund. Ultimately, efforts to install such a system failed because of the collapse of the Social Democratic–led government in early 1968 and the refusal of the successor bourgeois government to pursue the proposal (Petersen 1998: 217–21). The development of earnings-related supplementary pensions stalled until the late 1980s (see chapter 7).

Replacement rates for other transfer payments also fall rapidly as one moves above the income level of the average production worker. The character of the Social Democrats' union base contributed to this pattern.

The industrial unions, especially in the export sector, which were the main promoters of earnings-related benefits in Sweden and Finland, were weak, and the skilled and unskilled workers were divided in their interests. Thus, for example, the Danish LO, in sharp contrast to its Swedish and Norwegian counterparts, was ambivalent about earnings-related supplementary pensions with the unskilled workers favoring increased flat-rate benefits and the skilled workers favoring wage increases rather than increased pension benefits (Salminen 1993: 275–76). The petty bourgeois character of Danish employers is one reason, probably the main reason, why, in contrast to the other Nordic countries, employers' contributions to social security financing are very low and tax financing very high. That is, these employers are more worried about direct wage costs than their counterparts in other Nordic countries. As outlined above, the structure of industry and unions also discouraged structural rationalization policies and thus favored passive measures over active labor market policy. Finally, the Danish policy pattern included a combination of liberal dismissal rules and high unemployment insurance replacement rates and long duration of unemployment benefits, again arguably an adaptation to the need of small employers for flexibility in workforce management and the need of unions to compensate workers for the flexible dismissal policy (Benner and Vad 2000).

Despite these constraints, the Danish Social Democrats consistently promoted an improvement of the general level of welfare state benefits and an equalization of the treatment of blue- and white-collar workers. Against the resistance of the Conservatives and the Liberals, they increased unemployment insurance replacement rates beginning in 1960 until they reached an upper limit of 80 percent in the late 1960s (Petersen 1998: 227–28). Similarly, with the support of the Socialist Party and against the votes of the bourgeois parties, they increased sickness replacement rates in 1971 and a year later they eliminated waiting days and introduced indexation of benefits to inflation (Petersen 1998: 297–98). Finally, they pushed through social assistance legislation that obliged the state to maintain the customary living standards of those dependent on social assistance. In the case of some reforms, notably pensions, the Conservative and Liberal Parties ultimately did support legislation improving benefits, particularly when it was clear that the Social Democrats could muster majority support and that the reforms were popular, but in general they attempted to slow down the expansionary thrust of welfare state policy.

In women-friendly policies, Denmark was a leader. The women's movement that predated the emergence of the new radical feminist groups of the late 1960s had worked hard to influence policy and had initiated a public debate about gender roles. The child and youth care law of 1964 set the stage for a very rapid increase in public day care provision, which facilitated women's entry into the labor force. Thus, from a lower base in 1960 female labor force participation rates by 1973 had virtually caught up to those of Finland and Sweden, the two leaders among all advanced industrial countries. In 1981, Denmark had the highest proportion of union members who were women among fourteen European countries, slightly ahead of Sweden, with 43 percent of all LO members and 56 percent of all members of the white-collar central union organization being women (Lovenduski 1986: 170). Women's mobilization also increased in the political arena, with women working within the political parties, and by the end of 1984, 26 percent of parliamentary representatives were women (Lovenduski 1986: 152). Also in the 1980s, Denmark ranked highest in support for employment for mothers with children younger than school age (Gornick, Meyers, and Ross 1998: 40).

In 1965, the Social Democratic prime minister appointed a commission on the status of women, and one of the recommendations of this commission was that a state agency in charge of promoting women's rights be established. The bourgeois government rejected the proposal, but after the Social Democrats' return to power the prime minister created the Equal Status Council in 1975 (Borchorst 1995: 61). From the mid-1970s to 1990 Denmark resembled the other Nordic countries in generosity of maternity leaves (Gauthier 1996: 170–71) and later the introduction of parental leave. In sum, the Danish case illustrates well the interaction between growing labor force participation and growing political mobilization of women, incumbency of social democratic parties, and expansion of women-friendly welfare states.

### The Christian Democratic Welfare States of Northern Europe

As we pointed out in the previous chapters, the Christian democratic welfare states are as generous as the social democratic ones in terms of total cash transfers, but they are less universalistic and less service oriented, and much less gender egalitarian. The German, Austrian, and Dutch welfare states exhibit the essential characteristics of Catholic-corporatist welfare states, such as the existence of multiple insurance schemes for the same risk and for different employment categories, the reliance on the male breadwinner model, and the predominance of private provision of services combined with reliance on the family. These welfare state structures have important implications for gender roles; they assign the responsibility for care-giving predominantly to unpaid women's labor and thus keep women's labor force participation low.

The power constellations shaping the construction of these welfare states have been less favorable for labor than in the Nordic countries, with Austria coming closest to the Nordic situation and the Netherlands being furthest away from it. Deep religious cleavages historically divided the working class and its organizations. In Austria and Germany these divisions in the labor movement were overcome by the formation of unified labor confederations after World War II, but in the Netherlands they persisted. More importantly, in all three countries these divisions lived on in the party system in the form of strong Christian democratic parties. Christian democratic incumbency up to 1980 was strongest in the Netherlands, followed by Germany and then Austria; social democratic incumbency showed the opposite pattern, being much stronger in Austria than in the other two countries.

The constitutional structure effected a high degree of power concentration in Austria and the Netherlands, with Germany at an intermediate level because of federalism and bicameralism. The women's movements in the three countries did not become significant actors in welfare state issues until the 1970s. The 1970s were also a period of social democratic incumbency, alone in Austria and as the leading party in a coalition in Germany and the Netherlands, and thus first steps were made to improve the position of women in the social insurance systems and in the workplace. In all three countries, offices for women's affairs were set up at the national level. However, up to 1980 women's labor force participation in the Netherlands remained the lowest among all advanced industrial countries, rivaled only by Ireland; in Austria and Germany it was clearly below the levels of Scandinavia, Canada, Britain, and the United States. Thus, women's political mobilization and representation remained comparatively low also, and progress was slow.

The production regimes of Austria and Germany are clearly coordinated market economies; in the Netherlands coordination has been looser. Export dependence in Austria and Germany has been roughly similar to that of the Nordic countries, and in the Netherlands it has been even higher. The pressures for corporatist arrangements resulting from this dependence, though, were counteracted to some extent by the religion-based political divisions in the working class, most prominently in the Netherlands. Union density rates have been lower, as have contract coverage rates (table 4.2). Centralization of unions and employers associations has been actually higher in Austria than in the Nordic countries, but lower in Germany and even lower in the Netherlands. Corporatist arrangements in the sense of formal participation of representatives of labor and capital in quasi-governmental institutions have been strong in all three countries, but since the actual influence of labor on policy is heavily dependent on the incumbency of social democratic parties, this influence has been strongest in Austria and weakest in the Netherlands, with Germany in the middle.

The production regimes of all three countries differed markedly from the Nordic cases in the absence of active labor market policies. Germany was a partial exception in that active labor market policy did become a central component of reforms once the Social Democrats became the leading force in government in the late 1960s. In other aspects the production regimes of the three countries varied greatly among themselves. The Austrian production regime has been the most statist, with weak capital and a large nationalized enterprise sector. The German one has been based on strong coordination among large and medium-sized enterprises through active business associations, and between industrial enterprises and financial institutions, supported but not guided by the state. The Dutch production regime has been characterized by the presence of a few very large internationalized companies with weaker links to the domestic economy than the large German companies have to the German economy.

In the early post–World War II period all three countries pursued an industrialization policy based on low wages and undervalued exchange rates. In addition, Germany and the Netherlands provided mainly tax breaks for reinvestment, whereas Austria also relied heavily on direct investment grants and subsidies. All three governments also provided support for R and D, and some support for regional industrialization policies. These countries did not run budget surpluses like the Nordic ones in the Golden Age, but they generally balanced their budgets. They reached similarly high investment and economic growth rates in the 1960s and 1970s. Overall, the state's role in the production regime, both in promoting industrialization and full employment, was weaker in Germany and the Netherlands than in the Nordic countries; in Austria it was comparable to Norway and Finland, and stronger than in Denmark and Sweden.

### *Germany*

The central dynamics that shaped the German welfare state in the post–World War II period were the political competition between the Social Democratic Party of Germany (SPD) and the Christian Democratic

Union/Christian Social Union (CDU/CSU), and the efforts of the German Union Confederation (DGB), the German White Collar Employee's Union (DAG), and associations of employers and private insurance carriers and service providers to shape the social welfare system in such a way as to promote and protect the interests of their members. Policy legacies were important insofar as various groups, in particular white-collar employees and civil servants, were accustomed to having their separate privileged schemes and demanded no less from the new postwar social security system. Similarly, the representatives of previously existing insurance carriers, particularly in the health care field, mobilized to regain their roles. However, it is essential to put the impact of these policy legacies in the proper context of the balance of political power in postwar Germany. If labor had been stronger and the left had won the 1949 elections, the German welfare state would have been reformed and given a much more universalistic and solidaristic character. It was the failure of labor and the left to muster the political strength to implement their plans that opened the way for those with vested interests in the traditional corporatist social insurance system to reassert themselves and effect a restoration of these old structures.

The German welfare state, then, came to reflect the political predominance of the CDU/CSU, in coalition with the Free Democratic Party (FDP), in its critical formative years, but also the consistent pressures from the left and labor and the presence of a prolabor wing in the CDU. In the early post–World War II period an Allied plan for a comprehensive reform of the social security system failed because of determined opposition from private insurance, employers, employees, self-employed, doctors, and all political forces except the SPD, whose support, along with that of the unions, was only partial (Hockerts 1980: 23–131; Alber 1986; Baldwin 1990: 159–200). The plan envisaged a unification of the pension, sickness, and unemployment insurance systems, low flat-rate benefits, and financing exclusively through contributions, without any financing out of general revenue. Whereas blue-collar unions and the SPD and the Communist Party of Germany (KPD) strongly supported unification and inclusiveness of social insurance, they opposed the lowering of benefits compared to traditional standards and the elimination of state contributions.[19] After an initial delay in implementation of this plan, East-West tensions intervened to paralyze decision making in the Allied Control Council and to open the way for German interest groups to influence policy because the reform was left to newly elected German bodies. The 1949 elections to the Bundestag sealed the fate of the reform efforts, as the SPD and KPD together received only 36 percent of the seats and the CDU/CSU formed the first coalition government with the FDP and a small conservative party.

The new welfare state then came to be squarely based on pre-Nazi structures, with different insurance funds for different social risks and for different occupational categories, a funded system, and administration by self-governing bodies composed of the insured and employers.[20] The struggle over unification of social insurance became to some extent linked to the efforts to form a united trade union confederation for blue- and white-collar unions. A unified insurance scheme with a strong role for unions in its administration was seen as instrumental for trade union unity, but instead the failure of the social insurance reform gave momentum to the formation of a separate white-collar confederation, the DAG, shortly after the formation of the DGB in 1949. The DAG in turn became a strong advocate of separate insurance schemes. When advocates of separate schemes won the first elections to the administrative organs of the employees' insurance fund in 1953, DGB and SPD resistance against separate funds received a setback (Hockerts 1980: 145–46).

From this point on until the early 1970s, unification of different occupational schemes, and in particular equalization of provisions for blue- and white-collar workers, redistribution through inclusion of high-income earners in the compulsory schemes, a minimum pension, and improvements of benefits remained constant demands made by the SPD and the DGB (Alber 1986). The efforts at comprehensive reform were defeated time and again because of the minority political position of the SPD and the opposition from groups with vested interests in the existing system, but they did force the CDU/CSU to respond with their own reform plans, to improve pension benefits and gradually equalize pension benefits for blue- and white-collar workers. Certainly there was a strong prolabor, pro–welfare state wing within the CDU, but the elaboration of a CDU/CSU plan for comprehensive reform of the social security system was obstructed by internal struggles. After a considerable fight, the candidate of the labor wing who had supported a unified insurance scheme in 1946–47 won the appointment as minister of labor, but his deputy and other key officials were opponents of comprehensive reform (Hockerts 1980: 112–15). The ministry also remained understaffed, so that serious work on a comprehensive reform plan did not get under way until 1954–55 (Hockerts 1980: 116–17). Finally, the Ministry of Finance opposed most reform proposals because of their presumed impact on the economy.

To support the argument about the importance of SPD-DGB pressures and political competition with the CDU/CSU pushing the government toward reforms of social policy, it is necessary to present briefly the historical record for the period leading up to the big pension reform of 1957.[21] In 1950 the SPD presented a parliamentary initiative for pension increases; it was rejected, but the next year the CDU/CSU fraction presented a similar initiative that was accepted. In 1952 both the CDU/CSU and the SPD fractions made independent efforts to increase pensions, but the Ministry of Finance obstructed any legislation. In 1952 the SPD asked for the establishment of a Commission of Experts to study social policy reform with the purpose of coming up with a proposal that the big parties would be able to compromise on. When the government rejected this suggestion, the SPD developed and presented its own plan for a comprehensive social security reform inspired by the Beveridge Report. In 1953 an SPD proposal for financial equalization among different insurance funds was defeated. In 1954 the SPD initiated a debate in the Bundestag on the state of social security reform and thus made it clear that the government still had no proposal to present. Later in 1954 the Ministry of Labor proposed an increase in pensions only that was again opposed by the minister of finance. Only when the SPD presented its own legislation for a pension increase was the minister of labor's proposal accepted. The DGB added its weight to the insistent demands for reform through resolutions of its annual congresses.

By 1955, Chancellor Adenauer felt compelled to get personally involved in social security reform. He secretly commissioned four social scientists to elaborate a comprehensive conception of a social insurance system that would ensure social peace but preserve individual initiative and thus should be based on the Catholic principles of solidarity and subsidiarity. In April 1955 the Ministry of Labor presented a plan for increases in benefits only, still without suggestions for other reforms. A month later the report of the four experts was made public; this report, in turn, was opposed by the Ministry of Labor as impossible to implement. A special subcommittee of the cabinet continued to work on comprehensive reform, but the Ministry of Labor successfully directed this subcommittee toward giving priority to pension reform. Again, action was forced by an SPD parliamentary initiative that demanded periodic extra pension payments until a reform would be passed; the CDU/CSU presented a counterinitiative, and a compromise was unanimously passed by the Bundestag.[22] The most controversial issue within the government regarding pension reform was indexation; by the beginning of 1956 Adenauer endorsed "dynamic" pensions, i.e., periodic adjustments to maintain the standard of living reached during the working years, and his endorsement had significant influence on internal opinion formation. In January 1956 the SPD presented a legislative proposal for automatic pension adjustments that would guarantee 75 percent of previous earnings, thus taking up a demand made by the DGB on May 1, 1955. Finally, when the SPD presented a comprehensive legislative proposal for pension reform in April, it forced a response from the government in the form of a proposal from the Ministry of Labor that contained the basic contours of reform but still lacked many essential details, such as financing mechanisms.

In the political maneuvering over pension reform the Ministry of Labor and the left wing of the CDU/CSU sought compromises with the SPD, and the SPD on its part wanted to prevent the reform from being blocked by political confrontation and wanted to prove that the party was responsible and fit to govern. Thus, the SPD dropped its demand for a basic flat-rate pension financed out of general revenue in favor of entirely contribution-based pensions, and instead asked for a minimum pension for low-income earners. The method of pension adjustment, the extent of compulsory membership in the pension schemes, and the question of separate legislation for blue- and white-collar workers remained most controversial and led to significant mobilization on the part of the DGB, the DAG, and associations of employers, insurance companies, and banks. The final legislation was a compromise that brought a very significant increase in the real value of pensions, a transition from the funded to the pay-as-you-go system, separate legislation for blue- and white-collar workers but with identical provisions, a high but fixed income ceiling that excluded less than 4 percent of employees, and annual but not automatic adjustment to the development of wages (with productivity and national income as possible additional considerations for the body charged with the adjustment decisions). Again, both CDU/CSU and SPD unanimously supported this legislation, despite the bitter preceding battles.

It is important to note here the absence of agrarian allies for the SPD's push for basic flat-rate pensions financed out of general revenue. First of all, of course, there was no agrarian party comparable to the Nordic ones. Second, as early as 1946 farmers demanded their own pension scheme (Baldwin 1990: 192). Thus, rather than supporting the thrust for a universalistic basic pension, agrarian interests joined the camp of the advocates of a fragmented system. Their demands were met with the 1957 pension reform that established a separate scheme for farmers, with flat-rate contributions and flat-rate benefits.

In contrast to the pension reform, no general reform bill for the sickness insurance and health care system was passed. Several bills failed due either to determined opposition from the SPD and the unions on the one hand and health care providers and insurance funds on the other hand, or to great internal disunity in the governing parties. The central issues of contention here were equal treatment for blue- and white-collar workers with regards to earnings replacements, the income ceiling for compulsory insurance, the extent of cost sharing, the method of remuneration for physicians, and the rules for negotiations of fees between sickness funds and physicians. The political power constellation was further complicated in the health care policy area by the importance of the FDP as a coalition partner in government and by the fact that its electoral base included a large sector of health care providers, particularly physicians and dentists. The first step toward more equal treatment of blue- and white-collar workers in sickness insurance came in response to a massive regional strike by unions in support of demands for continuation of wage payments by employers during sickness, a benefit that white-collar workers already enjoyed while blue-collar workers only had a right to compensation from the sickness funds amounting to 50 percent of their wages, after three waiting days. The new rules gave workers 65 to 75 percent of their wages from the sickness funds and a supplement from employers to bring it up to 90 percent, with two waiting days (Hockerts 1980: 367–68; Alber 1986; Immergut 1986: 61–62). Full wage continuation by employers remained a consistent demand from unions and the SPD but could be introduced only by the Grand Coalition between CDU/CSU and SPD in 1969 when the CDU/CSU could be convinced by the SPD that concessions to the unions on this point were essential to save economic management through Concerted Action (Immergut 1986: 64–69).

After the reforms of 1957 there was a long period of only marginal innovation in social policy. In particular, the area of social services remained severely underdeveloped. The next big reform push came under the 1966–69 Grand Coalition and the subsequent SPD-FDP coalition governments. Most of the reforms under the Grand Coalition responded in some ways to the conjunctural economic difficulties. This is particularly true for the abolition of income ceilings for pension and unemployment insurance and the unification of the pension schemes for blue- and white-collar workers to balance their liquidity reserves (Alber 1986). Nevertheless, the effect of these reforms was to weaken the privileged position of white-collar employees in social insurance, a goal not only persistently pursued by the DGB and the SPD but also supported by the pro-labor wing of the CDU (Schmidt 1998: 92–93). The economic problems and the consequent need for union cooperation in Concerted Action also strengthened the SPD's hand within the Grand Coalition in pushing through the reform of unemployment insurance, which put much emphasis on active labor market policy.

The SPD-FDP government formed in 1969 presented broad-based reform plans for social policy. Schmidt (1998: 94) argues that the FDP left the social policy field by and large to the SPD, in part because its own support base benefited from the expansion of social insurance for the self-employed, and in part because the FDP concentrated on influencing economic policy and restraining the expansion of codetermination demanded by the unions. The SPD attempted again to implement a basic reform of the pension system aimed at unification, expansion, and greater redistribution, but had to settle for a compromise that significantly increased pension benefits and partially met the SPD's long-standing demands for a minimum pension, albeit only for people with a twenty-five-year record of contributions (Alber 1998). Voluntary coverage for housewives (blocked by the government in the 1957 reform) and the self-employed was introduced as well (Alber 1986). The most important part of the 1972 pension reform in the longer run turned out to be the introduction of a flexible age limit for retirement, which made early retirement possible at sixty-three. Under conditions of rising unemployment it came to be used increasingly as a tool to reduce labor supply, as we will discuss in chapter 7. The 1972 pension reform, like the 1957 reform, indeed became the object of intense party competition, with government and opposition seizing on the favorable projections of surpluses in the pension insurance to make ever more expensive proposals (Hockerts 1992). Health insurance benefits were improved in 1973 in a variety of ways, including provision of household assistance, and in 1975 coverage of birth control services was introduced, including abortion and sterilization (Leichter 1979: 142). Thus, the German welfare state was on its way to having more social democratic elements grafted onto the Catholic-corporatist structure, but before these reforms could go very far the economic difficulties of the post-1973 period intervened and put the issue of expenditure controls in the center of the agenda.

Women's labor force participation in Germany was comparatively high with 35 percent in 1950 (compared, for instance, to 29 percent in the United States in the same year), which was largely a result of the reconstruction effort, but from there it rose extremely slowly to 38 percent in 1982 (compared to 43 percent in the United States) (von Wahl 1999: 73). In the 1950s German policy put great emphasis on the male breadwinner model and women's responsibility for the home, and it allowed massive discrimination against women, particularly married women, in the labor market. Even the unions and the SPD took the view that women should work only in case of real economic necessity. The position of the SPD has to be understood in part in the context of the Cold War, as an effort to differentiate itself from the East German socialism/communism that promoted the integration of women into the labor force (von Oertzen 1999: 85). Though in the 1960s women's organizations worked for changing civil service legislation to allow for part-time work, efforts that were successful in bringing about such legislation in 1969 (von Oertzen 1999: 100), the women's movement was weak and gender equality was not on the agenda.

It was only in the late 1960s that a new independent feminist movement emerged that pushed for gender equality. At the same time, the women's group in the SPD began to adopt clearly feminist positions and achieved the adoption of a commitment to women's equality in the 1975 party program (Lovenduski 1986: 151). At the policy level, the SPD-FDP government established a women's policy machinery at the national level in 1972, and subsequently the Länder ruled by the SPD were the first to establish offices for women's policy (Ferree 1995: 98–100). In the 1972 pension reform the SPD pushed for a "baby year," that is, credit for pension insurance for a year without contributions after the birth of a child, but lost against CDU/CSU opposition by one vote (Hockerts 1992: 927–28). Despite further efforts to improve women's position in the labor market, including the adoption of the EU directive on equal treatment for women in paid employment in 1979, there was little effective progress in policies to promote gender equality in the 1970s. Also in 1979 paid maternity leave was introduced for employed mothers, for a period of six months.[23] The rise of the feminist movement outside and inside the SPD was followed very soon by the onset of economic difficulties and rising unemployment, and thus the male breadwinner model continued to dominate social policy.

The Germans had no policies specifically aimed at generating employment other than general policies aimed at creating growth until the Social Democrats managed to push through active labor market policies under the Grand Coalition in the late 1960s. Growth was the central goal of economic policy and employment was expected to grow as a by-product. Yet, despite spectacular growth unemployment remained at comparatively high levels in the 1950s. This was partly due to the particular growth model and partly due to the inflow of refugees from East Germany. The German production regime was a prototypical "flexibly coordinated system," with relatively long-term and high-trust relations within and among institutions at micro as well as macro levels (Soskice 1991: 48). The production regime was based on highly concentrated industries, strong links between large enterprises and banks, a strong coordinating role for business associations, tax incentives for reinvestment of profits, an undervalued currency that led to an export boom, and restriction of private domestic consumption through high taxes and low wages (Allen 1989; Zysman 1983: 255–56). The inflow of skilled and cheap labor from the East supported productivity growth with lagging wages. High industrial concentration and strong business associations facilitated cartel-like practices that strengthened the position of German enterprises in export markets. Strong links to banks that provided long-term financing enabled managers to take a longer-term view of industry needs rather than having decisions dictated by a concern with the short-run fluctuations of the stock market (Zysman 1983: 265).

The role of the state was mainly to provide a supportive environment for business and business-bank coordination, to provide high-quality education at all levels, to support research and development in cooperation with business, and to ensure a stable macroeconomic environment with general investment incentives, both direct subsidies and tax breaks. Though subsidies were substantial (Katzenstein 1987: 103), there was little direct investment by the state or direct guidance of private investment by the state. The CDU/CSU insisted on the primacy of the market, and with its 1959 Bad Godesberg Program the SPD abandoned plans for significant expansions of state ownership and control of the economy. In addition to ideological commitments, there were structural barriers to an interventionist economic policy. The federal government's powers were restricted and it depended on other actors for the execution of economic policies. To begin with, it faced a highly autonomous central bank with the sole mission of guaranteeing price stability. Moreover, federalism meant that the federal government controlled less than half of public spending and only about 15 percent of public investment (Katzenstein 1987: 101). In addition, wage bargaining is strictly bipartite. Participation in Concerted Action, the attempt to arrive at an incomes policy under the Grand Coalition, was voluntary and consisted mainly in the exchange of information, rather than the establishment of binding wage and price guidelines (Katzenstein 1987: 98).

By the early 1960s the combination of strong export growth, the stimulus for expanded trade from the formation of the EEC in 1957, and the end of the inflow of labor from the East due to the construction of the Berlin wall in 1961 led to full employment (Allen 1989). In fact, by the mid-1960s there was already a labor shortage that was filled by guest workers imported from the southern part of Europe, in contrast to what happened in the Nordic countries. The presence of these guest workers

then served as a cushion to maintain full employment during cyclical fluctuations through the simple mechanism of not renewing their work permits. In the late 1960s, though, the appreciation of the deutsche mark and
intensified competition from producers in developing countries began to
create structural unemployment and to necessitate structural adjustments. The German policy was less to offer subsidies and other forms of
protection to declining industries (though mining, steel, and shipbuilding
were important temporary exceptions) but rather to help firms find new
niches in high-wage industries and to support upgrading of skills of the
labor force. Support for growth industries took the form of massive public investments in research and development projects selected by joint
government-business committees, of provision of regional support to
shift resources out of declining and into growing sectors, and of local alliances among business, banks, and government agencies to promote
such industries (Zysman 1983: 257–58). The exercise of governmental
power by the SPD made it possible to complement this essentially mar-
ket-conforming mode of adjustment with an active pursuit of full employment through public support for occupational training and retraining
and for systematic labor market research, anchored in the 1969 reform of
the unemployment insurance system (Janoski and Alas forthcoming).

The German system of industrial relations was supportive of this high-
skill-high-wage employment regime. Despite only intermediate union
density, legal provisions ensured an organized labor presence at the enterprise level in the form of the works councils and extended the reach of
collective bargaining to virtually the entire labor force (Jacobi, Keller,
and Mueller-Jentsch 1992; Streeck 1997). Negotiations took place at the
industry level, and the negotiations in the metal industry typically served
as pace setters for other industries, resulting in a system with a high degree of economywide coordination of wage setting (Soskice 1991). The
vocational training system regulated at the national level by negotiations
between unions and employers' associations provided a labor force with
the high skill levels necessary to compete in quality-competitive markets.
From the point of view of the employers, investments in the skill level of
their labor force were sound because of the long average tenure of employees, which in turn was supported by the antidismissal bias of the institution of works councils (Streeck 1997). The strategy of competing
through high-quality production and product differentiation, supported
by the combination of the vocational training system and the wide reach
of collective bargaining, resulted in low wage dispersion across income
categories, sectors, and enterprises of different size, compared to Britain,
the United States, and for the most part also Japan (Streeck 1997). This

result came about in the absence of a deliberate wage policy of solidarity of the Swedish variety.

### Austria

The Austrian welfare state regime, like the German, was shaped by both Christian democratic and social democratic visions and power bases. The production regime, in contrast, was much more statist and assigned higher priority to full employment and thus was closer to a social democratic regime than the German one. The main reasons for this difference were the greater participation of social democracy in government, the greater relative strength of the state sector and weakness of private capital, and the greater strength of the organizational representation of labor. This constellation of forces was largely a result of the nationalization of large parts of the economy in order to avoid confiscation of German property by the Allied powers after World War II, of the early foundation of the Austrian Union Confederation (ÖGB) in April 1945—even before the formation of the provisional government (Talos and Kittel 1996: 109–10)—and its achievement of a monopoly position, and of the role assigned to peak associations by legislation.

In the Austrian case, compared to the German, it was less publicly visible political competition in parliament that drove social policy making than intracoalition negotiations. Nevertheless, as Talos (1981: 312–38) demonstrates, based on an examination of primary materials such as minutes of party congresses and congresses of peak associations, there were persistent differences between the parties and between the representatives of labor and capital. He argues that employers accepted generous social policy in the post–World War II period as the price to be paid for social peace, but consistently warned of dire economic consequences of employer contributions for the competitiveness of Austrian business. The Austrian People's Party (ÖVP), being a Christian democratic party, emphasized employment-based social insurance, individual responsibility and subsidiarity, whereas the Socialist Party of Austria (SPÖ) favored a universalistic, solidaristic, and generous welfare state regime. Like in Germany, the strength of the Christian democrats in the early postwar period, combined with the existence of policy legacies of a fragmented social insurance system, resulted in an employment-based welfare state with different schemes for different occupational groups, but under pressure from the SPÖ rules and benefits in the different schemes, most notably for blue- and white-collar workers, were gradually made more equal.

In the first elections, in November 1945, three parties were allowed to compete, the ÖVP, the SPÖ, and the Communist Party of Austria (KPÖ). The ÖVP came out of the pre–World War II Catholic-conservative camp, having chosen its new name to symbolize a greater distance from the Catholic Church. The ÖVP won a narrow absolute majority of seats in 1945, but secret coalition agreements had been concluded before the elections, and a coalition government was formed, even including the KPÖ with one minister, though the party had won only 5 percent of the vote (Enderle-Burcel 1996: 85–86).[24] The Grand Coalition between ÖVP and SPÖ lasted until 1966, and it was in this period that the foundations for the welfare state were laid and the institutions of cooperation among the social partners were cemented.

Like in the Netherlands, the experience of German occupation fostered a strong commitment among the leadership of the pre–World War II warring camps in Austria to peaceful coexistence and political cooperation. The coalition governments were one expression of this commitment; the Sozialpartnerschaft, that is, the cooperation among peak associations of capital and labor, was another (Enderle-Burcel 1996: 81–87). In the area of social policy, the same differences of vision were present as in the other countries. The ÖVP wanted to reestablish the old system with different provisions and different insurance carriers for different groups, and the SPÖ wanted to centralize and unify the old system in order for blue-collar workers to have the same rights as white-collar workers, and they wanted to introduce a citizenship pension that would also include the self-employed and professionals (Hofmeister 1981: 667).

The preliminary outcome of coalition negotiations on social policy was the 1947 transition legislation that established seven insurance carriers for accident insurance and pensions: a general insurance fund (for blue-collar workers in the public and private sectors), a white-collar insurance fund, a general insurance fund for invalidity, an insurance fund for agriculture and forestry, an insurance fund for the national railways, an insurance fund for mining, and an insurance fund for the notaries. In health insurance, there were no separate funds for blue- and white-collar workers, but also some occupational divisions, principally separate insurance funds for agriculture and civil servants, and in addition territorial and enterprise-based divisions. The principle of self-administration was reintroduced into the insurance funds, the representatives to be chosen by interest associations (Hofmeister 1981: 670–71). In the following years, social insurance benefits were gradually increased, as the economic situation improved, and significant steps were taken toward equalization between blue- and white-collar workers.

The next significant step in the development of the Austrian welfare state was legislation in 1955 that unified rules governing sickness, accident, and pension insurance; separate rules remained in effect for a few sickness insurance funds.[25] Again, this legislation was the outcome of intense negotiations inside the coalition, at the ministerial level, and it was passed by parliament in a special session only three days after the negotiations were concluded—demonstrating the marginal role that the legislature played in the formation of even major legislation (Hofmeister 1981: 674). The seven different insurance carriers were left unchanged except in name, but rights and benefits between blue- and white-collar workers were largely unified. The basis for calculating pensions was changed from actual contributions paid to past earnings. Subsequent reforms moved the insurance system toward greater inclusiveness, particularly of the self-employed, greater equalization among insurance funds, and greater generosity. An important step was the introduction in 1965 of an annual adjustment of pensions and of payments from accident insurance. Essentially, benefits were indexed to wage developments, with the option of delaying adjustments in economically difficult times.

Thus, like the German and Dutch welfare states, the Austrian reflected both Christian democratic and social democratic preferences. It was built on the principle of compulsory insurance, based on a person's economic activity, and indirect coverage through the family for the economically inactive; thus, it fully conformed to the male breadwinner model. Given the extremely low unemployment rates of the 1950s, 1960s, and 1970s, coverage became rapidly universal. Benefits were made earnings related, but for those not reaching a defined minimum, statutory supplements were available. Moreover, rules and financial resources among different categories and funds were equalized to a considerable extent, and benefits became generous. Services were largely confined to health care and provided privately; care giving was the responsibility of women in the family. Women's labor force participation in the 1970s was among the lowest in Europe.

There were no really major departures from these principles during the periods of rule by the ÖVP alone (1966–70) and the SPÖ alone (1970–83). Nevertheless, there was some movement away from prestructured compromise decisions and toward majority decisions, and a tendency toward more vigorous pursuit and implementation of social policy reforms under the SPÖ government (Talos 1981: 312, 324). The ÖVP government incorporated all previous regulations on support for families into new legislation, including a universal allowance for children and a universal birth allowance, without however modifying the male breadwinner model. The SPÖ government's agenda included a further expansion of the welfare state, along with expansion of higher education and an improvement of the position of women.

Women's labor force participation, like in Germany, was comparatively high in the early post–World War II period but then increased very slowly to the comparatively low levels typical of the Christian democratic welfare states. Part of the reason for the initially high levels was the size of the agricultural sector; in 1951, 44 percent of all working women still worked in agriculture, a proportion that was to fall by half by 1971 (Cyba 1996: 438). Clearly, work in agriculture has no positive impact on women's political mobilization, so Austria maintained a very traditional male breadwinner model of social policy. For instance, since 1980 Austria has had the highest family allowances as a percentage of the average male wages in manufacturing, and in 1990 it had the highest value of family allowances to a two-child family among advanced industrial societies (Gauthier 1996: 166–67).

In the late 1960s an autonomous women's movement emerged and at the same time feminist tendencies in the SPÖ women's group asserted themselves. The 1970s then were a decade of emerging challenges to the traditional gender model, and under the SPÖ government some legislation was passed to improve the position of women as mothers and workers (Rosenberger 1996: 363). In 1971 the rules were changed to count the twelve months after childbirth for pension purposes without the need to make contributions; in 1974 paid maternity leave was extended to sixteen weeks, and additional leave was made possible with a flat-rate payment. In the same year abortion laws were liberalized, and a year later new legislation changed authority relations in the family toward a more partnership-oriented arrangement. In 1979 a high-level office was created for women's affairs and legislation on equal treatment in wage setting was passed (Rosenberger 1996: 354–63). Nevertheless, it took the SPÖ until 1985 to commit itself to a quota of 25 percent of women for all offices, internal leadership positions as well as public office. In 1987 still only about 10 percent of legislators in Austria were women, the same level as in Germany, compared to 25 percent or above in the Nordic countries and close to 20 percent in the Netherlands (Norris 1987: 115).

The cooperation between organized interests, mainly capital and labor, but also agriculture, and their incorporation into the policy-making process, is very highly institutionalized.[26] There are both voluntary and compulsory associations, the former the ÖGB and several employers' associations, the latter the Federal Chamber of Labor (BAK) and the Federal Chamber of Industry and Trade (BWK), excluding only agriculture and the nontradeable public sector. The compulsory associations and the ÖGB have a representational monopoly, and they are highly centralized. The constituent units of the compulsory associations are regional and sectoral associations; the constituent units of the ÖGB are sectoral unions. Election to leadership positions is indirect and decision making concentrated at the top, which greatly facilitates bargaining and consensual policy making between the leaders of the peak associations (Tichy 1996: 218). The compulsory associations and the ÖGB are consulted in the process of elaboration of all major legislation, and given the traditionally close relations between the two major parties and these associations, they have been very influential. For instance, Katzenstein (1984: 61) cites 254 demands from the Bundesarbeiterkammer and the ÖGB for improvements in the 1955 social security legislation made between 1955 and 1961, 238 of which were adopted as government policy.

A central role in the Austrian production regime was assigned to wage-price agreements among the peak associations, first under the auspices of the tripartite Economic Commission and then of the Committee on Wage and Price Questions formed in 1957 (Talos and Kittel 1996: 118–19). This committee pursued a policy aimed at neutralizing struggles over the distribution of income between capital and labor; wages were to rise with productivity increases in the economy as a whole and inflation, and prices with costs so as to leave profits stable (Tichy 1996: 215–17). This committee and the enforcement of its decisions by the peak associations on their members were crucial for maintaining full employment while keeping inflation in check. The SPÖ government continued to assign priority to full employment in the economically difficult times of the 1970s, and the unions supported its policies with wage restraint, letting real wages decline in line with the deterioration of the terms of trade (Tichy 1996: 219). The main policy instruments used to maintain full employment were Keynesian demand stimulation in the state sector, promotion of exports, and subsidies for private investment (Eder 1996: 193).

The ability of the unions to enforce wage restraint was in large part a result of the strongly centralized and hierarchical structure of the ÖGB. The ÖGB encompasses the entire union membership in the country; it consists of fourteen member unions that cover the whole economy; ten of these unions organize the private sector, four the public sector. The ÖGB controls both finances and personnel of its member unions; it collects the dues and returns some funds to the unions—in the 1980s only about 16 percent (Traxler 1992: 278). Each union does its own bargaining, but the negotiations are coordinated by the ÖGB, and the Wage and Price Commission influences their timing (Traxler 1992: 292). Unlike their Nordic counterparts, Austrian unions have not used the collective bargaining process to promote wage equalization. Wage dispersion across sectors and skill levels has remained greater than in Scandinavia (Guger and Polt 1994: 147). Blue-collar metalworkers, and thus export-oriented industry, have set the pace for negotiations between other unions and employers (Traxler 1993). The three largest wage bargains, in Metal and Engineering, Public Service, and Trade, cover over 50 percent of the labor force (Guger and Polt 1994: 149).

Tichy (1996: 213–22) argues that it was the predictability of economic decisions that was the essence of Austro-Keynesianism. In addition to the predictable self-administration of wage-price policy, a predictable exchange rate and interest rate policy and generous investment subsidies helped prevent major fluctuations in demand and made traditional Keynesian corrections of short-term fluctuations less necessary. To the extent that such corrections were needed, they were effected largely through fiscal policy, as monetary policy was heavily oriented toward stable exchange and interest rates. The currency has been pegged to the deutsche mark since the 1970s, and it was formally fixed to the deutsche mark in 1982.

The Austrian economy in the early post–World War II period was still heavily dependent on raw materials–based industries and traditional consumer goods industries like food and textiles. The task for growth policy in the Golden Age was to modernize industry and bring productivity up to OECD levels. The economy was also characterized by a coexistence of large nationalized and small and medium-sized private enterprises. In 1977, the state employed 28% of the total workforce in industry, foreign capital employed 28%, and domestic private capital 44%; in the 1980s state sector employment declined to 26% and employment in foreign corporations increased to 36% (Kurzer 1993: 96). Through the nationalized banks, the state controlled a very large share of credit. Again, there was a difference of opinion between the coalition partners about economic policies; the SPÖ favored more planning and direct promotion of investment, the ÖVP more indirect measures (Tichy 1996: 221). The outcome was a compromise, with direct investment incentives to industry in the form of low-interest loans, interest subsidy schemes, and loan guarantees, and indirect investment incentives in the form of tax breaks on profits and income through accelerated depreciation reserves for investment and investment allowances (Grünwald 1982: 139–40).

Between 1963 and 1979, 16% of all industrial investment came from European Recovery Program funds administered by the government, which were loaned at 2% to 6% to investments creating high added value, in sophisticated technologies, and in regions suffering from labor market problems (Grünwald 1982: 139–40). Research promotion through loans, grants, and loan guarantees financed by the federal budget accounted for 5% to 6% of total research expenditures of industry. Enterprises facing difficulties due to structural changes were supported by subsidies for labor force training and the creation of new jobs (Grünwald 1982: 142–43). Nevertheless, there never was an industrial policy with planning like in Japan; rather, Austrian industrial policy was incremental and heavily reactive rather than proactive (Katzenstein 1982: 151–53). The state-owned enterprises are registered joint stock companies—they are members of the BWK—and their plans are not part of any macroeconomic plan. Their boards of directors from the beginning were elected according to party representation in parliament (Grünwald 1982: 143). Thus, they were responding to political concerns with full employment and regional policy, but they were never integrated into an overall economic blueprint. The success of the Austrian production regime is reflected in tables 5.2 and A.11; not only did Austria have one of the highest investment and growth rates in the Golden Age and beyond, but also one of the lowest unemployment rates.

### The Netherlands

In the Netherlands, social democracy was weaker in relationship to Christian democracy than in Austria and Germany. Underlying this political power distribution was a heavily religiously divided society. Union density was comparable to that in Germany, but the union movement was much more politically divided, with a stronger presence of Catholic and Protestant unions. Accordingly, the welfare state developed a typically Christian democratic character. Nevertheless, due to their inclusion in coalition governments in the formative period of the welfare state and then again in the 1970s, this time as leading coalition partners, the social democrats (PvdA) managed to introduce some universalistic elements and to reinforce the prolabor wing of the Christian democrats and thus push for ever more generous benefits.

In the pre–World War II period, the Catholic and Protestant parties had a clear political majority. The Liberals declined from a share of over 40 percent of the vote before the introduction of universal suffrage in 1917 to below 16 percent, and the PvdA remained isolated and without any significant influence. The unions were weak and politically divided, but the confessional parties recognized them as legitimate representatives of labor and integrated them into tripartite advisory bodies (Zimmerman 1986: 55–58). In these bodies, though, their role was strictly advisory and largely confined to matters of wages, working conditions, and social policy, not extending to economic policy. Welfare state schemes were restricted to low-income wage earners and to accident, illness, and disability, and they were administered by corporatist bodies. Social assistance was handled as charity through confessional organizations. The role of the state, then, was highly limited in social policy. In contrast to Germany, the Dutch corporatist welfare state system was not a statist design and it did not confer status through occupational classifications (Roebroek and Therborn n.d.: 5–10).

As in Germany, the end of World War II brought a conjuncture where universalistic and solidaristic reform seemed possible, but the left was too weak to take advantage of this opportunity. During World War II the government in exile in London commissioned a report on the desirable future form of social policy. The Van Rhijn Commission reported in May 1945 and proposed a new system, inspired by Beveridge, where the existing social insurance schemes would be made universalistic, new ones added, the benefits composed of flat-rate and earnings-related parts, and all schemes brought under unified state administration, though under the supervision of the Social Council and thus with interest group representation (van Kersbergen 1995: 129). The state would share in the financing of these social security schemes, along with employers and the insured. The PvdA strongly supported this plan, as did the social democratic unions (NVV), but the Catholic Party (KVP) and the other confessional parties and unions opposed it just as strongly (Roebroek and Therborn n.d.: 113–14). As a result, this report became just the starting point for a drawn-out battle over the principles of social policy.

From 1946 until 1958 Roman-Red coalition governments were in power, but the confessional parties together held a constant seat majority in parliament up to 1963 (Roebroek and Therborn n.d. 106). Thus, the confessional parties and organizations in civil society still outweighed those to their left and accordingly managed to put their imprint on the emerging Dutch welfare state. They pushed through the Social Insurance Organization Act of 1952, which firmly anchored the principle of administration of social security schemes through corporatist associations constituted on an industrial basis (Roebroek and Therborn n.d.: 115; van Kersbergen 1995: 129). They also continued to insist on paid employment as the basis for participation in social security schemes. Still, the PvdA had two important—related—successes as their minister of social affairs was able to engineer pioneering social security programs. The first was the passing of the Emergency Act for Old Age Provisions in 1946, which for the first time paid modest means-tested benefits for all persons over sixty-five. This act was immensely popular, and that popular support strengthened the hand of the PvdA minister of social affairs in the fight over a permanent pension scheme.

The PvdA had supported a universal pension scheme as proposed in the Van Rhijn Commission Report for decades, but since opposition against this report was overwhelming, the minister of social affairs appointed a second Van Rhijn Commission, with stronger union and confessional representation, and in 1948 that commission recommended a flat-rate pension based on flat-rate contributions from employees and the self-employed, not indexed and not intended to provide full subsistence. The NVV representatives objected to this plan and demanded income-related contributions and indexing and a linking to existing occupational pension schemes so as to provide an adequate pension. The final solution was a compromise, with flat-rate indexed minimum benefits for all residents, financed by special earnings-related contributions (van Kersbergen 1995: 131). This solution left ample room for occupational pensions and thus was very widely supported (Roebroek and Therborn n.d.: 118–19). The most important aspect, though, was that this pension scheme covered all men and single women and thus constituted a breakthrough to universal social insurance, following the precedent of the Emergency Act of 1946 but being no longer means tested.[27]

This success with the pension scheme contrasts sharply with the failure to transform social assistance in the same period. The ministries in charge of social assistance, first the Ministry of Home Affairs and then the Ministry of Social Work, were headed by conservative Catholics who wanted to keep the role of the state very restricted and public support for (heavily confessional) charities high (Cox 1993). The theoretical argument to be made to explain this difference and the more general pattern of development of the Dutch welfare state is that the balance of forces was tilted in favor of the confessional forces but the left constituted a serious challenge. In this situation, policy precedent and saliency to the public came to play an important role. Social assistance affected far fewer people than pensions, and there was no precedent for a universalistic public scheme. In contrast, strong public support for a state-guaranteed pension scheme, demonstrated in the wake of the Emergency Act, strengthened the position of the PvdA in the policy negotiations. Thus, the ability of the PvdA minister of social affairs to take advantage of the favorable early post–World War II conjuncture of high need for old-age assistance to push through a state-sponsored scheme had a favorable impact in the longer term on his successor's ability to engineer passage of a permanent universalistic and solidaristic scheme despite an overall unfavorable balance of forces for the implementation of such social democratic principles.[28] The competition with the left, in particular for the allegiance of unions, became an important factor pushing the KVP in the direction of supporting welfare state expansion after the breakup of the Roman-Red coalition in 1958.

In the 1950s the unions generally disagreed on the organizational forms of social security, with the confessional unions supporting corporatist, nonstatist forms based on employment and the social democratic unions state-administered schemes with a more universalistic thrust. By the 1960s, however, the Catholic unions came to support more inclusive and universalistic schemes, and the social democratic unions came to accept the strong role of labor market partners in the administration of social security. Thus, the unions became more effective as an interest group pushing for the expansion of the welfare state. In the late 1960s a general rapprochement between the Catholic unions and the NVV prepared the way for the joint action program of the early 1970s and the eventual merger in 1976. The KVP on its part saw the social base of confessional parties shrinking as Dutch society became increasingly secularized and depillarized, and thus the party became more concerned with maintaining the support of its working-class constituency. The majority held by the confessional parties shrank to one seat after the 1963 elections, and in 1967 they lost their majority status; by 1972 their total vote share had declined to just slightly over 30 percent. In order to prevent its union base from shifting more and more toward the PvdA, the KVP became more responsive to labor demands and gave its progressive minister of social affairs, Veldkamp, room to shape inclusive and generous welfare state policies.

Again as in Germany, there was broad agreement on the expansion of social programs, but disagreement on the extent of state financial contributions, the aim of redistribution, and the role of the state versus that of corporatist institutions in the administration of social policy schemes. Under the 1958–73 confessional-Liberal governments, important legislation was passed that improved benefits for widows and orphans, children's allowances, unemployment, labor disability, and health care. The dominant organizational form, though, remained fragmented and heavily reliant on employee contributions. The 1973–77 PvdA-led coalition government then increased the government share in financing. In 1974 this government also linked public sector wages and welfare benefits to private sector wage developments, and it raised the minimum wage, which meant an equivalent rise in the minimum benefit level in social insurance schemes (Hemerijck and Kloosterman 1994). The government also passed the 1976 National Disability Act, which was to assume great importance in the 1980s. This act abolished the distinction between occupational and other causes of disability and extended to all the disabled, regardless of the cause of disability, a flat-rate income assistance; in addition, disabled workers continued to receive an earnings-related supplement (Cox 1993: 165). With rising unemployment from the late 1970s on, this program came to be widely used as an alternative to early retirement, which led to a drastic escalation of costs. In the context of growing economic difficulties, the social democratic–confessional government already came under pressure from welfare state opponents, and under the post-1977 right wing–confessional governments an intense struggle ensued over the future of the social insurance system.

As in Germany and Austria, and in contrast to Sweden, the welfare state was built on and reinforced the male wage earner family structure. Under the influence of confessional parties, both Catholic and Protestant, the construction of benefits centered on a family minimum, and not only the standard unit for benefit calculation but also the unit for contributions to the national insurance schemes was the household (Sainsbury 1994b: 156). Family allowances as a percentage of average male wages in manufacturing in the period 1975–90 were among the highest in OECD countries (Gauthier 1996: 166–67). Child care outside the home was mainly done by confessional institutions and it was regulated by the Poor Laws until 1965 (Gustafsson 1994: 53). Up to 1980 women's labor force participation was consistently the lowest among all our cases in the quantitative analysis, and women were in a weak position to challenge this model.

In the late 1960s a new women's movement with reformist and radical wings emerged in the Netherlands, as elsewhere. The reformist wing, whose leaders had personal connections to the leadership of the PvdA, formally articulated demands for new policies to promote women's interests in 1973, and the PvdA-led government responded by setting up an advisory committee in 1974. This committee presented a five-year plan in 1976, which the government accepted, with little amendment, as a basic policy document a year later (Outshoorn 1995: 169–72). In that same year, however, the PvdA lost its position in government. The new government did set up a national-level office for women's affairs, but appointed as its head a woman who had not been an active promoter of women's equality (Outshoorn 1995: 169–72). A new period of activity followed under the short-lived left–Christian democratic cabinet in 1981, when the office for women's affairs was moved to the Ministry of Social

Affairs and Employment, and issues of economic independence of women moved to the center of concern (Outshoorn 1995: 174). In that year, a law on liberalization of abortion was passed, which was finally put into effect in 1984 (Gauthier 1996: 186). Otherwise, not much progress had been made on women's equality in social policy before retrenchment became the main concern.

The labor movement as a whole remained very restricted in its influence on social and economic policy despite the unions' inclusion in many tripartite bodies. Union density showed a slight but steady decline from 42% in 1950 to 39% in 1960 and 32% in 1980 (Visser 1992: 330). The fundamental problem, though, was the political division into three major and several smaller tendencies; the Catholic unions with 34% of total union membership in 1955, the Protestant unions with 18%, the social democratic unions with 37%, and among the smaller ones the syndicalist and communist unions with 4% (Visser 1992: 329). These divisions largely prevented unions from exerting strong pressures in these advisory bodies not only in social but also in economic policy. On the employer side there were also organizational divisions, with Catholic, Protestant, and nonconfessional employers' organizations at the industry level and the central federation level. During the occupation the central organizations of unions and employers had agreed to future centralized bargaining and negotiation. In 1945 the Foundation of Labor was founded for this purpose and recognized by the government as key advisory body in social and economic policy (Visser 1992: 324). In 1950, the newly founded Social and Economic Council, with representatives from unions and employers and independent experts appointed by the government, became the central advisory body on economic and social policy. However, in 1945 the government also claimed for itself large powers over the regulation of all aspects of labor relations (Zimmerman 1986: 75–80). Thus, governmental intervention substituted to some extent for the lack of unity and centralization on both the union and employer sides to ensure centralized wage setting.

During World War II a strong social consensus had developed on the need for rapid economic growth and modernization. From 1946 to 1958 the government successfully pursued a strategy of export-led growth and modernization, an essential component of which was a centrally coordinated, highly restrictive wage policy. In international perspective, Dutch wages were very low and investment ratios high (Zimmerman 1986: 85–87). From 1958 to 1963 wages became more differentiated, with different wage scales for different sectors, though wage restraint was still strong, but after 1963 full employment led to wage drift and began to erode the centrally directed restrictive wage policy. Neither the unions nor the employer organizations had sufficient central authority to enforce central wage bargains on their members (Flanagan, Soskice, and Ulman 1983:101). In the 1960s labor shortages induced employers to offer wages far above those negotiated (Visser 1992: 337), and wildcat strikes demonstrated opposition to union compliance with the government's incomes policy (Flanagan, Soskice, and Ulman 1983: 117). Moreover, most of the large multinational firms negotiated their own agreements, despite being members of employers' associations. In 1965 Philips accepted the principle of automatic price indexation of wages in a multiyear agreement, and in 1969 the Social and Economic Council (SER) accepted this principle as well (Visser 1992: 335–36). Nevertheless, ad hoc governmental intervention in wage regulation continued throughout the 1960s and 1970s.

Though high economic growth began to undermine the system of centralized wage setting in 1963, branch-level bargaining agreements remained subject to approval by the Labor Council, which operated within the macroeconomic parameters given by the SER (Zimmerman 1986: 127–30). However, unions and employers were increasingly unable to come to agreements. The government attempted to step in but repeatedly had to back off under strong union pressure (Flanagan, Soskice, and Ulman 1983: 115–17). The combination of increasing radicalization among rank-and-file union members, secularization, and rapprochement among the Catholic and social democratic unions induced union leaders to take a more assertive stance in the late 1960s and to demand genuine corporatist negotiations, such as about compensation for wage restraint through social policy. At the same time, employers were consolidating and professionalizing their associations. In 1968 separate business and employers' organizations merged into the Federation of Dutch Enterprises, and in 1970 Catholic and Protestant employers' federations merged into the Christian Employers' Federation.

The zenith of the efforts to arrive at genuine corporatist bargaining was the negotiation of a social contract in 1973 under the social democratic–Christian democratic government (Zimmerman 1986: 136). Attempts to implement centrally struck wage agreements in sectoral bargaining, though, ended in strikes, and from 1974 on central bargaining broke down every year (Flanagan, Soskice, and Ulman 1983: 137). In their 1976 program the unions asked for an active labor market policy and industrial policy in exchange for wage restraint. However, the post-1977 right wing–confessional governments made no efforts to support such bargaining. They did continue to insist on wage restraint but bypassed corporatist institutions in their efforts to address the economic deterioration. Instead, they relied on expert committees that were heavily composed of representatives of employers (Zimmerman 1986: 164–79).

In the 1940s and 1950s Dutch governments had pursued a strong proindustrialization policy, mainly by keeping both labor and capital cheap. Regional industrial policy took the form of investment grants for industry and subsidies for infrastructural improvement, along with special tax relief measures—all rather global and indirect measures (van der Knaap 1980: 121–31). The government did not engage in any direct intervention into investment and enterprise decisions, even after adopting a more active sectoral approach in the end of the 1960s (Braun 1987: 315). Even in the changed conditions of the 1960s and 1970s the government developed neither a proactive industrial policy nor an active labor market policy (Katzenstein 1985: 65–66) and thus was ill prepared to deal with rising unemployment. The Netherlands began to suffer economic problems and rising unemployment earlier and to a greater extent than our other cases (table A.12). The Dutch disease—that is, the negative effect of the overvalued exchange rate resulting from natural gas exports on domestic industry—combined with strong competition from NICs for the Dutch energy-intensive intermediate goods exports industry, and increasing investment abroad by Dutch companies, caused a significant decline of jobs in the private sector (Zimmerman 1986: 144–60). The appreciation of the exchange rate provided an additional incentive for capital exports, and foreign holdings of Dutch companies increased greatly in the 1970s (Lubbers and Lemckert 1980: 104). Unemployment rates in the double digits greatly increased budget deficits and made fiscal consolidation the primary concern of governments in their approach to the welfare state.

### The Antipodean Wage Earner Welfare States

As Castles (1985) has argued, the Antipodean working-class movements were among the strongest in the world at the turn of the century and, through alliances with liberals, forged perhaps the most far-reaching systems of social protection for workers of any countries in the world by the early 1920s. Moreover, largely as a result of the reforms of the Labour government of 1935–49, New Zealand's welfare state was one of the most advanced in the world in 1950. In contrast, by the end of the Golden Age, both of these countries could be seen as welfare state laggards in terms of the generosity of their social policy regimes in the narrow sense of legislated entitlements. Again, as Castles argues, the broader system of social protection was much more favorable to workers and the benefits delivered through a combination of the compulsory arbitration system, the high levels of per capita income, low levels of unemployment, and high levels of home ownership delivered workers a high and secure material living standard. However, this system was based on a protected manufacturing sector and proved highly vulnerable to the changes in the world economy in the past three decades.

To trace the development of the Antipodean systems of social protection, it is necessary to go further back in history than we have in the case of the European welfare states discussed earlier in this chapter, because the compulsory arbitration systems, the decisive element of the system of "social protection by other means," emerged at the turn of the century. At this point in time, both countries were agrarian export economies based primarily on the wool industry. The manufacturing sectors of both countries enjoyed the natural protection of distance as well as legislated tariffs, and before federation in 1901, the Australian colonies even erected tariff barriers among themselves.

Both countries were predominantly Protestant, and more important, without the legacy of established Catholic Churches, religious divisions were not as politicized as they were in Europe and no parallel to European Christian democracy developed.[29] The agrarian structure and the political structure, both of which differ somewhat across the two countries, contributed to the absence of an independent Protestant small farmers party, a "party of agrarian defense" (Lipset and Rokkan 1967; Urwin 1980) along Nordic lines. The Australian electoral system with the preferential or alternative ballot[30] for the House of Representatives and proportional representation for the Senate penalizes small parties (when compared to a straight proportional representation system) and encourages bloc politics. The domination of the countryside by large sheep estates meant that once an independent rural party did develop, it was dominated by conservative interests and was allied with the conservative Liberal Party. Though the average agricultural holding in New Zealand was considerably smaller, the single-member district plurality system resulted in a two-party system, and once Labour emerged as one of the two parties, most rural interests gravitated to the conservative Reform Party and its successor, the Nationals. However, in the pre–World War I period, before crystallization of the modern two-party system in either country, progressive small farming interests did ally with the emergent labor movement to support social reform. This was particularly important in New Zealand, but it also occurred in some Australian colonies/states, notably South Australia.[31]

By the mid–nineteenth century, the Australian colonies, though not quite fully democratic, were very democratic by European standards, and the nascent labor movement had contributed to the democratic push (Rueschemeyer, Stephens, and Stephens 1992: 136–37). After decades of vigorous growth, Australia entered a recession in the 1890s. In this economic context, a wave of strikes in the beginning of the decade ended in defeat for the unions. This stimulated a turn of the labor movement to political means to achieve its ends. In the 1891 elections in New South Wales, thirty-five labor candidates were elected and a parliamentary Labor Party was formed. By the end of the decade, labor was a significant force in the lower houses of every colony and in most cases it was the largest or second-largest political tendency, though it always was a minority. The two other factions were the protectionists and free traders, who differed on the level of protection, with the free traders favoring tariffs for revenue purposes only. Initially, labor was divided on protection and allied with either faction depending on its willingness to support pro-labor legislation. By the end of the decade, the labor parties had successfully supported the passage of favorable legislation in every colony except Tasmania, including the first modern social welfare legislation, the pension acts of New South Wales and Victoria (Clarke 1992: 171). In both cases, the legislation provided for means-tested, tax-financed, flat-rate pensions, though the labor members were opposed to the means test, arguing the pension should be a right (Kewley 1973: 46).

Of great significance for the subsequent development of social legislation were the provisions of the Commonwealth Constitutions, which were hammered out in this decade and went into effect with federation at the turn of the century. The constitution provided for a lower house and a senate. The powers of the senate are the same as those of the house except that it can only reject financial measures; it cannot amend them. Thus, though the government rests on the confidence of the house, the powers of the senate are considerable. The states are represented according to population in the house but in equal numbers in the senate. Moreover, as noted above, the electoral systems are different for the two houses. Lijphart (1984) categorizes bicameral systems in which the two chambers are relatively equal in power and are selected by different electoral criteria as strong bicameral systems. Given the different electoral systems, it is more likely that the two chambers will have different political compositions and thus one chamber will "veto" the legislation passed by the other. Indeed, this has not infrequently been the case in Australia. The Australian system is also federal, so the Australian political arrangements, along with the German, rank the highest of the cases examined in this chapter on the measure of veto points used in the quantitative analysis in chapter 3. A more nuanced measure would have rated Australia higher on this measure, as Australia is more strongly federal than Germany in the sense that more powers are reserved for the states. In particular, the constitution gave the federal government power to legislate on pensions and invalidity benefits, reserving all other areas of social welfare legislation to the states (de Garis 1974: 249). Until this provision was changed in 1946, it was an obvious obstacle to the development of federal social policy.

The pivotal turning points in the development of "social protection by other means" were the establishment of the federal arbitration court in 1904 and the Harvester decision of 1908. The arbitration court followed precedents in New South Wales and earlier in New Zealand. The establishment of the New South Wales court in 1901 was one of the achievements of the Labor Party in that colony and was in part a reaction to the failed strikes of the early 1890s (Clarke 1992: 171). Labor was also the main supporter of a strong federal arbitration court (Crowley 1974: 281). Following the New South Wales precedent, the court was composed of an employer representative, a union representative, and a jurist and was empowered to settle strikes and other disputes and make awards binding on an industry as a whole.

One immediate effect of the institution of the federal arbitration court as well as the state courts was a tremendous growth of union membership. Since the arbitration courts could deal only with organized associations, their establishment led to a trebling of union membership between 1906 and 1914 (Clarke 1992: 188–89). By the outbreak of World War I, union membership in Australia was 25 percent of the labor force,[32] the highest figure at that point in time of any of the current advanced industrial economies, which is all the more exceptional given the agrarian character of the economy (Stephens 1979b: 115).

The groundwork for the Harvester decision was laid by the turn of the Deakin Liberal government, which was supported by Labor, to the "New Protection." According to that doctrine, which was articulated in a 1907 government white paper, a manufacturer who benefits from federal protective tariffs should charge a reasonable price for the goods he produced and pay "fair and reasonable wages." The white paper declared: "The 'old' Protection contented itself with making good wages possible. The 'new' Protection seeks to make them actual" (quoted in Crowley 1974: 283). Though most of the New Protection legislation was invalidated by the high court, it was the basis for the Harvester judgment and the general concept of a "basic wage," a needs-based minimum wage.

In the Harvester judgment, the arbitration court ruled that the minimum wage for an unskilled worker should be determined by the "normal needs of the average employee, regarded as a human being living in a civilized community" and not on the grounds of the employer's capacity to pay (quoted in Crowley 1974: 284).[33] This "fair wage" was to be sufficient to afford a worker and his family, which was assumed to be a wife and three children, a living of exceedingly modest comfort (Clarke 1992: 188).

A final component of the new system of political economy was the restriction of labor supply, and the instrument was the White Australia Policy. Organized labor had long opposed efforts of landlords, particularly the Queensland sugar estate owners, to recruit Polynesian and Oriental labor and had also opposed "assisted" immigration of Europeans, that is, the granting of financial assistance for the passage to Australia for those intending to immigrate.[34] All parties supported White Australia policy, which effectively restricted immigration to Europeans and other whites, and it was made national policy at the first sitting of the Commonwealth Parliament (Crowley 1974: 274).

As Castles (1992) points out, arbitration court decisions in the early 1920s extended this system of social protection into another area covered by legislation in other welfare states, sick pay. Since docking a worker earning the basic wage for absence for illness would prevent him from bringing home a living wage, Justice Higgins, the author of the Harvester judgment, ruled in 1920 that absence due to illness could not be grounds for reduction of weekly pay. Employers successfully argued against the open-ended commitment implied in the judgment, and Higgins's successors limited it to six days, and it was later allowed to vary somewhat by industry. Nevertheless, Castles is correct in arguing that with a 100 percent replacement rate for short absences due to illnesses, Australia certainly had the most generous policy of any country at that time.

Before moving to the development of social protection, it should be noted here that outside of protection and arbitration, the role of the state in early economic development was limited to the vigorous development of infrastructure. Everything had to be built from scratch in this virgin continent and the colonial governments and later the states had extensive programs of public works to build the infrastructure for development. But this was accomplished in an otherwise very liberal political economy. For instance, financial markets were very open and the colonies/states borrowed extensively abroad to finance the projects they undertook.

As we turn to the development of social policy proper, it is necessary to carefully distinguish between what did develop and what might have happened had Labor been in a governing position more frequently. One of the aims of this chapter is to identify what features of the social policy promoted by organized labor and social democratic parties are generically "social democratic" and what features are variable due to the national context. Castles, who is rightly recognized as the most insightful interpreter of the development of Antipodean social policy, is ambiguous on this account. As we understand it, his principal argument is that the policy pattern resulted from the combination of a very strong labor movement that nonetheless was infrequently in office (Castles 1985; Castles and Mitchell 1993). Consistent with this, Castles argues that the much greater generosity of the welfare state in New Zealand as of 1950 was due in large part to the fact that labor was in power in New Zealand for a long period in the previous two decades. The clear implication here is that Australian Labor would have fashioned a different policy pattern had it been in office more often. At other points, he seems to imply that, given that effective social protection was delivered by the arbitration system, high levels of home ownership, low levels of unemployment, and high per capita income, Australian Labor favored the structure of the transfer system with its means-tested, tax-financed, and flat-rate benefits, though it would have preferred that they were somewhat more generous.

Based on the very detailed account of Kewley (1973: 28–169) of the period before the advent of the Labor government of 1941–49, we believe the evidence is quite clear. Labor favored tax-financed benefits and argued strongly against several Liberal proposals for the introduction of contributory social insurance. As to the structure of the benefits paid, Labor favored flat-rate *universal* benefits. Labor was the chief promoter of the 1908 invalid and old-age pension act, but the party favored universal rather than the means-tested benefits provided for in the bill presented by the Liberal government and passed by parliament with Labor support (Kewley 1973: 72–74, 83). By contrast, the Maternity Act of 1912 passed by the first majority Labor government provided for universal benefits (Kewley 1973: 103). Characterizing the whole period 1912–40, Kewley (1973: 99) states, "The Labor Party had come to favour the placing of benefits, where practicable, on a universal basis."

The inactivity of Australian governments in the area of social legislation in the period 1913–39 can be attributed to the infrequence of Labor governments at the federal level, which was due in part to splits in the Labor Party in the 1910s and 1930s, and to the division of powers between the states and federal government and the constitutional barrier to social legislation other than invalid and old-age pensions (Castles 1985: 70–71; Kewley 1973: 166). The Labor Party took over the reins of government in 1941 but was in a tenuous parliamentary situation until it emerged victorious in the 1943 election. The Labor governments of 1943–49 introduced and passed legislation providing for child allowances, unemployment benefits, sick pay, and health care benefits for the first time at the federal level, and they passed legislation improving pensions and maternity allowances. Most of this legislation was of dubious constitutionality when passed, as was the 1912 maternity benefit act, which, however, had not been contested. Thus, Labor submitted a constitutional amendment that would substantially broaden federal powers not only in social welfare but also in a broad range of areas related to economic management to a referendum in 1944. Like two similar constitutional amendments proposed by the pre–World War I Labor government, this proposal was defeated in the referendum. After its pharmaceutical benefits legislation was contested by the medical profession and struck down by the high court, Labor submitted yet another constitutional amendment to a referendum, which accepted it. This time the range of powers to be transferred was limited to social welfare legislation, albeit a wide range of areas with the only limitation being that the government would not have the powers of "civil conscription" in the area of medical and dental services.

The clause on conscription of medical personnel was designed to lessen the opposition of the Australian Medical Association to Labor's health care policies. It did not succeed in doing this. One provision of Labor's 1948 National Health Services Act was a maximum fee schedule, and this was met with determined resistance by the medical association. The act's other provisions were to set up a national insurance system to cover medical services and provide free hospitalization in public hospitals (which accounted for about 70 percent of total patient days) and subsidized care in private hospitals (Kewley 1973: 340–43). The act was framed in broad terms and the government intended to use its enabling powers gradually (Kewley 1973: 343). Labor's long-term goal was apparently to set up a national health service along the lines of Britain's new legislation (Castles 1985: 28–29). However, it did not even manage to fully implement its drug benefit or health insurance schemes due to the dispute with the medical association. Labor was defeated in the 1949 election and consigned to the political wilderness for the next twenty-three years. The new Liberal government replaced Labor's health care program with a scheme of federal subsidies for nonprofit health insurance.

The transfer programs passed by the Labor government mixed means-tested and universal benefits. The new child allowance was universal and the maternity allowance was made universal once again. Both the sick pay and unemployment benefits were means tested. In the area of pensions, Labor examined the possibility of superannuation but rejected it as excessively costly. For the same reason, the means test was retained but Labor went on record as favoring a gradual elimination of the means test. As an opposition party in the 1950s and 1960s, Labor repeatedly proposed that the means test on pension benefits be eliminated, though it should be noted that a significant minority of Labor parliamentarians favored retaining it on egalitarian grounds.

The coalition governments of the Liberals and the rural Country Party of the 1950s and 1960s accomplished very little in the field of social legislation until very late in their period in office. Benefits in the pension, unemployment, and sick pay schemes were periodically increased. In the case of pensions, these increases served only to keep beneficiaries up with the rise in wages; replacement rates were essentially stable (Palme 1990: 50–51; Kewley 1973: 399). Replacement rates in unemployment and sick pay did increase from under 20 percent of the average production worker's wage in 1950 but were still only slightly over one-quarter of that wage in 1970 (Kangas 1991: 75; Carroll 1999: 141).[35] Child allowances were allowed to fall to less than half their 1950 value by 1970 (Wennemo 1994: 132) and maternity allowances were left unchanged in nominal terms, thus, their real value was only a fraction of what it had been in 1949 (Kewley 1973: 445). In the area of health care, substantial portions of the population were still not covered by health insurance in the late 1960s, and only in the waning years of their long stay in office did the Liberal-Country governments, under considerable pressure from Labor under the leadership of Gough Whitlam, move to introduce legislation providing subsidized health insurance to low-income and other uncovered groups. Pressure from a revitalized Labor Party was certainly one reason for the increases in sick pay and unemployment compensation in 1970 and 1972. The one area of consistent progress under the Liberals was coverage in the national pension scheme: again responding to Labor's pressure to eliminate the means test, successive Liberal-Country governments passed legislation liberalizing the test. As a result, the proportion of the aged covered by the national plan rose from two-fifths in 1950 to over two-thirds in 1970 (Palme 1990: 47).

While Labor consistently called for more generous social legislation, its efforts picked up considerable vigor when Whitlam assumed the party leadership in 1967. In the 1969 election, Whitlam campaigned for the end of means testing on pensions, for a national superannuation scheme, and for universal national health insurance. These themes were repeated in the 1972 election, which brought Labor to power for the first time in over two decades. Like governments in other countries in this period, the Whitlam government entered office with the assumption that the economic conditions of the Golden Age would continue indefinitely into the future. As a result, the government laid out a very ambitious agenda of reform, especially in the area of social legislation.

The centerpiece of the government's social welfare program was Medibank, a universalistic single-payer national health insurance scheme. The Senate rejected the measure and three other major pieces of legislation, whereupon Whitlam dissolved both chambers and called new elections in 1974. Labor won the elections but failed to secure control of the Senate (Clarke 1992: 321–22). By calling a joint sitting of the two chambers, Whitlam managed to get Medibank and several other pieces of legislation passed. However, the Senate continued to refuse to finance the reform. Under increasing pressure due to the deterioration of the economy, the Labor government was out of office by the end of 1975, a victim of collusion on the part of the governor general and the leader of the opposition to dissolve both chambers through moves of dubious constitutionality.

The short-lived Whitlam government was not without its achievements in the area of social policy. The Fraser government that followed substantially altered the health care legislation, abolishing its universal character, but entitlements were still substantially better, especially for lower-income groups, than when Whitlam came to office. Labor did not deliver on its superannuation promise or its promise to end the means test, but it did take steps in that direction by eliminating the means test for older pensioners. It also improved sickness and unemployment compensation so that, along with the improvement introduced by the Liberal-Country government, the net replacement rate for these programs almost doubled to just under 50 percent for the average production worker (Kewley 1980: 124–25; Kangas 1991: 75; Carroll 1999: 141) between 1970 and 1975. Several other new cash transfer programs were also introduced.

Another achievement of this period, though only partly of Labor's doing, was the introduction of equal pay for women. This period has been seen as a turning point for the Australian women's movement as women's organizations, most notably the Women's Electoral Lobby, began to have an impact on the national political debate in general and the policies of the Labor Party in particular (O'Connor, Orloff, and Shaver 1999: 215 ff.; Curtin and Sawer 1996). In 1969, the arbitration Court ruled that women were to receive equal pay for equal work. Upon taking office, Whitlam requested that the Arbitration Commission reopen a recent wage case to permit the government to withdraw the Liberal-Country government submission on women's pay parity and replace it with one of its own. The Arbitration Commission agreed and later ruled that women employees must receive "equal pay for work of comparable value" (Clarke 1992: 319).[36] The combination of these two decisions led to very substantial increases in women's wages (O'Connor, Orloff, and Shaver 1999: 89). The Whitlam government further raised feminist expectations by appointing a special adviser for women's affairs who was charged with examining all cabinet submissions and evaluating their impact on women. However, she was given no staff and the government did not even manage to fulfill a promise made by Whitlam during the 1974 campaign to increase public finance of day care (Clarke 1992: 320–21). As we indicated earlier in this section, New Zealand differed from Australia in two important respects. First, the class of small farmers was larger; second, the governmental structure, a unicameral and unitary system, was highly favorable to rapid change. Both of these characteristics contributed to the development of a more generous social policy in New Zealand as of 1950. Indeed, it was a pioneer welfare state compared to other advanced capitalist democracies at this point.

The events of the 1890s were similar to those in Australia. The defeat of the unions in a miners and maritime strike in early 1890 led to a political turn on the part of the labor movement. In December of that year, five Labour members were elected to parliament along with thirty-eight others who were endorsed by unions. Labour formed a more or less durable alliance with the Liberals, who drew their support from small farmers and farm laborers, who expected to benefit from the land development schemes of the Liberals (Richardson 1992: 206). The Liberals ruled until 1911 and, particularly early in this period, passed the legislation that formed the basis of the arbitration system and New Zealand's nascent welfare state. In 1894, the government passed the Industrial Conciliation and Arbitration Act, which set up regional conciliation boards and an Arbitration Court with the power to make awards applying to a whole industry. As in Australia, the establishment of the arbitration system led to the rapid growth of unions (Richardson 1992: 207). In 1898, the government passed pension legislation providing for means-tested, flat-rate, tax-financed pensions.

Both the government and the conservative opposition advocated protection (Richardson 1992: 201). Perhaps for this reason, the tie between protection and the "fair wage" was not as firmly established in this period as it was in Australia. In fact, the fair wage itself, that is, a wage based on a worker's needs and not the employer's ability to pay, was not as firmly established in New Zealand until the advent of the Labour government of 1935–49, though the basic thrust of legislation and of Arbitration Court rulings went in that direction. In 1908, one year after the Harvester ruling in Australia, the New Zealand Arbitration Court issued a similar ruling, and in 1916 and 1925 it reaffirmed that the basic wage of an unskilled worker should be sufficient to support the worker, his wife, and two children (Easton 1980: 105). A conservative government in 1922 amended the arbitration act to allow the court to take into account the "economic conditions affecting any trade or industry" (cited in Richardson 1992: 221). With the onset of the Depression, a conservative coalition government in 1931 cut civil service salaries by 10 percent and amended the arbitration act to empower the Arbitration Court to amend any award if economic circumstances warranted and to allow the initiation of conciliation only if both parties to a dispute agreed. This was followed by a court ruling cutting wages by 10 percent and by wholesale wage cuts by employers who refused to permit disputes to go to the court.

In the 1910s and 1920s, party competition polarized into two camps with Labour advancing at almost every election and the parties of the right increasingly cooperating to stem the Labour advance. In the midst of the Depression, Labour won the 1935 elections by a huge margin over its conservative National Party opponents on a broad platform of reform: guarantee pricing for primary production, restoration of the wage cuts, a minimum wage, measures to insulate the economy from the world economy, increased control of the financial sector, and a range of social welfare legislation (health, education, increased pensions, and superannuation) (Chapman 1992: 352–53). The Labour government moved vigorously to implement its program as it restored the wage cuts, passed a minimum wage, and initiated public works to reduce unemployment. In 1936, the government amended the arbitration act, restoring full jurisdiction to the Arbitration Court, making union membership compulsory for anyone covered by an Arbitration Court award, and specifying that the basic wage was to cover the needs of a man, his wife, and three children. As a direct result, union membership trebled by 1938 and by 1939–40, 67 percent of nonagricultural employees were union members, by far the highest figure anywhere in the world (Stephens 1979b: 116).

A second landslide victory in 1938 by Labour was met with capital flight and, along with the rising cost of overseas machinery, depleted the country's sterling balances, forcing the government to introduce exchange controls. These controls became more or less permanent and, along with import licensing, also introduced in this period, provided the protection of the manufacturing sector, which complemented the family wage imposed by arbitration in New Zealand's version of social protection by other means.

The 1938 elections were fought on Labour's social security bill, and the election result was interpreted as a strong mandate for Labour's social policy legislation. The bill was passed soon after the election and was complemented with other legislation over the course of Labour's period in office, which ended in 1949. This package included increases in the means-tested pension; a flat-rate universal superannuation benefit; a universal family allowance with a flat-rate benefit for each child; and essentially free medical benefits.

The contrast with Australia at this point was in part due to the greater electoral success of Labour, which in turn can be linked to differences in agrarian class structure (Castles 1985: 71). But certainly the biggest factor was the difference in constitutional structure and, as Castles (1985: 28–29) argues, nowhere is this more evident than in the case of medical care. The labor parties began with similar intentions: a free medical care system with medical care delivered in large part by the state. In both cases, the medical associations were vociferous opponents of the proposed legislation. With the additional constitutional obstacles, the Australian Medical Association succeeded in blocking some of Labor's proposals and delaying others until the Liberal-Country coalition took power in 1949 and subsequently introduced legislation more to the association's liking. In New Zealand, the medical association succeeded in getting the important concession that outpatient care would be paid on a fee-for-service basis rather than on the capitation basis favored by Labour, but otherwise medical care became "as free as education," as proposed by Labour in the 1938 election (Castles 1985: 29; Easton 1980: 136; Laugesen 2000: chap. 3).

The National Party managed to reverse its electoral fortunes only by accepting the goal of full employment and the social security reforms of Labour (Chapman 1992: 370). However, that did not mean that social policy fared well under the Nationals, who ruled with one interruption from 1949 to 1972. The failure to raise the fees paid to general practitioners increasingly eroded the principle of free medical care, and replacement rates in transfer programs fell as successive National governments neglected to adjust them to the rising wage levels (Castles 1985: 29, 32). By contrast, the Labour government of 1956–60 raised family allowances by 50 percent (Chapman 1992: 379–80).

In 1972, central planks of Labour's election platform were a national superannuation scheme and no-fault accident compensation (McRobie 1992: 388). At that time, only 35 percent of employees were covered by occupational pension plans (Easton 1980: 63) and, with the only public program being means-tested pensions, it is clear that many white- and blue-collar workers suffered substantial declines in income in old age.

Labour won the election and delivered on both promises with programs that provided for earnings-related benefits. The Accident Insurance Act covered both work-related injuries and automobile accidents and provided an 80 percent income replacement rate. Benefits were raised in the means-tested pension program, and a universal, earnings-related, funded superannuation scheme was introduced (Easton 1980: 72–74, 96–97). The scheme was contributory and would not fully mature until 2015. The National Party responded with a promise to replace the superannuation plan with universal, flat-rate, tax-financed pensions with generous benefits for those with average incomes or below and an incredibly generous retirement age of sixty. The plan would pay full benefits immediately, and it was credited with having a large, perhaps decisive, impact on the election of 1975, which was won by the Nationals (Castles 1985: 39).

Progress on gender-egalitarian social policy was close to nil in New Zealand before the 1980s. Women's labor force participation as of 1960 was extremely low, second lowest after the Netherlands among all our countries, and it remained among the very lowest until 1980. In the period 1951–80, an average of only 5 percent of members of parliament were women (Curtin and Sawer 1996: 151). Moreover, for most of this time Labour was out of office. In the 1970s, new women's organizations, such as the Women's Electoral Lobby formed in 1975, appeared and gender issues became part of the public agenda for the first time (Curtin and Sawer 1996: 149), but with Labour exiting office that year, little was accomplished. For instance, there was no national scheme for maternity leave, as responsibility was left to employers. Of 900 collective agreements and awards registered between 1978 and 1981, though, only one-third contained maternity leave provisions (Gauthier 1996: 176).

### Comparative Analysis

In analyzing the development of the welfare state and production regimes in the different countries, we found a great deal of consistency among the goals, policies, and strategies of similar kinds of actors. To begin with the political actors shaping policy—political parties—the social democrats shared a commitment to universalistic, generous welfare states with a combination of basic, flat-rate, citizenship benefits and earnings-related benefits with high replacement rates and easy qualifying conditions. This is not to say that sympathy for means-tested programs was absent in social democracy, particularly in the beginning of the period. Faced with shortages of resources in the early postwar years, social democratic leaders often expressed the view that the few resources available should go to the neediest. However, they did insist that support for the needy be given as a matter of right, not subject to bureaucratic discretion. With the advent of vigorous growth in the postwar period, social democratic parties everywhere, including Australasia, preferred universalistic to means-tested programs. Where the immediate postwar reforms had resulted in a tier of flat-rate citizenship benefits ensuring "basic security" to the citizenry, as in Scandinavia, the social democrats pushed for earnings-related benefits with increasingly high income replacement rates, to assure workers "income security," the complement to basic security benefits in the "institutional" welfare state model.[37]

The comprehensive and unified welfare state model that the social democrats were able to build in the Nordic countries was also the type that they supported in early post–World War II proposals in Austria, Germany, and the Netherlands. After they lost out to the Christian democrats in those three countries, and different schemes for different categories of people were introduced—or mostly revived—they continued to push for an equalization of benefits and rules among the different schemes, particularly the schemes for blue-collar and white-collar workers, introducing universalism to the earnings-related tier through the back door, so to speak. In all three countries, the social democrats also pressed for a basic security complement to the income securities tier: in the Netherlands a minimum pension was introduced; in Austria mandatory supplements were made available to those not achieving a defined minimum; in Germany the introduction of a minimum pension remained a consistent demand of the social democrats, and its practical equivalent was finally introduced under the SPD-FDP government in 1972 for those with a long contribution record.

This characterization of generalized social democratic support for the institutional model with regard to transfer payments (but not services; see below) during the period of postwar affluence is somewhat problematic for Australia and New Zealand. There is no doubt that the push to earnings-related benefits was weaker there, a point we will comment on below. However, we contend that the means-tested character of many Antipodean benefits at the close of the Golden Age was not a product of labor movement preference for them but rather of labor's exclusion from power. Thus, with a longer period in office and concentration of power in the country's unitary, unicameral system of government, New Zealand Labour left office in 1949 with fewer means-tested benefits on the books than was the case in Australia. In opposition, both parties pressed for the removal of means tests and expressed at least some support for earnings-related superannuation benefits. In their brief periods in government, both parties moved to eliminate means-tested benefits or introduce superannuation in pensions.

Thus we contend that in pensions the two antipodean social democratic parties' preferences were not greatly different from those of their European counterparts. They were not different in favoring flat-rate child allowances not subject to a means test, which was the position of the social democrats in all cases. However, in our review of the historical literature, we found no mention of either the unions or the labor parties favoring the introduction of an earnings-related program for sickness pay or unemployment compensation. The absence of a push for income security in these areas from social democracy and the unions can partly be explained by the very low levels of unemployment. In this regard, they deviate from the Nordic cases in degree rather than principle, as there too the emphasis was on providing work, not cash assistance and, compared to the Christian democratic welfare states, high replacement rates in unemployment insurance were a rather late development in the Nordic countries.[38] In the case of sick pay in Australia, it is a very plausible hypothesis that the push for earnings-related benefits was muted by the fact that the arbitration system provided full pay continuance for short-term illness. Thus, the Australian worker achieved income security in case of illness "by other means."

During the Golden Age, the common commitment of social democrats in the area of social services concerned health. As in social insurance, the central goals were universal access to and equal quality of health care. In the Nordic countries, social democratic governments succeeded in realizing these goals by establishing national health services, and in New Zealand the Labour government established a single-payer national health insurance. In Australia Labor made major efforts in this direction, which however were largely thwarted. In Austria, Germany, and the Netherlands, where the social democrats had to accept social insurance, including health insurance, based on different schemes, they directed their efforts toward improving and equalizing the benefits under these schemes. Before the late 1960s, social services outside of education and basic health care were of minor importance anywhere and not on the political agenda. Social democrats, like all other political actors, accepted that care for children, the elderly, and the handicapped remains the responsibility of the family. The push for an expansion of new social services accompanied a turn of social democracy from support for the traditional family, with a male breadwinner and a female housewife, toward support for a two-earner family and greater gender equality, a push that was stimulated by a combination of increasing female labor force participation and feminist mobilization within and outside of the social democratic movement (see below). This change was most pronounced in the Nordic countries, less so and delayed but still discernible in Australia and New Zealand, and more muted or delayed among the social democrats in the rest of our cases.

With this turn, one aspect of the social democratic welfare state and production regime that was already present, an emphasis on labor mobilization—that is, on support for qualification and integration into the labor market—assumed even greater prominence. Active labor market policy, including training, retraining, and support for relocation, was the cornerstone of this policy of labor mobilization, and public care facilities for children and the elderly became an important additional component because they facilitated women's integration into the labor force. It is important to insist here on these central elements of the social democratic project in order to correct a widespread misinterpretation; the essence of the social democratic welfare state is not decommodification, but rather high qualification for and participation in the labor market. The concept of decommodification does capture one important element of the social democratic welfare state, the right to continuation of an adequate standard of living while involuntarily separated from the labor market, a right that is sorely lacking in liberal welfare states. This right is also given in Christian democratic welfare states though, and what differentiates the social democratic from the Christian democratic welfare state is precisely this emphasis on high labor force participation and qualification.

The common goals and broad strategies among social democrats with regards to production regimes were growth with full employment, industrial promotion policies, supply-side policies, and, as just mentioned, active labor market policies. However, there were many differences among them in the specific policies designed to achieve these goals, differences based on the structural conditions of their economies, the composition of their support bases, and the extent of their hold on political power. The most fundamental difference concerns the context of protection of the manufacturing sector in Australia and New Zealand, and the high openness to trade in our other cases. A policy made possible by the reliance of these economies on highly competitive primary product exports, industrial protection kept pressures for rationalization at bay and thus also the need for active labor market policies to deal with unemployment resulting from structural change. Active labor market policies were developed to the greatest extent in Sweden, followed by the other Nordic countries, and least so in the Netherlands and Austria, with Germany, where they were initiated by the Grand Coalition in 1969, in the middle. The restricted access of the social democrats to political power explains the absence of active labor market policies in the Netherlands and the later and more restricted development of such policies in Germany. In Norway and Austria, employment protection through direct subsidies of private enterprises or public enterprises substituted for active labor market policies during the Golden Age.

The extent to which industrial promotion and other supply-side policies involved direct state direction of investment and state ownership in industry and banks, or indirect stimulation and timing of investment and research and development, depended heavily on the structure and strength of capital. The most statist policies were pursued in Austria, Norway, and Finland, where private capital was weak, owning mostly small and medium enterprises. In Sweden, Denmark, Germany, the Netherlands, and Australia the social democrats' plans for more extensive state intervention in the economy were defeated politically, and they had to be changed in order for either the parties to win elections (Germany and the Netherlands) or incumbent governments to avoid political stalemate (Sweden, Denmark, and Australia).

The goals, policies, and strategies preferred by Christian democrats with regards to welfare state and production regimes were significantly less statist. They essentially wanted a social market economy built on the principle of subsidiarity (van Kersbergen 1995). They accepted the need to combat poverty and prevent significant declines in living standards, but they opposed the universalistic, unified, state-administered schemes promoted by social democrats, insisting instead on corporatist forms of contributory social insurance, supplemented by social assistance at the local level. In the area of social services, they accepted the need to guarantee access to health care for all, but they supported private delivery and insurance through a variety of funds. Other areas of care were to be the responsibility of the female members of the traditional family. The support of the traditional family was at the center of their policies, and consequently the system of social protection was to be built around the male breadwinner.

The production regimes preferred by Christian democrats were more market conforming than those preferred by social democrats, and their policies were more reactive and indirect. The most statist part of their policies, particularly noticeable in the Netherlands but also in Austria, was support for central wage setting to keep labor cheap. In labor market policy the emphasis was on passive measures, that is, on transfer payments to people who had lost their jobs. They also supported regional policies in the form of support for peripheral areas whose welfare was endangered by the decline of traditional industries.

Among our cases, agrarian parties were relevant actors only in the Nordic countries. They were not the initiators of major social policy, but rather reactively attempted to protect the interests of their constituency once a social policy reform was on the agenda. They supported universal coverage in social programs, flat-rate benefits, tax financing, and entitlement on the basis of citizenship, and their influence arguably brought the social democrats to support reforms built on these principles in several cases. Their position lent itself well to coalition agreements with the social democrats as in Sweden and Denmark, or it laid the groundwork on which later social democratic governments could build as in Finland.

The secular right parties in our cases offered varying degrees of opposition to the expansion of social policy. Their basic preferences were always less government, more market, and lower levels of taxation. Even where they did not strongly oppose a particular reform scheme, they always pointed to the danger of excessive costs for the health of the economy. Our boldfaced assertion on this point as well as that on the reactive role of agrarian parties has been contested to varying degrees by various authors writing on Scandinavia.[39] For example, they argue, and for the most part we do not contest this, that the Conservative Party in Sweden supported universalistic pensions in the 1940s discussions on pension legislation, or that all bourgeois parties in Norway supported virtually all of the basic social security legislations in the first three postwar decades. Or, as we ourselves have pointed out, the Swedish bourgeois parties, particularly the middle parties, embarked on a strategy of "outbidding" the social democrats on welfare state policy after they were decisively defeated in the supplementary pension struggle of the late 1950s. In part, we believe that these authors err in focusing only on the final stages of policy formation, such as the final parliamentary vote, and thus misread actors' preferences (see our discussion below). But much more important, they are operating on the basis of a false, if unstated, counterfactual, that policy would have differed little if the social democrats had been out of power. We discuss this more extensively in the closing paragraphs of this chapter.

Turning to the social bases of the different parties, one does by and large see the correspondence in preferences that one would expect. Blue-collar trade unions supported the same combination of minimum flat-rate and earnings-related, universal, unified schemes as did the social democratic parties in Scandinavia, Germany, and Austria; in the Netherlands this was the position of the social democratic unions. In Australia and New Zealand blue-collar unions supported flat-rate, universalistic, tax-financed, but—with few exceptions—not means-tested benefits; they only began to support earnings-related benefits in the late 1960s and early 1970s.[40]

The comparatively late support for earnings-related social insurance by the social democrats and organized labor in Australia and New Zealand has a parallel in the comparatively weak support for and limited scope of such schemes in Denmark and in the divisions between the socialists and the communists in Finland on this issue. What Australia, New Zealand, and Denmark have in common is the lack of a strong metalworking export sector whose workers were dominant inside the labor movement and were pace setting in centralized wage bargaining. In our other cases, these workers were relatively well paid within the blue-collar ranks but concerned about parity with white-collar workers, and they were powerful enough to make their position in support of earnings-related pensions that of the entire labor movement. It is obvious that flat-rate benefits in sickness and unemployment insurance cannot be so high as to provide a generous replacement rate for a production worker who is paid above the average, lest there be a strong incentive for workers paid below the average to become and remain sick or unemployed, as their income would actually increase in such cases. The alternative of earnings-related but privately negotiated occupational benefits was rejected by the metalworking unions because of the experience that white-collar workers generally did much better under such negotiated schemes. Where the metalworkers did not have a dominant position in the labor movement, the push for public, universal, earnings-related benefits remained weaker. The divisions between the Finnish social democratic unions, which included better-paid workers and the metalworking sector and who were the strongest supporters of earnings-related benefits, and communist unions, which were stronger supporters of raising flat-rate benefits, reinforce the generalization that support for earnings-related benefits is particularly strong in this segment of the working class.

Feminist movements became influential actors in shaping the welfare state and labor market policies relatively late in the cases and period considered here.[41] Even for Scandinavia, where they were most influential, Hernes (1987: 46) states that women were "traditionally the object of welfare policy, not its creators." Their basic concerns with regard to social policy concerned independent—from husbands, that is—entitlements to benefits for women and children, access for women to the labor market, equal pay for equal work, and social services facilitating female labor force participation. Major progress in all these dimensions was made in the Nordic countries from the 1970s on, following an increase in women's labor force participation and coinciding with a stronger presence of women in the leading organs of the social democratic parties and in parliament. In Australia, the Arbitration Court ruled positively on equal pay for equal work for women in 1969 and, upon prodding from the Labor government, for equal pay for work of comparable value in the early 1970s, both decisions that did increase women's wages significantly. In social policy areas and women's labor force participation, though, progress in Australia was slow, as it was in Germany, Austria, and the Netherlands.

What should be underlined about the contribution of women's movements to the welfare state in general and to the social democratic welfare state in particular is that it came from outside of, and to some extent, perhaps to a large extent, in opposition to the constellation of interests and forces that shaped other social democratic social policies. The social democratic welfare state was originally shaped around the interests of its core constituency, which in most cases was manufacturing sector workers, who if not the most numerous, were certainly the best organized and most highly mobilized group in the labor movement. And they were overwhelmingly men. The unions, in particular, were attached to the male breadwinner concept and for a long time resisted measures, such as part-time work and flexible work schedules, that would facilitate increased women's labor force participation as a threat to the wages of full-time workers.

With the expansion of nonmanual work, growth of the service sector, and expansion of higher education, women's labor force participation grew in all advanced industrial societies. However, as table 5.2 demonstrates, it grew differentially across different countries, in part dependent on the expansion of the service sector, public or private. The unions in all of the countries considered in this chapter were relatively strong as of the mid-1960s and were able to prevent the development of a low-wage market, which retarded the growth of private sector services. Only in the Nordic countries, with the social democrats in power and without the legacies of Christian democratic social policy, did the public service sector, and thus women's labor force participation, begin to grow rapidly in this period and then set off the feedback dynamic in which women's political mobilization led to social policies that further facilitated women's entry into the labor force described in the section of this chapter on Sweden. Thus, at the close of the Golden Age in the mid-1970s, women's movements had had a sizable effect on social democratic policy only in the Nordic countries, the notable exception being the Whitlam government's comparable pay policy. Even in the Nordic countries, the women's movement had to circumvent the social democrats' normal constituency, the unions, and mobilize directly in the party as well as in other parties, especially the left socialists and liberals. Thus, at that time one already saw a rise in women's representation in leadership roles within the parties but not in the unions.

Business associations, like their political allies in the secular right, preferred as little legislation and as much flexibility in social and labor market policy as possible. However, they were concerned not to waste political capital in opposition to reform proposals they were bound to lose on. In many cases, they concentrated their opposition on the method of financing and administration that imposed a burden on enterprises, on the overall level of the tax burden, or on the enlarged role of the public sector rather than on the proposed social policy itself. They were particularly opposed to and fought against large pension funds under government control in Sweden, Norway, and Finland. In fact, as our discussion of the Nordic cases showed, they offered advice to each other on where and how to engage in opposition to legislation.

Farmers did not have a unified position on social policy where small and large farming coexisted. In Denmark, small farmers were represented by the Radical Liberals and large farmers by the Liberals, and the former were more progressive than the latter on welfare state policy and thus more frequently allies of the Social Democrats. In Australia, large farming dominated, in contrast to New Zealand, where small farming was more widespread, and the result was a significant difference in the generosity of the welfare states in these two countries as of 1950. In Sweden, Norway, and Finland, small farmers constituted the base of the agrarian parties, whose universalistic thrust in social policy was discussed above. In Germany, small farming was the norm as well, but the farmers did not have independent political representation. They demanded their own scheme already in 1946, and in 1957 they received a scheme with flat-rate contributions and flat-rate benefits.

Doctors' associations were firmly opposed to governmental involvement in supervising the delivery and financing of health care services, insofar as such supervision invariably entailed cost controls. Thus, they fought not only the introduction of a national health service, as for instance in Sweden, New Zealand, and Australia, but also attempts to bring about the greater unification and state control of health insurance that were made in Continental Europe. Where private or semipublic self-administered insurance funds had an established position in the health care system, they typically joined the doctors in opposition to an expansion of the state's role.

Turning now to some general insights into the dynamics of welfare state formation that our analysis has yielded, we can begin with the argument about path dependency. As we argued in chapter 2, policy legacies clearly do influence future choices, but they do not determine policy patterns; rather, changes in power constellations, specifically incumbency of one rather than another set of political parties can modify established policy patterns. A given set of institutions entails the presence of a set of actors with their preferences, and other actors have to be stronger to impose their preferences against the status quo preferences of established actors. The Swedish example demonstrates that it is very difficult to change a system of privately delivered into publicly delivered health care, but that it is possible. Similarly, Finland underwent a system shift with the political shift and union reorganization of the mid-1960s, which moved it rapidly to a social democratic corporatist pattern of political economy and welfare state policy. Institutional change is possible, but only if the political power distribution and the constitutional structure are favorable. The party or parties supporting change need to have a majority in parliament, and the constitutional structure needs to concentrate power in parliament, such as to minimize access of the opposition to veto points.

Our treatment of the historical development of the Swedish case allowed us to outline the interaction of historical institutional constraints and policy legacies and employers', unions', and parties' resources, structure, and strategy in the shaping of the welfare state regime and the production regime. As we pointed out in chapter 4, viewed from any given single moment there appears to be a "functional fit" between these aspects of a country's political economy. Viewed in historical perspective, it is clear that at every point in time outcomes were created by economic and political actors' choices, but these choices were made in the context of institutional constraints and policy legacies, and of other actors' resources and strategy. Thus, to take a few examples, after the second victory of the social democrats in the 1936 Swedish election, it was clear to employers that they would have to face a strong and centralized trade union movement allied with a sitting social democratic government for the foreseeable future and that they would be forced to make concessions. The structure of agrarian interests, the Social Democrats' alliance with the Agrarian Party, as well as the dominance of the metalworkers' union within the LO and the dominance of the oligopolistic, export-oriented employers within SAF shaped the postwar policy pattern in decisive ways. The defeat of the Social Democrats in the planning debate and the business structure were decisive constraints on the unions' and Social Democrats' employment and growth policies that led to, without determining, the development of the Rehn-Meidner model and the relative absence of influence of the Swedish state on the direction of (as opposed to the volume of) investment, in contrast to the Norwegian, Finnish, and Austrian cases. Thus, our theory of social, political, and economic change, while positing a high degree of path dependence, can account for institutional transformation caused by actors' constrained choices.

A further example of path dependency within the context of a particular power constellation is the expansion of women's labor force participation and of the public social service sector in the Nordic countries. Women's labor force participation began to increase in the 1960s with the tight labor markets and the refusal of unions to allow massive importation of foreign labor, in contrast to what happened on the Continent. At the same time, women organized within and outside of the social democratic party and succeeded in eliciting a commitment of the party and the government to the promotion of gender equity. This entailed among other things the socialization of care-giving responsibilities and thus an expansion of the public social service sector. These new jobs in turn were predominantly filled by women, which strengthened women's political involvement and support for the welfare state, opening up a pro–social democratic gender gap in voting. In other words, the expansion of public health, education, and welfare employment changed the composition of actors and the preferences of actors in a self-reinforcing way. As we shall see in chapter 7, a similar dynamic might have emerged in New Zealand in the 1980s but was cut way short by a loss of power of the Labour Party and a reversal of many reforms by the subsequent government. Women's labor force participation did increase dramatically in this decade, women made advances in the Labour Party and in parliament, and the Labour government did increase funding for child care, but the change in the composition of actors and their preferences was not fast enough to prevent the election loss, and that loss stopped the whole process in its tracks.

A final example of path dependency is the development of the mutually supportive relationship between high skill levels of the labor force, a competitive economy, and a generous and redistributive welfare state in Sweden. The long-standing commitment of the social democrats to an elimination of poverty and reduction of inequality, both in material conditions and in access to high-quality education, resulted in an educational profile of the adult population that has an overall very high level and a comparatively very high floor (see the discussion earlier in this chapter). Clearly, this achievement is not due to investment in education alone but rather due to the combination of this investment with other policies designed to eliminate poverty and reduce inequality in living conditions. It is well known that poverty and high inequality are great barriers to educational achievement among the underprivileged. With these barriers greatly reduced, investment in education at all levels did have the desired effect of creating a highly qualified labor force. As endogenous growth theory recognizes, low levels of inequality and high quality of human capital are important determinants of economic growth (see e.g. Osberg 1995). In the Swedish case, they not only made industry highly competitive but also facilitated the elimination of low-skill-low-wage jobs and employers. The elimination of these jobs and employers in turn made it possible to build a generous and redistributive welfare state without creating perverse incentives and without having to face intense opposition from such employers. This welfare state, which includes generous education, training, and retraining allowances, in turn reproduces the conditions for the maintenance of the high-skill competitive economy.

A further insight with important implications is that there was often a discrepancy between actors' original preferences and the types of legislation they ultimately supported, due to their assessment of the strategic situation. For instance, in the prolonged struggle over pension reform in Germany, the SPD wanted to prevent a political stalemate and thus dropped its demand for a citizenship pension. Or, in Austria coalition negotiations led to the establishment of seven insurance carriers in 1947 and the unification of the rules governing sickness, accident, and pension insurance in 1955; the social democrats supported both packages of legislation, despite their original support for a unified system and a citizenship pension. The implications of this observation are that if comparative case studies focus on the short run only, such as on votes on final legislation, or even negotiations in the month or two before legislation is passed, they miss the important differences between actors' original preferences and the political struggles leading up to compromise proposals.

A related insight is that particular political and institutional constellations sometimes produced specific choices. For instance, in Finland the unions and the social democrats supported compulsory, earnings-related, but privately administered pensions, rather than a publicly administered scheme like their counterparts in the rest of the Nordic countries. This choice was a result of the traditional dominance of the agrarians over the National Pension Institute. The unions and the social democrats feared that existing pension funds, financed by employee and employer contributions, which were to be folded into the National Pension Institute with the establishment of earnings-related pensions, would be used by the agrarians to subsidize pensions for the rural population on a grand scale.

A final insight to draw attention to here is the importance of political competition with social democrats to push Christian democrats toward generous welfare state legislation. Our discussion of the process leading up to the 1957 and 1972 pension reforms demonstrated this very clearly in the German case. Competition on the basis of legislative proposals was less obvious in the Dutch and Austrian cases because of the inclusion of social democrats in coalition governments during the early formative period of the welfare state. Nevertheless, we saw in the Netherlands as well that the presence of a social democratic minister of social affairs, who managed to set a popular precedent with an emergency act in 1946, was crucial for pushing through a universalistic pension scheme. By pointing to the importance of this competition we do not mean to deny that Christian democrats had a welfare state project of their own. They did have a distinctive project that differentiates their welfare states clearly from the liberal and the social democratic ones. We simply want to indicate that competition made this project more generous. The importance of competition from a viable left, capable of making a credible bid for power, for pushing Christian democrats toward generosity in welfare state legislation is further underlined by the contrast between Germany, Austria, and the Netherlands on the one hand and Italy and France on the other hand. In the latter set of countries the left was divided and could not make a real bid for power until the 1970s, and accordingly the welfare state was on the average less generous than in the former set of countries.

Based on the comparative and historical material presented in this chapter, we can further elaborate on our comments about the development of the production regime and the fit between aspects of the production regime, particularly labor market policies, and the welfare state regime. As we saw in the last chapter, it is obvious that a country's economic structure and its situation in the world economy are critical influences on the development of the production regime. The Antipodes' dependence on primary product exports, particularly raw agricultural goods, Denmark's on processed agricultural product exports, the rest of the Nordic countries' on forestry and manufacturing exports, were points of departure that fundamentally shaped and limited the trajectory on which the country could develop. What we want to underline here is the degree to which the regimes, particularly the labor market policies and welfare state regimes, were shaped by the political actors relatively late in historical time, that is, since the Depression in the case of all countries except Australia and possibly New Zealand. Thus, we would argue that the cohesion of the four welfare state–production regime types outlined and the internal fit of the aspects of the regimes are more of a political creation than a functional necessity, and the clustering of the countries is largely due to similarities in political configuration.

Denmark is the most obvious case supporting this view, as it was not dependent on manufacturing exports like the other corporatist economies. Its production regime was relatively liberal at the outset and it could have developed in a yet more liberal direction. Yet unions were strong at an early point in Danish history (Stephens 1979b: 115–16), Catholicism and thus Christian democracy was essentially absent, and social democracy became the dominant though not hegemonic political force. As a result, Denmark developed a distinctly social democratic welfare state regime and labor market policy, yet other aspects of its production regime, such as industry-finance relations, remained liberal relative to the other coordinated market economies. More broadly, except for labor market policies, variations in production regime cut across our Christian democratic and social democratic types. Austria's production regime is more similar to Norway's, and Germany's is more similar to Sweden's than they are (or at least were, as of the end of the Golden Age) to each other's. From the point of view of the "functional necessities" of the preexisting production regimes, Austria and Germany could have developed social democratic welfare states and labor market policies and Sweden and Norway could have developed Christian democratic welfare states and labor market policies. This is most obviously true in the case of the development of public social services and the gender dimension of social policy, but it also applies to other aspects of social policy such as the universalistic basic income tier characteristic of the Nordic welfare states. On the other hand, the abyss between the coordinated and liberal market economies is much greater. Either Christian democratic or social democratic welfare and labor market policy would have to be greatly altered to accommodate a liberal market economy.

Our comparative historical analyses have strongly supported the quantitative results obtained in chapter 3, and they enable us to elucidate further some of the causal connections. They have fully supported the argument about partisan effects. Our analyses demonstrated great similarity in the policy preferences of social democratic parties and blue-collar unions on the one hand, and Christian democratic parties on the other hand, and they demonstrated that policy outcomes differed depending on who held governmental power.

Our quantitative analysis showed that social democratic cabinet participation is a stronger predictor of welfare state generosity than corporatism. Our case analysis confirmed this finding. We found that negotiations in corporatist institutions were important for shaping compromise designs for major social policy reforms in Austria when coalition governments were in power, but less so in Germany when the social democrats were excluded from government. In the Nordic countries, all major interest groups are consulted whenever major legislative measures are considered in an attempt to narrow the differences among all affected parties, but only by greatly stretching the concept could one characterize major social policy innovations as tripartite corporatist bargains and then only when the sitting government, employers, and unions agreed on the final legislation. On the other hand, adjustments of social policy by the government as part of an explicit bargain with the labor market partners in which wage restraint was achieved by compensating social policy measures was a constant feature of Finnish wage bargaining after the system shift of the mid-1960s (Wallerstein and Golden 1997) and was not infrequent in other Nordic cases. While the accumulation of such minor adjustments in social policy can have major effects in the long run, on the balance, the political power distribution remains decisive for the development of social policy. This is further underlined by the pre-1970s situation in the Netherlands, where unions were included in corporatist arrangements but had little effective influence on social policy. Corporatist negotiations have assumed greater importance in the retrenchment phase, but this will be the subject of chapter 7.

In chapter 3 we also found that social democratic incumbency was a much better predictor of welfare state generosity than union density. The comparative historical analysis of Australia and New Zealand indicates that union strength has only limited effects on social policy independent of social democratic government. In the period 1950 to 1970 the labor movements in these two countries were among the strongest in the world. Yet there was very little progress in building the welfare state in this period as Labour was out of power; on the contrary, bourgeois governments let the gains made under previous Labour governments erode by not adjusting benefit levels. The same happened in Australia after the ouster of the Whitlam government in 1975. These observations further support the primacy of political incumbency over other aspects of left-labor strength, such as corporatism and union density, as a causal factor in welfare state development.

The period analyzed in this chapter covered the beginning of the significant increase in women's mobilization into the labor force in the

Nordic countries. Increasing labor force participation facilitated increasing participation in politics and thus enabled women to become more effective in pushing for expansion of welfare state services. Our case material suggests that the interaction effect with social democratic incumbency we saw in the quantitative analysis is due to both the receptivity of social democratic parties to women's demands for greater representation in political leadership positions and the affinity between social democratic commitments to universal access and quality of welfare state programs and women's demands for an expansion of public delivery of welfare state services.

We also found demonstrative examples of the importance of the constitutional structure in the policy-making process. In Sweden, the pension reform that introduced a public, earnings-related scheme, with large publicly controlled pension funds, which engendered strong opposition from business, was passed by one vote in parliament. In Australia, a constitutional provision prevented federal social policy in areas other than pensions and invalidity until 1946, and it took two referenda to enlarge the federal government's authority over social policy. When the 1972–75 Whitlam government attempted to introduce a universalistic national health insurance and other social policy reforms, these reforms were blocked by opposition in the Senate. This experience contrasts sharply with the passage of free medical care under the 1938–49 Labour government in New Zealand with its unicameral parliament.

Finally, the historical and comparative materials contained in this chapter present evidence strongly supporting our contentions, elaborated in chapters 2 and 3, that the partisan effects on social policy cannot be measured by focusing solely on short-term effects of changes in government. First, the comparative analysis clearly demonstrates our "ratcheting up the policy peg" argument. Once instituted, most generous welfare state policies are popular, and certainly the policies that make up the vast majority of social spending—pensions, health care, and education—are very popular. Thus, each new policy passed ratchets up the policy peg and becomes the new point of departure for debate. Therefore, it is fallacious to observe, for instance, that the Swedish bourgeois government of 1976–82 accepted the whole edifice of the social democratic welfare state regime and did very little to change it, and then to infer that in Sweden changes in government did not and will not change welfare state policy. While it is certainly true that the partisan hypothesis would have been more strongly supported had the bourgeois coalition moved decisively to dismantle the welfare state, the behavior of this government is fully consistent with our policy ratchet argument. In fact, in our historical materials on Golden Age social policy development, we find no cases of conservative governments cutting social programs or benefits in major ways. Only in Australia and New Zealand did entitlements deteriorate in a significant way, and this was because the benefits were flat rate and thus were eroded by the failure of the governments to adjust them fully for inflation and increases in real wages. Moreover, this occurred over the course of the terms of many governments, not in a single term in office.

The policy ratchet argument is nicely demonstrated by a comparison of the Nordic countries and the Antipodes, particularly New Zealand, at the beginning and the end of the Golden Age. At the beginning of this period, the policy debates and the partisan differences were quite similar in the two regions. The social democrats attempted to construct a basic security income safety net and essentially free health care systems. While it is true that Antipodean labor parties relied more heavily on means testing, on the balance it cannot be said that there were fundamental differences in the policy preferences of the social democratic parties of the six countries. Indeed, according to the SCIP data, as of 1950, replacement rates in pensions, sick pay, and unemployment insurance were substantially better in New Zealand than in any of the Nordic countries and they were comparable in Australia (Palme 1990; Kangas 1991; Carroll 1999). Though the sequencing was somewhat different in the six countries, the parties of the right came to accept the basic social security reforms introduced by labor but continued to oppose public delivery of health care, increased taxes, and increased government regulation.

Moving ahead to the 1970s, with frequent participation in government in the Nordic countries, the social democrats and their centrist (mostly agrarian) allies had ratcheted up the policy peg while the Antipodean labor parties, banished in the political wilderness, had achieved little. Thus, the bourgeois coalitions in Denmark, Norway, and Sweden did little to change the welfare state policy regime, accepting policies, such as very high levels of taxation and national health services, that they had been very much opposed to two decades earlier. In Australia and New Zealand, not only did the parties of the right continue to be opposed to such policies, the labor parties would not have dared propose such policies, as they would have been too far beyond the policy frontier as defined by the existing policy peg.

The second problem with focusing narrowly on short-term partisan change discussed in chapter 2 can also be seen in the comparative historical evidence. We argued that once a welfare state–production regime is established, it tends to strengthen those who support it or can at least tolerate it and it weakens its opponents. Thus, the high-wage regimes of the

northern tier of Continental Europe and Scandinavia gradually eliminated one opponent, low-wage employers, while strengthening employers who, because they do not compete on the basis of low wages, can live
with high wages, generous social policy, and strong unions. For instance,
in Sweden employers in low-wage industries in the 1950s, such as textiles,
argued strongly against even the negotiated supplementary pensions proposed by the SAF leadership, contending that the costs would put them
out of business (Söderpalm 1980). Two decades later these industries had
largely disappeared from the Swedish scene, eliminating one source of
opposition to a generous welfare state.

The final two limitations in examining solely short-term partisan
policy differences, that a given change in government has only a limited
effect on the power balance among classes and on the hegemonic (ideological) balance in society, also explain why the Nordic bourgeois coalitions made few changes in welfare state policy, or for that matter why any
given government rarely makes large and enduring changes in social
policy in one period in office.

If one takes these four factors—the policy peg ratchet, the regime effect, the class power balance, and the hegemonic balance—and adds our
points about the effects of party competition on parties' policies and the
limitations of examining actors' positions on final legislative proposals, it
is easy to see how competent scholars examining legislative developments
over relatively short time periods in a single country have come to the
conclusion that partisan differences over social policy were relatively
minor, despite the very large differences in policy regimes that existed
by 1980, as shown in chapters 3 and 4. We agree with King, Keohane,
and Verba (1994) that the only valid test of the causal effect of one social
factor on another, in this case of partisan government on social policy
outcomes, is to rerun history changing only the factor of interest. Thus,
any causal inference involves a counterfactual that cannot be verified.
Nevertheless, we have enough historical information to construct highly
plausible explicit counterfactuals and engage other authors' implicit
counterfactuals.

As we indicated above, we think the authors who argue that partisan
differences over social policy were inconsequential operate with an implicit counterfactual in mind that we believe is false. They believe that the
policy position of an actor on final legislation, or in the more astute versions, the consistent policy position of an actor over the period of public
and behind-the-scenes discussions of the policy, is a valid indicator of
what the actor would have done if he/she or his/her allies were in office.

But this is deeply problematic. For instance, Swenson (forthcoming) argues, based on archival work, that Swedish employers supported legislation on basic pensions, sickness insurance, and active labor market policy, and he concludes from this that the correlation between social democratic incumbency and the social democratic welfare state is spurious. However, the fundamental question is whether employers would have supported the same policies under a long-term bourgeois government. Faced with labor shortages in the late 1940s, employers pressed for the importation of foreign labor (Swenson 1999: 26), which would have been a cheaper answer to their problems than active labor market policy. It is at least a plausible hypothesis that they would have been able to do so under a bourgeois government, as did their counterparts in Continental Europe some two decades later. Moreover, employers along with the bourgeois parties consistently warned about the consequences of rising social expenditures and thus taxes for the health of the Swedish economy. As we discussed above, bourgeois voters wanted lower taxes, these priorities were reflected in party programs, and it is most reasonable to assume that the bourgeois parties would have acted according to these priorities had they been in office. Under these circumstances, are we to assume that Swedish employers would have supported improvements in pensions and sickness insurance proposed by the social democratic opposition, along with the tax increases needed to pay for them?

Similarly, Baldwin (1990) argues that middle classes and bourgeois parties are responsible for the solidaristic social democratic welfare state. As we have pointed out, he is correct in arguing that the agrarian parties were the primary promoters of universalistic flat-rate and tax-financed benefits. However, what he fails to emphasize is that they played a primarily reactive role, ensuring that social policy reforms that were put on the agenda by the social democrats would benefit the farmers. Again, if we construct a counterfactual with bourgeois incumbency and consider particularly the Conservatives' and employers' preferences for low taxes, it is most unlikely that the agrarian parties would have found the support necessary to implement these universalistic tax financed schemes from a bourgeois coalition government.

Our argument about the difference between expected short- and long-term partisan effects implies also that we are interested in two different counterfactuals. Let us take the example of Norway since it is one in which the argument for the absence of partisan effects is strongest. We would want to know not only whether Norwegian social policy would have looked different in 1940 had the bourgeois parties been in office from 1935 to 1940, but also whether it would have looked different if the bourgeois coalition and not the Labor Party had been in power from 1935 to 1965. The fact that the bourgeois opposition supported most of the Labor Party's reforms in 1935–40 and later is relevant for assessing the partisan effects, but it is not the only relevant piece of information. The posture of the bourgeois opposition in the late 1930s could plausibly have been influenced by Labor's victory in the 1935 election, by the subsequent agreement with the Agrarian Party, and by the NAF-LO compromise that followed. The facts that the bourgeois governments that had preceded had done little in terms of social policy legislation and that Norway was a welfare state laggard in Europe as of 1935 are also relevant information for assessing the hypothesis that the Labor accession to power made a difference for social policy legislation as of 1940, as is the fact that Norway moved to the forefront in social policy legislation by the end of Labor's first period in office.

As to the long-term effects of partisanship, since we cannot rerun history with the Norwegian Labor Party in opposition, we have to resort to comparative analysis to elucidate the hypothesis. In the statistical analysis in chapter 3, we found very strong partisan effects on the social policy pattern when controlling for a broad range of other variables that have been hypothesized to affect the development of social policy. Thus, if Norway had had a bourgeois government for the period 1935–65 and still had the same policy configuration it developed under Labor, then it would be very much a statistical outlier, an anomalous case. In this chapter, we have seen that countries such as New Zealand, which was actually more generous in terms of social policy than Norway in 1949 but in which labor government was infrequent after that, fell far behind in terms of the generosity of social policy by the end of the Golden Age. We have also seen that countries with a similar pattern of partisanship, such as Sweden, ended up with similar welfare state regimes. And we have seen that Finland converged with its Nordic neighbors in terms of social policy when it converged with them in terms of partisanship and labor unity. All of this information taken together leads us to reject the hypothesis that the Norwegian social policy pattern would have been substantially the same had there been a bourgeois government and not a Labor government from 1935–65.

In sum, in this chapter we have examined the policy preferences and political actions of different parties and associated interest groups and social movements and found that, with few exceptions, social democrats, Christian democrats, and secular conservatives and their allies adopted positions that one would have expected them to, given the results of our analyses in chapters 3 and 4, albeit positions that were often modified in the course of struggles over legislation. Thus, the hypothesis of short-term partisan differences was supported. The comparative analysis across the cases also showed strong cumulative effects of long-term domination by one political tendency or another. Thus, the hypothesis of yet greater differences as a result of differences in long-term cumulative partisanship was also supported.

## CHAPTER SIX

◆

# Welfare State Retrenchment: Quantitative Evidence

It is by now a widely accepted view that the sea changes in advanced capitalist economies of the past two decades, above all the increasing internationalization of these economies, have constricted the policy options of the governments of these societies (e.g., see Scharpf 1991). The contested questions are just how much the range of options has been constricted and which options have been eliminated. Economic internationalization is assumed strongly to favor market solutions and thus to be particularly unfavorable to policies traditionally promoted by social democracy and organized labor. In the case of social policy, trade unions and social democratic parties expressed fears that steps to further economic integration, such as the Europe 1992 initiative or NAFTA, would result in pressures to reduce welfare state provisions to the lowest common denominator. Indeed, significant rollbacks in provisions in countries as different as Denmark and New Zealand have been linked to the impact of changes in the international economy and these countries' integration into it (Marklund 1988; Castles 1996). By contrast, Garrett and Lange (1991) and Garrett (1998) have argued that the constriction of political choice has been overstated and that in expenditure policies in particular there are still significant differences between governments of the left and right. Similarly, Moene and Wallerstein (1993) argue that though many aspects of the Norwegian and Swedish social democratic models have suffered in the new economic environment, the social policy provisions appear to be highly resistant to change.

In this chapter, we examine the politics of social policy in the post-1973 period through statistical analysis of a variety of measures of social expenditure and public employment. We focus on two questions. First, to what extent has there been a rollback of welfare state entitlements in the past two decades? Second, to what extent have the partisan differences on social policy that characterized the immediate postwar decades been

reduced or even eliminated? In other words, to what extent have governments of all colors been constrained to adapt their social policy to new
economic conditions? Finally, do the patterns in the cuts allow for any
identification of causal dynamics? Once we have answered these questions, we then turn in the next chapter to a comparative historical analysis to further examine and update our findings past the last data points,
and to begin to suggest some causes of these developments.

## Data and Methods

The quantitative data analyzed here are the same pooled annual data for
the eighteen advanced capitalist countries that were democracies since
World War II that we used in chapter 3. For the purposes of the analysis
here we divide the data set into four periods and examine differences in
change in welfare state effort across the nations during the four periods.
Again we do not use annual change as the dependent variable as this
would grossly underestimate partisan effects on welfare state outcomes.
However, when one turns to the problem at hand, the analysis of the
change in partisan impact on social policy in the past two decades as compared to the Golden Age, one cannot measure the dependent variable by
level since the primary determinant of level in the later periods is the preexisting level of expenditure. As a consequence, when one analyzes the
pooled data with levels of expenditure as the dependent variable, one
finds that a dummy variable for the post-1979 period is positively and
moderately strongly related to the level of expenditure when controlling
for a wide range of determinants of expenditure. As one can see from
tables A.1 through A.6, this is a result of the fact that the average level of
expenditure in the period is higher. In fact, the rate of change for this period is considerably lower than for the previous two periods.

Our solution is to examine change over relatively long periods of time
in order to tap long- as well as short-term partisan effects. The method
has considerable cost. By making the dependent variable change over the
whole period of the Golden Age, for example, we reduce the number of
data points to the number of countries in the data set, thus abandoning
the advantages of pooling. The resultant reduction of degrees of freedom
greatly reduces the number of control variables that can be introduced
into the analysis. However, conducting the analysis on the annual change
data will, as we demonstrated in chapter 3, greatly underestimate the political effects we are most interested in. One runs the risk that one accepts
the prevailing wisdom that there is little partisan impact on social policy
in the contemporary era when such effects do exist in the long run.

Data points for most of the dependent variables to be analyzed extend from circa 1958–61 to 1989–95. We employ the same dependent variables that we used in the pooled data analysis in chapter 3. Many of the indicators of "welfare effort" are measures of government expenditure or revenue expressed as a percentage of GDP (total expenditure, total revenue, the ILO social security benefits measure, transfer payments, and civilian nontransfer spending; see tables A.1 through A.4, and A.6). The pension measure divides public pension expenditure as a percentage of GDP by the percentage of the population over sixty-five to yield a measure of pension benefits per aged person (table A.5). As in the analysis in chapter 3, the health care measure is the public proportion of total health expenditure and not public health expenditure as a percentage of GDP (table A.8). Our best measure of public social service delivery is civilian public employment as a percentage of the working-age population (table A.7). Finally, we have one direct measure of entitlements available in sufficiently long time series, unemployment replacement rates. The measures used are the OECD measure of replacement rates for a person with average wages averaged across different family compositions (single person, married person with no children, etc.) and the same measure for a person with two-thirds of average wages (tables A.9 and A.10). The problematic French and Italian data are included in the tables but not in the regressions. Even in the case of the tables, any references we make to group averages refer to the averages that exclude Italy and France.

In our analyses of the pooled data in chapter 3, we found that governance by social democratic and Christian democratic parties were among the most important determinants of these measures of welfare effort. Partisan effects varied across the indicators in a systematic fashion, as hypothesized by recent work on welfare state regimes (Esping-Andersen 1990; Huber, Ragin, and Stephens 1993; Huber and Stephens 1993a, 2000a; van Kersbergen 1995). Social democratic welfare states are service heavy and thus social democracy was more strongly related to the variables that measure services (government nontransfer spending and civilian government employment). Christian democratic welfare states are transfer states (Kohl 1981: 314) and thus Christian democracy was more strongly related to transfers and pensions. Both social democracy and Christian democracy were very strongly related to total revenue, total expenditure, and the ILO social security benefits measure, which combines all transfers and some social service spending (mainly health care). Reflecting the great propensity of social democracy to run budget surpluses, the coefficient for social democracy was higher on the revenue variable and the coefficients for Christian democracy were somewhat higher for the expenditure variables. Neither one of these two political variables had significant effects on the health care variable nor on unemployment replacement rates.

Like most quantitative studies of welfare states, we found party cabinet share rather than parliamentary seats or votes to be the most powerful political determinant of social policy outcomes. As in chapter 3, we operationalize left cabinet share in the following fashion: We give a score of 1 for each year when the left is in government alone; in the case of coalition governments, we score a fraction calculated by dividing the left's seats in parliament by all governing parties' seats. Because our dependent variable is change over the period and not the level of the dependent variable, the political variables were operationalized as both current and cumulative cabinet share. Current cabinet share is measured by averaging the annual cabinet share data for the period. To measure the long-term partisan effects, we cumulate the cabinet shares from 1945 to the period in question following our analysis in chapter 3. After some experimentation with alternatives that combined long-term and short-term effects, we settled on running the whole analysis with both the cumulative and current cabinet share variables.[1]

Let us comment briefly on the relative merits of the two operationalizations in the light of the extended discussion in chapter 3. By operationalizing the dependent variable as change over a period of moderate length, we control for the effects of economic cycles. A case might be made that current cabinet during the period in question is the better operationalization given this operationalization of the dependent variable. Moving from annual to medium-term changes in the dependent variable does not only control out the economic cycle effects, it also reduces the data error problem. On the other hand, moving from levels to medium-term changes reduces the effect of the ratcheting up of entitlements and therefore the long-term partisan effects. However, the regime effects, power balance effects, and hegemonic balance effects discussed in chapters 3 and 5 will still be operative, and therefore long-term partisan effects are still important. The maturation effects vary by the dependent variable, being the greatest for the pension measure and the smallest for unemployment replacement rates. As a consequence we chose to present the analysis with measures for both medium-term (current cabinet) and long-term (cumulative cabinet) partisan incumbency in this chapter.

One additional independent variable, the level of unemployment, is included in the analysis because our comparative historical analysis (chapter 7) revealed that in most cases cuts in social programs were caused by increases in the rate of unemployment, which governments perceived to be permanent.[2] In the case of health care, we also control for the initial level of each dependent variable. Since the public proportion of health care expenses was in excess of 80 percent in many cases at the end of the Golden Age, there is a ceiling effect to how much it could rise later.

Work by Cusack and Garrett (1994) on the determinants of government spending and by Mjøset (1986) on the impact of the changing international environment on Scandinavian political economies has argued that the 1970s and 1980s were distinctly different in terms of the policies governments followed to deal with the domestic and international economies. Mjøset notes that the 1970s were a period of policy "fumbling" in which governments largely attempted to deal with the crisis with the old methods. In the 1980s, governments began to realize that the game had fundamentally changed and adjusted policy accordingly. Based on our comparative historical research, we add a fourth period, the 1990s. Several developments that had great impact on welfare state politics ushered in this period. First, the fall of the Berlin wall and the subsequent collapse of the Soviet Union—and the Soviet economy—deprived European countries that had developed trade relations with the Soviet Union of those markets and, as a result of German reunification, led to austere monetary policies on the part of the Bundesbank that affected all of Europe. Second, the criteria for convergence laid down in the Maastricht agreement imposed austere macroeconomic policy on all western European countries, thus aggravating the unemployment problem in the region. Third, the move to financial deregulation that had begun in the early 1970s was essentially completed in western Europe by the beginning of this period due to the Europe 1992 project. Fourth, the Scandinavian unemployment, and welfare state, crisis occurred in this period in part due to the developments just outlined. Our first period, then, stretches from the beginning of our data in the mid- to late 1950s to the first oil shock in 1973. The second period extends until the second oil shock of 1979, and the third from then to 1990. We chose 1990 as the final date in the third period because 1989 is the top of an economic cycle whereas 1990, like 1980, which is the beginning of the period, is in the middle of an economic downturn.

## Results

Tables A.1 through A.8 display the level of expenditure and taxes (A.1–A.4, A.6), the level of pension benefits (A.5), public share of health expenditure (A.8), and level of public employment (A.7) for the beginning and end of the three periods, as well as the mean annual change during the period. The general pattern for expenditure is relatively clear: The mean annual increase in almost all of the expenditure measures was higher for the 1970s than for the Golden Age and then lower for the 1980s than for either of the two earlier periods. While there are a number of individual country exceptions to this rule, once the countries are aggregated to the level of welfare state regime type, all groups followed this pattern.

By contrast, the mean annual change in revenue follows a different and less clear-cut pattern. However, if we compare the mean annual change in revenue to the mean annual change in expenditure, a much clearer pattern emerges. A comparison of the mean annual changes indicates that expenditure was increasing much faster in the 1970s in all regime types, whereas in the 1980s average annual increases in revenue exceeded those of expenditure in all three regime types.

Taken together these patterns of the development of revenue and expenditure support not only the general hypothesis that the three periods were distinct, but also that the Scandinavian pattern found by Mjøset (1986) may be a general one. Governments first responded to the economic difficulties by following traditional formulas that entailed maintaining or increasing entitlements and expenditure in an effort to fight recession and unemployment and mitigate their social consequences. After a decade of "fumbling," government after government regardless of political color embarked on new policies that often involved reining in the increase in expenditure and increasing revenue.

With regard to the 1970s, the increases in pension benefits, public share of health care, and public employment shown in tables A.5, A.7, and A.8 all indicate that the continued increase in all measures of social expenditure shown in the tables was not simply an artifact of increasing burdens on the welfare state caused by adverse economic conditions and demographic change. The OECD unemployment replacement rates shown in tables A.9 and A.10 also show that all of the group means for the welfare state regimes rise in this period and only a few individual countries declined, with the Canadian and Japanese declines being the only two of significance.

This is also confirmed by an examination of the graphs of replacement rates and coverage for pensions, sick pay, and unemployment compensation based on data collected by the Social Citizenship Indicators Project at the University of Stockholm (Palme 1990; Kangas 1991; Carroll 1999). These data are for five-year intervals and thus the periods do not correspond to those in our tables. If we ignore changes that were largely reversed in the next five-year period, the unemployment replacement rate data confirm a mean increase in benefits in the 1970s in the social democratic and the Christian democratic welfare states. They do indicate a deterioration in the liberal group in the 1975–80 period, a point that we will return to below. The sick pay data also show a pattern of aggregate increases across the two five-year periods of the 1970s. Only Denmark made substantial cuts in this period, Finland made a cut that was more than reversed by 1985, and many countries increased their sick pay replacement rates significantly in the 1970s. The pension data are yet more unambiguous; all groups and most countries increased their replacement rates in both minimum and average pensions in the 1975–80 period.[3] Thus, the SCIP data do not confirm the decline in pensions in Italy and the United States shown in table A.5. Since the SCIP data are a more valid indicator of entitlements for the reasons discussed in chapter 3, we conclude that no significant cuts in pension entitlements occurred in any country in this period.

While the expenditure data do indicate that fiscal policy was more austere in the 1980s and the growth in all categories of expenditure was lower than a decade earlier, it does not tell us to what extent, if at all, there was real retrenchment in the form of rollbacks in welfare state benefits. Making such an assessment is a matter of weighing the extent to which the more modest increases in expenditure failed to keep up with more rapid increases in recipient groups such as the aged and unemployed. Moreover, as the discussion of Sweden in our case studies below shows, it was possible even to reduce expenditure and increase entitlements by a combination of public sector economies, exchange rate policies, and economic revival. Thus, even the relatively widespread cuts in government nontransfer expenditure cannot be interpreted as indicating welfare state cuts, especially since government employment, the superior measure of welfare state services, shows continued increases in all but a few countries in this period.

Here we have a number of pieces of evidence that bear directly on the question of cutbacks in the 1980s. With regard to pensions, the pension benefits data in table A.5, which control for the growth of the aged population, do show cutbacks in a number of countries in the 1980s. Moreover, these data are subject to two sources of error, which might lead one to underestimate cutbacks. First, the maturation of pension systems pushes up expenditure without legislative changes, thus current cutbacks due to, say, changes in indexation may be masked by automatic increases legislated in the past. Second, the use of early pensions to combat unemployment would drive up our figures on pension spending per person over sixty-five, as those going into early pension would not be included in the divisor. The SCIP data, which unfortunately extend only to 1985, do not confirm the pattern of widespread cuts. They show large cuts in the Netherlands and small cuts in Australia in both average and minimum pensions, confirming the data in table A.5 with regard to these two countries. We note, however, that the latest figures in the SCIP data predate the installation of the Australian supplementary pension plan discussed in the next chapter, and that plan would not even appear in the ILO data that form the basis for table A.5 since the scheme is off budget. Of the other six countries for which our pension data indicate cuts, the SCIP data show minor cuts in minimum pensions in two cases, Switzerland and the U.K., and no cuts or increases in either programs in the other four. However, since most of the error in our measure would underestimate cuts and our data extend to 1989, we are inclined to believe that a number of countries did cut pension entitlements at least marginally in this period. Our comparative case studies do confirm that, in addition to the cuts in the Netherlands, Germany and Denmark did implement modest cuts of pension entitlements in the 1980s. Since, as we shall see, pensions are among the programs in which the public most resists cuts, the cuts in entitlements indicated by these data do appear to confirm a pattern of retrenchment in this period. With regard to the partisan pattern, the social democratic welfare states seemed most immune to cuts and the liberal welfare states most likely to cut. The partisan effects appear particularly strong given that Denmark, which recorded reductions, was primarily ruled by a bourgeois coalition in this period and Austria, which registered substantial increases, was governed by the social democrats alone or in coalition with the Christian democrats for the entire period.

With regard to health care, our data on the development of public share of health care expenditure show a different pattern than the expenditure as a percent of GDP variables (compare table A.8 with tables A.2, A.3, A.4, and A.6). The 1970s already exhibited a lower average annual increase in the public share than the earlier period and the public share actually declined in the 1980s. All but five cases exhibit such a decline, and in at least four cases the decline in the public share was quite significant. Since OECD data on coverage indicate very few decreases in coverage (OECD 1990: 143–45), these declines must be explained primarily by increased copayments and exit from the public system due to decreased services, long queues, and poorer quality services.

The unemployment replacement rate data also show cuts in entitlements in the 1980s in a number of countries (tables A.9 and A.10). In eleven cases replacement rates for persons with average wages continued to rise in the 1980s, but at a much slower pace than in the 1970s, and in six cases they fell (disregarding Italy and France because of data problems). Replacement rates for persons with two-thirds of an average wage were cut in five countries, remained stable in three, and were increased in nine. The only group where cuts dominated for both income categories was the group of liberal welfare states. The SCIP data confirm that the liberal countries as a group cut unemployment replacement rates in this period. The U.K. also appears as the country that implemented the largest cuts, cutting net unemployment replacement rates for the average production worker from around 60 percent to around 30 percent between 1975 and 1985. It is worth noting that the U.K. is the only country that recorded declines in welfare state effort on all but one indicator for which we have time series data, including unemployment replacement rates; transfer expenditure alone remained stable.

The SCIP data on replacement rates in sick pay also show cutbacks in some countries. We limit our attention to those countries that made changes of over 5 percent that did not simply reverse changes of the previous five years. Only Finland substantially increased sick pay in this period. The Netherlands and Australia lowered replacement rates, with cuts of less than 10 percent. The United Kingdom recorded a dramatic cut in the period 1975 to 1985, cutting replacement rates in sick pay by almost 30 percent, the same magnitude as the cut in unemployment benefits.

Our data on the development of public social services—the data on civilian public employment in table A.7 and from the WEEP data on public health, education, and welfare employment (Cusack, Notermans, and Rein 1989: 478)—both show that the social democratic welfare states experienced a significant increase even in the 1980s, whereas in the other two groups civilian public employment was essentially stable after increasing moderately in the previous two periods. Only the U.K., Ireland, the Netherlands, and Japan experienced a drop in the percentage of the working age population in civilian public employment, and there the decreases were quite small. The other countries experienced increases in civilian public employment but, save the Nordic countries, France, and Canada, of less than one percent for the group as a whole. The Nordic pattern is singular: civilian public employment increased between 2 and 3 percent in the 1980s in all four countries. The WEEP data on the percentage of the working age population in public health, education, and welfare employment from 1975 to 1985 confirm the overall pattern we found with the civilian public employment data.

With regard to the 1990s, the dearth of data and the comparatively short time period limit what we can say with confidence. The ILO data series on social security benefit and pension expenditure ends in 1989.[4] The revenue and expenditure data show few clear patterns, except for general austerity in the Christian democratic welfare states, where revenue clearly outpaced expenditures, and general expenditure cuts in liberal welfare states. In the social democratic group, there was a decline in revenue in Sweden and Norway, certainly an effect of the economic crisis of the early 1990s. Both Norway and Denmark reduced expenditures, but in Norway this went along with a decline in revenue, whereas Denmark raised revenue significantly in this period, a policy guided by the goal to meet the Maastricht criteria. The Christian democratic welfare states show a general pattern of increases in revenue, except for the Netherlands, and a very mixed picture in expenditures. The same pattern as in Denmark, of stronger growth of revenue than expenditures, is visible in Austria, Belgium, Netherlands, France, and Italy, all countries affected by Maastricht. The exceptions to this pattern are Germany and Switzerland, the latter not being a member of the European Monetary Union. The liberal welfare states show a uniform and rather large decline in expenditures, and a mixed pattern in revenue.

Transfer expenditures in the 1990s show an average increase in all groups; but each group has countries deviating from the overall trends. The average increase was about twice as high in the social democratic welfare states as in the Christian democratic and liberal ones. Nontransfer expenditures show a more mixed pattern in social democratic and Christian democratic welfare states; on average, such expenditures increased in the former group and even increased very slightly in the latter, in contrast to a uniform and sizeable decline in the liberal welfare states.

The civilian government employment data show a general pattern of cuts in Scandinavia; only in Norway did civilian government employment continue to grow. The Christian democratic welfare states present a mixed picture, but for the group as a whole stability dominates. In the liberal welfare states, we see large cuts in the U.K. but only small cuts or small increases in the other countries. The data on public share of health expenditure also show a pattern of retrenchment in Scandinavia; in this case Denmark is an exception with a stable share. The Christian democratic and the liberal welfare states do not show consistent patterns. Cuts outnumber increases and produce an average decline in the Christian democratic group. The average increase in the liberal group is driven by the increase in the United States and secondarily in Ireland. These overall mixed patterns suggest that there were significant attempts to reform welfare states in the various countries, but not necessarily with the primary goal of retrenchment, with the arguable exception of the liberal welfare states. The Maastricht criteria imposed strict austerity on the Christian democratic welfare states, but the policy instruments used to meet these criteria involved revenue increases as well as expenditure cuts.

Unemployment replacement rates show a rather diverse pattern if one is looking at individual countries, but the averages for all groups indicate a retrenchment for workers with both average and below-average wages, with the exception of a slight average increase for lower-paid workers in the social democratic welfare states. A unique and striking pattern is visible in the uniform cuts in unemployment replacement rates for lower-paid workers in the liberal welfare states; three of the four liberal welfare states under study instituted cuts for workers with average wages as well, the only exception being the United States. These cuts clearly correspond to the expansion of the low-wage sector in these countries. In contrast, the increases in unemployment replacement rates for both types of workers in Australia indicate an effort on the part of the government to cushion the effects of adjustment.

Regressions of the political variables and unemployment on the dependent variables available on an annual basis (all except unemployment replacement rates) are shown in tables 6.1 (with current cabinet share as an independent variable, pp. 214–15) and 6.2 (cumulative cabinet share, pp. 216–17). The general pattern of strong partisan effects in the Golden Age followed by attenuated partisan effects in the 1970s and then very little partisan differences in the 1980s and 1990s is striking. In the case of current Christian democratic cabinet, all of the coefficients for the 1980s are insignificant and many are actually negative. Current social democratic cabinet share does register a significant and moderately large effect on the civilian government employment variable in the 1980s. This coefficient taps the very substantial expansion of public social services in the Scandinavian countries in this period. As our statistical analysis in chapter 3 and the comparative historical chapters both show, this is in part due to the interaction of social democratic governance with the political mobilization of women. The regressions with cumulative cabinet shares show nuanced differences from the current cabinet share regressions but confirm the overall pattern of decline of partisan effects over the three periods and no partisan effects in the 1980s except in the case of social democracy on civilian government employment. The data for the 1990s have to be treated with considerable care because the period is very short. There are only two significant coefficients, for current Christian democratic cabinet and for unemployment on total government revenue. The positive effect of current Christian democratic cabinet on revenue arguably taps the efforts of these governments to cut budget deficits in order to qualify for the common currency under the conditions specified by the Maastricht accord.

The coefficients for unemployment exhibit the pattern traditionally hypothesized in the literature for the 1960s but a quite different pattern in the subsequent periods. The quantitative welfare state literature hypothesizes that unemployment is related to social spending because it increases the constituency for increased unemployment benefits and because increased unemployment automatically increases spending at any given level of entitlements since it increases need. The economics literature reverses the causal direction, arguing that the higher levels of entitlements, particularly unemployment benefits, increases unemployment because they increase the reservation wage. These expectations find modest confirmation for the 1960s as almost all of the coefficients for unemployment are positive and quite a few of them are significant as well. But in subsequent periods, most of the coefficients are negative, a few of them are negative and significant, and none are positive and significant. While the regression coefficients for unemployment indicate little difference between the 1970s and subsequent periods, if one combines them with inspection of the rates of annual change in the periods (tables A.1 through A.8), one sees a significant difference between the 1970s and subsequent periods. In the 1970s, all governments responded to the economic difficulties with increased efforts on all but a few of our indicators. However, those governments experiencing particularly high levels of stress from unemployment tended to increase spending somewhat less. In the subsequent period, many governments cut entitlements and slowed spending increases or even cut social spending, and the governments experiencing higher levels of unemployment were more likely to cut.

Turning now to the regressions with changes in unemployment replacement rates, we would not expect them to show us a pattern of declining partisan effects, given that the partisan effects were small in the period of welfare state construction to begin with, as we showed in chapter 3. Nevertheless, since unemployment rose to levels unprecedented in the post–World War II period during the 1980s and came to exert major pressure on the welfare state, as we will argue in the next chapter, it is worth looking at replacement rates in this increasingly central program here. The first point to note is that social democratic and Christian democratic incumbency continued to explain little about variations in replacement rates in unemployment compensation (table 6.3, p. 218). The one exception to this pattern is the significant coefficient for cumulative social democratic cabinet share in the 1970s. This can be interpreted as a regime, or power balance, or hegemonic effect; in other words, it was

**Table 6.1** Determinants of Changes in Welfare Effort by Period
(Current Cabinet Share)

| | 1960–72 | | 1973–79 | | 1980–90 | | 1991–95 | |
|---|---|---|---|---|---|---|---|---|
| | $\beta$ | $t$ | $\beta$ | $t$ | $\beta$ | $t$ | $\beta$ | $t$ |
| *Total government revenue (% GDP)* | | | | | | | | |
| Social democratic rule | .87 | 4.9 | .13 | .5 | .01 | .0 | .03 | .1 |
| Christian democratic rule | .08 | .5 | .44 | 1.7 | −.19 | −.7 | .40 | 1.7 |
| Unemployment | .30 | 1.7 | .04 | .2 | −.18 | −.6 | .38 | 1.6 |
| Adjusted $R^2$ | .55 | | .01 | | −.12 | | .10 | |
| N | 18 | | 18 | | 18 | | 17 | |
| *Total government expenditure (% GDP)* | | | | | | | | |
| Social democratic rule | .72 | 3.3 | .13 | .4 | .08 | .3 | −.03 | −.1 |
| Christian democratic rule | .25 | 1.2 | .22 | .8 | −.05 | −.2 | .23 | .9 |
| Unemployment | .23 | 1.1 | −.22 | −.8 | −.18 | −.6 | −.16 | −.6 |
| Adjusted $R^2$ | .36 | | −.10 | | −.15 | | −.11 | |
| N | 17 | | 17 | | 17 | | 18 | |
| *Social security benefit expenditure (ILO) (% GDP)* | | | | | | | | |
| Social democratic rule | .51 | 2.0 | .23 | .9 | −.03 | −.1 | | |
| Christian democratic rule | .08 | .4 | −.39 | −1.6 | −.15 | −.6 | | |
| Unemployment | .04 | .2 | −.04 | −.2 | −.33 | −1.1 | | |
| Adjusted $R^2$ | .08 | | .12 | | −.08 | | | |
| N | 18 | | 18 | | 16 | | | |
| *Social security transfer expenditure (% GDP)* | | | | | | | | |
| Social democratic rule | .42 | 1.7 | .15 | .6 | .19 | .6 | −.34 | −1.3 |
| Christian democratic rule | .41 | 1.8 | .32 | 1.4 | −.13 | −.5 | −.13 | −.5 |
| Unemployment | .20 | .8 | −.47 | −1.9 | .20 | .7 | −.07 | −.2 |
| Adjusted $R^2$ | .14 | | .17 | | −.15 | | −.08 | |
| N | 18 | | 18 | | 17 | | 17 | |

possible significantly to raise unemployment replacement rates only in countries where social democracy enjoyed a long-term established position of strength in shaping the policy regime.

When we introduce the level of unemployment we observe the following dynamics. In the Golden Age, the level of unemployment showed some, though not or only barely significant, positive association with changes in unemployment replacement rates. We interpreted this in chapter 3 as indicating that unemployment insurance enjoyed relatively low priority on the social policy reform agenda compared to the pressing issues of poverty in old age and health care. Once these issues had been dealt with in major social policy reforms, in most cases by the late 1950s,

**Table 6.1** *(continued)*

| | 1960–72 | | 1973–79 | | 1980–90 | | 1991–95 | |
|---|---|---|---|---|---|---|---|---|
| | β | t | β | t | β | t | β | t |
| *Public pension expenditure (% GDP per aged person)* | | | | | | | | |
| Social democratic rule | .20 | .7 | −.21 | −.8 | .34 | 1.2 | | |
| Christian democratic rule | −.04 | −.2 | −.29 | −1.2 | .10 | .4 | | |
| Unemployment | −.11 | −.4 | −.42 | −1.6 | −.02 | .1 | | |
| Adjusted $R^2$ | −.13 | | .08 | | −.07 | | | |
| N | 18 | | 18 | | 18 | | | |
| *Civilian nontransfer expenditure (% GDP)* | | | | | | | | |
| Social democratic rule | .68 | 2.8 | .05 | .2 | −.01 | .0 | −.15 | −.5 |
| Christian democratic rule | .01 | .1 | .12 | .4 | .04 | .2 | .09 | .3 |
| Unemployment | .35 | 1.5 | −.11 | −.4 | −.23 | −.8 | −.10 | −.4 |
| Adjusted $R^2$ ($N = 17$) | .25 | | −.20 | | −.17 | | −.18 | |
| N | 17 | | 17 | | 17 | | 17 | |
| *Civilian government employment (% working age population)* | | | | | | | | |
| Social democratic rule | .92 | 8.3 | .50 | 1.8 | .46 | 1.7 | .31 | 1.2 |
| Christian democratic rule | −.32 | −3.1 | −.08 | −.3 | −.29 | −1.2 | .15 | .6 |
| Unemployment | .25 | 2.2 | −.04 | −.2 | .10 | .4 | −.17 | −.6 |
| Adjusted $R^2$ | .85 | | .13 | | .14 | | −.03 | |
| N | 16 | | 16 | | 16 | | 16 | |
| *Public share of total health expenditure* | | | | | | | | |
| Social democratic rule | .19 | .8 | .33 | 1.1 | .19 | .7 | .02 | .1 |
| Christian democratic rule | .12 | .6 | −.31 | −1.3 | .15 | .6 | .01 | .0 |
| Unemployment | .01 | .1 | −.25 | −.1 | −.18 | −.6 | −.21 | −.9 |
| Initial level of public share | −.73 | −3.1 | −.09 | −.3 | −.34 | −1.3 | −.53 | −2.2 |
| Adjusted $R^2$ ($N = 18$) | .28 | | .14 | | −.07 | | .16 | |
| N | 18 | | 18 | | 18 | | 18 | |

β: standardized coefficient

| Significance levels for t | .05 | .1 |
|---|---|---|
| Two-tailed test | >2.2 | >1.8 |
| One-tailed test | >1.8 | >1.4 |

there was virtually full employment in the northern European countries and thus little pressure to adjust replacement rates in unemployment insurance. Where unemployment levels were higher, there was a slight tendency to adjust these rates upward, indicating a political response to the plight of the unemployed. This positive association between unemployment and increased replacement rates is also consistent with the reservation wage argument.

**Table 6.2**    Determinants of Changes in Welfare Effort by Period
(Cumulative Cabinet Share)

|  | 1960–72 | | 1973–79 | | 1980–90 | | 1991–95 | |
|---|---|---|---|---|---|---|---|---|
|  | $\beta$ | $t$ | $\beta$ | $t$ | $\beta$ | $t$ | $\beta$ | $t$ |
| *Total government revenue (% GDP)* | | | | | | | | |
| Social democratic rule | .91 | 5.1 | .45 | 1.8 | −.10 | −.4 | .18 | .7 |
| Christian democratic rule | .16 | 1.0 | .44 | 2.0 | −.12 | −.5 | .32 | 1.3 |
| Unemployment | .34 | 1.9 | .26 | 1.0 | −.23 | −.8 | .38 | 1.5 |
| Adjusted $R^2$ | .57 | | .31 | | −.13 | | .05 | |
| N | 18 | | 18 | | 18 | | 17 | |
| *Total government expenditure (% GDP)* | | | | | | | | |
| Social democratic rule | .85 | 4.1 | .63 | 2.6 | −.19 | −.7 | .06 | .2 |
| Christian democratic rule | .31 | 1.7 | .16 | .7 | .00 | .0 | .05 | .2 |
| Unemployment | .30 | 1.5 | .04 | .1 | −.30 | −1.0 | −.16 | −.6 |
| Adjusted $R^2$ ($N = 17$) | .48 | | .24 | | −.13 | | −.17 | |
| N | 17 | | 17 | | 17 | | 18 | |
| *Social security benefit expenditure (ILO) (% GDP)* | | | | | | | | |
| Social democratic rule | .78 | 3.6 | .48 | 2.0 | .06 | .2 | | |
| Christian democratic rule | .15 | .8 | −.25 | −1.1 | −.07 | −.2 | | |
| Unemployment | .17 | .8 | .00 | .0 | −.31 | −1.1 | | |
| Adjusted $R^2$ ($N = 18$) | .39 | | .18 | | −.10 | | | |
| N | 18 | | 18 | | 16 | | | |
| *Social security transfer expenditure (% GDP)* | | | | | | | | |
| Social democratic rule | .72 | 3.4 | .31 | 1.3 | .04 | .1 | .15 | .5 |
| Christian democratic rule | .48 | 2.5 | .31 | 1.4 | −.06 | −.2 | −.28 | −1.0 |
| Unemployment | .33 | 1.6 | −.35 | −1.5 | .11 | .4 | .02 | .1 |
| Adjusted $R^2$ ($N = 18$) | .40 | | .23 | | −.21 | | −.10 | |
| N | 18 | | 18 | | 17 | | 17 | |

In the 1970s, the association between levels of unemployment and change in unemployment replacement rates became negative and by the 1980s the strength of the negative association further increased and became quite large and highly significant. Again one has to combine the regression with the annual increases shown in tables A.9 and A.10 to arrive at the proper interpretation of the dynamics. In the 1970s almost all countries actually increased unemployment replacement rates, arguably in response to the rising unemployment as we shall see from the case studies in the next chapter. However, in those countries with the most severe unemployment problems, there appears to be some tendency for the increases to be smaller. At the very least, the positive relationship between

**Table 6.2** *(continued)*

| | 1960–72 | | 1973–79 | | 1980–90 | | 1991–95 | |
|---|---|---|---|---|---|---|---|---|
| | $\beta$ | t | $\beta$ | t | $\beta$ | t | $\beta$ | t |
| *Public pension expenditure (% GDP per aged person)* | | | | | | | | |
| Social democratic rule | .52 | 2.0 | −.20 | −.7 | .20 | .7 | | |
| Christian democratic rule | .02 | .1 | −.24 | −1.0 | .08 | .3 | | |
| Unemployment | .02 | .1 | −.47 | −1.8 | −.15 | −.5 | | |
| Adjusted $R^2$ | .09 | | .06 | | −.14 | | | |
| N | 18 | | 18 | | 18 | | | |
| *Civilian nontransfer expenditure (% GDP)* | | | | | | | | |
| Social democratic rule | .69 | 2.8 | .64 | 2.5 | −.31 | −1.1 | .32 | 1.2 |
| Christian democratic rule | .05 | .2 | .02 | .1 | .07 | .3 | −.02 | −.1 |
| Unemployment | .37 | 1.6 | .18 | .7 | −.34 | −1.2 | −.03 | −.1 |
| Adjusted $R^2$ | .24 | | .19 | | −.06 | | −.10 | |
| N | 17 | | 17 | | 17 | | 17 | |
| *Civilian government employment (% working age population)* | | | | | | | | |
| Social democratic rule | .80 | 4.2 | .93 | 7.6 | .50 | 2.0 | −.19 | −.7 |
| Christian democratic rule | −.21 | −1.2 | −.19 | −1.7 | −.34 | −1.4 | .22 | .8 |
| Unemployment | .22 | 1.2 | .14 | 1.1 | .09 | .4 | −.26 | −1.0 |
| Adjusted $R^2$ | .58 | | .82 | | .22 | | −.07 | |
| N | 16 | | 16 | | 16 | | 16 | |
| *Public share of total health expenditure* | | | | | | | | |
| Social democratic rule | .37 | 1.5 | .33 | 1.1 | −.08 | −.3 | −.19 | −.7 |
| Christian democratic rule | .15 | .8 | −.30 | −1.3 | .08 | .3 | −.19 | −.8 |
| Unemployment | .08 | .4 | −.24 | −.9 | −.28 | −1.0 | −.27 | −1.2 |
| Initial level of public share | −.80 | −3.6 | −.09 | −.3 | −.25 | −.9 | −.39 | −1.5 |
| Adjusted $R^2$ | .36 | | .13 | | −.10 | | .22 | |
| N | 18 | | 18 | | 18 | | 18 | |

$\beta$: standardized coefficient

| Significance levels for $t$ | .05 | .1 |
|---|---|---|
| Two-tailed test | >2.2 | >1.8 |
| One-tailed test | >1.8 | >1.4 |

unemployment benefits and unemployment predicted by the comparative welfare state and economics literature disappeared.

By the 1980s, the negative relationship between unemployment and change in unemployment replacement rates became very strong. Many countries did begin to cut replacement rates in this period, so it is clear that the sheer magnitude of the budgetary outlay for benefits stimulated economizing measures and the governments either cut replacement rates or at least responded with smaller increases than were occurring in

**Table 6.3**    Determinants of Changes in Unemployment Replacement Rates by Period

| | 1961–73 | | 1974–79 | | 1980–91 | | 1992–95 | |
|---|---|---|---|---|---|---|---|---|
| | $\beta$ | $t$ | $\beta$ | $t$ | $\beta$ | $t$ | $\beta$ | $t$ |

Replacement Rate for Person with Average Wages

| | $\beta$ | $t$ | $\beta$ | $t$ | $\beta$ | $t$ | $\beta$ | $t$ |
|---|---|---|---|---|---|---|---|---|
| *Current cabinet share* | | | | | | | | |
| Social democratic rule | .17 | .6 | .15 | .5 | .03 | .1 | −.08 | −.3 |
| Christian democratic rule | .26 | .9 | .00 | .0 | .04 | .2 | .16 | .6 |
| Unemployment | .39 | 1.3 | −.21 | −.7 | −.70 | −3.0 | −.06 | −.2 |
| Adjusted $R^2$ | −.07 | | −.14 | | .37 | | −.19 | |
| | | | | | | | | |
| *Cumulative cabinet share* | | | | | | | | |
| Social democratic rule | .29 | 1.0 | .53 | 2.0 | −.19 | −.9 | −.33 | −1.2 |
| Christian democratic rule | .23 | .8 | −.01 | −.1 | .00 | .0 | .01 | .1 |
| Unemployment | .42 | 1.4 | −.05 | −.2 | −.77 | −3.6 | −.13 | −.5 |
| Adjusted $R^2$ | −.07 | | .14 | | .41 | | −.10 | |

Replacement Rate for Person with Two-Thirds Average Wages

| | $\beta$ | $t$ | $\beta$ | $t$ | $\beta$ | $t$ | $\beta$ | $t$ |
|---|---|---|---|---|---|---|---|---|
| *Current cabinet share* | | | | | | | | |
| Social democratic rule | .28 | 1.0 | .06 | .2 | −.03 | −.1 | −.01 | .0 |
| Christian democratic rule | .20 | .7 | −.04 | −.1 | .11 | .5 | −.05 | −.2 |
| Unemployment | .38 | 1.3 | −.24 | −.8 | −.67 | −2.7 | −.23 | −.8 |
| Adjusted $R^2$ | −.07 | | −.16 | | .28 | | −.19 | |
| | | | | | | | | |
| *Cumulative cabinet share* | | | | | | | | |
| Social democratic rule | .32 | 1.1 | .50 | 1.8 | −.25 | −1.1 | .08 | .3 |
| Christian democratic rule | −.19 | .6 | −.06 | −.3 | .08 | .4 | −.03 | −.1 |
| Unemployment | .40 | 1.3 | −.07 | −.3 | −.73 | −3.2 | −.21 | −.7 |
| Adjusted $R^2$ | −.08 | | .10 | | .33 | | −.18 | |

$N = 16$
$\beta$: standardized coefficient

| Significance levels for t values | .05 | .1 |
|---|---|---|
| Two-tailed test | >2.2 | >1.8 |
| One-tailed test | >1.8 | >1.4 |

other countries. Countries with average unemployment above 8 percent in 1980–90 that instituted cuts in replacement rates for persons with average wages were Denmark, Belgium, Ireland, and the U.K.; and all of the countries with large increases in benefits, Norway, Finland, and Switzerland, had comparatively low levels of unemployment. On the other hand, the Netherlands also had unemployment rates of over 8 percent yet increased replacement rates substantially; the United States had lower unemployment rates and cut anyway. Moreover, the cuts in the U.K. were sufficiently steep that a regression scatter plot reveals that these were not "explained" by the unemployment level. Nonetheless, one can generalize that cuts in unemployment replacement rates in the 1980s appear to be heavily unemployment driven, a point that we will elaborate with regard to other programs in the next chapter.

## Conclusion

Our data analyses in this chapter showed that the expansion phase of the welfare state extended well into the 1970s. Both expenditure and entitlement measures indicate continued improvements in benefits. By the 1980s, though, it is clear that changed economic conditions shifted the agenda to austerity. Expenditure growth shows a general decline in the 1980s, compared to both the Golden Age and the 1970s. At the same time, revenue grew faster than expenditure in this period. As our case studies in the next chapter will show, governments everywhere became very concerned about fiscal imbalances and attempted to deal with them through different combinations of expenditure cuts and tax increases.

The data show that the countries that experienced the earliest significant increases in unemployment are also the countries that began to implement some cuts in the late 1970s already and intensified these cuts in various programs in the 1980s. Denmark and the Netherlands began to cut pensions, the public share in health expenditure, and sick pay replacement rates in the period 1975 to 1980 and continued with cuts in the 1980s. Other countries, such as Germany and Australia, followed the pattern of significant increases in unemployment and welfare state cuts in the 1980s; Scandinavia's unemployment problems reached crisis proportions in the early 1990s, and significant cuts became visible in the 1990s. We interpret this pattern as indicating that welfare state cuts were by and large unemployment driven; they were a pragmatic response to greatly rising burdens on welfare state programs and declining contributions to these programs from the working population. There is one very clear exception to this pattern, the United Kingdom, and a second weaker one, the United States.[5] In both of these countries, one could say that cutbacks were ideologically driven. Rather than being forced to institute cuts by dire economic straits, the governments in these two countries took the initiative to reduce the role of the state in favor of the private sector. Thatcher pursued a very ambitious and comprehensive privatization program, and Reagan created the fiscal constraints through profligate tax cuts. The U.K. both shows the largest cuts and is the only country with declines in all time series measures of welfare state effort save one.

The exception to the general rule of resistance to cuts until unemployment pressures became severe is indicated by the decline in the public share of health expenditure that began in the 1970s and continued in the 1980s virtually everywhere. We hypothesize that this decline was a result of the universal trend of particularly rapidly rising costs of medical services, which greatly added to the general fiscal pressures on all welfare state programs. The cuts in the public share reflect not only general austerity policies but also governmental efforts to bring these rising costs under control by shifting more of the burden to patients and thus turning patients into more cost-conscious consumers.

A final distinctive pattern of cuts is visible in the unemployment replacement rates in the group of liberal welfare states. These replacement rates declined already in the period 1975–80, and they continued to decline in the 1980s and 1990s. These declines mirror the vigorous expansion of the low-wage sector in these societies and the need to create incentives for unemployed workers to accept lower-wage jobs.

Partisan effects on a whole array of welfare state indicators declined in the 1970s compared to the Golden Age, and they disappeared virtually entirely in the 1980s. The only variable that continued to show a strong partisan effect in the 1980s was civilian government employment, with a strong positive association with social democratic rule. Cusack and Garrett (1994) found a significant effect of left-labor power (a variable that combines indicators of cabinet composition, union density, and union centralization) during the 1980s on changes in government civilian consumption. This dependent variable was the only social policy indicator on which significant political effects appeared in their analysis. Cusack and Garrett (1994) interpret this finding to indicate that investments in human capital remained an important component of the social democratic model in the 1980s. Based on the public employment data and particularly the data on public social service employment as well as our case studies, we offer the following somewhat different interpretation. The relationships between social democratic governance and both government civilian consumption and public employment in the data are largely produced by the growth of public social services. The data presented above indicate that this has been largely a Scandinavian phenomenon, and this is confirmed by Cusack and Rein's (1991) data on public social service employment for a larger group of countries, including Austria and Finland, for 1985. In the absence of policies explicitly supporting traditional family patterns such as those found in Catholic countries, in Scandinavia a reinforcing cycle was introduced in which the full-employment policies of the Golden Age brought women into the labor force and this in turn led to demands for supportive services, such as day care, and supportive transfer programs, such as parental leave (Huber and Stephens 2000a). Once enacted, these policies in turn enabled more women to enter the labor force, which, again in turn, led to further demands for expansion of supportive policies and to more generalized demands for greater gender equality. This pattern was also reinforced by the greater reluctance of the Scandinavian countries to permit employers to recruit foreign labor, which was clearly a product of the influence of unions on the shaping of, and administration of, labor market policy.

The centrality of gender equality and mobilization of women into the labor force in the expansion of public social service employment can also be seen in the fact that the one area of social insurance that all four Nordic countries expanded vigorously in the 1980s was parental leave (Hagen 1992: 143–48). Indeed, this was even true of Denmark, despite the onset of the employment crisis in the mid-1970s and initiation of cuts in other welfare state programs. There is no doubt that these developments have resulted in a Scandinavian welfare state pattern of investment in youth and the working population and thus in human capital rather than expenditure on the aged, as in the case of the Continental welfare states. Consequently, while it does have the productivist profile that Cusack and Garrett's interpretation indicates, this was more an unintended by-product of labor recruitment and gender equality policies than an intentional part of a policy to promote international competitiveness.

Nevertheless, though our analysis does demonstrate strong partisan differences with regard to expansion of public social services, the overall pattern is one of a sharp narrowing of political differences in the 1980s. Our interpretation is that this was a result of a shift of the political agenda: Once it was realized that the game had fundamentally changed as a result of the sea changes in the world economy, governments found themselves with dramatically fewer options. Above all vigorous expansion of entitlements was off the agenda. This contributed to shifting the politics of social policy to defending entitlements.

CHAPTER SEVEN

◆

# The Politics of Welfare States
# after the Golden Age:
# A Comparative Historical Analysis

In the last chapter, our examination of cross-national data on a variety of indicators of welfare state effort demonstrated that the era of welfare state expansion came to a halt in the 1980s. Though the indicators of expenditure or revenue as a percentage of GDP continued to rise due to increases in the clientele population, our other data as well as the social rights data from the OECD and the SCIP project indicated that modest cutbacks were widespread and that in a few countries, most notably the U.K., substantial cutbacks were made.[1] Moreover, we saw that the very strong partisan effects on welfare state effort documented in chapter 3 declined significantly in the 1970s and then yet more in the 1980s and 1990s. The only strong partisan effects that continued were in the area of public employment, where social democratic governments continued to expand whereas public employment in countries with Christian democratic as well as secular center and right-wing governments remained stable.

Our task in this chapter is to examine the nature of these apparent rollbacks in more detail and to inquire into their causes. Are these cuts in welfare state expenditures and entitlements more or less marginal, designed to put existing schemes on a firm financial basis, or are they part of a radical overhaul and curtailment of existing schemes? Are some types of programs more vulnerable than others? Are there differences among welfare state regimes in the types of programs that are most vulnerable? What were the domestic and international causes of changes in the politics of social policy? Again, as in chapter 5, we will focus specifically on the countries where the left and/or organized labor had a strong influence on the development of the welfare state and where the system of social protection is (or was) generous; the Nordic countries, Germany, Austria, the Netherlands, Australia, and New Zealand. In addition, we will need to make occasional reference to the experience of countries with liberal welfare states, to explore differences in vulnerability of programs in different welfare state regimes.[2]

Given the close interaction between welfare state and production regimes, we will need to analyze to what extent developments in the international economy have stimulated changes in national production regimes. Has the power balance underpinning the production and welfare state regimes changed? Have national institutions of coordination and corporatist decision making changed, and if so, why? Have governments changed their policies to stimulate growth and full employment, and has the effectiveness of these policies changed? Before turning to a comparative analysis of our cases, we will begin with an extremely brief overview of major hypotheses that link the changes in the international economy and domestic social structures to changes in national production and welfare state regimes. We shall then critique a number of these hypotheses and develop our own arguments regarding these changes and their effects on the regimes.

## Changes in the International Economy and
## Domestic Social Structures and Their Effects

### Current Hypotheses on the
### Causes of Welfare State Retrenchment

There is little question that in recent decades the advanced political economies did go through a sea change that can be conveniently dated as beginning with the breakup of the Bretton Woods system of fixed but flexible exchange rates in 1971 and the OPEC oil price increase of 1973. The sea change was produced by these events combined with a series of long-term secular changes: increasing internationalization of trade, internationalization and multinationalization of production, internationalization and deregulation of financial, capital, and currency markets, the decline of the industrial and rise of the service sector, and the decline of Fordist assembly line, semiskilled manufacture and rise of "flexible specialization" and skill-differentiated manufacture. These trends have been hypothesized to have fundamentally changed national production and welfare state regimes.[3]

The most prominent factor held accountable for pressures on the welfare state in general political discourse as represented, for instance, in publications like *The Economist* or *The New York Times* is globalization.

Globalization in an economic sense has three major components: increases in international trade due to a lowering of tariffs, nontariff barriers, and transportation costs; internationalization of production due to the growth of transnational corporations (TNCs); and increases in international capital flows due to deregulation of capital markets and technological advances in communications. Increases in international trade have been held to have a direct effect on social policy as the social wage adds to total labor costs and thus presumably makes products from countries with high labor costs uncompetitive. Unless payroll taxes for social security contributions are cut to reduce labor costs, the loss of competitiveness will lead to higher unemployment. Greater trade openness also reduces the effectiveness of demand stimulation in recessions as increased demand is more likely to generate increased imports compared to a more closed economy where it would have stimulated more domestic production.

Internationalization of production is held to exert a downward pressure on tax revenue, as countries need to compete for investment by making concessions on payroll taxes and taxes on corporate profits. Lower tax revenue will force a lowering of social expenditures. Politically, internationalization of production has made the threat of exit more credible and thus has greatly strengthened the leverage of capital vis-à-vis both unions and governments. The final component of globalization, the deregulation of international and domestic capital markets, has deprived governments of traditional tools for economic policy making. The free flow of capital means that governments cannot simultaneously control the interest rate and the exchange rate. If a government resorts to countercyclical expansionary monetary and fiscal policy, it will suffer an outflow of capital and thus a downward pressure on the exchange rate. In a context of fixed exchange rates, expansionary fiscal policy will lead to a risk penalty on the interest rate.

Among other factors not directly related to globalization that have put pressure on welfare states, the overall decline of growth in output and productivity since the 1970s is important. This decline is hypothesized to reduce the room for maneuver in a variety of areas. Most obviously, it makes raising taxes for welfare state expenditures politically more difficult. As long as productivity and real wages are growing, tax increases are not necessarily experienced as a reduction in take-home pay; once the growth stops, they certainly are. In the European context, the criteria for membership in the European Monetary Union have imposed austerity and deflationary policies on all countries and thus have further contributed to slow growth and exerted pressures for a lowering of social expenditures.

In all advanced industrial democracies, the transition to post-Fordism is said to have increased the need for greater skill differentiation and wage dispersion and for greater flexibility at the firm level in order to facilitate the rapid adaptation to changing demand conditions (Swenson 1991; Pontusson and Swenson 1996). The trend toward skill and wage differentiation and flexibility at the firm level has put centrifugal pressures on centralized collective bargaining. To the extent that centralized bargaining was considered a condition for wage restraint, this undermined the capacity of unions and governments to deliver such restraint. The failure of wage restraint in turn would have to increase unemployment.

The sectoral shift in the composition of the economy, consisting in the decline in manufacturing with high productivity growth and the increase of the service sector with lower productivity growth, is held responsible in part for the overall lower growth, and also for greater conflict within labor movements because of a growing diversity of interests between white-collar and blue-collar workers and between the sheltered and exposed sectors. Finally, changing demographics are cited as a heavy pressure on the welfare state, particularly on pension systems. Greater longevity and lower fertility are causing increasing dependency ratios and thus require ever greater contributions of the economically active to welfare state schemes, or a reduction of entitlements.

### *Narrowing the Argument: Some Cross-National Evidence*

Whereas some of the hypotheses we just laid out are supported by evidence, others need to be made more complex, and still others can be rejected outright. Furthermore, we need to assess the relative importance of the different factors and explore whether there are additional factors that have contributed to the pressures on welfare state and production regimes over the past two decades. In order to assess the relative importance of the different factors, we need to identify the crucial mechanism that links them to efforts to reduce welfare state expenditures and cut entitlements. Since our argument runs counter to some common wisdom and our evidence is extracted from detailed case studies, for the purposes of clarity, we present the argument here and present some cross-national evidence supporting our point of view and then discuss the cases before reviewing argument and evidence again in the conclusion to this chapter.[4]

We argue that the timing and severity of cuts in welfare state entitlements were primarily driven by increases in unemployment.[5] An increase in unemployment makes any given set of entitlements more expensive and reduces the number of people contributing to welfare state financing through payroll taxes, thus intensifying fiscal pressures. However, there was nothing mechanical and immediate about the relationship between changes in unemployment and welfare state cutbacks. First of all, the severity of fiscal pressures resulting from rising unemployment depended on the structure of welfare states; the greater the extent to which welfare state financing was based on payroll taxes, the more immediate the impact of rising unemployment. Second, fiscal pressures could be treated as cyclical for varying amounts of time. The turning point toward serious efforts at cutting entitlements came when politicians began to perceive that they were confronting permanently higher unemployment levels that made changes in welfare state financing and benefits unavoidable. Identifying unemployment as the Achilles' heel of generous welfare states helps us assess the contributing causes of its problems.

To begin with the hypothesis about trade competition, one can certainly observe that over the long run, since World War II, labor-intensive production, from textiles, apparel, and toys to shipbuilding, has moved from advanced capitalist countries to NICs and LDCs. However, if we look at the past two decades, which are generally considered the main period of globalization, we see no dramatic increase in trade for the most advanced industrial societies (see table 7.1, pp. 228–29). Moreover, the generous welfare states of northern Europe were built in highly open economies with workers in exposed sectors serving as wage leaders, as the performance of the export sector was pivotal for the economic welfare of these countries. In fact, in the mid-1990s, export industries were doing very well in most of these countries, at the same time as governments were cutting social benefits (Huber and Stephens 1998; Pierson 2000b). Export industries in these countries specialize in high-quality-high-skill production and have been able to hold their niches in world markets; for instance, German industry's share in growing world markets over the past twenty years remained relatively constant (Manow and Seils 1999). As we argued elsewhere (Huber and Stephens 1998), having a high social wage is like having high money wages; whether an economy can afford it or not depends on its productivity. Saying that loss of export competitiveness was not the cause of welfare state retrenchment only refers to a direct economic constraint; politically, the issue lent itself to powerful rhetoric from business and the right and thus may very well have contributed to legitimizing cuts (Swank 1998). Since there was no dramatic increase in trade in the most advanced industrial countries over the past two decades, we can also partly discount the importance of its depressing effect on countercyclical demand stimulation. Such stimulation has indeed become more difficult, due not only to trade integration, but also to the internationalization of financial markets, to which we shall return shortly.

Turning to the presumed effects of internationalization of production, the first fact to note is that by far the largest amount of direct foreign investment flows to OECD countries, not to NICs or LDCs (Stallings 1995). In other words, motives other than the search for cheap labor govern these investments. One of the key motives has been access to markets; for instance, Swedish companies began to invest massively in EU countries in the in mid-1980s, when it was not yet clear that Sweden would join. Companies specializing in high-quality production need a highly skilled labor force and an excellent infrastructure, factors most likely to be present in high-wage countries. Many of them also depend on a cooperative relationship with their workforce to sustain productivity growth and thus could not easily relocate to a country with a more antagonistic tradition of labor relations. It is of course true that within the circle of these countries with coordinated market economies (CMEs) total labor costs cannot be too much out of line over a long period before some shifting of production is likely to occur. Thus, there was some reason for Germany to worry about the rise in its total labor costs in the 1990s in the wake of reunification. The same holds true for the argument about tax competition. Ceteris paribus, a lower corporate and individual tax level will attract more investment and highly qualified personnel, but all other factors are rarely the same. As in the case of the argument about trade integration, then, internationalization of production is less of a direct economic constraint on CMEs with generous welfare states than a rather significant political constraint. It is certainly true that globalization of production has strengthened capital politically vis-à-vis both unions and governments by making the threat of exit more credible and thereby has enabled business to extract concessions by arguing that a given country's business climate was noncompetitive.

The most detrimental aspect of globalization for the maintenance of generous welfare states has been the internationalization of capital markets and the increase in the volume of capital flows. As one can see from table 7.1, the changes in both the degree of capital controls and the volume of flows since the early 1970s has been dramatic. Indeed, by the early 1990s, almost all advanced industrial countries had eliminated controls on international capital movements. With open capital markets, governments cannot control both the exchange rate and the interest rate. Thus, countries that were dependent on domestic capital controls to deliver low (and below world market) interest rates to stimulate investment could continue to use such controls only if they were willing to take the consequences of a depreciating currency, the negative consequences of which

**Table 7.1** Selected Indicators of Economic Openness

| | (1) (2) Degree of Liberalization of Capital Controls | | (3) (4) Trade Openness | | (5) (6) Outward Direct Foreign Investment | | (7) (8) Borrowing on International Capital Markets | |
|---|---|---|---|---|---|---|---|---|
| | 1960–73 | 1990–94 | 1960–73 | 1990–94 | 1960–73 | 1990–94 | 1960–73 | 1990–94 |
| *Social democratic welfare states* | | | | | | | | |
| Sweden | 2.4 | 3.8 | 46 | 59 | 0.5 | 6 | 0.17 | 10.54 |
| Norway | 1.5 | 4 | 82 | 72 | 0.1 | 1.9 | 1.37 | 5.01 |
| Denmark | 3 | 4 | 60 | 65 | 0.2 | 1.6 | 1.01 | 3.91 |
| Finland | 1 | 3.5 | 45 | 54 | 0.2 | 1.5 | 0.92 | 9.63 |
| Mean | 1.98 | 3.83 | 58.3 | 62.5 | 0.25 | 2.75 | 0.87 | 7.27 |
| *Christian democratic welfare states* | | | | | | | | |
| Austria | 2.2 | 3.5 | 53 | 77 | 0.1 | 0.8 | 0.39 | 4.16 |
| Belgium | 3 | 4 | 77 | 138 | 0.3 | 3 | 0.35 | 2.77 |
| Netherlands | 3 | 4 | 92 | 99 | 1.3 | 6.6 | 0.41 | 4.01 |
| Germany | 4 | 4 | 40 | 62 | 0.3 | 1.2 | 0.05 | 1.85 |
| France | 2.9 | 3.6 | 27 | 44 | 0.2 | 1.9 | 0.09 | 2.69 |
| Italy | 2.9 | 3.6 | 31 | 39 | 0.3 | 0.7 | 0.42 | 1.91 |
| Switzerland | 3.9 | 4 | 61 | 69 | 0 | 4.4 | 0.06 | 2.21 |
| Mean | 3.13 | 3.81 | 54.4 | 75.4 | 0.36 | 2.66 | 0.25 | 2.80 |

**Table 7.1**  (continued)

| | (1) (2) Degree of Liberalization of Capital Controls | | (3) (4) Trade Openness | | (5) (6) Outward Direct Foreign Investment | | (7) (8) Borrowing on International Capital Markets | |
|---|---|---|---|---|---|---|---|---|
| | 1960–73 | 1990–94 | 1960–73 | 1990–94 | 1960–73 | 1990–94 | 1960–73 | 1990–94 |
| *Liberal welfare states* | | | | | | | | |
| Canada | 3.8 | 4 | 40 | 56 | 0.3 | 0.9 | 1.69 | 4.91 |
| Ireland | 2 | 3.3 | 78 | 119 | 0 | 0.7 | 0.73 | 7.15 |
| U.K. | 1.9 | 4 | 41 | 51 | 1.1 | 4.5 | 0.45 | 4.61 |
| U.S.A. | 3.7 | 4 | 10 | 22 | 0.6 | 1.4 | 0.1 | 1.81 |
| Mean | 2.84 | 3.83 | 42.3 | 62.0 | 0.50 | 1.88 | 0.74 | 4.62 |
| *Wage earner welfare states* | | | | | | | | |
| Australia | 2.3 | 3 | 30 | 37 | 0.2 | 0.9 | 0.35 | 3.7 |
| New Zealand | 1.5 | 3.5 | 46 | 58 | 0.1 | 6.5 | 0.67 | 4.12 |
| *Japan* | 2 | 2.8 | 20 | 18 | 0.2 | 0.7 | 0.09 | 1.46 |
| Grand mean | 2.61 | 3.70 | 48.8 | 63.3 | 0.33 | 2.51 | 0.52 | 4.25 |

Data sources: (1, 2) Quinn and Inclan 1997; (3, 4) Huber, Ragin, and Stephens 1997 from OECD; (5, 6) see table 3.1; (7, 8) Swank 1998 from OECD and IMF sources.

became increasingly apparent. Moreover, the increased internationalization of capital flows and dismantling of external capital controls also made it increasingly difficult to maintain the more interventive forms of domestic capital market regulation, the removal of which in turn made it more difficult to privilege business investors over other users of credit. Governments wishing to stimulate business investment directly were forced to resort to subsidies instead, which are not only more expensive but are also for the most part illegal in the EU and to a lesser extent under the rules of the Uruguay round of GATT.

The effect of capital market liberalization on the effectiveness of fiscal policy is rather more complicated than it is generally portrayed in the globalization literature. On the one hand, fiscal stimulation should be more effective in an open economy than in a closed economy, because in a closed economy, government borrowing will drive up interest rates and crowd out domestic investment. On the other hand, in an economy open to both financial flows and trade, the government either will have to cancel out fiscal stimulation with monetary austerity or will be faced with a depreciating currency, depending on the exchange rate policy. With fixed exchange rates, government deficits will drive up interest rates, thus counteracting the fiscal stimulation. With floating exchange rates, deficits will drive down the exchange rate, thus increasing domestic inflation, which, if not checked, can threaten to turn into a wage-price-devaluation spiral.[6]

One might assume that these two effects of increased financial openness might simply cancel each other out, but the wider international economic environment of the 1980s and 1990s arguably made fiscal stimulation more difficult than it was in the 1960s. As a result of the combination of deregulation, the accumulation of public debt since the 1970s and competition from non-OECD countries for investment funds (Rowthorn 1995), real interest rates have risen across the board (see table 7.2). Thus, deficit spending is costly. Moreover, the interest rate premium paid for deficit spending is particular high because budget deficits are among the most important indicators that investment managers take into account when they consider the purchase of government bonds. Based on interviews with financial market portfolio managers Mosley (1998: 14) finds that the most closely watched indicators are "a narrow set of 'big numbers' outcomes—the government deficit/GDP ratio, the rate of inflation, and (sometimes) the foreign exchange rate and government debt/GDP ratio. This set of aggregate indicators is assumed to capture default and inflation risks, and, therefore, to predict relative bond performance."

Thus, there is a kernel of truth to the thesis linking globalization to the current problems of the welfare state. However, many other factors

**Table 7.2** Real Long-Term Interest Rates

|  | 1960–73 | 1973–79 | 1979–89 | 1989–93 |
|---|---|---|---|---|
| *Social democratic welfare states* | | | | |
| Sweden | 1.4 | −1.1 | 3.8 | 5.4 |
| Norway | | −0.4 | 5 | 7.5 |
| Denmark | | | 7.1 | 6.6 |
| Finland | | −2.4 | 2.5 | 8.3 |
| Mean | 1.4 | −1.3 | 4.6 | 7.0 |
| *Christian democratic welfare states* | | | | |
| Austria | | | | |
| Belgium | 2.6 | 0.9 | 6 | 5.3 |
| Netherlands | 0.1 | 1.3 | 5.6 | 5.7 |
| Germany | 2.6 | 3.1 | 4.5 | 4.1 |
| France | 1.8 | −0.2 | 4.8 | 6.1 |
| Italy | 0.6 | −4.2 | 2.6 | 6.1 |
| Switzerland | −1.0 | 1.1 | 0.7 | 1.9 |
| Mean | 1.1 | 0.3 | 4.0 | 4.9 |
| *Liberal welfare states* | | | | |
| Canada | 2.6 | 0.0 | 5.7 | 7.1 |
| Ireland | | 0.1 | 4.4 | 7.9 |
| U.K. | | | 3.5 | 4.1 |
| U.S.A. | 1.5 | −0.6 | 5.1 | 4.4 |
| Mean | 2.1 | −0.2 | 4.7 | 5.9 |
| *Wage earner welfare states* | | | | |
| Australia | | −1.9 | 5.1 | 8.2 |
| New Zealand | 1.0 | −3.9 | 2.3 | 7.7 |
| *Japan* | | −0.1 | 4.6 | 4.0 |
| Grand mean | 1.3 | −0.6 | 4.3 | 5.9 |

Data source: OECD 1995b: 108.

have contributed to the dramatic rise in unemployment in the 1980s and 1990s, the proximate cause of most welfare state retrenchment. There is, of course, a huge unresolved controversy in economics and political economy on the causes of the post-1973 decline in growth and rise in unemployment in advanced capitalist democracies, and we cannot claim to resolve this debate and make any definitive statements here. Nevertheless, we would like to draw the readers' attention to those contributions in this debate that seem compelling theoretically and are consistent with our understanding of the cases. One could certainly begin with the contention that lower growth has contributed to lower employment. One key factor underlying the decline in growth is the decline in productivity growth, which in turn is certainly a product of a lower level of investment and the shift in sectoral composition of the economy (on the sectoral shift see Iversen 2000; Pierson 2000b; Maier 1985). Lower investment levels in turn are in part, probably in large part, a result of the greater cost of borrowing and the higher risk of investment in an increasingly open and volatile economic environment.

Many economists argue that capital stock has no impact on unemployment and inflation, and that the problem of job creation is to be solved through the stimulation of more employment on existing capital stock by making labor markets more flexible.[7] However, as Rowthorn (1995) argues forcefully, there are good theoretical reasons and strong empirical evidence linking the growth of capital stock to growth of employment. Rowthorn develops his argument within a nonaccelerating inflation rate of unemployment (NAIRU) framework and assumes no central coordination of wage and price setting. In his model, additional capital stock reduces the inflationary conflict over income distribution and thus allows the NAIRU to stabilize at a lower level. Growth in capital stock causes productivity growth, which in turn permits growth in real wages and reduces the saliency of the struggle over the share of labor versus capital income. His model works in the context of noncoordinated bargaining, and it is even more plausible that the labor market partners in a coordinated economy would take advantage of higher growth rates to opt for relative wage restraint in the interest of higher investment and employment levels. Empirical support for these arguments is provided by a regression analysis estimating the effects of growth in capital stock on unemployment in ten OECD countries in 1960–92, which shows a large statistically significant effect (Rowthorn 1995: 33–34).

Our own data show a fall of gross fixed capital formation from 24 percent of GDP in the 1960s to 21 percent of GDP in the 1980s (see table 5.1). Three important immediate causes of this decline in investment are a decline in the rate of profit on productive investment, a decline in net savings, and an increase in real interest rates discussed above (see table 7.2).[8] We would add the role of financial deregulation in restricting governments' use of policies to stimulate investment as a fourth reason. Our argument is supported by the fact that the coordinated market economies, most of which relied on some form of capital controls, experienced a significant decline in gross fixed capital formation from the 1960s through the 1980s, whereas the liberal market economies experienced no such decline. Nevertheless, as one can see from table 5.1, the level of gross fixed capital formation in the CMEs remained above that of the liberal market economies (LMEs).[9] In Germany, where capital controls were not a factor, financial internationalization has also had a negative effect on the traditional model of investment financing, in so far as the special long-term relationships between banks and corporations are becoming weaker (Streeck 1997; Seils and Manow 2000).

As to consequences of lower growth, it is certainly true that a faster-growing pie offers more opportunities for redistribution through taxation and welfare state expenditures, and for bargaining in which unions agree to wage restraint in exchange for employment growth. One might also hypothesize that lower growth meant lower employment growth and thus, ceteris paribus, higher unemployment. However, as Glyn (1995: 2) points out, it is not true that employment growth in the OECD was significantly faster in the period 1960–73 than in 1973–93;[10] the data show conclusively that observers who explain the current problem as one of "jobless growth" miss the mark completely. While this may be true of manufacturing, if anything the opposite is true of the economy as a whole: Given that average annual per capita growth was significantly lower in the post-1973 period (see table A.11), these economies were clearly producing more jobs for each percentage of growth than they were in the 1960s. As sectoral composition of the economy has shifted from the high-productivity growth manufacturing sector to the lower-productivity growth service sector, each percent of increase in growth results in a larger increase in employment precisely because of the greater labor intensity of services. While we would agree with the contention that the lower growth rates caused by the sectoral shift have had a direct impact on social policy because higher growth rates facilitate the simultaneous expansion of private and public consumption, the sectoral shift has not exerted pressures on the generous welfare states by causing increasing unemployment.

Since the growth of the working-age population is actually lower in the period after 1973 than before, it must be that rising participation rates explain part of the rise in unemployment. Glyn correctly observes that this goes far in helping us to explain the secular trend within countries, but is of more limited use in explaining the differences among countries. From table 5.2, we can see that in the earlier period the entry of women into the labor force was entirely offset by the exit of men from the labor force. Since this was an era of full employment, it is a good guess that the exit of men was almost entirely voluntary and due to the lengthening education and declining retirement ages. By contrast, in the more recent period, women have entered the labor force at double the rates that men have exited. Moreover, we know that in this period, a significant portion of the exit of men was involuntary as they were forced into early retirement by high unemployment. Part of the reason that Christian democratic welfare states experienced larger increases in unemployment than the liberal or social democratic welfare states is their inability to absorb the increasing entry of women into the labor force for the reasons pointed out in chapter 4. The small increase in women's labor force participation in Switzerland and Austria, which was counterbalanced by declines among men, helps explain why these two countries fared better in their unemployment rates than the other countries in this group. In the social democratic welfare states, the big increase in women's labor force participation occurred while these countries maintained close to full employment.

In the European context, conjunctural factors have depressed growth and aggravated unemployment beyond what had to be expected from the secular changes discussed above. In terming them "conjunctural developments," we don't mean to imply that these developments are necessarily cyclical and transitory; rather, we want to distinguish them from secular changes that are more or less impervious to political action. With regard to conjunctural elements of the present employment crisis in Europe, then, one can begin with the contribution of the debt buildup of the 1970s to the current high levels of interest rates noted above affecting all countries. With only two exceptions, the countries included in our quantitative analysis increased expenditure faster, in most cases much faster, than revenue in the 1970s and then did the reverse in the 1980s, but not enough to erase the debt, and in many cases not even the deficits, inherited from the 1970s. This legacy, plus the development of the EMS, the collapse of the Soviet Union, German reunification, the Maastricht accord, and the development of the EMU led, in sequence and in combination, to the extremely austere monetary and fiscal policy now prevalent in Europe (Hall 1998; Soskice 2000). The collapse of the Soviet Union and with it the Soviet economy sent a negative shock to all countries with exports to the Soviet Union, a shock that was a major blow to the Finnish economy and a minor one to a number of others. The budget deficits caused by German reunification stimulated an exceptionally austere response on the part of the Bundesbank, which was then communicated to the rest of Europe.[11] The convergence criteria contained in the Maastricht accord pressed further austerity on all member governments. Even those governments not committed to becoming EMU members, such as Sweden, and even those outside of the EU, such as Norway, were constrained by international capital markets to adhere to the austerity policies of the future EMU members. As our case studies will demonstrate, in the cases of Finland, Sweden, and to a lesser extent Norway, government policy mistakes strongly contributed to, and indeed may have created, the crisis.[12] The economic recovery of the Scandinavian countries in the second half of the 1990s supports the assessment that conjunctural factors and policy mistakes were important factors behind the crisis.

The effect of the change to post-Fordism on centralized or coordinated bargaining and the capacity of unions to deliver wage restraint has by no means been uniform. For instance, the system of collective bargaining underwent major changes in Sweden but virtually none in Austria. The pressures for change were strongest where centralized bargaining was linked to wage compression across skill levels, such as in Sweden, Norway, and Denmark. Essentially, efforts to use centralized bargaining to reduce wage differentials between skill levels had to be abandoned. However, only in Sweden did the employers association go as far as to disband its collective bargaining unit and withdraw its representatives from a number of tripartite consultative bodies. As we will explain below, this can be attributed to a combination of structural and historical factors peculiar to the country. More important from the point of view of the effects of abandoning centralized bargaining at the national level is the possibility that bargaining at the sectoral level might produce wage restraint as well in the presence of a strong independent monetary authority with a track record of nonaccommodating policy, so that the labor market partners bargain with expectations of very low inflation and with expectations that inflationary wage settlements will be punished by the monetary authority, as some authors argue (e.g., Iversen [1998]; Hall and Franzese [1998]). We doubt that such institutional arrangements per se can deliver wage restraint without some sort of central coordinating agency as in the Danish case, which we shall discuss below.

The argument that the sectoral shift to services means a lower capacity for increasing productivity in the economy as a whole has gained wide currency. Whereas we would agree that this sectoral shift certainly has contributed to a lowering of productivity growth compared to the Golden Age and that it will continue to have this effect for the near future, the argument has often been taken too far. What is obvious is that the service sector is very heterogeneous, ranging from hair styling, where options for productivity increases are definitely minimal, to business services, where technological advance has just as definitely been tremendous. Looking at public social services, it is not clear that productivity in some of these services could not be increased faster in the medium future due to technological developments.

Similarly, the simple hypothesis about the effect of changing demographics on the welfare state has to be made more complex. The most frequently cited figure for "demographic burden" is the ratio of the working age population to the aged population shown in the first three columns of table 7.3 (p. 238). However, since youth are also dependent on welfare state services, particularly education but also day care, the figures in the next three columns are also relevant for assessing demographic burden. While those figures certainly err in the opposite direction, understating the impact of demographic change on the welfare state, since the expenditure per aged person is certainly much higher than expenditure per young person, they are a useful corrective to the conventional figure. However, neither of the two dependency ratios measures the "supporting population" accurately since the divisor is all adults including the unemployed, disabled, early retirees, and those on social assistance, in labor market training, and in education and thus dependent on welfare state expenditure, along with those adults not in the labor force, mainly housewives, and thus not contributing taxes to the support of the welfare state. The total dependency ratio in the last three columns of the table (the employed population divided by the unemployed and inactive population of all ages) gives a more accurate picture of the ratio of welfare state dependents to welfare state supporters. These dependency ratios heavily depend on the total number of active labor force participants and thus on changes in labor market participation. There is wide variation across the welfare state groups both in present dependency ratios and past changes. If one compares this table and table 5.2, it is apparent that the present variation is heavily due to differential labor force participation rates of women. This suggests that in countries with low female labor force participation there are possibilities for improving dependency ratios over those now projected.

Here we need to introduce an additional causal dynamic that has put stress on many established pension systems, a change in the basic parameters on which pay-as-you-go (PAYGO) systems were built in the early post–World War II decades (Myles 1997; Myles and Pierson 2000b). Even if they were designed to include some buildup of pension funds, these systems were essentially generational transfers in which the current generation was taxed to pay for the pensions of the aged. In PAYGO systems entitlements are generally not determined directly by contributions to the system but by the level of earnings in all or certain best earning years and by the length of contributions and then indexed to the cost of living to guarantee the pensioner a given replacement rate. These are "defined benefit" systems. This design was quite rational from the point of view of both generations in an era in which real wage growth was high and the return on capital, particularly on government bonds or similar conservative instruments (which was the destiny of most public pension investment), was low by comparison. Each generation would benefit from rapidly rising wages and receive a higher pension than if the generation's contributions had been invested in bond markets and it had "paid for its own pension." The rise in real interest rates and decline in real wage growth that occurred after 1970 reversed this relationship. Now the PAYGO systems became problematic in the long term because real wages do not increase fast enough to cover the defined benefits of past generations. The increased rate of return on capital made it seemingly more attractive for each generation to pay for its own pensions by investing contributions in capital markets, even in quite conservative and secure investments.

Finally, a rarely cited but certainly important reason for the slowing of the expansion of the most generous welfare states, such as the Dutch or Scandinavian ones, is that they had "grown to limits," to borrow the title of Flora's (1986) comparative study. These welfare states were comprehensive, covering all major program areas, and in each program coverage was universal or near universal, replacement rates in transfer programs were very high, and, in the case of the Scandinavian countries, publicly provided services enjoyed a near monopoly in their sector. As a result, tax burdens were very high and thus the room to increase taxation limited. However, it is worth pointing out here that it is not clear to what extent this growth to limits constitutes an absolute economic constraint, or to what extent it constitutes a politically formed perception and thus is susceptible to modification.

In the arguments laid out above, there is a straightforward connection between the developments outlined and welfare state retrenchment or, at least, slowed expansion. These same developments have been hypothesized to reduce partisan differences in governmental policy because they constrain the policy latitude of any government. We showed in the last chapter that partisan differences indeed did decline. The literature on the question of partisan differences in the current era contains a number of nuanced distinctions. The most common position assumes that the agenda of parties of the left will be most constrained because it involves substituting "politics for markets" while these trends, especially internationalization of the economies, push in the opposite direction. By contrast, Garrett and Lange (1991) argued that, while there has been a

**Table 7.3** Ratios of Active to Dependent Populations

| | Working-Age Population per Elderly Person | | | Working-Age Population per Dependent Person | | | Ratio of Working Population to Nonworking Population | | |
|---|---|---|---|---|---|---|---|---|---|
| | 1960 | 1990 | 2020 | 1960 | 1990 | 2020 | 1960 | 1980 | 1989 |
| *Social democratic welfare states* | | | | | | | | | |
| Sweden | 5.5 | 3.6 | 3.0 | 1.9 | 1.8 | 1.6 | .92 | 1.04 | 1.11 |
| Norway | 5.7 | 4.0 | 3.6 | 1.7 | 1.8 | 1.7 | .67 | .88 | .94 |
| Denmark | 6.0 | 4.3 | 3.3 | 1.8 | 2.1 | 1.8 | .81 | .95 | 1.06 |
| Finland | 8.5 | 5.0 | 2.9 | 1.7 | 2.1 | 1.7 | .92 | .97 | 1.01 |
| Mean | 6.4 | 4.2 | 3.2 | 1.8 | 2.0 | 1.7 | .83 | .96 | 1.03 |
| *Christian democratic welfare states* | | | | | | | | | |
| Austria | 5.4 | 4.5 | 3.3 | 1.9 | 2.1 | 2.0 | .87 | .69 | .78 |
| Belgium | 5.2 | 4.5 | 3.1 | 1.8 | 2.0 | 1.8 | .64 | .61 | .61 |
| Netherlands | 6.8 | 5.4 | 3.2 | 1.6 | 2.2 | 1.8 | .57 | .56 | .71 |
| Germany | 5.8 | 4.6 | 3.3 | 2.1 | 2.2 | 2.0 | .89 | .78 | .81 |
| France | 5.3 | 4.7 | 3.0 | 1.6 | 1.9 | 1.7 | .76 | .68 | .65 |
| Italy | 7.0 | 4.7 | 2.7 | 1.9 | 2.2 | 1.8 | .74 | .60 | .60 |
| Switzerland | 6.2 | 4.5 | 3.2 | 1.8 | 2.0 | 1.8 | 1.00 | .98 | 1.10 |
| Mean | 6.0 | 4.7 | 3.1 | 1.8 | 2.1 | 1.8 | .78 | .70 | .75 |

**Table 7.3** (continued)

| | Working-Age Population per Elderly Person | | | Working-Age Population per Dependent Person | | | Ratio of Working Population to Nonworking Population | | |
|---|---|---|---|---|---|---|---|---|---|
| | 1960 | 1990 | 2020 | 1960 | 1990 | 2020 | 1960 | 1980 | 1989 |
| *Liberal welfare states* | | | | | | | | | |
| Canada | 7.7 | 5.9 | 3.1 | 1.4 | 2.1 | 1.8 | .53 | .81 | .92 |
| Ireland | 5.2 | 5.4 | 4.0 | 1.4 | 1.6 | 1.8 | .59 | .51 | .45 |
| U.K. | 5.5 | 4.2 | 3.5 | 1.9 | 1.8 | 1.8 | .86 | .82 | .88 |
| U.S.A. | 6.5 | 5.3 | 3.6 | 1.5 | 1.9 | 1.8 | .61 | .80 | .93 |
| Mean | 6.2 | 5.2 | 3.6 | 1.6 | 1.9 | 1.8 | .65 | .74 | .80 |
| *Wage earner welfare states* | | | | | | | | | |
| Australia | 7.2 | 6.0 | 3.7 | 1.6 | 2.0 | 1.9 | .66 | .76 | .86 |
| New Zealand | 9.0 | 5.8 | 4.1 | 1.4 | 1.9 | 1.9 | .58 | .68 | .78 |
| *Japan* | 11.2 | 5.8 | | 1.8 | 2.3 | | .91 | .90 | .99 |
| Grand mean | 6.7 | 4.9 | 3.3 | 1.7 | 2.0 | 1.8 | .75 | .78 | .84 |

Data source: OECD 1994a: 100, supplemented by calculations by the authors based on UN 1996.

narrowing of macroeconomic policy choices, there are still marked partisan differences in social expenditure policies. The overall policy agenda has moved to the right, but there are still significant partisan differences. Others have suggested that the multiclass Christian democratic parties find it less difficult to abandon Keynesian full employment welfare state policies than the working class–trade union based social democratic parties. In this case, one might hypothesize continued partisan differences.

We have argued (Huber and Stephens 1993b; Stephens 1996), as has Pierson (1996), that the politics of welfare state retrenchment are different from those of welfare state expansion. Once instituted, social policies develop support bases in addition to those groups that supported their original enactment.[13] The broad social coalitions supporting the welfare state status quo prevent centrist and even right-wing parties from implementing, or even advocating, significant cuts in entitlements. Thus, to the extent that economic difficulties mean the agenda in most countries is not expansion but rather retrenchment, one should expect narrower partisan differences than in the past. The narrowing of differences is a result of constraints both on the right and the left.

The effect of the increasing international constraints outlined above is mediated in part by ideology or, more narrowly, beliefs about which policies can achieve a given goal under present conditions. These beliefs could of course be wrong, or at least alternative policies that do not involve retrenchment might be equally effective. Given this importance of beliefs about the consequences of different policies, one must assume that the rise in the international hegemony of neoliberal economics contributed to the tendency of retrenchment in state expenditures and direct involvement in social policy and to a decline in partisan differences. Moreover, since the neoliberal view of the world is highly congruent with the interests of capital, its rise to hegemony has further strengthened the leverage that capital has been gaining from globalization vis-à-vis governments and unions, by way of legitimizing the claims of capitalists regarding constraints on social policy in the eyes of the mass public.

A final point of complexity needs to be raised in this introductory discussion. Not all adjustments to social policy of the past two decades, even quite dramatic ones, involve "retrenchment." In many cases, we will find that new conditions made the old policies unviable and they were changed as a result. These changes usually involved reductions of benefits, increases in qualifying condition, and/or increases in taxes or contributions. If the solution to the problem is only an increase in taxes or contribution and these are levied in a fashion that does not make the system less redistributive across class and gender, then we will term the change a "reform" or "adjustment" and not a "cutback" or "retrench-ment." The latter terms will be reserved for cuts in benefits or changes in benefit structures or taxes that make the system less redistributive. Gen-erally, increases in qualifying conditions also indicate "cutback" or "re-trenchment," but there are ambiguities here. For instance, an increase in the number of years of contributions required to acquire a full pension is, in principle, no different from an increase in the rate of contributions and thus might reasonably be equated with a tax increase. We shall now turn to a comparative examination of such adjustments and cutbacks and their causes in our nine cases.

## The Nordic Social Democratic Welfare States

### Sweden

As in the other Scandinavian countries, Swedish governments initially treated the new economic era as if it were a temporary downturn.[14] Thus, the Social Democratic government reacted with countercyclical mea-sures. As the difficulties wore on, the series of bourgeois coalition gov-ernments, which took power in 1976, introduced a combination of re-strictive and expansive measures that Mjøset (1986) characterizes as "fumbling." These governments were eager to defend employment levels and welfare state entitlements to prove Social Democratic propaganda against them to be incorrect. While no major social policy innovations were passed, neither were there any significant rollbacks. To fight unem-ployment, the governments subsidized some industries and took over failing ones. As a result, unprecedented budget deficits mounted. In part in reaction to the deficits, but also as a result of a neoliberal turn on the part of the conservatives and the aggressive neoliberal posture of SAF, the government began to introduce some very modest entitlement re-ductions in 1980, such as reducing compensation for part-time pensions and introducing one waiting day for sick pay (Marklund 1988).

That the sick pay waiting day became a major issue in the 1982 election that brought the Social Democrats back to power indicates both the wide-spread support for the welfare state in Sweden and also the new regime's policy mandate. The new government knew that it faced a changed world and new policies would be necessary. Before entering office, leading So-cial Democratic economic analysts had come to the conclusion that it was impossible to expand public expenditure as a percentage of GDP. Thus, any reforms would have to be financed by other cuts in public spending,

public sector efficiency gains, or GDP growth (Feldt 1991). In office, the
Social Democrats not only cut spending as a percentage of GDP (while,
remarkably, actually introducing some new reforms), but also cut state intervention in the economy in other ways, notably deregulating financial
markets in 1985–86, directing all state enterprises to make profitability
their only goal, partially privatizing some state enterprises, and introducing market principles in public sector service provision.[15]

There is no doubt that some of these policies followed the preferences
of Finance Minister Feldt and his advisors, whose neoliberal (at least, neoliberal within the context of Swedish Social Democracy) bent went further than many in the labor movement, above all the LO leadership and
the LO economists, would have gone had they controlled policy. However, with regard to the size of the welfare state, there was agreement.
Prior to the 1986 LO conference, a group of LO policy experts (who
would hardly count among Feldt's allies) issued a report that argued that
it was not necessary for the welfare state to grow as a percentage of GDP
in order for it to achieve its goals (security, equality, etc.). In part, this report simply stated that the Swedish welfare state was fully developed: it
was already comprehensive, coverage was universal or near universal in
all programs, and replacement rates were very high. Putting the LO report and the Feldt group's assessment together, one can say that, seen in
comparison with earlier periods, the promoters of the welfare state in
Sweden had less to do but, because taxes and expenditure had reached
close to saturation level, they had less to do it with.

While still in opposition, the Social Democrats supported a tax reform, proposed by the Center-Liberal government, that lowered marginal rates in the middle and higher brackets. This prefigured the
1989–90 "tax reform of the century," in which the Social Democratic government in cooperation with the Liberals reduced the rates of marginal
taxation for those in higher income brackets, cutting them to 50 percent,
apparently turning its back on redistribution and accepting bourgeois
arguments about the relationship between marginal taxation and work
motivation.[16]

The "Third Road" (between Keynesian reflation as pursued by the
French Socialist government in its early months in office and Thatcherite
austerity policies) pursued by the Social Democrats during their tenure
in office was a response to these developments. By devaluing the
Swedish krona by 16 percent, on top of a devaluation of 10 percent the
previous year, the Social Democratic government created a substantial
competitive edge for Swedish industry. They followed this up by secur-
ing wage restraint from the unions and cutting the deficit, and so on,

as mentioned above (thus restraining consumption), creating a profits boom and a redistribution of income from labor to capital. Aided by the turnaround in the international economy, the policy appeared very successful as the economy picked up and unemployment and deficits fell. Based on this performance, the Social Democrats won the 1985 election and by the 1988 election, the Third Road seemed wildly successful: The budget deficits, which had been 8 percent of GDP when the Social Democrats had come into office, had been eliminated; unemployment was under 2 percent; the balance of trade was in surplus; and new social reforms had been passed. The expansion of gender-egalitarian policies was a key area of innovation in this decade as parental leave was extended to nine months, public day care and preschool were expanded, and paid absence to care for ill children expanded from twelve to sixty days (Bergqvist 1998; Hagen 1992). The women's movement within the Social Democratic Party was a pivotal force behind these changes and in this period women's presence in the Social Democratic Party was increased, eventually achieving parity with men. With these successes as a base, the Social Democrats campaigned in 1988 on promises of a new round of social reforms: the introduction of a sixth week of vacation (the favored reform of the unions) and extension of parental leave insurance from nine to fifteen months and provision of public day care places for all preschool children over the age of one and a half (favored by the women's movement).

Within a year of their reelection, the bubble burst. In the face of the economic crisis that the government encountered during its period in office, it failed to deliver on any of these promises. In response to the sharp deterioration of the economy, the government introduced an austerity package in February 1990 that called for a pay freeze and a strike ban, reversing its commitment to noninterference in relations between unions and employers. Though the government fell due to lack of parliamentary support for the package, it reconstituted itself, and two months later, with Liberal support, it passed a similar austerity package (though without the offensive labor market features) that among other things reduced the replacement rate for sick pay from 90 percent to 65 percent for the first three days and to 80 percent for days four through ninety. In the fall of 1990, the Social Democrats reversed their stand on the EC, now favoring membership, joining the Liberals and Conservatives, who had long held this position.

Given that Swedish Social Democrats' electoral success had been largely built on the public perception that they possessed a unique capacity simultaneously to institute social reforms and manage the economy effectively, it is not so surprising that their apparent failure to do either resulted in the 1991 election in their worst defeat since 1928. The economy continued to worsen under the Conservative-led minority bourgeois coalition. Open unemployment increased from 1.6 percent in 1990 to 8.2 percent in 1993; counting those in active labor market measures the increase was from 2.1 percent to 12.5 percent (OECD 1994b: 36). GDP growth was negative in 1991, 1992, and 1993. The government, with the support of the Social Democrats, was initially committed to defending the value of the krona, which had been fixed since the 1982 devaluation. During the European currency turbulence of the fall of 1992, the government and Social Democrats went to extraordinary lengths to defend the krona, agreeing to two "crisis packages": austerity measures that included significant reductions in entitlements, such as a cut in the sick pay replacement rate, the introduction of a waiting day for sick pay, and the reduction of pensions. In the end, the measures were unsuccessful and the krona was floated. Though the decision to float meant that the basis for the agreement was now absent, it was clear that all political actors regarded the economic situation as a crisis and agreed that cuts in entitlements would be necessary. What made these cuts necessary was the widespread conviction that Sweden would not be able to return to anywhere near the 2 percent open unemployment (with no more than an additional 1 percent in labor market measures) in the foreseeable future. The fact that the new policy of self-financing of the unemployment insurance system assumed a normal rate of unemployment of 5 percent shows that policy was being made on this assumption as early as 1993.[17] Thus, though the budget was in surplus in 1989 before the social benefits cuts of the early 1990s, it was assumed to be in structural (and not just cyclical) deficit when the bourgeois government left office.

Before outlining the changes instituted in response to the crisis and further changes in the Swedish welfare state, it is important to point out that a number of reforms were already planned prior to the crisis. Three are worth mentioning here.[18] First, the earnings-related tier of the pension system (ATP) faced a future crisis due to demographic changes that will occur with the retirement of the baby boom generation and due to the shift in wage developments relative to the return on capital. ATP was only partially funded; fundamentally it involved a generational transfer. Moreover, as in PAYGO pension systems in other countries, entitlements were not determined directly by contributions to the system but by a combination of best years of earnings and length of contributions and then indexed to the cost of living. In Sweden as elsewhere, the decline in the wage and productivity growth invalidated the calculations on which the system was based.

Sweden's old system combined a flat-rate citizenship pension, a partially funded earnings-related defined-benefit PAYGO plan (the ATP plan discussed in chapter 5), and a supplement for those who had accumulated few pension rights in the earnings-related plan.[19] The new system expanded the funded component by introducing fully funded individual accounts. It combines (1) an earnings-related notional defined-contribution PAYGO plan, (2) a defined-contribution fully funded individual accounts system with centralized administration, and (3) a pension-tested supplement for retirees with few pension rights in the earnings related plans. The notional defined-benefit PAYGO component is the biggest innovation in the new system. A retiree's pension from this system is calculated on the basis of total lifetime contributions, the rate of wage growth, and average life expectancy in the population at the time of retirement of the individual. It is more resilient to demographic or wage growth changes than a defined-benefit system because of the adjustments for wage growth and average life expectancy of the population. The whole system is expected to yield approximately the same replacement rate as the old system at presently forecast levels of wage growth and life expectancy though, of course, the benefits deriving from the funded portion will depend on the performance of the investment.

Since the plan that emerged would have to hold for long periods of time, all of the parties in the parliamentary committee working on the plan committed themselves to working out a broad compromise. A quickly agreed-upon baseline was that, in the new system, each generation would have to pay for its own pensions. A full pension would be based on forty years of contributions with no special consideration for best earning years; benefits are to be based on lifetime income. In a fundamental change of principle, the new system will be one of defined contribution not defined benefit. Also in contrast to the previous system, which was financed by an employer tax, the new system will be funded by equal contributions of employers and employees: each will contribute 9.25 percent of the payroll. As compared to the ATP system, this basic design benefits full-time, full–life cycle (read male) manual workers. It was immediately recognized that women and to a lesser extent workers with higher education would be disadvantaged by the system and that adjustments had to be made. Therefore, the bill agreed upon in principle in 1994 by the governing parties and the Social Democrats and finally implemented in 1999 provided for extra pension points for child care and studies, as well as compulsory military service. Some redistribution is built into the system as there is a benefits threshold (indexed to real economic growth) above which contributions would be paid half the rate of the payments below.

Second, the rapidly rising costs of both sick pay and work injury insurance had already evoked considerable concern by the late 1980s. In the case of work injury insurance, court decisions in the early 1980s liberalized qualifying conditions, which led to rapid increases in the number of claims and the costs without compensating adjustments in financing. The abolition of the waiting day for sick pay and improved compensation was accompanied by increased absenteeism and increased costs (though, interestingly, the increase in absenteeism was greatest among the long-term ill, whose benefits were not changed). Before the emergence of the employment crisis, some reform of these systems was imminent, in the direction of the "work line" that emerged from the Working Environment Commission of the late 1980s as a possible way to economize while maintaining generous benefits. According to this view, the costs of work injury insurance and early pensions and, by extension, sick pay could be reduced by rehabilitation and other efforts to keep people in the workforce. One approach to this would be to provide workers with the proper incentives to keep working (and employers with the proper incentives to keep people working) rather than resorting to social insurance. For instance, shifting the cost of work injury insurance, sick pay, and early pensions to employers with high incidences of work-related injuries and sicknesses would provide an incentive for them to improve the working environment.

Third, in the course of the 1980s, the delivery of public services came under fire. Consumers of social services increasingly expressed dissatisfaction with the delivery of welfare state services in general. Specifically, a significant number of citizens in their roles as clients, patients, and parents felt that they had no choice as to which types of service to obtain and where to obtain them. Local government and the service providers themselves made decisions about locating service centers, about opening hours, etc. This left many consumers with a feeling that they could have little or no influence on the delivery of these services. Large sectors of the population came to perceive the providers of welfare state services as distant bureaucrats and their agents, rather than human beings caring about the welfare of those in need of the services they were charged with providing. In addition, with the budget constraints politicians became increasingly concerned with the cost of all public services, including welfare services.

The Conservative answer was to promote privatization and competition in order to improve the quality of delivery of services and reduce their cost, while the Center Party promoted decentralization. The Social Democrats in general, and party leader Palme in particular, attributed the electoral losses of the 1970s in part to the issue of an unresponsive and distant public bureaucracy (Feldt 1991), and they were eager to address the issue once they returned to office in 1982. After some false starts, the government settled on a program of action that emphasized decentralization of authority in the delivery of services to lower levels of government and introduction of market models in the public service, such as payment by output (Olsson 1990; Rothstein 1992).

Initially, the Social Democrats resisted any movement toward the privatization of public services, especially welfare services. For the first time in a very long time, the bourgeois parties won a debate on basic principles of future development of the welfare state, that is, that private alternatives should in principle be allowed to compete with public providers of services.[20] Let us be clear here: Swedes favor allowing choice between public and private providers. They do not think that private providers would necessarily be better. On the contrary, in the case of every major service except child care, very large majorities believe "state or local authorities" are "best suited" to deliver the service in question; even in the case of child care, a plurality thinks state and local authorities are best suited, followed by the family (Svallfors 1991, 1992).

The Social Democrats have come to accept the option of private providers competing with the state, albeit within the parameters of state regulation and financing, but the extent of the private role is still a point of controversy within the party. The Conservatives on their part have backed off from their neoliberal ideal of privatization and deregulation and come to accept the need for continued state regulation. Nevertheless, subtle but important differences remain with regard to the importance attributed to the goal of equality for the recipients of services. Many Conservatives favor allowing private individuals and families to pay extra for services, whereas the Social Democrats are firmly opposed to this on the grounds that this would create a system of two (or more) classes of services. Furthermore, the Social Democrats and most Liberals insist that any private alternatives must avoid the problems of selectivity and social dumping. For instance, they oppose admissions tests by schools that could lead to a situation where private schools admit only good students and students with any kind of learning or behavioral problems would be dumped on public schools.

Three important changes in service delivery have been introduced so far. First, in education, the bourgeois government introduced a voucher system under which parents can choose any public or private school. For those choosing a private school, the government will provide a voucher equivalent to 85 percent of the cost of educating a student in a public school. Schools are not allowed to charge fees beyond the amount provided by the vouchers. Second, the option for private providers to offer day care under the same conditions as public providers was also introduced. Third, a so-called house doctor system was introduced that, by allowing individuals to freely choose their own doctor, expanded the possibilities for private practice. As of the mid-1990s, it cannot be said that private providers have assumed a major role in any of these areas. In 1995, almost one in eight day care places were in nonmunicipal facilities, most of them in worker or parent cooperatives (Pestoff 1998: 174–75), while only 8 percent of health care and 1.5 percent of schooling were provided by private producers.[21] But, regardless of the political coloring of the national government, it does seem relatively clear that the long-term trend will be toward more variation in the delivery of publicly financed social services with private entrepreneurs, consumer cooperatives, and producer cooperatives competing with the communes and regions. This seems likely in part because the responsibility for making decisions about the delivery of services is in the hands of the communes and regions, which are often governed by different party coalitions than the national government, and in part by the movement of the Social Democrats to a more favorable view of alternative providers. By late 1998, Prime Minister Persson, several other leading politicians, and even union leaders in the communal workers union, traditionally the center of resistance to such moves, were advocating private and cooperative alternatives within health care with the proviso that this be done within the frame of "solidaristic" financing (*Dagens Nyheter,* www.dn.se, November 16, 1998).

The bourgeois government elected in 1991 implemented a number of cuts in social benefits, most of them with Social Democratic support.[22] Early retirement pensions will no longer be given due to slack labor markets. Sick pay was reduced to 80 percent after ninety days. Pensions were adjusted downward to 2 percent below the base amount; that is, the basic pension would now be 98 percent of the base amount. Industrial injury insurance was coordinated with sick pay, which entailed a reduction of the replacement rate. Qualifying conditions were sharpened for both benefits. Employers must now pay for the first two weeks of sick pay.

Since this was accompanied by a corresponding decrease in employer contributions to the system (and thus no savings for the government), this move was primarily designed to reduce absenteeism by increasing employer surveillance of employees' claims. A five-day waiting period for unemployment benefits, which was eliminated by the Social Democratic government of the 1980s, was reintroduced and replacement rates were reduced to 80 percent. As in the case of the new supplementary pension system, employees will now make contributions to the sick pay insurance scheme. While the Social Democrats opposed the changes in the unemployment system and many of the changes in the work injury system, once in government, they lowered the replacement rate for parental insurance from 90 percent to 80 percent to make it consistent with the unemployment compensation, sick pay, and work injury insurance. Subsequently, in a deal with the Center Party in 1995, they lowered replacement rates to 75 percent, only to raise them again to 80 percent in response to protests from the unions and falling support in opinion polls. As part of their efforts to cut the budget deficit, the Social Democrats also introduced employee contributions to social insurance in some programs and increased them in others.

The cuts in replacement rates and increases in qualifying conditions in the sick pay, work injury, and unemployment insurance systems were accompanied by increased spending on active labor market policies. The Social Democratic government directed yet more resources to the development of human capital, including active labor market policy, adult education, and higher education to raise the skill level of the workforce and to increase employment. Thus, taken as a package, these reforms can be seen as an effort to follow the work line mentioned in chapter 5. However, the emphasis has changed from the original formulation. In that version, employees were to be provided with increased training and rehabilitation and other positive incentives to remain in the active workforce, while employers were to be provided both carrots and sticks to reduce absenteeism and work injury. The policies passed in the past few years contain a lot of sticks along with a few carrots for employees; they entail modest steps toward an increase of the market incentive to remain employed and, when employed, to stay at work—steps toward recommodification of the Swedish welfare state. Clearly, the change in emphasis was in large part motivated by the savings that the cuts entailed and thus can be directly connected to the economic crisis and rise in unemployment and the resultant huge increase in the government budget deficit.

The sequencing of events offers compelling evidence that the rollbacks in the Swedish welfare state in the early 1990s were a product of the rise in unemployment and the belief that unemployment will not return to its previous levels. The argument that entitlements per se make Swedish industry uncompetitive is untenable particularly after the float of the krona, which reduced Swedish wage costs by one quarter in a year. In 1994, Swedish export industry had a banner year with most enterprises reporting record profits, and continued to perform at a high level through 1999. However, with unemployment still high and the budgets in deep deficit, the Social Democratic government elected in 1994 continued the cuts in entitlements and services begun by the bourgeois government, and it raised taxes. Only when the combination of tax increases, budget cuts, and the recovery of domestic demand and the consequent fall in unemployment brought the budget into surplus late in the government's term in office, did reversal of some of the entitlement cuts come back on the agenda

This turns our attention to the causes of the problems of the production regime in the post–Golden Age era. The problems faced by social democracy in Sweden were products of the structural changes in the advanced industrial economies sketched at the beginning of this chapter and a series of policy mistakes.[23] As Moses points out in his comparison of Norway and Sweden (1994), the current era is one of financial *and* trade openness in contrast to the interwar period (in which trade was regulated) and the postwar Golden Age (in which financial flows were regulated). Thus, neither capital controls nor trade regulations (tariffs, quotas, etc.) can be deployed to defend the external balance leaving governments one tool shorter than in these two earlier periods.

The internationalization of Swedish business and of financial markets led to a successive deregulation of Swedish financial markets, beginning under the bourgeois government of 1976–82 and completed by the Social Democrats in the 1980s. This deregulation of capital flows made it impossible for the Swedish government to control both the interest and the exchange rate. Thus, this deregulation along with the increase in international interest rates led to real interest rates in the 1980s that were two and a half times as great as those of the Golden Age (see table 7.2). The subsequent deregulation of domestic capital markets made it more difficult to privilege productive investment over other uses of capital, such as real estate speculation or consumption. Active labor market policy was increasingly the sole tool the government could rely on.

The development of Swedish industry had broader ramifications for the Swedish production and welfare state regimes as it changed the interests of capital and the balance of power between labor and capital. Because of increasing export orientation, multinationalization, decreasing dependence on Swedish raw materials, and increasing reliance on self-financing of investment, Swedish business became markedly less interested in a compromise with domestic labor which entailed an increase or just maintenance of domestic consumption, more interested in lowering wage costs, more concerned about competition for labor with the growing public sector, and more concerned about access to foreign markets. These developments along with the reaction to the labor offensive on codetermination and wage earner investment funds were the roots of the new political offensive beginning in the late 1970s of the employers' federation, SAF, and other business organizations, criticizing the welfare state and advocating privatization, deregulation and EC membership (Pestoff 1991; Pontusson 1992a).

The decline of centralized bargaining, a central feature of the Golden Age model, has been dramatic in Sweden. VF, the organization of export-oriented engineering employers, met with its first success in its drive to decentralize the bargaining process in 1983, when it convinced the important metal workers' union to sign a separate agreement. This was followed by renewed centralization but with supplementary bargaining at lower levels carried out with the threat of industrial action, in contrast to past practice. In 1990, SAF, as a result of the initiative of VF, appeared to have dealt a death blow to centralized bargaining when it disbanded its bargaining unit, but this was followed by a wage round in which a government-appointed commission successfully concerted a centralized agreement, which was later extended to 1995. The following bargaining round was again decentralized, as was the 1998 round, despite LO efforts to coordinate union demands.

The changes in occupational structure and union structure help explain the unions' weakened ability to resist decentralization. Segmentation of the labor market as a result of the decline of industry, growth of services, and growth of white-collar employment has fragmented labor interests and led to difficulties in coordinating labor demands (e.g., see Hernes 1991; Kjellberg 1992). In Sweden and in Norway, the Golden Age wage bargaining model (the EFO or Aukrust model) called for export industry to set wages in line with the country's competitors and then for other sectors of the economy (domestic industry, the public sector, etc.) to follow suit. This was easily accomplished in the 1950s and 1960s when LO was by far the dominant confederation on the labor side; within LO, private-sector workers were dominant; and among those unions the metalworkers' union was by far the dominant force. Today, LO dominance has declined, and so has, within LO, the weight of private-sector workers relative to public sector workers. What makes this argument compelling is that TCO opposition to a recentralization of bargaining proposed by LO in the Alliance for Growth negotiations in the fall of 1998 was decisive in preventing a recentralization.[24]

However, decreasing union solidarity would not have resulted in decentralized bargaining in the 1980s if the employers had not pressed for it. This was a sharp reversal of their position at the origins of the system, when they were the originators of centralized bargaining, as they hoped that it would help restrain wages (Swenson 1991). As Swenson (1991) points out, VF's main concern then was that wage increases in the protected sector, particularly construction, would generate wage inflation in the export industry, thus damaging the competitiveness of Swedish industry. By centralizing bargaining and making wage increases in other sectors dependent on the situation of the export sector, they could control this source of wage inflation. Thus, wage restraint was the principal motivation for the centralization of bargaining, which fits the mainstream view in comparative political economy on the effects of centralized wage negotiations.

By the early 1980s, VF's position had changed. According to Pontusson and Swenson (1996), and following them, Iversen (1996), changes in the nature of production from assembly line to "diversified quality production" led to increasing skill differentiation in the industrial workforce and consequently to increasing emphasis on the part of engineering employers on wage differentiation as a tool to attract and motivate skilled labor. In both accounts, the factor that links the decline in centralized bargaining to the advent of post-Fordist production is wage compression between occupations. This does not explain why Sweden differed from Norway with regard to the decline in centralized bargaining. Moreover, it does not explain why Swedish employers were willing to give up one of the apparent benefits of centralized bargaining, wage restraint.

Our interviews with union and employer economists in Sweden do confirm Pontusson and Swenson's contention that the decline in Fordist production led employers in the crucial engineering sector to set a higher value on wage flexibility than in the past and thus to oppose centralized bargaining and the solidaristic wage policy, particularly LO's extension of the solidaristic wage policy to stage two, from equal pay for equal work to equalization of pay between skill levels (also see Olivecrona 1991). Trade union economists we discussed this issue with contend that the demands for greater wage flexibilization could have been accommodated within centralized bargaining. However, employers did not believe that LO would give up its attempts at wage compression. Such perceptions on the part of employers clearly play a role in explaining why they concluded that it was necessary to dismantle centralized bargaining in order to end wage compression policies in spite of the fact that comparisons with Danish, Finnish, and Austrian bargaining indicate that there is no necessary link between the two. Finally, and maybe most importantly, Swedish employers contend that the centralized bargaining system no longer delivered wage restraint. On the contrary, they claim that the clauses compensating workers for wage drift in other sectors that had progressively been built into the central agreement actually resulted in wage inflation (Olivecrona 1991: 15–28).

The degree of power shift from labor to capital also serves to distinguish Sweden from Austria, Finland, Denmark, and Norway, which also had centralized bargaining at the outset of the 1980s. As mentioned above, Swedish industry was not only initially more export oriented and multinational but also became increasingly so in this period, which made Swedish business less interested in a compromise with domestic labor. Along with the growing strength of the bourgeois parties, this served to increase the power of Swedish capital vis-à-vis labor, which certainly contributed to the perception on the part of employers that their drive to decentralize bargaining, as well as the broader SAF political offensive, was likely to succeed.

As Martin (1991) has pointed out, weakening the role of LO in the bargaining process, SAF's primary goal, also weakened LO's political clout. We contend that this was more than a desirable by-product from SAF's point of view. LO's resort to legislation instead of negotiated compromise with SAF in the struggles in the 1970s over workplace democracy and even more so wage earner funds deeply alienated SAF and was, by all accounts, a central motivation for SAF's political offensive of the late 1970s and 1980s.[25] There can be no doubt that the desire to weaken LO's political clout was a prime motivation for SAF's broader push to weaken Swedish tripartism in general, as indicated by the withdrawal of its representatives from the boards of all state agencies in 1991. The fact that the SAF representatives were replaced by business representatives, in many cases the same people who were often debriefed by SAF on their activities, indicates that the move was designed to force LO representatives and not trade union representatives in general off the boards and thus to weaken the political clout of the central organization (Pestoff 1999).

What is disputed is the role that the political motivations played in the decision to press for the decentralization of bargaining. Wallerstein and Golden (1997), Martin (2000), and we (Huber and Stephens 1998) give this argument considerable credence, whereas Swenson, the only one of these scholars to examine the SAF archives (though only up to 1978), finds no evidence that the weakening of LO's political clout motivated VF's action in this period.[26] Nevertheless, we remain inclined to attribute a role to the complete undermining of trust between the SAF and LO leaderships caused by the labor offensive of the 1970s and consequently to political motivations. We have three pieces of evidence to support our point of view. First, de Geer, writing also largely based on the SAF archives but also on the basis of feedback on his work from the SAF leadership, finds some evidence that weakening the political clout of LO was a motive for decentralization (e.g., see de Geer 1989: 133, 224). Second, in an interview in 1999 conducted by one of the present coauthors, discussing the failure of the Alliance for Growth, a senior SAF economist explained the sources of employer resistance to LO's proposal for a recentralization of the wage bargaining system. In doing so, he specifically referred to the political weakening of LO as one reason for the decentralization of bargaining. Third, Jan Herin, vice general director and chief economist at SAF, gave a similar motivation for decentralization at a conference in 1995. Responding to a presentation on the Swedish economy by the American economist Richard Freeman, he asserted that the weakening of LO's political clout was an important motivation on the part of employers for the move to decentralization.[27]

The reaction to LO's politicization and to the political clout centralized bargaining gave the organization helps explain differences with other countries. While organized labor became radicalized all over Europe in the late 1960s and 1970s, in none of the other corporatist countries did the principal labor confederation make such a fundamental break with the corporatist bargaining procedures of the past or seriously propose a measure that would mark as fundamental a transformation of relations between labor and capital as the original wage earner funds proposal did.

To turn to policy errors, by 1989 the benefits of the devaluations had been eaten up due to insufficient wage restraint, which was only in part due to the structural changes such as the decline in the hegemony of blue-collar private-sector unions and the weakening of centralized bargaining. The large devaluation, which boosted profits in the export sector, combined with a tight labor market encouraged employers to offer wages above the negotiated levels. The government's continued expansion of public-sector employment in this context aggravated the situation. Above all, the deregulation of credit markets was poorly timed. This was done in 1985 when there were still generous tax deductions for consumer interest payments, and it fueled an unprecedented credit boom and consumer spending orgy at a time when the economy was already beginning to overheat. Part of this credit boom was accounted for by cross-border flows of loans, clearly an effect of deregulation of international capital flows.[28] As the Rehn-Meidner model would predict, this boom of export profits and of credit made wage restraint impossible. With wage increases far above productivity increases, Swedish export industries did become uncompetitive. Yet the government and its bourgeois successor refused to float the krona until the fall of 1992, when the economy was already in deep recession and much damage in terms of failed businesses, lost markets, and lost jobs had been done.

In the early 1990s, both the Social Democratic and bourgeois governments continued to follow policies that inadvertently had strong procyclical effects on consumer behavior, this time in the context of a deep recession. The combination of a reduction of the tax rate on capital income, falling inflation, and stable nominal interest rates resulted in a substantial increase in real after-tax interest rates. The bust after the real estate boom added to the situation by reducing the wealth position of many households below the probable desired level. All this contributed to a household savings rate of 10 percent in 1993, by far the highest level in over two decades, and a correspondingly depressed level of personal consumption in the midst of a depression (OECD 1994b: 16–17). On the side of the banks, this same set of circumstances—the asset boom and bust caused by speculation in the wake of financial deregulation—left many banks holding sufficient bad debts that they became insolvent. The government bailout operation cost the public coffers seventy-four billion kronas (5 percent of GDP) in 1991 and 1992 alone, thus adding to the already spiraling budget deficit (OECD 1994b: 129).

Our arguments contrast with those of Erixon (1996) and Pontusson (1992a) on one point. In their view, the high-profits policy was not only a departure from the Rehn-Meidner prescriptions but it was the key source of the failure of wage restraint in the 1980s, just as the model would predict. Thus the advantages of the devaluation were eaten up by wage inflation by the late 1980s, and Sweden was in an uncompetitive situation again. However, in the aggregate, profits were not higher in the 1980s than in the 1960s. The figures on net operating surplus in table 5.1 indicate this.[29] Moreover, since the Rehn-Meidner policies could not control profits in the export sector, it is not plausible to argue that they were the key to the failure of Third Road policies. While high profits in the export sector along with the tight labor markets and the decline in centralized bargaining did contribute to wage inflation in the early 1980s, as of the mid-1980s Sweden still enjoyed much of the competitive edge it had gained from the devaluation. By far the most important causes of wage inflation in the late 1980s were the consumption boom and overheating of the economy as a result of the deregulation of the credit market and the government's failure to take corrective steps.

An additional factor here might be the transitions from a centralized bargaining system to coordinated industrial level bargaining. Iversen (1998) and Hall and Franzese (1998) argue that systems of coordinated industry-level bargaining will deliver wage restraint and thus low unemployment if the monetary regime is characterized by an independent central bank charged with targeting inflation. However, for the system to work, it is clear that the government's fiscal policy also has to coordinate with monetary policy and wage bargaining so that the signals about future inflation that the central bank is attempting to send are not undermined by fiscal policy. In Sweden in this period, this did not occur.

The economic situation in Sweden in the period 1993–95 illustrates the difficulties of countercyclical management in the contemporary international economic regime. Export performance was extremely strong beginning 1993, sufficiently so that Sweden registered positive numbers in the balance of payments account beginning 1994. However, partly due to the very high levels of personal savings, domestic demand was extremely depressed and this was a stumbling block to getting open unemployment below 8 percent. Despite this, the Social Democratic government elected in 1994 has continued austerity policies: cutting public spending and raising taxes. All possible economic stimulation policies had a downside: Decreasing interest rates to stimulate investment and consumer spending would result in depreciation of the krona followed by import-induced inflation and compensation demands by the unions in the next wage round. Both decreasing interest rates and increasing the fiscal deficit would increase demands for imports leading to a balance of payments deficit and thus to currency depreciation and so on.

Nonetheless, the performance of the Swedish economy since the Social Democrats returned to power underlines that governments are not without instruments to manage the economy in the current era.[30] It also demonstrates how much of the Swedish crisis was caused by a combination of economic cycles and governments' failed management in the face of them. In 1994, the economy noted positive growth; it experienced average per annum growth rates of 2.8% in 1994–99, and the OECD projected growth rates of 3.0% for 2000 and 2.7% for 2001 (*Dagens Nyheter,* www.dn.se, November 17, 1999). By 1996, inflation had been brought down to below 1 percent. Renewed growth and a combination of tax increases and budget cuts enabled the government to cut the deficit from

7.9% of GDP in 1995 to a 1.9% surplus in 1998 and 1999, and debt as a percentage of GDP fell from a high of 76% in 1996 to 66% in 1999 (SCB 2000, www.scb.se/ekonomi/ekonomi). Budget surpluses of 2% are projected for 2000 and 2001 (*Dagens Nyheter*, www.dn.se, November 17, 1999). The austere budgets and the falling deficit brought down interest rates and the krona–deutsche mark interest rate differential substantially in the same period, stimulating investment and further growth. Renewed growth and active labor market policies resulted in a fall of open unemployment to 7.2% for the year 1997 and to 5.7% by January 2000 (Statistiska Centralbyrån, www.scb.se/snabb/akaswe.asp, March 9, 2000), and it is projected to fall to 4% in 2001, missing the government's goal of 4% in 2000 by only one year (*Dagens Nyheter*, www.dn.se, November 17, 1999). The one area of concern was wage inflation as the 1995 round of bargaining, in which negotiations were carried out at an industrywide level, failed to produce wage moderation. The graveness of this failure given prevailing monetary and exchange rate arrangements was realized by labor market actors and the government, and the 1998 round (also industry-level coordinated bargaining) did produce moderate wage increases, as the literature on central bank independence and bargaining centralization would predict. However, senior economists for unions and employers whom we interviewed in June 1999 expressed concern that the wage bargaining system as presently constructed would not deliver wage restraint once the economy approached full employment, though they disagreed on how to remedy the situation.

### Norway

Due to the inflow of funds from the oil sector, exports of which now account for 16 percent of GDP, Norway has avoided the severe unemployment crisis of the other Scandinavian countries and thus has also escaped the welfare state rollbacks that occurred recently in Sweden and Finland and earlier in Denmark. On the balance, the past decade and a half cannot be characterized as either one of rollback or innovation. On the one hand, there have been significant expansions of maternal leave in 1986, 1987, and 1993. The new provisions provide for fifty-two weeks with 80 percent income replacement (or forty-two weeks at full pay), second only to Sweden in generosity. In addition, since 1990 qualifying conditions for unemployment compensation have been liberalized. On the other hand, indexation of benefits has been modified; the replacement rate in the supplementary pension plan has been cut by 3 percent; work requirements for unemployment compensation have been strengthened; the qualifying conditions for disability tightened; and the strictly medical criteria for disability pensions reintroduced. While the Norwegian authorities are now also committed to a work line, this has only been manifested in the stricter qualifying conditions for unemployment, disability, and sickness benefits and greater efforts at rehabilitation. In contrast to the other Nordic countries, replacement rates have not been cut nor have waiting days been increased. For instance, the replacement rate for sick pay is still 100 percent, and there are no waiting days.

Underlying this mixed picture are difficulties in the Norwegian production and labor market regimes, similar to those suffered in Sweden and Finland, partially masked by revenues from the oil sector.[31] Financial liberalization has weakened the ability of the government to direct credit and investment, though the resources from the oil sector still give the state considerable leverage compared to Sweden. As in Sweden and Finland, deregulation of credit markets in the mid-1980s led to a consumer spending boom that was followed by a spate of bank failures and consumer retrenchment. As in Sweden, governments of different political coloring pursued hard currency policies that certainly aggravated the competitiveness problems of industry until Norway was forced to float the krone in the fall of 1992 (though with less dramatic consequences for the currency's value than took place in Sweden). Even the Labor government has prioritized fighting inflation over unemployment (Moene and Wallerstein 1993).

Unlike in Sweden, peak-level tripartism has not weakened. After briefly considering withdrawing from public committees like its Swedish counterpart, the Norwegian employers association joined an initiative of the Social Democratic government aimed at promoting industrial innovation that includes leaders of business, the government, and LO (Mjøset et al. 1994: 71). The contrast with Sweden is certainly partly related to the character of national capital in the two countries. Norwegian capital is not only less multinational and more tied to domestic resources than the Swedish, but also the state owns the most important natural resource, oil. Thus, both the power of Norwegian capital vis-à-vis labor and its interest in domestic class compromise are different from those of its Swedish counterpart. Though local-level bargaining accounts for a larger proportion of wage increases (Moene and Wallerstein 1993), centralized bargaining was preserved until the 1998 wage round.

The consequences of these economic developments have been that unemployment began to rise in the mid-1980s, reaching a high of 5.9 percent in 1992 with an additional 3 percent in active labor market measures. From this point, economic developments turned sharply positive. The tripartite initiative of the government, known as the Solidarity Alternative, designed to produce wage increases in line with those of Norway's major trading partners, did produce wage moderation and facilitated positive developments across the economy until the 1998 wage round. The economy boomed, growing at a vigorous 4.1% per annum in 1994–97, and then cooled in 1998, growing at 2.3% with about 2% growth projected for 1999–2000. The general government budget averaged a substantial surplus of over 6% of GDP in 1996–99 (OECD 1999d). By 1998, unemployment stood at 1.9% and many sectors reported labor shortages. Government policy aggravated these shortages as the Center–Liberal–Christian Democratic minority coalition eased early retirement and introduced cash benefits for parents of toddlers who do not send them to public day care. Against this backdrop, it is perhaps not surprising that the outcome of the 1998 bargaining round, conducted at the industry level, was inflationary, though the supplementary bargain the following year resulted in modest wage increases. The reasons for this are unclear; we speculate briefly on this in the conclusion of the book.

## *Finland*

As we pointed out in chapter 5, Finland's period of vigorous social reform extended well past the end of the Golden Age (Marklund 1988: 35–38). This is not surprising precisely because not only was Finland a laggard and thus there was no ceiling effect (that is, the welfare state had not grown to limits) but also because Finnish economic growth rates were good compared to those of other OECD countries. In fact, in 1979–89, Finnish economic growth at 3.2 percent per capita per annum was even higher than the Japanese (see table A.11). Finland did experience higher unemployment than Norway or Sweden in the 1970s and 1980s, as it moved to over 5 percent in the early 1980s and then back to 3.6 percent by 1990. This helps explain why this period of welfare state expansion was punctuated by bouts of retrenchment. Nonetheless, things looked rosy as late as 1989, when, after the revaluation of the markka, statisticians of the Industrialists' Association announced that Finland had surpassed Sweden and Norway in per capita income (Andersson, Kosonen, and Vartiainen 1993: 30). In welfare state development, Finland also caught up with the other Nordic countries. For example, the gap between Finland and the other three countries on Esping-Andersen's decommodification index for 1980, a good measure of the generosity of pensions, unemployment compensation, and sick-pay, was closed by the end of the decade (see table 4.1).[32] As in the other Nordic countries, the development of gender-egalitarian policies and the expansion of social services were particularly vigorous in this decade.

The crash was as catastrophic as it was rapid; GDP growth fell to 0.4% in 1990 and turned negative in 1991 (−6.4%) and 1992 (−3.6%) (OECD 1993b: 14). Unemployment increased dramatically from 4% in 1990 to 18% in 1993. Significant cuts in expenditure that have affected a wide range of transfers and social services have been instituted. Stricter qualifying conditions for unemployment benefits have been passed and the replacement rate cut by 3%.[33] The replacement rate for sick pay has been reduced (from 80% to 67% in the case of the average production worker), contributions increased, and waiting days increased from seven to nine. Replacement rates for parental benefits have been cut from 80% to 67% and the benefit period cut from 275 to 263 days. Subsidies to prescription drugs have been significantly reduced. The replacement rates for the earnings-related tier of public employee pensions has been cut from 66% to 60% and an employee contribution of 6% of income introduced. Further cuts in the replacement rate for all employees to 55% or even 50%, and a change in the calculation of the replacement rate on the basis of lifetime and not final income are planned. A number of new taxes and fees have been introduced. Employee contributions to the employment-related pensions, previously financed entirely by the employers, were introduced. As in Sweden, the universal flat-rate pension was abolished and replaced by a supplement tested against other legislated pensions. A basic sickness allowance payable to those without income, such as students and homemakers was abolished. Most of these retrenching reforms were carried out by the five-party government formed in the wake of the 1995 election, led by the Social Democrats but including the Conservatives.

Part of Finland's problem was idiosyncratic: the collapse of Soviet trade. Otherwise we see a pattern now familiar from recent Swedish and Norwegian developments. Deregulation of financial markets led to a (procyclical) boom in consumer borrowing, inflation of asset prices, and overheating of the economy followed by banking collapse and consumer retrenchment. The banking crisis was more severe in Finland than in Sweden and Norway, as indicated by the fact that the bailout operation imposed a cost on the government and central bank equal to 7 percent of GDP. As in Sweden and to a lesser extent Norway, the economic difficulties were further aggravated by the attempt to follow a hard currency policy, which ultimately failed as Finland was also forced to float. In Finland, the traditional procyclical policies of the government added to the economic plight (Andersson, Kosonen, and Vartiainen 1993).

These policy errors certainly contributed to the situation but should not be allowed to obscure the fact that the same long-term changes in the domestic and international economy that altered the conditions for the Swedish and Norwegian models did the same for the Finnish. Financial internationalization and deregulation and high international interest rates undermined important features of the supply-side policies. On the demand side, the decline in demand for Finnish exports in the core capitalist countries was temporarily compensated with Soviet trade, which is no longer an option. Finnish business, like Swedish, became increasingly internationalized, especially in the second half of the 1980s, as direct foreign investment increased substantially. Thus, even to the extent that government policy could encourage investment, it was less able to ensure that it occurred in Finland.

However, as in the other Nordic countries, proclamations of the end of the Finnish model appear to be premature. Per annum growth rates were a vigorous 4.3% from 1994 to 1998, stimulated by the expansion of foreign demand, moderate wage increases, and an easy money policy that was possible due to an initially undervalued and appreciating currency. A 3.4% increase in GDP was projected for 1999 and 2000 (OECD 1999c). The Social Democratic–led government (which includes the Conservatives) brought the deficit down to 1.4% in 1997, and a surplus was projected in subsequent years. This has further brought down interest rates and eliminated the markka–deutsche mark differential. These positive economic developments, along with the government's Employment Program of 1995 and massive early retirement programs, helped move the unemployment rate down to 9% by November 1998.[34]

The Finnish wage bargaining system remained centralized during this period and both the 1995 and 1998 bargaining rounds were characterized by incomes policy agreements between the unions, the employers association, and the government, which produced moderate wage increases. These agreements helped push inflation under 1% by 1996. The Finnish decision to join the European Monetary Union in 1999 was announced several years prior to that date; thus the past two bargaining rounds have operated in a monetary environment in which Finnish monetary policy is de facto set by the Bundesbank. By contrast, efforts to keep the 2000 bargaining round centralized failed due to the dissatisfaction of some unions with the inability of centralized bargaining to address sector-specific problems, such as outsourcing.[35] The metalworking industry set the pattern with modest wage increases of 3.1 percent and other unions followed suit, though at this writing the round has not been completed, with the paper industry, an important export sector, among others, still outstanding. Thus, in Finland, wage moderation has been produced under central bank independence with both centralized and sectoral but coordinated bargaining. One must, of course, keep the still high level of unemployment in mind.

### Denmark

Danish unemployment began to rise almost immediately at the end of the Golden Age after the first oil shock. Unemployment rose from 0.9% in 1973 to 5.1% in 1975, continuing to a peak of 10.5%, subsiding in the 1980s, only to increase to a new peak of 12.2% in 1993 (table A.11; see also Furåker, Johansson, and Lind 1990: 148). Denmark's liberal economic policies, its lack of an industrial policy and active labor market policy, and its concentration on consumer exports all contributed to its greater international vulnerability and to the rise in unemployment. In fact, its period of full employment lasted only a decade and a half and can be attributed to a combination of foreign consumer demand in the Golden Age and the rise in welfare state employment in the 1960s.

The economic difficulties and particularly the rise in unemployment made existing entitlements increasingly expensive. Successive Danish governments responded with significant welfare state cuts that have nonetheless only prevented social security benefit expenditure and total government expenditure from rising as fast as it otherwise would have. A variety of measures have been employed in this effort: increases in the selectivity of benefits, introduction of income testing, modifications of indexing, temporary deindexation, increases in qualifying conditions, increases in copayments for health care and day care, and introduction of waiting days. Many of the cuts have been directed at the system of unemployment compensation, with the result that the effective replacement rate has fallen dramatically from a peak of 72 percent in 1979 to 58 percent in 1987 without actually lowering the nominal replacement rate for a worker with average wages (Marklund 1988: 31–35; Nørby Johansen 1986).[36] As one can see from the OECD data (tables A.9 and A.10), lower-paid workers have been shielded from these cuts. Some improvements of benefits have also been made, but aside from the substantial increase in maternity leave (from 98 to 144 days) and increases in pensions, these too have been responses to the unemployment crisis: eased conditions for preretirement pensions, increased subsidies for industries employing new workers, increased severance pay, and introduction of active labor market measures (Hagen 1992: 145; Nørby Johansen 1986).

Most of the cuts and improvements mentioned in the previous paragraph, were carried out by the bourgeois governments of 1982–93, and the cuts were generally protested by the Social Democrats (Green-Pedersen 1999). However, once it returned to office in 1993, the Social Democratic government did not roll back the cuts; on the contrary, as part of an effort to deepen the Danish version of a work or active line, the government implemented large cuts in the duration of unemployment benefits, though at two years, it is still long by Nordic standards. The activation policy features a combination of positive incentives (e.g., improved vocational and job training) and negative incentives for workers (ceilings on wages for public employment programs, the cuts in duration of unemployment benefits) and employers (responsibility for the first two days of unemployment compensation). In a significant departure from past principles, the citizenship pension for those over seventy was subject to an income test beginning 1994.

One segment of the system of social protection was created after 1985, the system of earnings-related pensions. As we explained in chapter 5, Denmark lacked an earnings-related tier with high income replacement rates characteristic of the other Nordic countries. Given the budgetary situation and the expense of the comprehensive earnings-related schemes the unions were demanding, politicians were reluctant to enact legislation in this area. Beginning in the mid-1980s and extending into the 1990s, the unions successfully negotiated for such schemes sector by sector. Given the high levels of union density and contract coverage, these schemes came to cover a very high percentage of employees. Indeed, a government investigation of the need for legislation in this area in the late 1990s concluded that coverage was sufficiently high that no legislation was necessary.

The move to a more active labor market policy was not the only change in macroeconomic management Denmark made in this period. Denmark adopted a hard currency policy and a policy of fiscal restraint designed to produce moderate wage increases. The new bourgeois government introduced an active industrial policy in 1983 (Benner and Vad 2000). Initially, the policy was selective, aimed at supporting export-oriented business—in the Danish context primarily small and medium enterprises, especially in higher technology, with R and D support, export credits, and risk capital. In the 1990s, these selective measures were replaced with general measures (e.g., workforce qualifications, infrastructure, taxation) and oriented to increasing service sector employment.

Initially wage restraint proved difficult to implement. As in the past, the labor market partners often could not agree and the negotiations were referred to a state mediator who in turn was not able to produce an agreement, whereupon the Danish parliament would impose a solution. Even with this political intervention the increases in unit labor costs were above those of Germany in the 1970s and 1980s (Benner and Vad 2000). Then the Danish wage bargaining system underwent a very significant transformation in the late 1980s and the 1990s (Wallerstein and Golden 1997; Iversen 1996). The current system of a small number of sectoral-level bargaining cartels can be characterized as highly coordinated sectoral-level bargaining, "coordinated decentralization" as it is referred to in recent literature on Danish labor relations.[37] We say "highly coordinated" since the strong role of the public mediator makes inflationary wage increases much less likely than in countries with sectoral-level bargaining and the export manufacturing sector acting as a wage leader as in Germany or recent rounds in Sweden, Finland, or Norway. The mediator has the right to link together the voting procedures to approve the settlement, so that both sectors that have concluded agreements and those still negotiating constitute a single entity. Thus, even if the members of unions still bargaining rejected an agreement (concluded by the union or fashioned by the mediator), the agreement would be ratified as long as a majority of all members in the linked bargain voted in favor of the agreement. The changes made in the bargaining system have apparently been effective, as the increase in unit labor costs in Denmark in 1989–96 was low (1.9%) and below increases in Germany. However, the 1998 bargaining round was characterized by conflict and produced inflationary increases, but there was a return to moderation in 2000.

The macroeconomic figures attest to the success of the new Danish policy parameters, as Denmark, like the other Nordic countries, experienced an economic revival in the mid-1990s. GDP grew 3.1% per annum in 1994 to 1998 with a fall to 2.0% per annum forecast in 1999 and 2000. The budget moved into surplus in 1998 and 2% surpluses were expected in 1999 and 2000 and unemployment fell to 6.5% in 1998 and was forecast to fall to 5.9% in 2000 (OECD 1999b: 32–33).

Some observers (e.g., see Benner and Vad 2000, Scharpf 2000) have seen Denmark as a model for how a social democratic welfare state might survive and even prosper in a postindustrial economy operating in a highly internationalized competitive economic environment. In particular, it offers a formula for how a very generous welfare state might be combined with employment creation in private services in which labor costs figure prominently. Most of these policies, such as no employer payroll taxes and liberal dismissal rules, are legacies of the Golden Age welfare state, in which generous welfare policies were adapted to the needs of small and medium enterprises. Others, such as strengthening active labor market policies, weakening of policies that allow permanent welfare dependence, and the off-budget pension reform, have been added or augmented in the crisis period.

## The Northern Continental
## Christian Democratic Welfare States

### Germany

In Germany unemployment reached 4% in 1975, up from a customary pre-1973 level of below 1%, and economic growth slowed from an annual average of 3.5% in the period 1960–73 to 2.6% in 1973–79 (see table A.11). The SPD-FDP government continued expanding welfare state entitlements up to the mid-1970s, but then the economic changes led to first efforts to contain rising welfare state expenditures, through a combination of letting adjustments lag and increasing contributions. Economic conditions worsened in the 1980s and under the CDU/CSU/FDP government that came to power in 1982 cutbacks were intensified. Economic growth slowed to 1.6% in 1979–89 and unemployment reached a level of 8% in 1983 and stayed there until 1985. An economic recovery in the late 1980s let unemployment decline to 4.2% in 1991, but reunification with East Germany and a renewed severe recession in 1993 resulted in massive losses of jobs, particularly in the manufacturing sector, and an unemployment rate of 10.3% by mid-1996 (OECD 1996b: 100). As in the Netherlands, many older workers went into early retirement and the labor force participation rate of male workers between sixty and sixty-four years of age fell to 31.5% in 1986 (Hinrichs 1991). In addition, between 1970 and 1986 the share of the unemployed among all recipients of social assistance increased from less than 1% to 33%, as many long-term unemployed people saw their unemployment benefits exhausted.

The Social Democratic–Liberal government began to curtail expenditures in 1977 by changing indexation rules and the calculation formula for pensions, raising contribution rates for pensions and user fees for prescriptions, reducing some health insurance benefits and promoting concerted corporatist action to control health expenditures, and tightening controls on recipients of unemployment benefits. The post-1982

Christian Democratic–Liberal government then pursued similar types of changes but of a greater magnitude. It introduced individual contributions of pensioners to sickness insurance and of recipients of cash sickness benefits to pension and unemployment insurance, tightened eligibility conditions for unemployment benefits and for full invalidity pensions, increased copayments for medical services and prescriptions, reduced unemployment benefits in a variety of ways, reduced benefit levels for social assistance and weakened entitlements to social assistance in favor of stronger administrative discretion. Several of these measures meant significant cuts in benefits;[38] in general, pensions were less affected than unemployment compensation. Adjustments in pension policy were essentially a corporatist affair, decided by a group of experts representing the major institutions, and accepted without major dissent (Hinrichs 1991). This was also true of the pension reform of 1989 (going into effect in 1992), which was designed to consolidate the financing of the pension scheme for the future, in the face of an aging population. The reform phased out early retirement plans and introduced a partial pension to facilitate gradual retirement, changed indexing from gross wages to net wages (i.e., gross wages minus taxes and social security contributions), fixed federal subsidies at 19 percent, changed the practice of revaluating contributions from very low-income earners that had de facto functioned as a minimum pension plan, and changed the pension formula in many other ways (Schmidt 1998: 108–11). Alber (1998) points out that by 1997 pensions were 22 percent lower than they would have been under the rules in effect in 1977, but that the real value of pension benefits had nevertheless kept increasing. This phenomenon goes a long way in explaining the relatively protest-free process of cutting entitlements. This consensus regarding pension policy was eroded by the severe challenges that German reunification posed, and it came to an end with the pension reform in 1997, which introduced an adjustment for life expectancy in the annual pension adjustment formula in order to reduce the average replacement rate in accord with rising life expectancies, a reform measure that the SPD and the unions opposed (Hinrichs 1998).

Other areas of reform, particularly in the 1990s, were more controversial; for instance, the austerity program in social assistance and social services pursued by the government in 1993 met with considerable opposition. As part of this austerity program, the adjustment of standard rates for social assistance was fixed in advance until June 1996, thus reducing the real income of recipients by letting the increases lag behind anticipated inflation (Ploug and Kvist 1994). However, up to that point, social assistance benefits had actually increased and the distance to average wage earners decreased (Alber 1996). Unemployment replacement rates had suffered a series of cuts; from 90% to 80% in 1975, to 68% in 1981, to 63% for persons without children in 1983. They suffered further cuts in the 1990s: down to 60% of net wages for people without children for unemployment insurance and 53% for unemployment assistance; the replacement rates for those with children declined to 67% of net wages for unemployment insurance and 57% for unemployment assistance (Alber 1998). Unemployment assistance was restricted to one year, after which recipients become dependent on income-tested, locally monitored social assistance that is widely regarded as stigmatizing.

There were a few innovations in the 1980s in the areas of labor market policy and gender policy. Active labor market policy received a boost from increased support for (re)training, and so did passive labor market policy from a lengthening of the benefit period in unemployment insurance for older workers (Schmidt 1998: 104–5). Legislation in the area of gender policy was hardly of the Nordic gender-egalitarian variety, though. Despite a continuing increase in women's mobilization during the 1980s and 1990s, the level of mobilization remained clearly below the levels characteristic of the Nordic countries, and of course women faced a government committed to a very traditional notion of the family and woman's role in it. Women's labor force participation increased from 51% in 1980 to 62% in 1994, among the highest levels in the Christian democratic welfare states but still some 10% lower than the average for the Nordic countries (table 5.2). Women's representation in parliament increased from 8% in 1980 to 21% in 1990, also clearly below the 33% to 39% in the Nordic countries at the same time (Borchorst 1994: 41).[39] Moreover, under pressure from women's groups inside and outside of political parties, there was a rapid proliferation of offices for women's affairs in state and city governments. However, the actual power of these offices was heavily dependent on support from the executive and/or legislature that created them and appointed the officers, and thus the policies pursued by these offices largely reflected the policy of incumbent governments (Ferree 1995: 102–4). In some places, this meant that real progress was made in nondiscrimination in employment, for instance, but at the national level very little progress was made in gender-egalitarian social policy.

Rather, couched behind a discourse of parental responsibility and women's choice, the actual reform measures were much more favorable toward nonworking women. In 1986, the CDU/CSU/FDP government replaced the paid maternity leave for employed mothers with an education allowance for any parent, employed or not, taking care of a child after birth. This allowance was a low flat-rate benefit, equivalent to about one-fourth of an average female blue-collar worker's wages, to be paid to all for six months. After six months, the benefit became income tested. The benefit could be combined with part-time work of up to nineteen hours a week. This benefit structure was clearly most beneficial for one-breadwinner families, and secondarily for families with a second small supplementary income. It was clearly biased against the main breadwinner taking any of the leave, and in fact nearly 99 percent of the benefit recipients were women (Kolbe 1999: 160–65). The only unambiguously women-friendly reform in the 1980s was the lowering of the minimum required contribution period for pension entitlements to five years (Schmidt 1998: 104–5). Another one was the introduction of pension credit for time spent rearing children—a reform the SPD had already wanted in the 1972 pension reform. However, the combination of this reform with the education allowance was double-edged; people who combined the education allowance with part-time work lost these pension credits (Kolbe 1999: 160). The duration of the means-tested education allowance was gradually extended to two years, and parents had the right to job protection for an additional year of unpaid leave. Since the flat-rate benefits were not adjusted, however, they eroded in value during the first decade of their existence. Moreover, due to strong opposition from employers and from within the ruling coalition, job protection was less than absolute (Kolbe 1999: 161–62). In short, this reform did little to support labor force participation among mothers of small children.

How difficult labor force participation for mothers of small children is becomes clear if one considers the availability of child care. As of 1993, child care facilities were available for 2 percent of children under three years of age only. For older children, coverage was 78 percent, but this was not all-day care (Bussemaker and van Kersbergen 1999: 37). Rather, preschool care is typically offered for a few hours a day, and children are expected to eat lunch at home. The pattern of lunch at home is for the most part valid for elementary school as well, which makes it all but impossible for both parents to have full-time jobs. Adaptation to this West German pattern meant a real step backward for women from the former German Democratic Republic. The combination of lack of support for the maintenance of child care facilities with rapidly rising unemployment meant that women with small children and women over fifty were particularly likely to be pushed out of the labor force, and women came to account for some two-thirds of the unemployed (Ferree 1995: 109).

The only innovations in social policy in the 1990s (as opposed to cutbacks in existing programs) have come in response to rulings by the constitutional court, or in response to significant new social problems, or as temporary measures to deal with the extraordinary economic situation.[40] In 1990 the constitutional court determined that a minimum subsistence level for children was to be exempt from the tax liability of parents and in 1992 it ruled that the tax-free amount was too low to fulfill its constitutionally mandated goal of guaranteeing a minimum subsistence level. Accordingly, tax deductions for lower-income people were raised, the child tax allowance was increased, and the child benefit for the first child was increased. Two significant new social problems have been German reunification, with the consequent need to integrate the new Länder into the social security system, and the increase in aged persons in need of nursing care from nonfamily caregivers. The extension of the West German pension system to the East was a response to the former problem, the introduction of nursing care insurance in 1995 a response to the latter. Nursing care insurance is financed by employer and employee contributions and is compulsory for all those for whom statutory health insurance is compulsory. Finally, the recession of 1993 induced the government to extend unemployment insurance benefits for short-time work from six to twenty-four months until the end of 1994. Ideological differences with regard to the welfare state intensified in the early 1990s, under the financial pressures resulting from reunification and under the impact of the growing strength of neoliberal tendencies within the Christian Democratic Party. At the rhetorical level, the ruling Christian Democratic–Liberal coalition advocated a transition from the welfare state to the achievement state (Leistungsstaat), based on individual responsibility and contributions and on the market, whereas the Social Democrats advocated a continued strong role of the state, particularly in employment policy and more generally as guarantor of social peace.

The results of these efforts up to 1990 were a containment of the increases in general public expenditures and in transfer payments. Looking at the total social budget, one sees an increase from 26.5 percent in 1970 to 32.6 percent in 1980, and then a slight decline to 29.5 percent in 1990. The obvious reason why expenditures did not fall any more, despite significant cutbacks, is the rise in the number of claimants of benefits. The social rights data in 1975–85 show a general pattern of stagnation or slight declines. One can guess that these data would show stronger declines if they were available for 1990 and 1995. The most serious restrictions were not imposed until after the change in government in 1982, and many of them did not yet have a highly visible impact by 1985. Reunification then put new upward pressure on expenditures and thus led to additional cutbacks in the 1990s. These cutbacks would have been larger, had it not been for state structure and partisan incumbency. From 1990–91 on, the opposition SPD had a majority in the upper house, which enabled them to block cutbacks that they considered excessive and particularly burdensome for the lower income sectors (Schmidt 1998: 145). Schmidt (1998: 137) cites a governmental estimate of total savings in the magnitude of 2.8 percent of GDP as a result of all the cutbacks undertaken by the CSU/CSU/FDP government from 1982 to 1997.

Economic problems in general, unemployment in particular, and thus budget pressures were greatly aggravated by the attempt to integrate the former East Germany through the wholesale transfer of West German institutions. With the loss of the Eastern markets, manufacturing in the eastern part of Germany collapsed; the share of manufacturing in employment declined from 40 percent to 16 percent in 1995 (Carlin and Soskice 1997). About one-third of the firms in manufacturing in eastern Germany, employing about 16 percent of the workers in industry, acknowledge paying wages lower than those in industry agreements, and the real number is estimated to be much greater (OECD 1996b: 118). Nevertheless, few firms in the eastern part of the country have managed to break into the top-end quality manufacturing characteristic of the western part and thus to become competitive at prevailing wage and benefit levels. In the mid-1990s eastern Germany accounted for about one-third of total unemployment with only one-fifth of the total labor force (OECD 1996b: 106). In 1994 61% of the GDP of the eastern part of Germany was still imported, and roughly half of total investment was financed by the public sector (Carlin and Soskice 1997). Industrial subsidies increased from 5.4% of GDP in 1989 to 7.1% in 1993, and the share of the eastern part increased from 35% in 1991 to 43% in 1993. Similarly, active labor market policy measures became a major new kind of transfer program in the eastern part, particularly through subsidized work schemes (OECD 1996b: 82, 129).

Of course, such massive transfers to the eastern part increased government expenditures and required new revenue. Total government expenditures rose from 45% in 1989 to 50% in 1993, and social expenditures shot up to a world high of 68% of GDP in the East German Länder by 1992 (Schmidt 1998: 137–38). As Czada (1998) points out, the general government budget and the social insurance schemes were in a very strong financial position in 1989, and unemployment was at 8% and thus below the European average. The transfers to the former East German Länder then put tremendous pressures on all of these schemes and required increases in contributions and in the share of financing coming from general taxation.

Taking taxes and contributions together, the increase in the tax burden on labor incomes was 3.5 percentage points between 1990 and 1994; this increase would be even higher if the 7.5% temporary solidarity surcharge, which was reintroduced in 1995, is taken into account (OECD 1996b: 73). These increases led to conflict with the conservative Bundesbank and to policy-induced recession. Essentially, the Bundesbank had imposed a firm monetarist policy mandate; every year since 1974 the bank has published a firm target for the increase in the money supply and thus bound both governments and unions to restrain expenditures and wage demands respectively (Streeck 1994: 123). In response to the financial burden of reunification, both the government and the unions exceeded these restraints and were punished by the Bundesbank with an extremely restrictive monetary policy. Tax increases to finance reunification motivated unions to press for significant money wage increases, and the unions were successful in collective negotiations in 1991 and 1992. In reaction, the Bundesbank raised interest rates and let the exchange rate appreciate, until the economy suffered a severe recession in 1993 (Carlin and Soskice 1997). This recession aggravated the unemployment problem in both the eastern and the western parts, and the slow recovery in the following two years failed to lead to an improvement in the unemployment rate (OECD 1996b: 4), despite wage restraint on the part of unions. Total unemployment reached a high of 11.6 percent at the beginning of 1998, though unemployment had stabilized in the West at below 10 percent. The healthy economic growth had such a weak impact on investment and employment because that growth was concentrated in the export sector while domestic demand remained depressed and structural change had caused both labor and capital to be used more efficiently (OECD 1998b: 15–34).

As mentioned in chapter 5, Germany did develop an active labor market policy from the late 1960s on, but this policy remained much weaker than in Sweden. A temporary exception was the approach to unemployment in the eastern part, where in the second half of 1990 15% of the labor force were supported by labor market policy measures, such as retraining, additional training, job creation, wage subsidies, shortened work weeks, and early retirement. This figure climbed to a high of 23% in 1991 and declined again to 10% in 1995 (Schmidt 1998: 140). Still, passive measures continued to outweigh active ones by far; in 1994, total labor market expenditures amounted to 4% of GDP, and direct expenditures on active labor market policies to 1.1% of GDP (OECD 1996b: 129). The increase in active labor market policy measures in the 1980s was partly successful, but what success these policies had was negated by reunification. After

declining from the early 1960s to the beginning of the 1980s, the employment rate actually recovered by some 3% by 1989, but in the 1990s the
downward trend resumed (OECD 1996b: 100). As in the Netherlands,
early retirement became a widely used tool to deal with unemployment
among older workers. However, again as in the Netherlands, the burden on
the transfer system grew to levels high enough to elicit reforms designed to
increase labor market participation. In the mid-1990s the government
moved, for instance, to increase the age for early retirement at full pension,
to stiffen requirements for social assistance recipients to accept jobs, and
to revise the labor code to promote active job search.

A major problem for the German production regime and thus the
welfare state is the sluggish job growth in both public and private services, a problem that Germany shares with other Continental European countries (Scharpf 1997, 2000). As Scharpf (2000) argues, personal and corporate income taxes have no effect on private-sector
employment, whereas social security contributions and consumption
taxes have strongly negative employment effects on private services,
which means that they are particularly problematic in countries where
the huge majority of welfare state programs is financed by employer and
employee contributions, as in Germany. Seils and Manow (2000) take
this argument a step further and link the lack of job growth in private services to the strategic interaction of unions, employers, the central bank,
and the government in Germany. They argue that the primary response
to economic difficulties is to reduce the labor supply by shifting workers
into welfare state programs. This, however, puts budgetary pressure on
welfare state programs, and since the government is under pressure from
the central bank to keep the deficit low, these pressures are met with increases in social security contributions, which in turn put downward pressures on employment in low-productivity private services, the very sector
where jobs particularly for the lower-skilled would need to come from.
The strength of the unions in turn has prevented a lowering of wage levels at the bottom, which would allow employers in the service sector to
shift some of the social security costs onto the workers.

Despite pressures for greater wage flexibility, unions and the majority
of large employers have continued to insist on coordinated sectoral bargaining and have firmly—and successfully—resisted the emergence of
low-wage sectors. To deal with unemployment and obtain compensation
for wage restraint, the unions since the late 1970s have pursued a variety
of qualitative demands, in particular a reduction of working hours and increasing support for training. They were partially successful with their
demands for a reduction of working hours, particularly in the metal-

working industry. As Thelen (2000) makes clear, employers are split on the issue of coordinated wage bargaining. Particularly the high-quality manufacturing firms, where active participation of a skilled workforce in work organization and innovation is crucial, do not want to risk a deterioration of the cooperative relations they have built up with their works councils, a deterioration that could result from the decentralization of collective bargaining to the enterprise level. Nevertheless, in the East the entire system of collective bargaining is being challenged by the decline in membership of both unions and employers associations (Czada 1998: 41) and by noncompliance with wage bargains.

The new SPD government attempted to give a boost to employment creation by setting up the tripartite Alliance for Jobs in December 1998, a permanent tripartite institution with different working groups and regular top-level talks between the leading representatives of employers, unions, and the government. The alliance was a departure from traditional patterns of industrial relations, insofar as the talks necessarily involve issues to be included in collective bargaining, and collective bargaining has traditionally been strictly bipartite. In January 2000, the alliance, under the chairmanship of Chancellor Schroeder, adopted recommendations for an employment-oriented bargaining policy (http://www .eiro.eurofound.ie/2000/01/features/DE0001232F.html). However, subsequent statements by union leaders and employer organization representatives made it clear that the two sides had rather different interpretations of the agreed-on principles, which were that the available wage funds should be determined by productivity growth and should be used primarily for job-creating agreements. Thus, the alliance by no means superimposed more binding central coordination on the pattern of sectorally coordinated bargaining, but rather it issued at best morally guiding recommendations for the sectoral bargaining rounds.

### *Austria*

Compared to our other cases, Austria did not really suffer an unemployment crisis and a crisis of the welfare state, though the need for austerity became a constant theme by the mid-1980s. Up to the late 1990s, unemployment levels remained moderate, at an average of 4.3% in 1982–91, 6% in 1992–95 (OECD 1997a: 21), and 7% in 1996–98 (OECD 1999a: 132). Accordingly, cuts in welfare state entitlements remained moderate as well, and there were even some new programs being introduced. Social spending rose from 26% of GDP in 1980 to 29% in 1993 (OECD 1997a: 133). To some extent, this difference between Austria and the other countries is accounted for by structural differences, and to some extent by the avoidance of the policy mistakes made in the Scandinavian countries. First, Austria was a laggard in productivity in the European context and thus maintained strong productivity growth while catching up from 60% of the OECD average in 1950 to slightly above that average in 1991 (OECD 1993a: 77). Second, Austrian business is much less internationalized than, for instance, Swedish business. The big exporting firms are nationalized, and the private sector consists primarily of smaller, domestically oriented firms. Historically, investment abroad has been very low; as late as 1987, investment abroad amounted to 1.9% of GDP only, compared to 7% for Sweden (Kurzer 1993: 95). Third, Austria benefited from a strong growth in gross capital flows since the early 1970s, particularly from Germany, Switzerland, and the Netherlands (OECD 1993a: 55). Fourth, tourism is an important contributor to the Austrian economy, and tourism is naturally bound to the country and is labor intensive. Finally, women's labor force participation grew only very moderately and thus exerted comparatively little pressure on the supply of employment.

With regard to policy choices, Austria liberalized capital flows gradually and avoided the procyclical policies that characterized the Scandinavian cases in the late 1980s and early 1990s. In 1991 Austria abolished the last foreign exchange regulations, but this had no dramatic impact. Austria had pursued a hard currency policy since 1973 (Scharpf 1991: 61–63) and officially pegged the schilling to the deutsche mark in 1982. In 1980 an attempt was made to stimulate investment by lowering interest rates slightly below German levels, but this attempt resulted in an immediate and substantial outflow of short-term capital and thus had to be abandoned (Haschek 1982: 196–97). Thus, despite the fact that de jure Austria did not have an independent central bank, de facto the government had all but abdicated its control of monetary policy. With the interest rates removed as a policy instrument, the Austrian government successfully boosted investment by offering new tax breaks for reinvestment and increasingly by directly subsidizing investment, thus moving to a greater reliance on the type of selective supply-side policies that are still feasible in the internationally open financial environment (but, we should note, not permissible under current regulations of the European Union). These policies are certainly one factor behind the continuation of a high reinvestment ratio in Austria in the 1980s. Overall interest rates have also been comparatively low, in accordance with German levels (OECD 1997a: 37).

With the shift to a hard currency policy, successful wage restraint has been all the more essential, and the continued practice of centrally coordinated bargaining has facilitated such restraint. The system of cooperation between the peak associations has also continued to provide the basis for consensual fiscal and social policy making. By 1986 the budget deficit had reached a peak of 5 percent of GDP; it was brought down to 3.25 percent by 1992; in the late 1980s this was done mainly through expenditure cuts, in the early 1990s through tax increases (OECD 1993a: 34–38). The concern with the budget deficit in the mid-1980s led to reforms to strengthen the financial basis of social insurance, comprising both increases in contributions and decreases in expenditures in 1984, and decreases in expenditures only in 1987. A major reform of the pension system was introduced in 1993, designed to make the system financially sound without increasing contributions or government's obligations. Among other measures, the reform included new rules for pension adjustment and incentives for delayed retirement. In the same year, a new insurance scheme for long-term care was introduced on the one hand, and eligibility requirements for unemployment insurance were tightened on the other (Talos 1996a: 548–50).

Progress on gender-egalitarian social policy was slow; the pattern of women's labor force participation and political mobilization resembled the German pattern very closely, and though the social democratic SPÖ were in government, they were in a coalition with the Christian democratic ÖVP from 1986 on and thus had to strike compromises to accommodate the latter's commitment to the traditional male breadwinner family. Women's labor force participation increased from 49 percent in 1980 to 62 percent in 1994, the same as the German rate; and women's representation in parliament climbed to 22 percent in 1990, one percentage point ahead of the German rate (Borchorst 1994: 41). A major effort to address gender issues in social policy was the "family package" of 1989. It was a package precisely because it contained provisions each of which in isolation would have been unacceptable to one or another of the coalition parties. Among other things, it introduced paid parental leave instead of maternity leave and extended the period from one to two years, albeit at a low replacement rate; it introduced support for the reintegration into the labor market of women who had taken time off to raise children; and it increased social assistance for low-income families. As in Germany, five years after the introduction of the legislation fewer than 1 percent of those who took parental leave were fathers (Rosenberger 1996: 364–65). Parental leave legislation was curtailed in the consolidation package of 1996–97 that limited the period of leave that one partner could claim to eighteen months (OECD 1997a: 49).

More progress was made in 1992 with legislation designed to reduce inequalities in the material positions of women and men. The impetus for this package came from a ruling of the constitutional court that held gender-differentiated age requirements for pension entitlements to be unconstitutional. The consequent need for parliament to revise pension legislation was taken advantage of by women's rights advocates to demand additional provisions to equalize material conditions for women and men in the labor market and in social insurance. These provisions included goals for hiring 40 percent women in every employment category in the public sector, an expansion of the notion of discrimination, the goal of equal pay for work of comparable value, an expansion of leave to take care of ill relatives from one to two weeks, improvements in the conditions of part-time work, pension credits for raising children, and payment of family allowances to mothers rather than the wage earner (Rosenberger 1996: 366). Again, in practice the hiring quotas have not been met, and the absence of child care facilities remains a major obstacle for women's integration into the labor market on an equal footing with men.

A recession let the deficit climb back up to 4.7 percent of GDP in 1993, and in the coalition negotiations after the 1994 elections, plans to trim the deficit assumed a crucial role. In 1995 austerity measures were imposed, such as a reduction of overtime and other extra pay for civil servants, higher pension contributions by civil servants, restrictions on family benefits and unemployment benefits, and higher pension contributions by farmers and the self-employed (OECD 1997a: 43). In fact, disagreements between the SPÖ and ÖVP coalition partners over the type of austerity policies to pursue induced the ÖVP to break up the coalition and force new elections as soon as 1995. The SPÖ improved its position by 3 percent of the vote and again became the lead party in a Grand Coalition. In the shadow of the Maastricht agreement, the new government agreed on the most stringent austerity plan in recent Austrian history, designed to reduce the budget deficit from 5 percent in 1995 to 3 percent over two years. The plan encompassed both tax increases and cuts in spending on personnel in the public sector, in transfer payments like pensions and family allowances, and efforts to increase the average retirement age (OECD 1997a: 47–49). These measures were successful in reducing the government deficit to 2.7 percent in 1997 and keeping it there for 1998 (OECD 1998a: 42; 1999a: 133). In 1997 parliament approved a pension reform that further reduced early retirement pensions, harmonized the calculation of public sector pensions with the general system, and extended the obligation to pay social security contributions to all labor income, including casual jobs, but also brought an improvement in the form of an increase in the imputed pension value for child-raising periods (OECD 1998a: 7–8). Wage restraint remained a crucial tool in the search for continued economic upgrading and growth of employment. The quest for productivity improvements was successful as productivity in the exposed sectors became one of the highest in the OECD by the early 1990s. Austria also maintained one of the highest investment rates in the OECD (OECD 1993a: 45). It is worth pointing out here again that top-level coordination of sectoral bargaining coexisted with significant wage dispersion and some wage drift at enterprise levels (Traxler 1993). Wage agreements usually only set minimum conditions and it has been up to individual works councils to improve upon these terms, with the result that highly profitable enterprises have generally paid higher than negotiated rates. In response to increasing commercial pressures, though, wage drift has fallen significantly since the mid-1980s (OECD 1997a: 127–28). The possibility of concluding enterprise level agreements made overall restraint compatible with the flexibility some employers wanted to attract highly skilled workers.[41] There has also been a tendency for works councils and enterprises to conclude agreements on more flexible work practices, albeit without a firm institutional and legal basis (OECD 1997a: 118).

A major area of contention was the modernization and privatization of the state-owned enterprises. The ÖVP assumed some neoliberal stances in the 1980s and began to push for more competition and privatization partly for ideological reasons; the unions mainly opposed privatization, and the SPÖ took a mostly pragmatic position in the middle (Müller 1988). Professionalization of management, rationalization, and partial privatization did take place after the mid-1980s, initially with the stipulation that 51 percent ownership had to remain in public hands. When there were renewed large losses in the sector in the early 1990s, the process of privatization assumed new urgency. In addition, as reducing the public debt became a goal, proceeds from privatization came to be relied on for this purpose (OECD 1997a: 58).

As the use of public-sector enterprises to shelter employment decreased, Austria put greater effort into an active labor market policy to support retraining and relocation of laid-off employees. Still, active labor market policies remained comparatively modest; in 1994 spending on active labor market policy measures amounted to only 0.2 percent of GDP (OECD 1997a: 145). As in Germany and the Netherlands, early retirement became a widely used tool to reduce unemployment among older workers. Since 1970 the average retirement age has gradually declined

from about sixty-two to fifty-eight years, without any changes in the statutory retirement age (OECD 1997a: 54, 6). As a result, labor force participation among older workers is among the lowest in the OECD; only 24
percent of the population ages fifty-five to sixty-four are in the labor force
(OECD 1997a: 143).

The 1990s posed two new economic challenges: the inflow of workers
from the former Eastern Bloc countries, and the entry into the EU as
of 1995. Despite attempts to stem the flow from the east, large numbers
of workers came to Austria in search of jobs. By 1994, almost 9 percent of wage and salary earners were foreigners (OECD 1997a: 115). At
the same time, increasing trade with the eastern European countries
stimulated new investments and jobs in Austria. One of the important
consequences of EU membership was that the government could no
longer use investment subsidies as a major tool to promote economic
growth. Such subsidies are only allowed in very limited cases.

Probably the biggest challenge to the Austrian model is political. The
two main parties have consistently been losing votes, so much so that
they lost their joint two-thirds majority in parliament in the 1994 elections, and the ÖVP fell behind the FPÖ to third place in the elections
of October 1999, which eventually led to the controversial coalition government between the ÖVP and the FPÖ. In 1983, the SPÖ received
48% of the vote and the ÖVP 43%, for a joint total of 91%; by 1994
these figures had fallen to 35%, 28%, and 63%, respectively.[42] The FPÖ
obtained 22.5% of the vote in 1994, the Greens 7%, and the Liberal Fo-
rum, a split-off from the FPÖ, 6% (Dachs 1996: 292). The erosion of the
preeminent position of the two big parties also weakened the legitimacy
of the entire system of incorporation of peak associations into the policy-making process. The opposition parties, lacking ties to the interest
associations, have attacked their legitimacy, particularly their compulsory nature and method of financing (Dachs 1996: 299). Some of the indicators of a slow decline in the preeminence of peak associations are
the decline in voter turnout in internal BAK elections, the decline in the
number of bills submitted by the government—and vetted by the peak
associations—as a proportion of the total number of bills passed by parliament, and the decline in the number of members of parliament who
also hold positions in the peak associations (Crepaz 1994). An additional factor weakening the position of organized labor is the fact that if
one takes into account nonemployed persons, the density of Austrian
unionization has declined, by 15% between 1980 and 1988 alone
(Traxler 1992); union membership as a percentage of all employees declined from 59.6% in 1980 to 51.6% in 1995 (Traxler 1998: 244).[43] To the

extent that the position of the peak associations and the two main parties is challenged, then, the chances for a continuation of the consensual pattern of policy making, of shared benefits and sacrifices, are reduced.

## The Netherlands

The case of the Netherlands has attracted wide attention because of its recovery—some have called it miraculous—from a severe unemployment and welfare state crisis. Unemployment in the Netherlands in the 1970s and 1980s was higher for a longer period of time than in any of the other eight cases of generous welfare states that we discuss here, and the fiscal pressures on the welfare state were correspondingly intense. The particular measures chosen to deal with unemployment—expansion of early retirement and of disability pensions—led to a real and perceived crisis of inactivity. Recovery was brought about by a combination of centrally agreed-on wage restraint, cutbacks of entitlements, and structural reforms of the welfare state. However, it is crucial to note that these cutbacks and structural reforms left intact the comprehensive character of the Dutch welfare state and its effective approach to lowering poverty; they did not amount to a transformation of the Christian democratic into a liberal welfare state regime.

As we discussed in chapter 5, the Dutch growth model in the 1940s and 1950s was primarily based on keeping labor and capital cheap; a specific industrial policy or active labor market policy never existed. Already in the 1960s the wage restraint policy eroded and in the 1970s centralized bargaining broke down altogether and wages began to exceed productivity gains (OECD 1996c: 48). The difficulties faced by all European countries in the wake of the 1973 oil shock were aggravated by the "Dutch disease," the appreciation of the exchange rate because of natural gas exports. The high exchange rate hurt Dutch exports and made capital exports more attractive. Efforts to renegotiate gas export contracts after 1973 to reflect higher energy prices (and increase government revenue from the exports) met with limited success, as many multiyear contracts had been signed at fixed prices in the scramble for export markets in the late 1960s (Lubbers and Lemckert 1980: 99). Accordingly, budget and balance of payments pressures intensified and unemployment increased. In 1975 unemployment reached 4%, up from a customary pre-1973 level of between 1% and 2%. Economic growth slowed considerably as well.

The PvdA-led coalition government that came to power in 1973 kept expanding welfare state entitlements and expenditures up to the mid-1970s. Like many other governments, it interpreted the crisis in the wake of the 1973 oil shock as temporary and saw expansionary fiscal policy as the appropriate way out of the crisis (Visser and Hemerijck 1997: 132). However, by 1976 the economic changes forced first efforts to contain rising welfare state expenditures, mainly by letting adjustments lag behind inflation. Economic conditions worsened in the 1980s, governmental power shifted to the right, and cutbacks were intensified, contributions increased, and eligibility criteria and enforcement provisions for a wide variety of programs stiffened. Economic growth slowed further, and unemployment fluctuated between 8 percent and 12 percent in the 1980s. Whereas full employment had remained in the center of the political debate in the 1970s and governments provided subsidies to ailing firms and supported the creation of jobs in labor-intensive public infrastructure and construction, the post-1982 Lubbers government made it clear that budgetary concerns were much more important, and it scaled back these job creation and preservation measures and abandoned them by 1985 (Visser and Hemerijck 1997: 159–60). Unemployment figures only tell part of the story, though. Many older workers went into early retirement and many claimed disability pensions. As a result, the labor force participation rate of male workers between sixty and sixty-four years of age fell from around 70 percent in 1973 to 22 percent in 1991 (Hemerijck and Kloosterman 1994). In addition, many of the long-term unemployed whose benefits were exhausted came to rely on social assistance. Between 1970 and 1986 the share of the unemployed among all recipients of social assistance increased from 3 percent to 67 percent (Esping-Andersen 1996c).

In 1974 the Den Uyl PvdA-led government linked public-sector wages and welfare benefits to private-sector wage development, which in turn was determined by collective agreements with automatic cost-of-living compensation (Hemerijck and Kloosterman 1994). The post-1982 Lubbers government severed this link and embarked upon a series of cutbacks to reach its primary goal, a reduction of the budget deficit. Salaries and benefits in the public sector were frozen in 1982 and remained frozen in subsequent years, as did the minimum wage and the social benefits tied to it (Visser 1992: 344). In 1984–86 pensions and family allowances were frozen; in 1984 unemployment and disability benefits were cut by 3% and the next year the replacement rate in these programs was lowered from 80% to 70%; in addition, the length of the benefit period for disability and unemployment was reduced, which meant that recipients had to shift to social assistance where benefits were lower (Cox 1993: 178–83). The result of all these cuts was that the gap between average wages and average benefits increased by 12 percent in 1983–89 (Visser and Hemerijck

1997: 134). As in other cases, these cuts were not experienced as a full 12 percent reduction in real income by beneficiaries; rather, they represent the gap between the real income and a hypothetical situation of increases under the old rules. It is also worth noting that coverage through private negotiated pension plans kept increasing in the 1980s and 1990s, from 84 percent of all employees, public and private, to 91 percent in 1997 (Wierink 1997).

The loss of jobs, particularly in the industrial sector, took a toll on union membership. Union density declined from 40% in the 1960s to 32% in 1980 and 23% in 1986 (Visser 1992: 330); in the late 1980s it picked up again to reach 30% in 1996 (Visser and Hemerijck 1997: 84). After the failure of collective agreements as well as of government-imposed wage restraint in the 1970s, the loss of jobs and of union members finally induced employers and unions to arrive at a bipartite agreement in 1982 that set the precedent of moderation in wage demands in exchange for acceptance of the goal of a reduction in working hours (Hemerijck and van Kersbergen 1997). Between 1982 and 1985, real wages fell and after 1987 they recovered slowly until 1993, when increases again came to be kept below inflation (Visser and Hemerijck 1997: 101–6). However, as Visser and Hemerijck (1997: 102–4) point out, the reduction of working hours for full-time employees made very slow progress; and it became increasingly difficult for unions to maintain a united front on the issue. In 1982–93 the average work week fell from 40 to 37.5 hours (Visser and Hemerijck 1997: 102–4). What did happen was the creation of large numbers of part-time jobs. Though central agreements were no more than nonbinding recommendations for bargaining at the sectoral level, and even at the sectoral level agreements became more flexible than before, allowing tailoring to the needs of individual enterprises (Visser 1992: 351), the overall corporatist agreement on wage moderation was a crucial trendsetter. Central supervision and guidance of decentralized bargaining have remained important, as all negotiations continued to be carried out by full-time officials and deviance continued to be sanctioned (Visser and Hemerijck 1997: 112). Thus, the Netherlands presented a constellation of centrally coordinated sectoral bargaining with an independent central bank and successful wage restraint.

The 1982 agreement significantly improved the competitiveness of Dutch exports and reduced the wage bill in the public sector, thus contributing to economic growth, job creation, and a recovery of public finances. The overall wage restraint contributed to a job creation rate from the mid-1980s to the mid-1990s that was more than four times that of the average in the European Union (Hemerijck and van Kersbergen

1997) and to a decline in the unemployment rate after 1987, down to a low of 5.3 percent in 1992 and 5.8 percent in 1997 (OECD 1998c: 20). Other factors, of course, contributed to renewed economic growth and employment creation. The Dutch disease was to a large extent overcome and upgrading was successful in traditionally strong sectors such as agri-foods, chemicals, and financial services (OECD 1996c: 75). In the 1980s there was a clear trend in favor of capital income and to greater inequalities in wages, but the increase in wage inequality has remained modest in comparative perspective (Visser and Hemerijck 1997: 40).

Despite these favorable developments in growth and open unemployment and despite the cuts already imposed, welfare state expenditures continued to weigh heavy on public finances. Increasingly, and correctly so, the problem of the Dutch welfare state came to be defined as one of excessive inactivity and the solution as an overall increase in labor force participation. In 1985 the government had launched a major attempt to reduce fraud and abuse in the social assistance and disability programs. Inspectors were sent out to check on household income of social assistance recipients, but due to intense public criticism this program was dropped again. Abuses in the disability program to relieve unemployment were rampant because the criteria were lenient and both employers and unions, the actors controlling the program through the bipartite industrial boards, had a strong interest in shifting older and less productive workers more or less painlessly out of the labor force in this way. As a result, the program supported some nine hundred thousand people by 1990, having been conceptualized to serve no more than two hundred thousand (Hemerijck and van Kersbergen 1997).

After the PvdA was included in Lubbers's third cabinet in 1989, the government embarked on a very serious reform of the sickness and disability schemes. It instituted financial incentives for employers to restrict the use of these schemes. It imposed new eligibility criteria for the disability scheme, lower benefit levels, a shortened period of full benefits, and more stringent conditions regarding acceptance of alternative employment (Visser and Hemerijck 1997: 141). The government also urged physicians to apply more stringent standards and demanded reexaminations of the disabled for improvements, as well as reemployment of the partially disabled (Cox 1994). These measures led to a decline in the number of disabled from a peak of 925,000 in January 1994 to 861,000 in December 1995 (OECD 1996c: 16). The sickness insurance reform stipulated that beginning in 1994, employers had to continue wage payments to sick or disabled workers at 70 percent of the previous wage for six weeks (two weeks for small firms), and they were charged with "providing guidance" to the sick or disabled individuals through company doctors or the social security administration. This, together with a bonus system for employers who kept on or hired partially disabled persons, provided strong incentives for employers to scrutinize sickness and disability claims carefully. It also created a greater role for private insurance as employers can insure themselves against sickness and disability claims. These changes led to the negotiation of supplementary sickness and disability insurance in collective agreements, and an overall increase in the importance of private insurance (Hemerijck and van Kersbergen 1997). In other programs, a trend begun in the 1980s toward more emphasis on household income testing and greater reliance on flat-rate rather than earnings-related benefits was continued. Income testing had been introduced into the pension system when minimum pensions were set in 1987 at 70 percent of the social minimum plus an allowance of up to 30 percent of the social minimum for the younger partner, depending on the income of the younger partner. In 1994 this ratio was changed to 50:50; i.e., half of it was made subject to income testing. The gap between the average income of active and inactive people continued to grow; from 1983 to 1993, it increased by some 20 percent (OECD 1996c: 52–54), and the freezing of benefits in the pension and unemployment insurance schemes in 1993, 1994, and 1995 let that increase grow even further.

The implementation of these reforms met with strong resistance and discontent; the unions organized the largest postwar protest demonstration in The Hague in response in 1991, and in the 1994 elections the governing parties paid heavily (Visser and Hemerijck 1997: 141–46). Since the Christian democrats lost even more votes than the PvdA, the latter became the largest party and its leader, Vim Kok, became the prime minister in a new coalition government with two liberal parties, the VVD and D66. Despite their heavy losses, the social democrats remained committed to social security reform. They promised to leave the level and duration of benefits untouched, but to change the institutional structure of social security and to continue with a primary emphasis on increases in labor force participation. Essentially, up to the early 1990s all the changes had left the essential principles of the existing programs intact; the changes had been aimed at putting these programs on a sounder financial base and at curbing abuses of the programs. In 1993, however, a Dutch parliamentary committee in which all parties were represented issued a report that looked at the totality of social programs and made proposals for significant changes in these programs and their administration, and the left-liberal coalition then implemented many of these changes. The essence of the administrative changes was to strengthen political supervision of the social security schemes that had been administered by unions and employers. Among the most important changes were the establishment by the government of an independent political body to monitor the administration of social insurance schemes and a shift of partial administrative and financial responsibility for social assistance from the central to local governments, with the aim of tightening supervision to curb abuses. Furthermore, in 1997 the National Social Insurance Institute was created with independent members, employers' and trade union representatives, and a government-appointed chair and charged with setting the yearly premiums for the different social security schemes (Visser and Hemerijck 1997: 149). In other areas, eligibility criteria for unemployment compensation were tightened again and linked to active participation in the search for employment and in retraining (OECD 1996c).

Finally, all responsibility for sickness cash benefits was transferred from the state to employers in 1996; employers have to continue wage payments equivalent to at least the social minimum for one full year, and additional benefits are to be negotiated in collective agreements. This gave employers an incentive both to reduce absenteeism and to seek private insurance to cover their risk and thus amounted essentially to a privatization of sickness insurance (Hemerijck and van Kersbergen 1997). In 1998 this general trend continued with a law on disability that set premiums for disability insurance according to the past record of incidence of disability of employers, but also gave employers the option of leaving the public disability scheme and taking out private insurance (OECD 1998c: 13). However, employers will still be bound by the benefit rules set by legislation. In early 2000, the government granted the social partners more influence in the implementation of reintegration of unemployed and disabled people in the labor market by allowing collective agreements to include provisions obliging companies to help former employees find another job. Such agreements can be declared generally binding for the entire sector by the minister of social affairs (eironline; http://www.eiro.eurofound.ie//2000/02/InBrief/n10002175.html.).

With the increasing emphasis on raising labor force participation rates, the lack of an active labor market policy came under scrutiny during the 1980s and efforts were made to strengthen the Public Employment Service and involve the labor market partners. Still, as late as 1990, 85 percent of all expenditures on labor market policy were passive, that is, they went to transfer payments in compensation for income losses. Finally in 1991 a new tripartite employment service was set up, but in a public evaluation in 1994 it was criticized very heavily and as a result its functions were restricted to particularly vulnerable groups, the long-term unemployed, the young, and ethnic minorities (Visser and Hemerijck 1997: 165–72). The main instruments used are fiscal measures to subsidize low-paid employment at the bottom end of the labor market in both the public and private sectors (OECD 1997b: 63–64). An active labor market policy focusing on employment measures, vocational education, and training on a large scale is still missing. Crucial for the reduction in unemployment and the increase in labor force participation rates were clearly the increase in part-time work and the efforts to improve conditions of part-time work with regards to benefits. The share of part-time work in total employment increased from less than 15% in 1975 to 35% in 1994; 75% of part-time jobs are held by women, which in turn meant a substantial increase in female labor force participation (Hemerijck and van Kersbergen 1997). New jobs were created predominantly in the service sector, where employment grew by more than 13 percent from 1990 to 1995, while it decreased by almost 5 percent in industry. Still, one has to keep in mind that even after the welfare state reforms there remains a great amount of hidden unemployment in the Netherlands, and total labor force participation is still comparatively low. In full-time equivalents the employment rate at 52% is not much above the 1984 low of 48% (OECD 1998c: 34). Moreover, the rise in total working hours after 1987 was associated with a slowdown in productivity growth, indicating that marginal productivity in newly created jobs has been relatively low (OECD 1997b: 80).

Women's labor force participation remained the lowest in the OECD countries until 1980, and the welfare state strongly supported the male breadwinner family pattern. Between 1980 and 1990 it increased dramatically by Dutch standards, but still remained behind the levels of Germany and Austria. Moreover, more women were holding part-time jobs than in any other of the fourteen major OECD countries (Sainsbury 1999b: 196). Along with increases in labor force participation came increases in political mobilization and representation. The decline in union membership among male workers that occurred at the same time as women joined the labor force and thus unions in increasing numbers meant that women constituted the largest part of new union members and came to constitute an overall larger share of the union membership. Accordingly, unions began to take up issues such as child care and sexual harassment in collective bargaining (Outshoorn 1995: 185). Women's activity in political parties increased as well, as did their representation in parliament, to a level comparable to those in Germany and Austria.

Considerable women-friendly progress in social policy did occur, though the Netherlands had a very long way to go and the history of discrimination in the labor market and the traditional male breadwinner model have remained very difficult to overcome. Reforms in the 1980s ended the formal discrimination against married women in disability insurance, the public pension system, and extended unemployment benefits. The pension reform had the widest-ranging effect, as it gave both partners equal entitlements, but it left working women at a comparative disadvantage as they have to pay contributions whereas housewives do not but have the same entitlements. In 1985 the unit of contribution to all national insurance schemes was changed from the household to the individual, but health care remained exempt, and the unit of benefits for means-tested programs remained the household (Sainsbury 1996: 184–87). In 1991 parental leave, consisting of the right of father and mother to lower working hours to twenty per week for six months, was introduced in the private sector, but it remained unpaid and thus an unattractive option; in the public sector it was introduced two years earlier and is paid (Sainsbury 1996: 188–89). Maybe the most important area of progress was the extension of social benefits to part-time work by lowering the thresholds for entitlements. Finally, in 1990 the Childcare Stimulation Act was passed, which provided subsidies for child care centers, day care host parents, and care for young schoolchildren. The care arrangements remained largely privately provided. However, the impact of this legislation was highly limited; between 1990 and 1993 it increased the proportion of children in subsidized day care only from 2 percent to 4 percent (Gustafsson 1994: 55).

## The Antipodes

Changes in the world economy had a much more fundamental impact on the Antipodean systems of social protection than they did on the social democratic welfare states of Scandinavia or the Christian democratic welfare states of Continental Europe. However, the Australasian story does not conform very well to the image of the motors of change portrayed in the usual versions of the globalization thesis. In that view, technological change and deregulation in other countries lead to increasing openness of trade and financial markets, which puts competitive pressures on exports of countries that have resisted the deregulation process and then, once those countries do deregulate the external sector, the pressures of cost competitiveness put a downward pressure on wages and welfare state entitlements. The second half of this scenario does bear some resemblance to the Antipodean experience, but the initial impetus was quite different and bears much greater similarities to shifting terms of trade problems faced by third-world primary product producers in earlier decades.

In chapter 5, we saw that Australia and New Zealand developed unique systems of social protection that were predicated on rents transferred from highly competitive primary sector exports to workers and entrepreneurs in protected manufacturing sectors. The two settler colonies developed as part of the British imperial system and the Sterling area. At the beginning of the 1950s, this was still their character: 75% of Australia's exports and 88% of New Zealand's were primary products and 31% of Australia's exports and 65% of New Zealand's were destined for Britain (Easton and Gerritsen 1996: 25–26). It was inevitable that this would change with the decline of the empire, the relative decline of Britain, and the two countries' locations on the other side of the globe from Britain. Britain's entry into the EC hastened that transformation. By 1982, only 4% of Australia's exports and 15% of New Zealand's were headed for Britain. Yet the two countries were still very dependent on primary product exports (57% of Australian exports and 62% of New Zealand's), though in Australia's case over half of this was now mineral products rather than agriculture. Both countries now counted on tourism as a major foreign exchange earner. The terms of trade for these Antipodean exports deteriorated in the postwar period. This was one cause of the relatively poor economic performance of the two countries: From 1950 to 1980 the Australian economy grew at an average annual rate of 2.1% per capita and New Zealand's at 1.6%, both well below the average for industrial democracies of 3.2%. In the case of New Zealand, the situation was particularly dismal: Its growth rate was the worst in this group of rich countries and it fell from fourth place in terms of per capita income to sixteenth.[44]

Relying on transfers from primary product exports to support national affluence and the system of social protection had clearly become an unviable strategy. These world market developments led to major changes in economic strategy, industrial relations, and social policy in both countries, with the common thread being a move to market regulation of relationships that had previously been politically controlled. Interestingly, this deregulatory process was initiated by the labor parties, though in both cases subsequent conservative governments deepened the process, particularly in those areas bearing directly on the system of social protection–social policy and the industrial relations system. Moreover, as of this writing, because of the longer period of conservative rule, differences in the constitutional structures and differences in the labor parties, the outcome in New Zealand was a radical system shift in the social protection system. By contrast, the Australian Labor Party, which was in power from 1983 to 1996, attempted to cushion the impact of economic deregulation by maintaining substantial elements of the wage regulation system and by introducing compensatory social policy changes.

In Australia, prior to the advent of the Hawke Labor government in 1983, the response of both of the major parties to the changes in the world economy associated with the post–Golden Age period was partisan politics and policy as usual.[45] As we saw in chapter 5, the Whitlam government came to power with an ambitious social policy agenda though, without control of the senate, it was able to implement little other than the centerpiece of this agenda, the Medibank universal health insurance system. The Fraser Liberal-Country government rolled back the Medibank reform and, in general, moved to retrench social expenditure. While the emphasis on fighting inflation and allowing unemployment to rise might be seen as a departure from the past in a neoliberal direction, the Fraser government did not move to deregulate the economy in any significant way. Indeed, its initiatives in areas of energy and minerals development might be seen as an increase in state regulation. Thus, the Australian case also fits the pattern we encountered in the quantitative data and in the other case studies of continued, if somewhat diminished, partisan differences, and policy "fumbling" as governments failed to grasp the fundamentally altered nature of the new world.

Like the Social Democratic government elected in Sweden the year before, the Hawke government came to office with a fundamental change in direction in mind and, as Schwartz (1994a, 1994b) shows, in both cases this involved increasing reliance on markets in both the private and public sector. This was, of course, a much more fundamental change in direction in Australia (and New Zealand) than in Scandinavia. At first glance, it appears as a curiosity that this move would have been made by a labor government, but as Easton and Gerritsen (1996: 28) point out, the conservative parties had been in power almost continuously from 1949 to 1983 and were so deeply entwined with the old elites that benefited from the prevailing arrangements that it was difficult for them to make a decisive change of direction despite the widespread perceptions that these arrangements no longer worked.

The basic parameters of policy change had been worked out before the election with the cooperation of the Australian Confederation of Trade Unions (ACTU) by Hawke, who was a former president of the union confederation. The centerpiece of economic management was the Prices and Income Accord, usually referred to as simply the Accord, an agreement between the government and ACTU, in which the unions agreed to restrain wage growth in return for government efforts to increase employment and introduce social policy changes favorable to workers. In the course of the Hawke and Keating Labor governments the Accord was renegotiated eight times, the first five of which were ratified by the arbitration commission or its successor, the Australia Industrial Relations Commission (AIRC). Initially, fiscal and monetary policy were expansionary, but declining foreign balances and increasing orthodox views from the treasury led to the targeting of monetary policy on inflation fighting and eventually to orienting fiscal policy to produce balanced budgets over the economic cycle. Thus, Australian Labor came to adopt fiscal and monetary stances similar to those of the Nordic social democrats.

The Accord was intended not only to compensate labor for wage restraint, but also to cushion the effect of the extensive deregulation of the economy and the resulting economic dislocations on employees. The government moved progressively to substitute market regulation for government intervention in the domestic economy. In the public sector, firms were corporatized or privatized, the production of formerly government-supplied goods and services was contracted out, public monopolies and publicly regulated companies were subjected to competition, and user fees were introduced or increased (Schwartz 1994a, 1994b; OECD 1996a: 121–23). In the private sectors, markets were deregulated and subsidies to private business (except labor market measures aimed at increasing employment) were cut. The domestic financial sector was deregulated in the mid-1980s. In external relations, the dollar was floated and protection, a cornerstone of the old system, was substantially reduced, though it is important to recognize that some industries, notably the automotive, footwear, textile, and clothing industries, still enjoy significant protection (OECD 1996a: 125).

The Accord process is credited with effectively restraining wage growth, as real compensation per employee in the business sector increased by a cumulative 8 percent in 1983–95, while productivity increased by 16.5 percent (OECD 1996a: 83). Easton and Gerritsen (1996: 41, 45) argue that the Accord process has resulted in rapid employment growth in Australia, which was almost twice the OECD average for 1985–92. However, because of rapid natural population increase, increasing female labor force participation, and immigration the impact on unemployment has been very modest. Unemployment fell from 9% when Labor took office to 6% in 1989 but then increased with the recession to 11% and then fell to 9% by the time of Labor's loss in the 1996 election. Moreover, a significant portion of the increase of employment is accounted for by part-time workers and casual workers, which each made up one-quarter of the workforce in 1995, though it should be noted that 70% of casual work was part-time, so that together the two categories make up about a third of the labor force. While most of the part-time work is voluntary, a quarter of part-time workers would have preferred to work more hours (OECD 1996a: 71–72).

By contrast to the "marketization" of the rest of the economy, the Labor governments moved much more carefully in the area of industrial relations. In the initial years of the Accord, the old arbitration system was essentially maintained but directed to a new end. With the balance-of-payments and currency crisis of the mid-1980s and subsequent turn in macroeconomic policy, the wage-setting process was gradually decentralized and wage increases made dependent on productivity increases at the enterprise level except for the bottom end of the wage scale (Bray and Nelson 1996: 80, 84; OECD 1995a: 53–57; OECD 1996a: 80–83). The Industrial Relations Acts of 1988 and 1993 enabled firms and employees, unionized or nonunionized, to negotiate agreements within the broad frame of the centrally determined award as long as the agreements met a "no disadvantage test," that is, the agreement, taken as a whole, was no worse than the award, with the AIRC making this determination. As of 1996, 62 percent of workers in the federal awards system were covered by such agreements. Awards are still important in fixing the minimum wage and, under the Accord, the AIRC has been particularly vigilant in protecting the interests of low-paid workers. Though business interests strongly supported this move to decentralization, Bray and Nelson (1996: 81, 84) insist that "ACTU accepted, indeed championed" the changes in the bargaining system.

The Labor government assigned to social policy changes the role of compensating those adversely impacted by the economic deregulation process and of compensating labor for the wage restraint agreed to in the Accords. The central thrust of social policy has been to serve a clientele that was increasing as a result of demographic change as well as of economic restructuring, within the constraints of the government's commitment to controlling the growth of expenditure. The means chosen to do this were increases in targeting and selectivity. Income and asset tests were reintroduced for pensioners over seventy. The formerly universal child allowance was subjected to a means test.

To combat family poverty, an additional child allowance and a very substantial enhancement of the rent allowance were introduced for low-income families (Castles 1996: 107).

Feminists inside and outside of the Labor Party fought for and won increases in day care: The number of publicly funded day care places increased 60 percent (albeit from a small base) in the first two years of the Labor government and fourfold by 1993 (Curtin and Sawer 1996: 162). As we have seen, the Whitlam government had already established a toehold for feminist concerns in the government bureaucracy and the Labor governments expanded this, most notably establishing the Women's Budget Program (later entitled Women's Budget Statement), which required departments and agencies to report the impact of their activities on women. A maternity allowance, advocated by women's organizations as well as the trade unions, was included as part of the Accord process in 1994 (O'Connor, Orloff, and Shaver 1999: 216–17). However, as Curtin and Sawer (1996: 155) point out, the Labor Party's commitment not to increase public expenditure led to a contraction of community services important to women. By the same token, an aggressive expansion of public social services and parental leave, as occurred in the Nordic countries in this period, was not on the agenda.

By far the most significant policy innovations of the period, medical insurance and supplementary pensions, were direct products of the Accord. As part of the first Accord agreement, the Hawke government introduced Medicare, a universal health insurance scheme, essentially the same as the Medibank scheme introduced by Whitlam and abolished by Fraser. In 1986, the arbitration system delivered an earnings-related superannuation system that was subsequently expanded and codified into legislation by the government. When fully matured in 2031, it would have provided benefits equal to 60% of preretirement income. It was to be funded by employers' contributions of 9% of payroll, employee contributions of 3%, and government funds matching employee contributions. Similar to the Finnish earnings-related tier, because it is privately administered, the pension outlays do not appear as government expenditure and the employer and employee contributions do not appear as taxes. Thus, the Labor government managed to introduce, or at least midwife, a very expensive social policy innovation and yet keep its promise not to substantially raise taxes.

With regard to taxation, the Labor government's posture was consistent with its overall policy direction of introducing neoliberal reform while cushioning the distributive outcomes. The highest marginal tax rates of 60 percent were lowered to 49 percent, but a capital gains tax and a progressive tax on business fringe benefits were introduced. Notably, in contrast to New Zealand, an attempt by then–treasury minister Keating to introduce a goods and services tax in order to reduce income taxes was turned back by opposition from inside the ALP and the unions.

In 1996, the Liberal-National party coalition led by John Howard won the election on a relatively moderate program but then, on assuming office, presented a strongly neoliberal program, including a radical change in the industrial relations legislation along the lines of the 1991 Employment Contracts Act in New Zealand (see below) (Schwartz 2000). The Howard government capped the employers' contribution to the new pension system at 7 percent and cut active labor market spending. In the area of gender policy, the government abolished the Women's Budget Statement, cut the budget and the mandate of the Office for the Status of Women, and cut day care support while introducing a tax rebate to the primary breadwinner (O'Connor, Orloff, and Shaver 1999: 218). More radical neoliberal changes in social policy and even more so in the proposed labor relations legislation were averted only by the government's minority position in the Australian senate. The government was returned to office in 1999 but by the slimmest of margins, losing the popular vote to Labor and finding itself in a yet more weakened position in the senate.

As we saw in chapter 5, the end of the Golden Age was marked by politics as usual in New Zealand, as the Nationals trumped Labour's superannuation plan with an incredibly generous, and expensive, pension plan of its own.[46] Partly because of a favorable move in the terms of trade before the first oil price increase, there was no immediate sense of crisis despite the poor postwar growth record. Upon taking office, the National prime minister, Muldoon, authoritarian in style and populist and interventionist in policy, did identify high inflation, consistent balance of payments deficits, low savings rates, and rising unemployment (though still low by later standards) as persistent problems. Though it was increasingly recognized that the highly regulated and protected agrarian export economy was unsustainable, Muldoon's solution was not to move primarily in a neoliberal direction. Some market regulations were removed, but his primary thrust was interventionist. The second oil price increase stimulated the National government to initiate a number of projects in natural gas and hydropower development designed to make the country 60% self-sufficient in energy (McRobie 1992). As inflation reached 17.6% in 1982, Muldoon introduced wage and price controls for twelve months and then extended them for another eight months. He subsequently responded to a sharp rise in interest rates with controls on home mortgage interest rates. These policies along with the underlying structural weakness of the economy put increasing pressure on the N.Z. dollar. The government countered by depleting its foreign reserves and credit lines and forcing a closing of the Reserve Bank of New Zealand immediately after the 1984 election, which was handily won by Labour.

Labour Party leader David Lange became prime minister in 1984, but the key figure behind the turn in policy direction and policy developments of Labour's 1984–87 term in office was Finance Minister Roger Douglas, backed up by doctrinaire neoliberal top bureaucrats in the treasury. Outside of industrial relations and social policy, the government introduced neoliberal marketizing reforms with breakneck speed: the currency was floated; state-owned enterprises were ordered to behave like private enterprises and then many were privatized; tariffs were progressively reduced; import licensing was eliminated; subsidies to industry and agriculture were progressively eliminated; where feasible, government departments were corporatized and in some cases privatized; the financial and banking system was deregulated; the Reserve Bank was made more independent and ordered to focus on price stability as its overriding goal. In the field of taxation, top marginal income tax rates were reduced from 66% to 33%; the tax base was broadened by cutting deductions; and a goods and services tax of 12.5% was introduced to make up for the revenue shortfall. These radical and rapid changes moved the New Zealand economy in 1984 from the most regulated economy among OECD countries to one of the least regulated at the end of Labour's second term in 1990. The process produced massive layoffs in the protected and subsidized sectors of the economy; unemployment rose from 5.7% in 1984 to 7.7% in 1990, and many more people experienced disruptions in their careers.

During Labour's tenure in office, social policy and industrial relations remained insulated from the neoliberals' reforming zeal. The Nationals' profligate pension reform had been responsible for large increases in the deficit in 1978–79, which continued into the 1980s (Dahlziel and Lattimore 1996: 52). Labour did cut this program, raising the retirement age to sixty-five in a phased-in fashion and introducing a tax surcharge of 20 percent on high-income earners. Active labor market policy was also cut back. On the other hand, support for low-income families was broadened. As in Australia, feminists inside and outside the party successfully pushed Labour to increase public funding of day care substantially, despite strong pressures for a general decrease in social expenditures, and also successfully pressed for an extension of maternity and parental leave, which, however, remain unpaid (Curtin and Sawer 1996: 156–62). Over the opposition of neoliberals in the government and bureaucracy, female party leaders spearheaded the effort to pass the Employment Equity Act of 1990, which strengthened statutes against gender discrimination in pay and set up a mechanism to assess comparable worth of predominantly female and male occupations.

In the case of industrial relations, Labour restored compulsory unionism, which had been eliminated by the previous National government. The aim of the Labour Relations Act of 1987, which among other things set a minimum union size, was to rationalize and streamline labor relations, not to weaken the unions' hand in bargaining. Nonetheless, due to ongoing restructuring of the economy, union density did decline somewhat under Labour, falling from 44 percent of wage and salary earners in 1987 to 42 percent in 1991 (Crawford, Harbridge, and Hince 1998).

The Nationals, who had converted from the interventionism of Muldoon to a neoliberalism more doctrinaire than that of the neoliberals in Labour, were swept into office in 1990 as a result of discontent with Labour. They turned their reforming zeal onto the areas that Labour had left untouched, industrial relations and social policy. They immediately repealed the Employment Equity Act of 1990 and proceeded to pass a piece of industrial relations legislation, the Employment Contracts Act of 1991, that so radically changed industrial relations that Castles (1996: 106) has characterized it as marking "the end of the wage earners' welfare state in New Zealand." Its main provisions were (1) the elimination of compulsory unionism and blanket coverage; (2) the elimination of compulsory arbitration; (3) the elimination of the obligation of employers to negotiate with a union authorized by the employees of the firm; (4) prohibition of collective agreements covering employees not explicitly authorized by the parties to the agreement; and (5) prohibition of support strikes against multiple employers even when the employers were part of the same corporate entity (Dahlziel and Lattimore 1996: 79–80; Kelsey 1995: 180–82). The impact on unions was immediate as union density fell from 42% of the workforce in May 1991 to 35% in December 1991 and continued to fall to 20% of the workforce in 1996 (Crawford, Harbridge, and Hince 1998).

In the 1991 budget, unemployment, sickness, and family support benefits were cut by 3% to 25%, depending on the age and family status of the recipient, with most household units receiving an 8% to 9% cut (Easton 1996: 117; Kelsey 1995: 276). In the budget, the Nationals announced a move in principle from a universal welfare system to one in which the top third of income earners would pay for most of the cost of their social services (Dahlziel and Lattimore 1996: 90–91). Reforms in this direction were implemented in tertiary education, health care, family support, and pensions. The universal family support system was replaced with one targeted on low-income groups. In the case of health care, publicly provided care was targeted at families eligible for family support, low-income singles, and pensioners with no private income; all others were subjected to a copayment (Kelsey 1995: 276). As for pensions, these were to become tightly means tested and the increase of the pensionable age to sixty-five was to be accelerated. However, the Nationals were forced into partial retreat as a result of protests from the elderly and, in their second term with their precarious position in parliament, the government agreed to yet more generous modifications in an agreement with Labour and the Alliance, a new party to the left of Labour.

Elaborating somewhat on Castles's characterization of the Australasian systems, the historically developed systems delivered social protection by a combination of high levels of national affluence, full male employment, a family wage for the male breadwinner, low levels of wage dispersion, and high levels of home ownership. Underpinning the system was the arbitration system and high levels of unionization. In both countries, this system of social protection was severely undermined before the advent of the conservative governments by a combination of the changing world economy, above all the long-term deterioration of the terms of trade for primary-sector exports, and the growth of the postindustrial economy. Growth rates, which were low by international standards—anemic in the case of New Zealand—decreased the relative level of national affluence. Postindustrialization, changes in the world economy, and the restructuring of the economy as a result of labor's reforms ended male full employment and resulted in declines in unionization and increases in enterprise-level bargaining. All of the foregoing weakened the family wage and increased wage dispersion. As Castles (1996: 106) points out, the demise of social protection by other means resulted in greater reliance on traditional welfare state policy. Both labor governments made some movement in this direction by increasing support for low-income families and increasing day care places. In Australia, the new earnings-related pension system and the universal Medicare scheme represent large strides in the direction of increased reliance on traditional welfare state policy.

The outcomes with regard to poverty and income distribution in the two countries are what one might expect. The "cushioning" reforms of the two labor governments did not fully compensate the lowest income groups, and poverty increased in both countries, surprisingly somewhat more in Australia than in New Zealand under labor, though it is difficult to tell since the figures are not comparable across the countries. With the advent of the New Zealand National government, the poverty and inequality figures increased steeply in New Zealand between 1990 and 1992, showing clearly the combined effect of the Employment Contracts Act, the social benefits cuts, and the increase in unemployment. The neoliberal supporters of the New Zealand experiment would not, of course, justify their project in terms of its impact on poverty and certainly not inequality. However, the aggregate figures on growth, productivity, employment, and unemployment give them little to cheer about (table A.11; see also OECD 1996d: 180; 1997a: 198; 1999e: 16–19). Over the past decade and a half, average per capita GDP growth in New Zealand was below that of Australia and the average of advanced industrial democracies. Unemployment was at levels comparable to Australia's and better than the OECD average, but employment growth was considerably below that of Australia and other OECD countries, as was productivity growth.

In assessing the Antipodean experiences under labor, it is important to keep in mind that they are not without parallels elsewhere. We saw in our discussions of the Nordic countries that social democrats instituted marketizing reforms in the public sector, privatized state-owned enterprises, and so on while preserving the system of industrial relations and social welfare as much as possible. What makes the reforms under Australian Labor appear more radical is that the starting point was a much more regulated economy and the system of social protection was more dependent on those regulations. In terms of the outcome it is probably safe to say that, if anything, the market as a whole is still more regulated in Australia and certainly it enjoys more external protection. On the other hand, it has hardly caught up to the Nordic countries in traditional social policy, so the citizens of Nordic countries now enjoy much higher levels of social protection than the citizens of Australia.

By contrast, the market reforms of the New Zealand government under Labour go much further that anything we have seen in the other countries we have examined, including Australia. Virtually all of the contributors to Castles, Gerritsen, and Vowles 1996 (also see Schwartz 2000) who compare New Zealand and Australia under labor point to the party-union relationship and the constitutional structure to explain the differences. The constitutional structure in New Zealand allowed the government to do what it wanted unchecked by an upper house or state governments. The party-union relationship, with the much greater formal role for the unions in the Australian Labor Party, was the underpin-

ning of the Accord, which not only checked some of the suggested neoliberal reforms, such as the 1985 tax policy of then–finance minister
Keating, but also was responsible for the two big social policy innovations
of this period, universal medical care and earnings-related pensions. Easton and Gerritsen (1996: 34) add that the personalities of the prime ministers and finance ministers of the two countries contributed to the differences as did the party structures, with the existence of organized
factions in Australia being a check on the neoliberal ambitions. The existence of organized factions can in turn be traced back in part to the constitutional structure (as well as the sheer differences in scale of the countries), as the state-level parties are a nurturing ground for the factions.
Even the effects of the personality differences are magnified, indeed
made possible, by all of the foregoing structural differences. It is hard to
imagine that Roger Douglas would have gotten as far as he did with his
agenda in the face of organized factions, union integration into the policy-making process, and checks from an upper house and state governments. As it was, divisions in the party over his policy resulted in his departure from the government in 1988.

While many analysts argue that the Labour government paved the way
for the National government reforms by legitimizing reforms guided by
doctrinaire neoliberalism, most agree that it was the National government's reforms that effected a system shift particularly with regard to the
welfare state, the main focus of this book, and the industrial relations system, the mainstay of the Australasian system of social protection. New
Zealand is the only country among our case studies that effected a system
shift, and among the advanced industrial democracies covered in our statistical analysis only the United Kingdom under Thatcher and Major
made a comparable shift.[47] We have argued that welfare state policies
once implemented are very popular and thus even conservative parties
are reluctant to implement cutbacks beyond those that appear to be essential as a result of fiscal stress caused by rising unemployment, increasing demographic burdens, and so on. In New Zealand, the cuts were not
popular. Citing a study of public opinion, Kelsey (1995: 301) points out
that between the 1987 and 1990 elections opinion on governmental economic policy shifted strongly and "a large majority of the population
thought that it was either going too fast or headed in the wrong way."
Surveys in 1989 and 1993 show that in 1989 very large majorities of New
Zealand favored "increased spending meaning higher taxes" for all social policies save support for Maori and Pacific Islanders and social assistance. By 1993 public support for every category of social spending
had increased as had public support for income redistribution and state

intervention to control large companies and multinationals and to protect the environment, precisely in a period when the National government's policy was moving in the opposite direction.

As Pierson (1994) points out, the Thatcher government's social policy cutbacks were not popular, and in many cases the government had to retreat from its more radical proposals in the face of public protest, as did the New Zealand National government in the case of the pension reform. But both governments did implement many unpopular policies, which begs the question of why they were able to do this. The two governments share four characteristics—and they are the only two governments that share them—that explain why they were able to implement system-shifting cutbacks: (1) the presence of a secular conservative party alone in government, (2) constitutional structures with no veto points, (3) single-member districts and plurality elections, and (4) the worst postwar economic growth records among OECD countries. Of these, the last is probably the least important but arguably did contribute to a sense of crisis in which the electorate would tolerate changes it would not have otherwise tolerated. The parties were secular conservative and thus unconstrained by a Christian democratic legacy that might have made the victory of the radical neoliberals in the party less likely. The contrast with Australia during the Howard government demonstrates nicely how the absence of veto points enabled the National government to implement such extensive changes in a single term (1990–93). The electoral system of single-member districts and plurality elections allowed governments in both the U.K. and New Zealand to build large parliamentary majorities on the basis of a minority of voters, thus effectively insulating themselves from the median voter. The Conservatives under Thatcher never received more than 44% of the vote but amassed huge seat majorities in parliament. The New Zealand National Party, having received 48% of the vote, won 58 of 99 seats in 1990; in 1993, with 35% of the vote, the party received 50 of 99 seats.

New Zealand voters recognized that governments were unresponsive to public opinion in part because of the electoral system and demanded a change. For obvious reasons, the dominant parties were reluctant to do this but were forced to by a sequence of events that would take us too far afield to recount. Thus, the 1996 elections were held under a mixed-member proportional system designed after the German system, which results in exact proportional representation for any party gaining more than 5% of the vote. Not surprisingly neither Labor (31%) nor National (37%) came anywhere close to a parliamentary majority, and the centrist New Zealand First Party (14%) held the pivot of the system and the role of kingmaker. The National–New Zealand First government considerably slowed the pace of neoliberal reform and actually reversed it in the case of health care, in which public hospitals became public non-profit institutions rather than public corporations. The 1999 election returned a Labour-led center-left coalition committed to a cautious expansion of the welfare state (Schwartz 2000).

## The Impact of Retrenchment

In concluding this chapter on retrenchment, an attempt should be made to gauge whether the retrenchment of the welfare state and labor market deregulation have been significant enough to have an impact on the outcomes discussed in chapters 3 and 4. Unfortunately, of the sixteen countries for which we presented income distribution and poverty data based on the LIS surveys, comparable data through time for at least a decade are available for only seven. Moreover, since these are surveys, they are subject to some sampling error, particularly for smaller subgroups, such as single mothers. Given these problems, we can draw firm conclusions only from consistent and significant patterns of movement in the various indicators. In the LIS data, the only unambiguous, large changes between the first surveys in the late 1970s or early 1980s and the surveys in the early to mid-1990s occurred in the U.K. and the U.S. In the U.K., the overall poverty rate increased from 6% in 1979 to 11% in 1995, and poverty among single mothers from 11% to 28%; in the U.S., the overall poverty rate increased from 17% in 1979 to 19% in 1994, and poverty among single mothers from 42% to 49%. Inequality increased significantly as the post-tax-posttransfer Gini index in the U.K. increased from 0.27 in 1979 to 0.35 in 1995, and in the U.S. from 0.31 in 1979 to 0.37 in 1994. In the case of the U.K., the change moved it from the average for advanced industrial countries around 1980 (see table 4.4) to the second most inegalitarian after the U.S. in the mid-1990s. Unfortunately, there are no LIS surveys for New Zealand, but the available data show a significant increase in poverty and inequality in the early 1990s (Easton 1996). The OECD wage dispersion data show a parallel pattern, with big increases in wage dispersion in the 1980s and 1990s among full-time employed people in the U.S., the U.K., and New Zealand, and very little change in all other industrial countries.

The changes in the other countries are much smaller. The Dutch data show an increase in inequality from 0.27 to 0.30 and poverty among single mothers from 7% to 16%, but the lack of a clear trend across the three surveys makes one skeptical of inferring too much from the data. Norway and Sweden show some increase in inequality (from 0.22 to 0.24 and from 0.20 to 0.23 respectively) but a decline in poverty among single mothers and stability in poverty rates among other groups.[48] Australia shows an increase in inequality (0.29 to 0.32), while it remains stable in Canada (at 0.29). Both countries record declines in poverty among single mothers: from 45% to 30% in Australia and from 42% to 32% in Canada, indicating that the increased targeting of benefits to vulnerable groups in both countries had some effect. Perhaps what is most impressive about the LIS data for all of the countries (not just the seven surveyed here), except the U.K. and U.S., is how little the retrenchment and particularly the large increases in unemployment in the 1980s and 1990s have affected the levels of poverty and income distributions, which is a tribute to the effectiveness of the social safety nets in these countries.

## Conclusion

The country studies presented in this chapter as well as our research on other industrialized welfare states support but nuance the conclusions of our quantitative study in the last chapter. The country studies and source materials confirm that cutbacks in benefits were widespread but in large part modest, or at least not system transforming, except in the United Kingdom, which stood out in the statistical materials as having implemented deep cuts, and New Zealand, which did not appear in our statistical materials because of missing data especially for the 1990s.[49] Nonetheless, no one who has studied New Zealand's development would deny that the social protection regime has experienced a system shift, and most observers would agree that its neoliberal reforms were the most radical implemented in any industrial democracy. The data on outcomes indicate that labor market deregulation and welfare state retrenchment in these countries did substantially increase poverty and inequality.

The inequality and poverty data also indicate large increases in the United States, and some students of American social policy, such as Francis Fox Piven, would add the United States to our group of radical retrenchment cases.[50] While we do agree that the United States, along with the United Kingdom and New Zealand, is a case of ideologically driven rather than unemployment-driven retrenchment, we would argue that the welfare state cuts and labor market deregulation in the United States was much less extensive than in the other two countries. The cuts in the United States were largely limited to the social assistance programs, whereas in the United Kingdom and New Zealand they also hit universalistic welfare programs such as pensions, health care, sick pay, and unemployment compensation. In the area of labor market deregulation, the Reagan administration's neoliberal reforms were largely limited to what could be accomplished by appointments and executive orders, while the labor market reforms in both New Zealand and the United Kingdom were yet more radical and thoroughgoing than the welfare state cuts. Deindustrialization combined with an already quite weak union movement, not legislative changes, bears the primary responsibility for the trend toward inequality in the United States. As King and Wood (1999) point out, federalism and divided government blocked the Reagan administration from achieving its full agenda in Thatcherite fashion. Of course, the United States was already quite an outlier among industrial democracies in its system of social protection as the only country with no national health insurance, legislated sick pay, or child allowances, and with one of the weakest if not the weakest union movement. Thus, the U.K. and New Zealand converged on the U.S. regime, but as of the mid-1990s at least, the U.K., for which we have comparable data, had not reached U.S. levels of poverty (11% vs. 19%), especially among vulnerable groups such as single mothers (28% vs. 48%), leaving the U.S. still in sole possession of an ignominious social achievement award.

Our case studies also confirm that in most countries there were few really major cutbacks that went into effect before the mid-1980s; the exceptions are the United Kingdom, Denmark, and the Netherlands. Strenuous efforts to curtail expenditures did not come until the 1980s and early 1990s, when rising levels of unemployment caused sharply increasing expenditures under existing entitlements and let the number of contributors to social insurance schemes decline. Most countries had instituted some economizing measures in the 1970s, such as delays in adjustments to inflation, changes in the rules for indexing, and increases in contributions and in user fees. In the 1980s such measures were almost universally intensified, additional measures such as increased waiting days for benefits were introduced, and entitlements themselves came under scrutiny. Significantly, as late as the late 1980s, Norway, Sweden, and Finland, all of whom had avoided the unemployment crises characteristic of the rest of the case studies, had not only not cut programs, they had increased entitlements. As noted, the most significant increases were in gender-egalitarian social policies such as parental insurance and public social services.

In general, pension systems remained the best-protected parts of the welfare state. Changes in indexing and in calculation formulas led to some decreases in real pensions in virtually all countries, and early pension programs were phased out in some. However, with the notable exceptions of the United Kingdom and New Zealand (with its incredibly generous retirement age of sixty), no significant and clearly visible lowering of real benefit levels was imposed. The major cutbacks in entitlement programs came in sickness pay, disability pensions, and unemployment compensation.

Overall, then, by the late 1980s and early 1990s a picture of widespread cuts emerges, in some cases at least of considerable magnitude. However, this picture has to be qualified from two points of view. First, outside of the U.K. and New Zealand, there were very few programs in any country where benefits in the mid-1990s were more than marginally lower than they had been in 1970. Second, the basic institutional features of the different welfare states were preserved. Only in those two cases could one speak of a basic transformation of the welfare state pattern that had been shaped during the Golden Age. One must be careful with this assessment, though; small to moderate cuts, changes in indexing, small shifts toward more means testing and partial privatization, etc., may over the long run erode the foundations of existing welfare state regimes and transform them in the direction of residual regimes.

Our case studies also confirm the existence of three phases of economic management, and by extension phases of change in the production regime, which appeared in the quantitative data: After the Golden Age, in which Keynesianism held sway, the countries initially responded to the shocks of the 1970s with stimulative policies, as if the developments were simply a new economic downturn, and then to the combination of inflation and stagnation with a mix of stimulative and restrictive polices. In country after country, traditional demand-side stimulation was abandoned in the 1980s as a primary tool for fighting unemployment, and increasingly over the next decade and a half even governments of the left began to target inflation. The deregulation of financial markets internationally and domestically in country after country added new pressure to turn around macroeconomic policy as it also eliminated the possibilities of simultaneously controlling interest rates and exchange rates and of privileging productive investors over other potential users of capital. In the context of the European Community and then European Union, even subsidizing investment, which was done successfully in Austria, for example, became increasingly impossible. Financial deregulation in turn stimulated a shift in central bank policy orientation toward targeting inflation, and then a trend toward central bank independence in countries in which central banks had been subject to the control of the sitting government.

In this same period, there was an almost uniform trend to "marketization" in the public sector as publicly owned firms were reorganized to operate on profit-making market principles, and market principles were introduced into public administration and services as much as possible. Moreover, even social democratic governments in countries as diverse as Sweden, New Zealand, France, and Austria moved to partially or entirely privatize firms, a policy pursued more vigorously by conservative governments. Tax systems also underwent change as governments of different political coloring followed the example of the Reagan tax reform and lowered rates, cut deductions, and broadened the base in personal and corporate income taxes (Swank forthcoming). While this did not necessarily involve a cutting of the tax burden, it was a concession to neoliberal arguments that high marginal rates and extensive deductions led to work disincentives and to undesirable distortions in markets for capital and labor.

Outside of New Zealand, the United Kingdom, and to a lesser extent Australia, labor market institutions underwent relatively modest changes (Golden, Wallerstein, and Lange 1999). The most dramatic change was the shift to industry-level bargaining in Sweden, where a combination of highly internationalized business, a recent acrimonious relationship between business and the manual workers central organization, and the wage compression policies of the unions led business to an aggressive campaign that included the decentralization of collective bargaining. However, in other coordinated market economies in which previously accommodating central banks were replaced with independent central banks, new production techniques called for more wage flexibility, and changes in the composition of the union movements made centralized bargaining more difficult, institutional stability hid changes in the actual process of wage setting, as wage setting became more decentralized and locally flexible and occurred in an environment in which strongly nonaccommodating signals were being sent by the monetary authorities. Otherwise the structures of the coordinated market economies—market training, business-labor cooperation at the firm level, interfirm relationships, and bank-firm relationships—remained intact, though there were signs of the weakening of "patient capital" in countries such as Germany.

It is worth underlining that the rises in unemployment were not the driving force behind these changes in the production regimes of the coordinated market economies. This can most clearly be seen in the cases of Austria, Finland, Sweden, and Norway, which experienced no or little rise in unemployment in the 1980s and continued welfare state innovation throughout the decade. Yet, all the changes in production regimes—market reforms in the public sector, privatization, the deregulation of financial markets, the movement to central bank independence, and the movement to more austere fiscal policy—substantially predated the unemployment crisis and were well under way by the mid-1980s. They even predated the announcement of the Single European Act and thus are not attributable to the acceleration of European integration after 1985. The initial causes of the changes in the production regimes, including macroeconomic policy, were the internationalization of the economy, above all the domino decision of country after country to deregulate financial markets in the wake of the breakup of the Bretton Woods system in 1971, and changes in production techniques and in the domestic social structure, particularly the postindustrialization of the occupational structure. Moreover, there is good evidence that governments reluctantly made choices that they perceived to be the only alternative as the result of the growing hegemony of neoliberal economic theory when, in fact, alternative courses of action were possible. We do not mean to dismiss unemployment and European integration as additional causes of the changes in the production regimes of coordinated market economies: There is no doubt that both the rise of unemployment in Europe and the quickened pace of European integration did accelerate the process of change. Indeed, the latter made the move to central bank independence and consequent changes in the wage bargaining process virtually compulsory.

In contrast to the coordinated market economies of Europe and liberal market economies of Europe and North America, the production regimes of the Antipodes did undergo a system shift as a result of changes in the international economic environment. As a result of long-term secular changes in commodity prices, the Australasian production regimes became unviable because they were based on rents transferred from the primary product sector to a protected manufacturing sector. These rents were highly adversely affected by the changes in international markets. In both countries, the wage regulation system, which was the core of the system of social protection, was changed substantially—in New Zealand totally transformed—and this, along with the rise in unemployment, exposed workers to much higher levels of risk of poverty than had earlier been the case. Add to this other marketizing reforms (see Castles, Gerritsen, and Vowles 1996; Schwartz 1994a, 1994b, 1998), and it becomes apparent that the production regimes of the Antipodes have converged on the liberal type. However, there are strong differences between the two countries with regard to not only the extent of labor market deregulation but also changes in the social policy regime proper. In Australia, Labor attempted to compensate those hit hardest by the ongoing changes with targeted programs, and it also introduced two universalistic policies, medical care and supplementary pensions, that make the Australian social policy regime one of the most generous in the liberal group. By contrast, the conservative government elected in 1990 in New Zealand and unchecked by veto points in the country's unicameral unitary system carried out deeply unpopular reforms that completely deregulated the labor market and substantially cut social benefits.

The case studies considerably nuance our picture of the decline of partisan differences. While they do confirm the general pattern that partisan differences in social and economic policy declined dramatically by the 1980s (with the exception of the continued social democratic expansion of social services, maternity leave, and other gender-egalitarian policies in the Nordic countries), they suggest that saying that these differences virtually disappeared, even in the Nordic countries by the 1990s, is an overstatement. It is true that both the left and the right were more constrained, the right because the welfare state was popular and the left because, once the unemployment crisis set in, the economic situation prevented new social policy innovation. The low levels of growth are an additional constraint on social democratic reform, as any government finds it exceedingly difficult to raise taxes when there is little or no income growth and therefore increased taxes would lower people's nominal as well as real income. Moreover, it is certainly true, as Garrett and Lange (1991) argue, that macroeconomic policy was particularly constrained; our case studies identify the deregulation of financial markets as the factor that was most responsible for constraining the range of macroeconomic policy alternatives. Demand stimulation via deficit spending and interest rate cuts was ruled out except in exceptional circumstances.

However, in social and labor market policy our case studies did reveal continued partisan differences in some of our nine countries. In Sweden, the bourgeois government of 1991–94 cut taxes and entitlements, whereas the Social Democratic government that followed continued to cut entitlements and social service spending but increased taxes in order to limit the extent of those cuts and in order to bring the budget into surplus. As the budget moved into surplus, more policy options appeared and by the 1998 election the partisan landscape followed the pattern observable in previous decades: The Social Democrats favored devoting most of the forecast revenue surpluses to a reversal of cuts, especially in social services, while retaining a budget surplus amounting to 2 percent of the GDP; the Left Party favored smaller surpluses and quicker reversal of cuts; on the other end of the spectrum, the Conservatives favored greater tax cuts; and the middle parties were situated in between. In Norway and Denmark, similar, restricted but evident, partisan differences could be detected. By contrast, in Finland, the political response to the deep crisis of the 1990s was the formation of a multiparty coalition stretching from the Conservatives to the Social Democrats to implement the austerity program; thus partisan differences did virtually disappear. In Australia and New Zealand, partisan differences were substantial as both labor and conservative governments introduced market-oriented reforms, but the labor governments attempted to insulate the welfare state and, to a lesser extent, the labor market from the reforms, whereas conservative governments subjected both to neoliberal reforms. Indeed, in Australia, the Labor government did not simply preserve the welfare state, it actually introduced or at least husbanded two of the largest innovations in social policy occurring in any country in this period, the Medicare universal health insurance and the supplementary pension plan.

On the surface, it appears that a case could be made for the disappearance of partisan differences in the three Christian democratic welfare states examined in this chapter. This can be attributed to the fact that coalition governments in Austria and the Netherlands served to obscure differences that might have resulted from a clear change of government, whereas in Germany the Christian Democrats were in power for virtually the whole period and the Social Democratic government is still rather new to allow for an assessment of its policy. It is also arguable that Christian democratic parties operating within coordinated market economies do not find a neoliberal turn as attractive as secular conservative parties, particularly those operating in an uncoordinated market economy. The fact that the newly elected Kohl government did not follow Reagan and Thatcher and embark on a neoliberal turn, despite the rhetoric indicating the intention of such a turn at the time, is evidence that this is the case. However, there is also evidence of continued partisan differences in the policies favored by social democrats and Christian democrats, such as the deep differences over austerity measures that broke up the Austrian coalition government in 1995, or the blocking of cutbacks by the SPD-controlled upper house in Germany in the 1990s. What is difficult to determine is the extent to which these differences were manifested primarily for electoral purposes or whether they would have translated into actual policy differences had one or the other party been able to govern alone.

As to the sources of the cuts, we have to distinguish between the ideologically driven cuts and the unemployment-driven cuts. The ideologically driven cuts were all carried out by conservative parties in uncoordinated market economies with weak or absent Christian democratic political presence: the Bolger government New Zealand, the Thatcher-Major government in the United Kingdom, the Reagan administration in the United States, and the Howard government in Australia. However, only the governments in New Zealand and the United Kingdom were able to implement deep, system-shifting cuts. We argue that the exceptional nature of these two cases can be traced to their political systems, which concentrate power (unicameral or very weakly bicameral parliamentary governments in unitary political systems) and make it possible to rule without a majority of popular support (single-member districts and plurality elections, which allow parties with a minority of votes to enjoy large parliamentary majorities). In both countries, the governments implementing the deep cuts were elected by a minority of voters but nonetheless commanded large parliamentary majorities. Thus, in both cases, the conservative governments were able to pass legislation that was very unpopular.

In the remaining countries, large and apparently irreversible rises in unemployment were the driving force behind the cuts. Only in Australia was increased trade exposure a major reason for rising unemployment, though. As in New Zealand, Australia's industry had been protected from import competition, and once trade policy was liberalized, the less efficient sectors of that industry came under pressure to rationalize and shed labor. The European countries had already had a high degree of trade openness during the Golden Age and their welfare states were built around the interests of workers and employers in the export sector. For these countries, we categorically reject the argument of neoliberals that increasing trade openness exposed the economies to increased competition, which revealed the costs imposed by generous welfare state entitlements on their export sectors. The export sectors of countries such as Germany and Sweden were doing extremely well in the mid-1990s, at precisely the same time that the governments were cutting welfare state entitlements; thus, somehow linking the cuts to export uncompetitiveness, directly or indirectly, is implausible.

In attempting to explain the rise in unemployment, we enter the contested terrain of explaining the lower levels of growth in the post–Bretton Woods era and their consequences. Without giving a definitive answer to that question, we can point to evidence from our cross-national survey at the beginning of this chapter and from the case studies that we believe narrows the controversy considerably. We contend that had economic growth been higher, ceteris paribus, more employment would have been created and, in identifying sources of lower economic growth, we also identify sources of lower employment growth.[51] An important proximate cause of growth is the level of investment, and investment has been lower since 1973 than before. This, in turn, can be linked to the higher level of real interest rates and the decline in government regulation and subsidies directing credit at businesses for investment. The rise in real interest rates is a product of financial deregulation and of the buildup of world debt in the wake of the two oil shocks. The removal of government targeting of business investment is a direct outcome of financial deregulation. Financial deregulation was most damaging to those countries in which financial regulation had been a key element of Golden Age growth policies—Austria, Sweden, Norway, and Finland among the cases examined here—but also countries as diverse as France and Japan.

The significant role of financial deregulation in the explanation of the decline in growth, especially for those countries in which financial regulation played an important role in their Golden Age growth policies, turns the neoliberal thesis on internationalization and unemployment on its head. In the neoliberal view, removing the barriers to the movement of factors of production will raise aggregate welfare but there will be winners and losers, with the most regulated economies being the losers and the least regulated being the winners. We would concur with this view in the area of trade among OECD countries, but would simply remind the reader again that the generous welfare states of northern Europe have been very open to trade, more open than the liberal welfare states (Katzenstein 1985). By contrast, the deregulation of financial markets has resulted in lower levels of investment, especially in countries where financial regulation was part of the Golden Age growth model, and thus has lowered aggregate growth.

A further reason for lower economic growth is the shift to the service sector, where labor productivity is generally lower than in manufacturing. On the other hand, for the same reason, the expansion of the service sector meant that the decline of economic growth did not lead to a commensurate decline of employment growth. In fact, it is simply not true that the post–Bretton Woods period was one of "jobless growth" as some observers have claimed. Despite the lower levels of economic growth, the growth of employment was only slightly lower after 1973 than before. However, labor force growth was faster than employment growth, as labor force participation among women rose faster than labor force participation among men declined after 1973, whereas these developments had counteracted one another earlier. The higher levels of unemployment in the Christian democratic welfare states are at least in part due to their failure to absorb increasing women's labor force participation in an expansion of the public social service sector, as in the social democratic welfare states, or in private services, as in the liberal welfare states. Within the Christian democratic group, the low level of unemployment in Austria and Switzerland is partly attributable to the low level of female labor force expansion.

Our comparative case studies have also demonstrated the impact of conjunctural factors on economic problems in the 1990s, and in the case of the Nordic countries the impact of policy errors. Essentially, the combination of German reunification, the standards set by the Maastricht agreement, and the discipline of international financial markets imposed restrictive monetary and fiscal policy regimes on all the European countries. Even within these constraints, the Nordic governments managed to overcome the worst effects of earlier policy mistakes and return to a scenario of budget surpluses, economic growth, and falling unemployment, which in turn opened the possibility of restoring some previously cut benefits.

If one compares the dynamics of this period to the period of welfare state growth examined in chapters 3 and 5, the most striking change is the decline in the role of partisanship.[52] The flip side of the decline of partisanship is the increased importance of policy legacies. The existing policy arrangements create supporters, the beneficiaries of those arrangements. Given the broad coverage of core welfare state programs, such as pensions, child or family allowances, parental leave, health care, education, and so on, the resistance to entitlement cuts is widespread. We have pointed to this as the primary reason why the retrenchment era does not simply move the political spectrum to the right, with conservative parties favoring a return to the social policy arrangements of three decades ago. Moreover, if one were to examine the details of policy, such as the structure of benefits, the financing, etc., which we have not done in this chapter, one would find that these details also produce interested constituencies that resist change to these structures.

By contrast, constitutional arrangements, which we found to be so important in our analyses of welfare state expansion in chapters 3 and 5, continued to have strong effects in the retrenchment period, but the direction of policy change was reversed, that is, absence of veto points facilitated retrenchment. One might rephrase the argument and say that the absence of veto points facilitates rapid and radical change in policy in either direction. Constitutional structures have figured prominently in our explanation of the radical retrenchment in New Zealand and the United Kingdom, but it should be underlined here that one can see their effect in many other cases, both among those examined in this chapter and others not examined here. In their study of neoliberal reform in the United Kingdom and the United States, King and Wood (1999) argue that the same features of constitutional structure that we identify as creating veto points were a strong contributing factor in explaining the fact that Thatcher was able to achieve much more of her program than Reagan. Bonoli and Mach (2000) point out how the Swiss constitutional structure, which along with the United States scores highest on our measure, made it possible for the Social Democrats and the unions to block attempts at retrenchment that commanded parliamentary majorities. We would argue that the unicameral unitary systems of Sweden, the Netherlands, Denmark, and Finland made it possible for governments in those countries to impose austerity or carry out significant reforms of welfare policy while Germany, with its bicameral federal system, has not been able to overcome the budgetary burden of reunification. The contrast between Sweden, which moved from a 12% of GDP budget deficit in 1993 to a surplus in 1999, and Germany, which could not reduce a 5% of GDP deficit below 2% in the same period, is telling.

For the first decade of the period covered in this chapter, the Nordic welfare states were still in a period of expansion and the most important field of expansion was in policies that enable citizens to have a family and work at the same time, with extension of parental leave and expansion of day care being only the two most obvious of these policies. The main beneficiaries of these policies were women, and as we pointed out in earlier chapters, they were double beneficiaries because many of them found work in the expanding public sector. Increasingly women's movements, in cooperation with the social democrats, were the main agents of these changes. By the end of the period, gender gaps in voting and welfare state support opened up across the Nordic countries. However, our Antipodean case studies show that this was not merely an idiosyncratic Nordic phenomenon. In Australia and to a lesser extent New Zealand, the same alliance of labor parties and women's movements inside and outside of the parties was responsible for the passage of gender-egalitarian legislation. In the Christian democratic welfare states as well, we saw that much of the limited progress in gender-egalitarian legislation was made under social democratic–led governments at the national level and at the level of the German Länder.

In chapter 2, we were critical of theories that attribute important roles to bureaucrats and policy experts in the formation of social and economic policy, not so much because we contended that they were uninfluential but because such theories present no clear hypothesis that might explain long-term change within a country or patterns across countries. That is, the role of bureaucrats might appear in post hoc explanations of policy development but not as a predictive hypothesis. An exception is the recent literature on "femocrats," women placed in policy positions in government, often in special offices or even ministries, charged with vetting proposed legislation's effect on women and/or proposing new legislation promoting women's equality. Since the charge of these bureaucrats is to move policy clearly in one direction, our critique does not hold in this case. Our case studies indicate, and Stetson and Mazur's (1995) much more comprehensive study of two-thirds of the advanced industrial democracies confirms, that the conditions for major influence of femocrats are similar to those we have identified for gender-egalitarian policies in general: a combination of active femocrats with left government and a strong women's movement, particularly within the dominant party of the left.

In the case materials, we detected another instance of influence of policy analysts, though these were often not bureaucrats but policy advisers who were either career politicians or academics with party links who were appointed by the sitting government to their position and who exited with the government. As Schwartz (1994a) points out in his study of Sweden, Denmark, New Zealand, and Australia, in all four of these countries, as well as most advanced industrial countries both within and outside of our group of nine countries we might add, key agents of neoliberal reforms were economists or bureaucrats or policy analysts with economic training located in the ministry of finance or treasury. These policy advisors' thinking was clearly influenced by trends in the international economics profession, which has its center of gravity in the United States. The case studies strongly indicate that these advisers did have an independent effect on the direction of policy, but this is more properly classified as an autonomous effect of ideas. Furthermore, their effect was to push policy further toward marketization than was required, once retrenchment and marketization were on the agenda; they did not put these issues on the agenda by themselves.

# CHAPTER EIGHT

$\blacklozenge$

# Conclusion

## Summary of Arguments

### Substantive Issues

The first of the central arguments we have developed and supported in this book concerns the importance of political choice for the formation of welfare states. The relative strength of different political tendencies with different power bases in society fundamentally shaped the character of welfare states in advanced industrial societies in the post–World War II period. Two political tendencies, social democratic and Christian democratic, supported the construction of generous and comprehensive welfare states, in contrast to secular center and right-wing parties, which kept the role of the state in social protection more restricted and favored a residual welfare state only. There were significant differences between social democratic and Christian democratic welfare state designs, reflecting the interests of their respective power bases in society. Social democratic parties had their power bases predominantly in organized labor, including white-collar workers and their unions, whereas Christian democratic parties had more heterogeneous power bases, reaching across all classes, and including business as well as labor wings. Thus, Christian democratic parties pursued a politics of compromise, accommodation, and mediation of a variety of interests, whereas social democratic parties promoted primarily wage earner interests.

These different political preferences were translated into different policies when these parties held political power and thus resulted in welfare states with different characters. Where social democracy was the dominant force, the welfare state was built on a combination of universalistic, flat-rate, tax-financed, and employment-based, income-related, contribution-financed programs. Where Christian democracy dominated, the welfare state was built mostly on the latter type of programs. In addition, social democratic parties presided over the introduction of extensive public funding and public delivery of social services, including care for children and the elderly. In contrast, Christian democratic parties provided for public funding of a more restricted range of privately delivered services, leaving caregiving responsibilities to the family (that is, women). These choices had profound implications not only for the status of women but also for overall activity rates and thus for the resiliency of the two types of welfare states in the changing economic environment of the 1980s and beyond, two topics to which we shall return below.

In addition to pressures from its own labor wing, it was particularly competition with social democratic parties that pushed Christian democrats to embrace stronger commitments to welfare state expansion. In our case studies, this dynamic was particularly visible in the German and Dutch cases, whereas in Austria it was somewhat less obvious because public competition on the basis of policy proposals was to a considerable extent replaced by negotiations within the coalition. Another telling example is Italy, where the national health service was introduced in the 1970s, only after the left had managed to make a credible bid for power. Both the generosity and the specific nature of the welfare state regime profoundly shaped the material well-being of the populations. Social democratic and the generous Christian democratic welfare states of northern Continental Europe performed much better than liberal welfare states in keeping people out of poverty, and they also produced lower inequality in income distribution, with the social democratic having a clearly more egalitarian impact than the Christian democratic welfare states. The welfare state regimes in the Nordic and northern Continental European countries then further reinforced the more egalitarian income distributions resulting from their production regimes. It is important to repeat here that in our quantitative analysis years of Christian democratic rule were strongly associated with welfare state generosity but not with redistribution, whereas years of social democratic rule were strongly associated with both sets of indicators. To the extent that the countries we classified as having Christian democratic welfare states showed more egalitarian outcomes, our quantitative results suggest that these particular outcomes were due to the influence of social democratic parties, reinforcing the effect of the structure of the production regimes.

The construction of generous welfare states required support from cross-class coalitions. In the case of the Christian democratic welfare states, the Christian democratic party itself was capable of assembling these coalitions within the party, given its cross-class base. In the case of social democratic welfare states, these coalitions were built in the early stages between blue-collar workers and small farmers, through alliances between social democratic and agrarian parties. As we showed in our comparative historical analysis, the worker part of these coalitions was responsible for the expansion of welfare state programs, but the agrarian part was responsible for the emphasis on the universalistic, flat-rate components of the social democratic welfare states. As industrialization advanced, agriculture declined, and farmers lost importance as an electoral force, these original coalitions were replaced by coalitions between blue- and white-collar workers, or between the working class and sectors of the middle classes. In part, support for social democratic parties among white-collar workers grew, and in part white-collar workers pressured centrist parties to be more supportive of wage earner interests. Both blue- and white-collar workers had an interest in improving welfare state benefits by making them earnings related. However, pressure for legislation on earnings-related schemes came mainly from the blue-collar unions, as the blue-collar unions perceived correctly that negotiated—as opposed to legislated—social benefits were generally better for white-collar than for blue-collar workers.

Corporatist arrangements were important features of the production regimes in the Nordic and northern Continental European countries during the construction of the welfare states. However, the key factor for welfare state construction was partisan incumbency. Essentially, tripartite negotiations included social policy provisions along with questions of wage setting and economic policy only under social democratic governments. Moreover, legislation that introduced major new social programs was virtually never the result of such tripartite negotiations. For instance, before the 1970s unions in the Netherlands were included in corporatist arrangements, but their influence on economic and social policy was de facto highly limited. The first real corporatist bargain was struck under the PvdA-led government in the 1970s.

Corporatist arrangements were crucial for the successful functioning of these welfare states and associated production regimes in world markets. As we pointed out, the generous social democratic and northern Continental Christian democratic welfare states were embedded in production regimes that were highly open to trade. Thus, the ability to achieve wage restraint was essential, and corporatist institutions provided the mechanisms for successful negotiations. Two types of arrangements successfully provided wage restraint—centralized bargaining at the national level, practiced in the Nordic countries and Austria—and bargaining at the industrial level, with informal wage leadership of exposed sector industrial unions and an independent central bank, practiced in Germany. Other important features of the production regimes of the Nordic countries and Austria were capital controls, budget surpluses, and gov-

ernment promotion of investment through a variety of supply-side policies, such as provision of preferential credit to industrial investors, or direct state investment. It is important to point out here that the experience
of these countries contradicts the generally held assumption that the
combination of fiscal conservatism, emphasis on supply-side measures,
wage restraint, and openness to trade—that is, the combination associated with structural adjustment—is incompatible with social democratic
redistributive reform. In addition, the Nordic governments pursued active labor market policies to maintain full employment. In Germany,
preferential relations between enterprises and banks provided long-term
investment capital, and government support for R and D and structural
adaptation helped maintain high levels of employment. In the Nordic
countries and Germany, labor training was an essential feature of the successful pursuit of high-skill-high-wage production for export markets, a
market niche that these countries have defended successfully after the
Golden Age.[1]

We pointed out that there has been an overall correspondence between
these production regimes and the welfare state regimes. Despite considerable variation in specific relations between enterprises, the government,
and labor, and in specific policies, welfare state regimes with generous
replacement rates and qualifying conditions in sickness and unemployment insurance are embedded in production regimes supporting high-
skill-high-wage production and having highly regulated labor markets. We
have called this a "mutually enabling fit" as a production regime oriented
toward high-skill-high-wage production provides the financial basis for a
high social wage on the one hand, and a generous social safety net keeps
the reservation wage high and thus is an incentive for employers and
unions to improve productivity on the other. Another kind of mutually enabling fit exists between highly regulated labor markets and the service intensiveness of welfare states in the context of rising women's labor force
participation. Where women's labor force participation increases, the
need for social services increases. In liberal production regimes, such services came to be provided mainly by low-wage jobs in the private sector. In
coordinated production regimes, labor market institutions prevented the
emergence of a low-wage service sector, and women directed demands for
social service provision to the state, thus promoting the growth of public
social service provision.

Aside from having mutually enabling features, welfare state and production regimes also have some common antecedents. As we noted, political incumbency is not as central to the development of production regimes as it is to the development of welfare state regimes, but somewhat

more distant antecedents are, particularly the strength of labor organization. High levels of labor organization in turn have been linked to various causes, prominent among them high trade openness, dependence on manufacturing exports, high levels of economic concentration, and strength of employer organization. Certainly, all these factors also favor the path-dependent emergence of coordinated production regimes. Success in world markets for manufacturing products requires innovation, increases in productivity, and investment in human capital. Achievement of these goals in turn is facilitated by government support in the form of investment incentives and support for R and D and human capital development, and by cooperation among employers in labor training. Organized employers and strong labor movements facing each other, as well as competitive world markets, in turn are constrained to find some kind of accommodation, which favors the emergence of centralized or centrally coordinated sectoral bargaining. Emphasis on increasing productivity and wages is then extended to producers for the domestic market through these bargaining arrangements, which leads to the gradual disappearance of low-productivity-low-wage employers in manufacturing, prevents the emergence of a low-wage private service sector, and reinforces the high-skill-high-technology orientation of the economy.

We showed both in our quantitative and in our comparative historical analyses that women's labor force participation and mobilization were an additional important factor shaping welfare states. Initial labor market decisions set off an interactive dynamic between rising women's labor force participation and social service expansion. During the period of full employment in the 1960s, Christian democratic governments in coordinated market economies, committed to the traditional family model with a male breadwinner, opted for the importation of foreign labor, whereas the social democratic governments in the Nordic countries restricted this practice with the result that women's labor force participation began to increase rapidly. Increasing labor force participation led to increasing mobilization and a stronger political presence of women, inside and outside of the social democratic parties and, to a lesser extent, the unions. Pressures from mobilized women pushed the social democratic parties to extend their commitment to equality between classes to include equality between genders, to relieve women from private caregiving responsibilities through the expansion of social services, and to pass legislation enabling parents to combine work with child rearing. The expanding public social service sector in turn provided more jobs for women, and this interaction then gradually resulted in the service-heavy, women-friendly Nordic welfare states.

In countries where Christian democracy was dominant, women's labor force participation remained much more restricted, as did the public financing and provision of social services and policies facilitating the combination of work and family. In the liberal welfare states, embedded in liberal production regimes, a low-wage—predominantly private—personal and social service sector developed, which provided jobs occupied mostly by women. Women in these societies, particularly those in social and health service jobs, also came to favor expansion of the welfare state. However, their political influence on welfare state formation remained much weaker than in the social democratic cases, as they were much less likely to be unionized and had no powerful political allies embracing an agenda of generous public funding and provision of social services and of policies supportive of combining work with parental responsibilities. Finally, in the case of the wage earner welfare state regimes we saw a dynamic parallel to that in social democratic welfare state regimes, of women's mobilization inside and outside of a sympathetic party—the Australian and New Zealand labor parties—incumbency of these parties, and resulting gender-egalitarian legislation, in this case for equal pay for comparable work. Thus, as for policies redistributing resources among classes, the decisive factor in shaping policies redistributing resources between genders was political choice, carried by a power base rooted in organization in a combination of political parties, labor unions, and social movements.

The translation of political preferences and political power into policies, of course, is heavily shaped by the nature of political institutions. Political institutions regulate access to the policy-making process. We have shown—again in both comparative historical and quantitative analyses—how constitutional provisions that concentrate power facilitated, and provisions that disperse power obstructed, the passing of major pieces of welfare state legislation. This was true both for the construction of welfare states and for welfare state retrenchment. Some of the clearest examples in the construction of welfare states were the passage of the supplementary pension plan in Sweden, a major project that passed parliament on the basis of a one-vote majority, and the contrast between Australia and New Zealand in the passing of legislation on medical care. The labor parties in both Australia and New Zealand favored the introduction of national health insurance, and in the unitary political system in New Zealand the party, once in office, was able to implement this plan, whereas legislation to the same effect introduced by the Labor government was defeated in the upper house of the Australian federal system. Other examples are defeats of legislation on national health insurance in the federal systems of

Switzerland and the United States. In Switzerland, mandatory health insurance was delayed considerably through the availability of veto points, and the United States has remained the only advanced industrial democracy without mandatory health insurance. In Switzerland the introduction of mandatory maternity insurance was rejected again in a referendum in 1999, which makes Switzerland, along with the United States, another anomaly among advanced industrial democracies. Examples of the importance of political institutions from the retrenchment phase are the radical cuts implemented by the Thatcher government in the U.K. and by the National government in New Zealand, both cases of extreme power concentration. The cuts in these two cases present a stark contrast to the carefully negotiated reform packages of the 1990s in Switzerland, which combined cuts with improvements in order to forestall or win a potential referendum against the reforms in this system with extreme power dispersion (see Bonoli 1997; Bonoli and Mach 2000).

Beginning in the 1970s, secular changes in advanced industrial economies along with the internationalization of capital markets and of production began to challenge the coordinated production regimes. Growth rates declined and unemployment increased, which in turn put financial pressure on the generous welfare states. The reasons for the rising levels of unemployment are complex, of course; they are certainly not only a matter of excessive labor costs as some economic theories would have it. In agreement with those economists who emphasize investment levels as determinants of unemployment, we have argued that the lower investment levels in the 1980s and 1990s compared to the Golden Age are related to higher unemployment. We have linked lower investment levels in coordinated market economies, in turn, in part to financial internationalization, since the deregulation of international and national capital markets deprived governments of policy instruments to promote investment. In the German case, financial internationalization weakened the preferential relationships between enterprises and banks. Other reasons for the lower levels of investment are the higher real cost of capital and lower corporate profits. We noted that growth of the labor force was generally faster than growth of employment, in part due to rising labor force participation rates among women, but that the fastest growth of women's labor force participation occurred in the Nordic countries, where women were absorbed into the rapidly expanding social service sector and unemployment remained low until the late 1980s.

Secular changes, namely the shift from manufacturing to services and within manufacturing from standardized mass production to flexible production, combined with internationalization of production, also began to undermine centralized collective bargaining and wage restraint. They undermined the hegemonic position of blue-collar unions in export-oriented manufacturing, traditionally the pace setters in centralized negotiations, and generated stronger demands from employers for greater flexibility of wages and increased control over wage formation at the level of the firm. These demands could still have been accommodated within an essentially centralized bargaining framework, but they did make a policy of wage compression across skill levels, as pursued in Sweden and Norway, impossible. Where employers made demands for flexibility and decentralization of bargaining, these demands assumed special weight because of the shift in power relations in favor of capital caused by internationalization of production. As shifting investments and production from one country to another has become easier and the threat of exit has become more credible, capital has gained leverage vis-à-vis both labor and governments in negotiations over wages, taxes, and issues of control. It is worth repeating here that internationalization of trade did not constitute an important challenge to the Nordic and northern European coordinated production regimes, as trade openness had already characterized them during the Golden Age.

The effect of these secular changes on unemployment and thus the welfare state in Europe was greatly aggravated by conjunctural factors in the 1990s. In the Nordic countries policy mistakes further magnified the negative effects of secular and conjunctural factors. Our choice of the term "conjunctural" does not indicate that these were simply factors causing a particular economic cycle and likely to be overcome within a couple of years. However, they are different from the secular changes insofar as their causes are more narrowly political and their effects may eventually be overcome by political decisions. The combination of the debt buildup of the 1970s, German reunification and the reaction of the Bundesbank to the consequent rising expenditures, the Maastricht criteria, and the development of the EMU led to the pursuit of extremely austere monetary and fiscal policies by European governments (Hall 1998; Soskice 2000). The collapse of the Soviet Union deprived several countries of export markets and constituted a particularly important loss for Finland. Finally, in Finland, Sweden, and to a lesser extent Norway, the timing and extent of financial deregulation and the handling of exchange rate policy allowed an exorbitant consumer boom and wage inflation, which ended in a deep recession and bank insolvency and thus imposed great financial burdens on these governments. The turnaround of these Nordic countries in the late

1990s supports the argument that policy mistakes had been an essential cause of the crisis and could be corrected.

The emerging economic challenges in the 1970s were met initially with largely traditional countercyclical responses and then austerity measures, in more or less a trial-and-error pattern. By the 1980s it had become clear that a serious adaptation of economic and social policies to the new conditions was called for. In particular, the rising levels of unemployment were putting financial pressures on the generous welfare states and began to force welfare state retrenchment. With the exceptions of the United Kingdom, New Zealand, and the United States, the timing of benefit cuts clearly showed that unemployment levels were the driving forces. In the U.K., New Zealand, and the U.S. we saw ideologically driven cuts, instituted before significant increases in unemployment, in tandem with tax cuts, or going beyond what changes in unemployment seemed to require. The cuts in the U.K. and New Zealand amounted to real system transformations, undermining the universalistic basic security aspects that had existed and moving the welfare states toward residualism. In the other countries the cuts remained more moderate and system preserving, and they were often counterbalanced by increases in contributions and sometimes even improvements in entitlements. In some countries, such as Denmark, Australia, and Switzerland, the systems of social protection were completed in the 1980s with the expansion of earnings-related occupational pensions. In Denmark these pension schemes were negotiated but achieved near universal coverage because of the high union density, and in Australia and Switzerland they were made mandatory through legislation. In all three cases, these pension schemes were financed by employer and employee contributions and were treated as separate programs, administered by nongovernmental institutions. Thus, even in the period of retrenchment these pension benefits, which imposed significant costs on employers, could be introduced, precisely because they were off budget for the government.

The exceptions to the pattern of moderate cuts combined with increases in contributions were programs that were clearly abused and perceived as responsible for reducing activity rates, such as early retirement and disability pensions in the Netherlands. Nevertheless, some kinds of nonvisible cuts, that is, cancellations of improvements that had not taken full effect and whose elimination therefore did not lower the real value of currently received benefits, were in part very steep, over 20 percent in the case of German pensions, for instance. Moreover, the introduction of greater means testing and the privatization of some aspects of the safety net, such as in the case of the sickness and disability insurance in the

Netherlands, may have the potential to undermine the solidaristic aspects and the comprehensive character of these welfare states in the longer run.

In the changed economic environment of the 1980s it became clear that the active, service-oriented social democratic welfare states were in a stronger position than the passive, transfer-oriented Christian democratic welfare states to make adaptations to the new conditions. Rising unemployment aggravated the differences between active and passive welfare state regimes, as Christian democratic welfare states handled it by attempting to reduce the labor supply through early retirement and, in some countries, generous disability schemes. In the extreme case of the Netherlands the use (or abuse) of these schemes generated a perceived crisis of inactivity. In contrast, the effects of the service-oriented social democratic welfare state programs were higher labor force participation and investment in youth and labor, which greatly reduced the proportion of people with low skills, who became hard to employ. Some improvements in activity levels in the Christian democratic welfare states could be achieved through part-time work, as demonstrated by the Dutch experience, and this in turn required an adaptation of social policy regimes to extend benefits to part-time workers.

Despite these continued differences between welfare state regimes, we noted a reduction and then the disappearance of partisan effects on welfare state efforts in our quantitative analysis, as all parties and governments have been operating under severe constraints. Rhetorically, differences have continued, in some countries quite pronounced differences, but electoral constraints have kept the right from implementing radical cuts and the left from resisting cuts altogether and raising taxes in a significant way. Nevertheless, in our case studies we saw instances of clear shifts in orientation when governments changed, such as when the Swedish social democrats came back to power in 1994, or when labor and conservative parties replaced each other in Australia and New Zealand in the 1980s and 1990s.

### Methodological Issues

Our central methodological concern was to demonstrate the fruitful nature of a close dialogue between two major research traditions, cross-national quantitative analyses and comparative historical analyses. Existing theory informed our use of both of these approaches, as it guided our choice of variables for the quantitative analyses, as well as our hypotheses for the comparative historical parts of the study. With quantitative analyses we established generalizable effects of specific variables across cases and the average magnitude of these effects. We showed that partisan composition of government, constitutional structure, and women's labor force participation had the most consistent and substantively most important effects on the development of various dimensions of welfare state regimes. The comparative historical analyses then enabled us to elucidate causal mechanisms mediating the observed effects and to establish agency. We provided evidence for the political struggles over the formation and passing of welfare state policy and for the particular problems faced by welfare state legislation in political systems with a dispersion of power. Knowledge gained from the comparative historical studies also helped us make theoretically informed choices when we were forced to eliminate variables due to multicollinearity. It also suggested particular operationalizations, such as the construction of the index of constitutional structure and the interaction effect between women's labor force participation and social democratic incumbency.

Another major methodological concern was to demonstrate the need for broadly comparative analyses and analyses over long periods of time in order to properly assess causal factors behind welfare state construction and retrenchment. Single-case studies and studies of dynamics over short periods of time obscure the impact of the balance of power in society and between different political tendencies and instead privilege actors or economic fluctuations as decisive factors for welfare state legislation and expenditures. This holds true for both quantitative and comparative historical analyses. We distinguished four kinds of causal mechanisms that mediate the long-term effects of incumbency and that tend to be obscured in short-term analyses: structural limitation, ideological hegemony, the policy ratchet effect, and regime legacies.

Structural constraints are formed mainly by the balance of power in society, that is, between capital and organized labor, women's movements, professional associations, and other social movements and interest groups, as well as among different political parties.[2] They are shaped by the basic constellation of collective actors. Ideological hegemony refers to the center of gravity of public opinion regarding the shape of a desirable social order, including the proper form and functions of the welfare state. In other words, it refers to the distribution of basic preferences among actors. The policy ratchet effect refers to the rapid growth of support for welfare state policies after their introduction, specifically for universalistic policies that benefit a large proportion of the population, which then turns these policies into the new point of reference for discussions on further welfare state development. This we can conceptualize as an effect that changes the distribution of preferences among actors.

The regime legacies effect, finally, refers to the impact of specific policy regimes on the strength of social actors and their capacity to shape further welfare state developments. This effect, then, changes the constellation of actors. Each of these four factors affects actors' perceptions of a realistic and legitimate range of debate on social policy, and of their own capacity to shape policy in accordance with their preferences, and therefore their political strategies. Accordingly, actors with essentially the same preferences, say employers with preferences for lower taxes and social security contributions, will take very different official positions and pursue different political strategies, in countries where they are confronting an electorally highly successful social democratic party that presided over significant welfare state expansion and that is based on a strong labor movement, than in countries where they are facing electorally dominant secular center and right-wing parties that kept the welfare state highly restricted and an organizationally and politically weak labor movement. By the same token, progressive bureaucrats in the former situation can contribute to the formulation of much more generous policy than equally progressive bureaucrats in the latter. A single-case study of either situation might conclude that it was employer or bureaucratic support or opposition that accounts for welfare state outcomes. A further implication of this argument is that a focus on parliamentary votes, even if the analysis covers longer periods of time, is misleading, because mostly political struggles take place before the final vote and are heavily shaped by the four factors just discussed.

## Speculation and Prescription

We argued that both secular trends and conjunctural elements have been underlying the unemployment problems of the 1990s in Europe. The main secular trends are the decrease in economic growth and investment, the shift from the manufacturing to the service sector, and the internationalization of capital markets and of production. The main conjunctural elements are German reunification, the collapse of Soviet trade, the Maastricht accord and the development of EMU, and procyclical mistakes in economic management in the Nordic countries in the late 1980s and early 1990s. There the timing of the financial deregulation contributed to an overheating of the economies and thus to severe problems for wage restraint, and then the continuation of the fixed exchange rate policy despite the failure of wage restraint, combined with the effects of changes in tax policies on consumer behavior, deepened the recession. The diagnosis of conjunctural causes, and the substantial recovery of the

Nordic countries in the second half of the 1990s, allows for some degree of optimism that they might be overcome and that unemployment can be brought down, which would relax some of the most immediate pressures on the generous welfare states.

Most discussions about the future of the welfare state begin with the problem of the increasing demographic burden caused by the combination of higher life expectancy and declining fertility. In the political discussion, the opponents of the welfare state often portray this problem as a time bomb that is certain to destroy welfare states as we know them. However, as we pointed out in the last chapter, there is significant variation among countries in the increase of the projected aged dependency ratio. Moreover, we argued that the relevant figure is the total active- to inactive-population ratio, that is, the ratio of those actually supporting the welfare state through work and thus a contribution to the tax base, to the unemployed and inactive population of all ages, which in turn is at present and will be in the future heavily dependent on labor force participation ratios. In this comparison, the social democratic welfare states do best, followed by the liberal welfare states, then the wage earner welfare states, and finally the Christian democratic welfare states. Underlying these figures are the by now familiar differing levels of women's labor force participation, and the two sets of figures combined also underline another advantage of social democratic welfare states: not only are their active-to-nonactive ratios very favorable, the demands on the economies to produce more jobs due to the entry of women in the labor force will decline in the future as these countries are approaching a situation in which the adult female population is fully active in the workforce.

What are some of the policy alternatives that could support increases in employment, in active-passive ratios, and thus in the financial situation of generous welfare states? If one assumes that technological progress and productivity increases in the manufacturing sector continue and keep the rate of job creation relatively low despite increased investment, one needs to look to the service sector as the major potential creator of jobs. The OECD Jobs Study has argued that low productivity growth in this sector means that these jobs must be low-wage jobs (OECD 1994b). The OECD, pointing to the American example of the "job machine," the creation of large numbers of low-wage jobs in the private service sector and concomitant lowering of the unemployment rate, has been pushing for an essentially neoliberal route of deregulating labor markets, increasing wage dispersion, and cutting social benefits, such as unemployment compensation, which raise the reservation wage. However, there are five major problems with this prescription.

First of all, the American model is not nearly as successful as its supporters would have it. Freeman (1995) argues that if one adjusts the unemployment rates for the increase in incarceration, which has trebled since 1980, the U.S. performance does not look so outstanding. Western and Beckett (1999) have estimated that an inclusion of the prison population would raise unemployment levels among males by a negligible amount in Europe but by almost 2 percent in the United States. Freeman also presents extensive data demonstrating that increased wage dispersion in the United States did not contribute to employment growth. Second, it is not clear that efforts to imitate the U.S. experience through deregulation of labor markets, an increase in wage dispersion, and lowering of social benefits would generate large numbers of jobs. The experiences of the two countries that made the most dramatic moves in the direction suggested by the OECD, the United Kingdom and New Zealand, do not support the view that the American experience is replicable. Both countries have had modest upturns in employment recently but both are still above 6 percent in unemployment and thus are not faring better than the Netherlands, Denmark, or Sweden. Third, the costs in terms of poverty and inequality are high, as demonstrated by the experiences of the United States, the United Kingdom, and New Zealand. We presented the figures in the last chapter; suffice it to repeat here that the increase in inequality in the United Kingdom was the largest recorded in the LIS data and moved the United Kingdom to a position second only to the United States as the most inegalitarian country among the eighteen analyzed in this book. Fourth, as we discussed in chapter 4, there is a strong relationship between inequality and skill levels at the bottom; in countries with more inegalitarian income distributions, the lowest performing groups perform worse than their counterparts in countries with more egalitarian income distributions. This indicates that an increase in inequality is most likely to lead to a deterioration of skill levels among the lowest income earners over a generation or two. Fifth, the presupposition that productivity in the service sector is necessarily low and therefore wages have to be low across the board is dubious. The service sector is very heterogeneous, and productivity improvements are certainly possible in some subsectors, most notably business services.

If deregulation of production regimes and residualization of welfare states are not a desirable option from the point of view of poverty and inequality, what are the options for increasing employment in coordinated production regimes and solidifying the financial position of generous and comprehensive welfare states? An essential step certainly has to be to increase domestic levels of productive investments. This can be achieved in part by restructuring parts of the social insurance systems to have them funded and to have these funds invested domestically. Such reforms have already begun in some social insurance systems in the Nordic countries and in the Canadian pension system. Even the current reforms are far from fully funded if one defines fully funded as the level of funding characteristic of American private pension schemes. Although it would be impossible to fund the current Nordic or Austrian earnings-related pension schemes at this level, because such schemes would quickly overwhelm the capacity of the national capital markets to absorb this amount of capital, substantial increases in the level of funding could be implemented.[3] There is little doubt that these social insurance funds would quickly become the dominant owners of stocks, bonds, and money markets in the countries in question. Given the political reaction of business to the Swedish unions' bid for societal control of capital via the wage earner funds, it is obvious that these funds would have to be constructed in such a way as to ensure only a passive ownership role for the social insurance funds. Funding social insurance systems more fully would not only create new sources of investment but also make these systems more resilient to cuts in the face of adverse economic developments and in the long run facilitate wage restraint. It would facilitate wage restraint because a growing share of the shift of income from labor to capital effected by wage restraint would accrue to wage earners themselves via the returns to their social insurance funds.

Another policy to support higher investment levels is to return to budget surpluses so as to bring down domestic interest rates. Furthermore, since selective investment incentives, such as differential tax rates for invested as opposed to distributed profits, tax breaks for industrial credit but not consumer credit, countercyclical investment funds, and so forth, have been effective, they should be revived to the extent possible under EU rules. Certainly, promoting wage restraint remains an additional essential policy priority in the quest for higher investment levels, particularly if complemented by policies to encourage reinvestment over distribution of profits. Wage restraint is beneficial not only in the tradable sector, but also in the nontradable sector, both in the public and private sectors. Wage restraint in the public social service sector can increase public savings and investments, and in the private sector it can be traded off for investment commitments.

The same essential logic as to wage restraint applies to a policy of lowering employer contributions to social security schemes by changing the structure of financing of these schemes. Payroll contributions can be lowered and replaced by increasing reliance on financing through general revenue in exchange for investment commitments on the part of employers. Since it would be most impractical to have negotiations with individual enterprises over such trade-offs, these policies could take the form of automatic rebate schemes, i.e., rebates on payroll taxes contingent on investments. Clearly, a shift from reliance on payroll taxes to financing out of general revenue would require an increase in other forms of taxation. Scharpf (2000) finds that private sector employment is not affected by levels of personal and corporate income taxes, in contrast to levels of social security and consumption taxes, which suggests that increases in personal and corporate taxation would be appropriate solutions. Of course, there are limits to the capacity to raise these types of taxes as well, limits set by competition among OECD countries in general and EU member countries in particular for investment and highly qualified employees.

Reductions in payroll contributions could also expand jobs at the bottom of the pay scale. As Scharpf (2000) points out, in systems with social assistance programs that assure subsistence and thus imply relatively high reservation wages, high payroll taxes can price jobs with low labor productivity in the private sector out of the official labor market. He assumes that earned income is generally counted against social assistance, and that therefore all taxes and social insurance contributions on wages at that level have to be absorbed by the employer. However, social assistance schemes themselves could be changed to take account of this problem, insofar as additional earned income could be allowed with a phased reduction of benefits.

Another promising approach to the promotion of higher labor force participation, as exemplified by the Dutch case, is through the creation of part-time jobs, opportunities for job sharing, and flexibilization of work schedules. In the context of generous welfare states and coordinated production regimes, this requires an extension of social benefits to part-time employees and their coverage through collective wage agreements. Even though the creation of part-time jobs and job sharing obviously have a more limited effect on aggregate activity levels than the creation of full-time jobs, they have at least two desirable effects. First, from the point of view of equity, two people employed half-time are certainly preferable to one being employed full-time and the other one unemployed. Second, in the former scenario, both people maintain an uninterrupted connection to the labor market and thus continued employability, which should reduce frictional unemployment and thus increase the aggregate number of hours worked and the total value of goods and services produced.

In Christian democratic welfare states, where the problem of low labor force participation rates is most severe, an essential step toward alleviating this problem is to make labor force participation compatible with raising children by measures such as changing school schedules (so children don't come home for a couple of hours in the middle of the day), introducing generous paternal leave, and expanding social services in the area of care for preschool and school children. In line with the Christian democratic tradition, such services could be funded and regulated by the state, and they could be delivered by private nonprofit institutions. In either case, an expansion of care services would of course also create jobs in these services. The obvious objection is that this would cost money and thus would require tax increases, a very difficult proposition in the present environment. However, some of these changes, such as the introduction of a continuous school day, would not burden the government budget. Others should become acceptable if preceded by wage restraint and accompanied by higher investment and some overall employment growth and a consequent enlargement of the tax base.

A further important component of a comprehensive approach to increasing labor force participation levels is investment in training and retraining of the labor force, particularly of low-skilled labor. An accompanying measure in coordinated production regimes with wide bargaining coverage is to allow for lower entry-level wages of unskilled labor, with a time limit lest these become permanent low-wage jobs. Similarly, employment of the long-term unemployed in the private sector could be subsidized for a period of time, until they have successfully reintegrated into the labor market. A further set of measures that may favor employment creation in such production regimes, following the Danish model, is to allow more flexibility of hiring and firing in small and medium enterprises. These production and welfare state regimes are well prepared to cover the social costs of higher job turnover through well-developed unemployment compensation and retraining programs.

The move from passive unemployment compensation to labor activation policies would appear to be similar to the workfare approach pursued in the liberal welfare states, particularly the United States and the United Kingdom. In reality, our proposals here are radically different. In those cases, the primary motivation has not been to increase the overall activity rate in order to sustain a generous welfare state, but rather to purge the welfare rolls and make long-term dependence on social assistance impossible in order to reduce the burden on residual welfare states.[4] What is lacking in the residual welfare states and uncoordinated production regimes is a comprehensive support system for the integration of welfare recipients into the labor market. Most prominently, these countries lack comprehensive systems of training and retraining, with the result that welfare recipients generally have extremely low skill levels and have difficulty improving those skills. The roots of the problem go even deeper. We noted in chapter 4 the relationship between degrees of inequality in the society and educational achievements. Given the ranking of the United States and the United Kingdom as the two most unequal among the advanced industrial societies, it is no surprise that the basic educational levels of welfare recipients are so low. Add to this the weakness of the system of vocational training, of active labor market policies in the form of income support during periods of retraining, and of public provision of care for the young and the elderly, and it becomes clear why these workfare programs have had only very limited success. A serious part of the problem is that former welfare recipients typically end up in jobs at the bottom of the wage scale, which in these uncoordinated production regimes is very low, and consequently integration into the labor market is not a ticket out of poverty.

Esping-Andersen (1999) makes the important point that changes in family structures and in life cycles have created new risk structures that are difficult to address through the traditional social insurance schemes, particularly those characteristic of Christian democratic welfare states. He suggests that more spending is needed on the young and on working-age people for education and training and that spending needs to take more differentiated forms to meet the needs of different groups. Clearly, such spending needs to be financed predominantly out of general revenue. These suggestions seem to imply a move toward more targeted forms of programs, which stands in tension with the proven strength of political support for universalistic programs. Similar support for such new programs might be built if they grant entitlements on a statutory, not discretionary basis, and if they are clearly targeted on support for periods in education and training. As such, they would have a universalistic character, available by right to all who are engaged in particular educational and training activities.

The fact that wage restraint will remain an essential ingredient of any successful coordinated production regime–welfare state regime combination draws attention to the need for adjusting the systems of collective bargaining in the context of the new crucial role played by the European Central Bank. In theory, the transfer of monetary authority from the national to the European level should change the important positive relationship between coordinated bargaining, an independent monetary authority, and wage restraint pointed to by Iversen (1998, 1999) and Hall and Franzese (1998). The amalgamation of several national bargaining units into a single currency area should lower the overall degree of coordination of bargaining. However, as Soskice and Iversen (1998) argue, the situation in Europe is different, as the de facto power over monetary policy was already exercised by one agency, the German Bundesbank. They outline two scenarios that could result from the transfer of monetary authority from the German Bundesbank to the European Central Bank: (1) the ECB targets the European, rather than the German, inflation rate, departing from previous Bundesbank practice; or (2) the ECB takes account of the impact of German wage development on European inflation and in part targets German as well as European inflation. Under the first scenario, German wage bargainers have less incentive for restraint than they used to have, and an inflationary settlement would increase European inflation. This would likely induce the ECB to take restrictive measures in response, which then would affect the rest of the EMU countries as well and lead to a rise in unemployment across Europe. Under the second scenario, there would be continued incentives for German labor market partners to bargain with restraint, and thus the signals and incentives for bargaining rounds in other countries would remain largely unchanged. Certainly, the first couple of years after the transition present difficult challenges, as national actors need to learn to anticipate the behavior of the ECB.

Moreover, Soskice and Iversen's more positive scenario may be too optimistic as it is based on the assumption that the German system of central bank independence and coordinated sectoral-level bargaining produced low unemployment as argued by Soskice (1990) and Hall and Franzese (1998). These authors point to the success of the German system in the 1980s, which produced 5.5 to 6 percent unemployment. Though this was below the European average, it did not reach the 2 to 3 percent levels aspired to by the Nordic union movements. Indeed, the Swedish LO has argued that the present Swedish system of sectoral-level bargaining, an independent European monetary authority targeting inflation, and a common currency or fixed exchange rates will not produce wage restraint as the economy approaches full employment. Particularly for the smaller countries in Europe, the present system has deficient controls on the wage demands of sheltered sector unions as the European Central Bank is unlikely to impose austerity on all of Europe in response to a large wage increase negotiated by, say, the Swedish Commercial Workers Union (Handels), because that agreement is unlikely to affect Europe-wide inflation. The Danish, Finnish, and Austrian systems provide for stronger central level controls either through state mediators, governmental intervention, or central coordination by the unions.[5]

Finally, what can we say about the politics of reforming welfare state and production regimes? In other words, what are the political structures and processes most conducive to a successful adaptation of welfare states and production regimes to the new economic and demographic conditions? We would define successful reforms as those making welfare states and production regimes capable of keeping more than 90 percent of the population out of poverty, providing everybody with adequate health care and education, preventing the emergence of permanent groups of outsiders, and being sustainable financially and in terms of political support. This last criterion makes obvious the need for wide support or at least acceptance of any such reforms. Support or acceptance of reforms that entail curtailments of benefits in the interest of employment creation, just like acceptance of wage restraint, are greatly facilitated by a shared perception of the severity of the unemployment and welfare state problems and of the probability that the reforms will be successful. Obviously, the severity of the crisis itself influences such perceptions. Procedurally, the achievement of such shared perceptions is facilitated by the inclusion of major parties and/or major peak associations in negotiations of reforms. In contrast to the period of welfare state construction, then, corporatist arrangements have come to play a crucial role in welfare state retrenchment and restructuring (Ebbinghaus and Hassel 1999). The experience of most European countries has demonstrated that union support for or at least acquiescence to reforms was essential. Exceptions to this pattern were conjunctures where there was a widespread perception of crisis, unions were on the defensive, and political systems provided for high power concentration, such as in the United Kingdom, the Netherlands, and New Zealand; there, governments could push through highly unpopular reforms despite union opposition.[6] However, at least the United Kingdom and New Zealand have failed by our criteria of success for reforms, as poverty has increased above the 10 percent level.

## Contributions to Theories of the Welfare State

Our analyses have provided support for our theoretical framework that bases the explanation of welfare state development on the crucial role of political parties, the underlying organization of subordinate classes and the subordinate gender, the constitutional structure of the state, and the impact of the international economy. Our power constellation framework is related to the class struggle–power resource mobilization theoretical approach but provides important amendments to the approach, in part based on the recognition of the pivotal role of incumbency of different political tendencies, and in part based on the feminist critiques of the class struggle–power resource mobilization approach. It also accepts parts of the state-centric view of welfare state development but suggests amendments to that view as well. Confirmation of the validity of our framework was provided both by the cross-national quantitative and comparative historical analyses, which showed the importance of political parties with different power bases and of the strength of labor movements. Our framework and the evidence amend power resources theory by emphasizing the importance of political incumbency and by including women's organizational power based on mobilization in unions, political parties, and women's movements as an important determinant of the size and character of the welfare state. Women's mobilization and organizational power in turn were strongly supported by increasing labor force participation.

Our framework incorporates the constitutional structure of the state and policy legacies, two factors at the core of the state-centric approach to the study of welfare states, as important determinants of welfare state development. Our quantitative analyses as well as our case studies provided strong support for the impact of state structure on welfare state expansion and retrenchment. Constitutional structures with wide power dispersion clearly slowed down both processes. Our framework proposed amendments to the traditional state-centric view by giving the policy legacies argument a directional character for the construction phase of the welfare state and by insisting that bureaucrats and the relative success of their actions be seen in the context of the power distribution in society and political incumbency. The general arguments about policy legacies tend to emphasize inertia and thus predict difficulties in retrenchment, particularly of universalistic policies, but they fail to generate directional hypotheses for welfare state construction. Inertia in principle could apply to generous and universalistic as well as to residual and means-tested types of policies. We have tried to generate directional hypotheses in our discussion of long-term effects of partisan incumbency, and we have suggested that the general effect of policy legacies is upward, toward more generous programs, but that partisan incumbency is the decisive variable. Our evidence supported this view, as there was a general trend toward an improvement of entitlements under both social democratic and Christian democratic regimes before the changing economic conditions began to dictate austerity in the late 1970s.

We argued that the influence of bureaucrats on social policy formation is highly contingent on power relations in society and on the political orientation of the government, and the evidence from our cases supports this argument. First of all, certain positions in the bureaucracy, such as bureaus for women's affairs, were only created in response to social and political pressures. Second, the request to bureaucrats for the elaboration of proposals for welfare state policies typically came from the minister in charge of social policy, and this minister was of course appointed by the party or parties in power. For the most part, the minister also set out the basic parameters of the goals of the policy. The chance that any given policy proposal elaborated by bureaucrats would get a sympathetic reception depended on the degree of conformity of the proposal with the preferences of this minister, the rest of the cabinet, and ultimately the legislature. Other studies showed that occupants of state positions charged with promoting women's rights have been most effective where they had strong allies in government, which in turn was mostly the case if the government was formed by a left-wing party that had a strong internal women's group and was in addition pushed by a strong external women's movement (Stetson and Mazur 1995). Our argument and evidence concerning the contingency of bureaucrats' policy influence on wider power relations in the society and on political incumbency are fully consistent with the compelling analysis of the National Labor Relations Board in the United States by Stryker (1989).

We also found support for our intermediate, or mild, version of path dependency in welfare state development. In chapter 2 we rejected the strong, critical junctures version of welfare state development, according to which the formation of welfare state and labor market institutions in the early post–World War II period set countries on a path from which there was little deviation later on. We later demonstrated how New Zealand fell from the position of having the most generous and comprehensive welfare state in 1950 to the position of being a laggard and ultimately of having the welfare state regime transformed into a residual one. Or, in a movement in the opposite direction, we saw how in Germany and Austria initially rather stratified welfare state regimes became more egalitarian by eliminating differences between white- and blue-collar workers, mainly due to pressure from the social democratic parties and the union movements. However, in chapter 2 we also argued that there is considerable path dependency, that the effect of the underlying causes of welfare state formation is not uniform over time, but rather that incumbency in the formative period of welfare state institutions is more crucial than at later points in time, and that the ratchet effect and the regime legacies effect cause path dependency. In chapter 5 we demonstrated that incumbency of Christian democrats in the early post–World War II period was crucial for the revival of occupationally based multiple insurance schemes, which competed with plans for the introduction of more unified schemes promoted by social democrats in Germany and the Netherlands. We also demonstrated how social policies that benefited large sectors of the population, once introduced, became widely accepted and set the base point for discussion about further policy reforms, a phenomenon we called the ratchet effect. We further showed that the combination of generous unemployment benefits and wide union contract coverage led to the marginalization of low-wage employers in the Nordic and northern Continental European countries and thus to the loss of influence of opponents of generous welfare state regimes, and we called this a regime legacies effect. On a more general level, we showed that same effect in that prolonged incumbency of social democratic parties and the consequent firm institutionalization of a generous welfare state regime caused employers to adjust their expectations accordingly and not waste political capital in fights opposing welfare state programs that they could not win, though they continued consistently to oppose the level of taxation that these programs entailed.

Our conceptualization of the ratchet effect is compatible with the concept of policy legacies, but it is not the same. The conceptualization of policy legacies emphasizes inertia, or the difficulty of changing to different policies because of the stakeholders in the existing policy regime. Thus, policy legacies can have a depressing as well as an expansive effect on welfare state development. Our policy ratchet effect denotes an upward trajectory only, that is, an expansive effect. In our discussion of the period of retrenchment, then, we used the concept of policy legacies, since the struggle became mainly one over preserving what had been achieved. Expansion was by and large off the agenda, but policy legacies could greatly slow down retrenchment.

Our categorization of welfare states built very heavily on Esping-Andersen's (1990), except that we added the fourth world of wage earner welfare states and renamed his conservative-corporatist category. However, our analysis brought to the fore one fundamental disagreement with his conceptualization of social democratic welfare states. He sees decommodification as a defining feature of the social democratic welfare state regime, whereas we have emphasized the strongly labor-mobilizing features of that regime. Of course it is true that the social democratic welfare state regime aims at offering a safety net that preserves a person's living standard when that person is separated from the labor market. However, the emphasis is on involuntary and temporary separation from the labor market, except in the case of old age, and on maximum support for reintegration. Moreover, the social democratic welfare state and associated coordinated production regimes have aimed at integrating a maximum proportion of the population into the labor market, principally by making paid work compatible with child rearing.

Neither our quantitative analyses nor the comparative historical studies provided much support for the logic of industrialism thesis.[7] It is clear that demographic factors, that is, dependency ratios that turned unfavorable, have been and will continue to be challenges for welfare states. However, as we showed, dependency ratios depend not only on the relative size of different population groups, but also on overall activity rates that vary greatly across countries. It is also clear that growing needs drive up expenditures under any given set of entitlements, be it an increasing number of pensioners driving up pension expenditures or an increasing number of unemployed driving up expenditures for active and passive labor market policies. However, we found very little evidence outside of the United States that suggested a role for the organizational power of pensioners per se in shaping pension entitlements, independent of unions or political parties, and we found no such evidence for the unemployed.

Despite the widely accepted claims that the politics of retrenchment are very different from the politics of welfare state development, and despite our own agreement with the proposition that policy legacies are important, we found a significant degree of continuity in determinants of welfare state generosity. The most marked continuity we found was in the impact of state structure. This impact manifested itself both in the context of radical cuts, which occurred only under conditions of power concentration, and in the blocking or watering down of reforms in bicameral parliaments or by referenda. One clear change we found was a reduction of partisan differences due on the one hand to high support for the welfare state, which made cuts politically difficult, i.e., a policy legacies effect, and on the other hand to economic constraints, which made expansion very difficult. Yet, in the case studies we also found evidence that the political composition of governments and power relations in society continued to make a difference in the phase of retrenchment. All of the ideologically driven cuts were carried out by secular right-wing parties in societies with declining union movements and without significant Christian democratic presence. On the other side of the political spectrum, social democratic governments attempted some restoration of benefits that had been cut by center-right governments, once economic conditions and the fiscal situation of the state had improved enough to make this feasible.

We further amended existing welfare state theory by widening our perspective to include production regimes. We emphasized the importance of the connection to production regimes both for an understanding of the emergence and continued viability of generous welfare states. Coordinated production regimes are crucial for the affordability of generous welfare states, as such welfare states require a strong tax base and thus an expansion of employment in high wage production. In a developmental sense this relationship is to be seen as an argument about path dependency, insofar as coordinated production regimes make the establishment of generous welfare states more likely. Embeddedness in a coordinated production regime is not a precondition for the establishment of comprehensive pension and medical insurance, as shown by the example of Australia in the 1990s, but it is a facilitating condition for the expansion of such programs and even more so for other transfers and services. What we have called a mutually supportive or enabling fit applies to transfer programs for the working-age population, as well as to services for the young and the working-age population. High transfer benefits for the working-age population imply a high reservation wage and thus obstruct the expansion of low-wage jobs. High-quality services in education, labor training, retraining, and employment searches in turn promote the ready availability of a qualified labor force for high-quality-high-wage production; and child care services enable women to become part of that labor force. Coordinated production regimes in turn maintain a generally high wage level through high bargaining coverage.

Coordinated production regimes also used to sustain higher investment levels than uncoordinated production regimes on the basis of preferential credit provided through government policies or through special relationships between enterprises and banks. Higher investment levels in turn are linked to growth of employment and thus to the viability of generous welfare states, another example of the mutually enabling fit. A further essential characteristic of coordinated production regimes is coordinated wage setting. Coordination of wage setting is important for the exercise of wage restraint—within the context of high-wage economies—in the interest of sustaining competitiveness against other high-wage countries. We noted that the transfer of de facto monetary authority in Europe from the Bundesbank to the European Central Bank introduces at least transitional uncertainty as there are no established patterns of policy making of the European Central Bank that could serve as guidelines for wage bargainers.

Finally, our theoretical framework drew attention to the impact of the international economy on the development of the welfare state, and we have addressed theories, or better, a loose set of propositions, concerning the impact of globalization on welfare states. We have taken issue with the argument that an increase in trade openness made economies with generous welfare states unviable. We pointed out that the most generous welfare states had been constructed in highly trade-open economies and that there was only a modest increase in trade for these countries over the past fifteen years. We did find the internationalization of capital markets to be a serious problem for coordinated production regimes and thus indirectly for generous welfare states. Internationalization of capital markets made the pursuit of traditional investment promotion policies more difficult or even impossible, and it also obstructed the pursuit of counter-cyclical management. The third aspect of economic internationalization, internationalization of production, we found to be predominantly a political problem. Most direct foreign investment flows to other highly developed countries, and investments that require high skill production find the most hospitable environments in other high-skill-high-wage economies, not in the developed countries with the lowest wage levels. However, the higher credibility of the exit threat resulting from internationalization of production clearly gives more leverage to capital and thus puts downward pressures on employer contributions to welfare state programs and on corporate taxation.

### Contributions to Theories of the State

In the initial elaborations of power resources theory, it was presented as a theory of the state, an alternative to pluralism and orthodox Marxism (Korpi 1978, 1983; Stephens 1979b). The theory argued that, in the absence of working-class organization, the orthodox Marxist theory was essentially correct: Public policy was formed according to the interests of capital. While the theory did see an important role for active participation of capitalists in the policy-making process, the primary mechanisms by which the rule of capital was secured was through the structural dependence of the state on capital, that is, the dependence of state policy makers on capital's willingness to invest, and through hegemony, ideological domination. The latter was viewed not in a conspiratorial fashion, though conscious efforts to influence the public's political consciousness were ever present, but rather importantly as influenced by inertia. As Mann (1973) points out, socialism, or any other ideology that imagines a substantially different way of organizing society, is learned. Thus, ceteris paribus, everyday consciousness will reproduce itself and thus is a conservative force. An important part of the organizing task of the working-class movement was to promote a counterhegemony, an alternative image of how society might be organized. The theory hypothesized that the state would respond to changes in working-class organization, and the main mechanism by which this response was effected was electoral: the working-class movements organized and propagandized for electoral support for social democratic parties, which, when in office, would pass legislation favorable to working-class interests.

Even in the original formulations, the theory envisioned this as a process of coalition making, and, in the analysis of Scandinavia for instance, saw a shift from a farmer-worker coalition to a wage earner alliance as the farming population declined and postindustrial capitalism rose (Korpi 1978, 1983; Stephens 1979b; Esping-Andersen 1985). Even at that time, the postindustrialization of society had created new social movements, and subsequent formulations of the theory have sought to include these as bases for challenging the rule of capitalist interests and market principles of allocation. In this book, the women's movement has figured most prominently; had we examined environmental policy rather than social policy the environmental movement would have been more central.

Our analysis of welfare state expansion and even more so retrenchment provides support for the structural dependence of the state on capital thesis, which power resources theory shares with neo-Marxist analysis, such as Block (1977) and Lindblom's (1977) neopluralism. Even in the Golden Age, when countries imposed controls on the mobility of capital, governments of all political colors in all advanced capitalist societies were dependent on business investment to stimulate growth, which limited the degree to which governments could tax capital or impose regulations that would reduce profitability. Thus, in sharp contrast to the strong partisan effects on social policy, one does not find strong partisan effects of the level of corporate income taxes, for example, even in this period. The deregulation of financial markets and the multinationalization of production has further increased the political leverage of business. While it is difficult to detect any trends to lower business taxation in the data (Swank 1998), our case studies show that at the very least governments, including social democratic ones, believe that concessions to business in tax policy and regulation were necessary to keep business in the country and to stimulate further investment (also Ganghof 2000).

The first attempts to apply power resources theory to variations in the welfare state were explicit about the link between the theory and the variables employed to operationalize working-class strength, union organization, and left party rule but not very explicit about the relationship of the control variables and the related theories (e.g., logic of industrialism) to any theories of the state (Korpi 1983; Stephens 1979b). In his book on pension policy, Myles (1984) made this link explicit, and it soon became typical for analyses of welfare state variation to frame them as tests of state theory (e.g., see Pampel and Williamson 1988, 1989). It was the link to theories of the state that made empirical works in comparative social policy relevant to a much wider audience of political sociologists, political economists, and political theorists and explains why they found their way into the leading journals in sociology and political science.

What then are the implications of our results for the theory of the state in advanced capitalist democracies? In the case of the logic of industrialism theory, we must first briefly review the theory and its conventional operationalization, as the theory of the state is implicit rather than explicit. In the operationalization and testing of this approach, the aged proportion of the population and the level of economic development have figured prominently as the main predictive variables. According to the theory, the level of economic development operates largely indirectly through its effect on the changing demographic and occupational structure, though it was also hypothesized to enable social policy innovation by increasing the total pool of resources. The main hypotheses linking the theory to theories of the state are the transformations of demographic and occupational structures. According to the theory, industrialization creates "new needs," groups in need of temporary income support (unemployed and ill workers) and permanent income support (pensioners) who depended on the agrarian extended household before, as well as those in need of services required by or enabled by industrial society, such as education and medical care. The theory, in its bare bones, is structural functional and thus without agents. Wilensky (1975: 26–27) provides the agents, primarily the needy themselves, but also those on whom the needy would be dependent (offspring, parents, etc.). Thus, the theory implied a theory of the state—that the state responded to the demands of its citizens—essentially a pluralist theory of the state.

Though one might identify many needy groups, the only one that found its way into the quantitative studies was the aged. The initial studies, both cross-sectional (Wilensky 1975, 1976) and pooled time series (Pampel and Williamson 1988, 1989) appeared to confirm that there was a strong relationship between social spending and the proportion of the population aged net of a number of control variables. But these studies failed to distinguish between the automatic effect that the growth of the aged has on expenditures at any level of entitlements and an actual effect of the proportion aged on entitlements, and it would be necessary to show the latter in order to support the pluralist theory of the state as Pampel and Williamson intended it to. Our regressions on pensions standardized by the aged proportion of the population, which control for the automatic effect of the proportion aged, show no effect of the aged on pension generosity, the one policy for which one would hypothesize the effect to be strongest.[8]

State-centered theory received some strong support in our analysis but not when it made claims that detached state effects, even if only in relative terms, from the structures of power in society and partisanship in governance. Heclo's (1974) strong statement of this view, in which the activities of bureaucrats are the primary determinants of policy outcomes and electoral outcomes are irrelevant, received no support. By contrast, Stetson and Mazur's analysis, in which femocrats were influential in policy making but only in combination with left government and women's mobilization, is completely consistent with the picture painted by our analyses. Likewise, the case studies of retrenchment in the last chapter made it clear that strong effects of constitutional structure on social policy generosity were contingent on partisan governance and the world economic conjuncture. In the retrenchment era, concentration of government power facilitated moderate retrenchment and, when combined with right-wing government and plurality elections and single-member districts, it enabled radical neoliberal cutbacks.

Thus, our results give extremely strong support to our power constellation theory and indirectly to its precursor, power resources theory. While one might question the link between Christian democratic governance and power resource theory (see below), the strong effect of social democracy on all of our dependent variables does provide unambiguous support for the theory. Moreover, power resources theory's main prediction is not that social democratic welfare states will spend more, but rather that they will be redistributive and poverty reducing, as well as, based on the incorporation of gender into the theory, gender egalitarian. While we found some Christian democratic governance effects on poverty reduction, they were much smaller than the social democratic effects, and Christian democracy had no effects on redistribution and, of course, was negatively related to gender-egalitarian outcomes.

As in the case of constitutional structure, we consider our analysis of gender to be a modification of the original power resources approach rather than derivative of it. We do not believe that patriarchy can be derived from the structures of capitalism, but rather that it is an autonomous structure of inequality that interacts with the class structure. But from there there are many parallels and interactions in our analysis of gender and class. They both involve struggles of subordinate groups against dominant groups, and the method of struggle is organization. Perhaps even more so in the case of gender, a focus of the political struggle is to develop counterhegemony, to alter consciousness about the appropriate relations between the genders, and this in turn influences the policy process largely, though hardly entirely, through the electoral mechanism. Finally, both struggles are focused on substituting political decisions on allocation for market allocations, and it is around this link that the alliance of feminism and social democracy is formed.

Our empirical results are quite clear, but we are mobilizing them here to support a theory of the state and a view of the American state that is radical and will be rejected out of hand, particularly by most Americanist political scientists. This theory of the state argues that it is the distribution of class power that is most influential in determining policy outcomes, particularly those with distributive implications. Even in the best conditions—that is, best for organized labor, women, and social democracy—the result of the policy process is a compromise between capital and labor. Even in the Nordic countries, capital has considerable hegemonic power and states are structurally dependent on capital. On the other end of the spectrum, in the United States, the policy configuration is much less favorable to workers, especially to working-class and poor women, and is much more favorable to capital, the wealthy, and the professional and managerial upper middle class. In our view, this outcome is the result of a distribution of class power that is much more favorable to capital and its affluent allies. Perhaps belaboring the point, but making its implications for American democracy clear, this means that the great limitations of American social policy work to the benefit of a wealthy minority by keeping the tax level exceedingly low and, in this sense, that the United States is less democratic than countries where working-class movements are stronger.

This interpretation will be unpalatable to many and thus we anticipate that either our empirical results will be dismissed or, more likely given their unambiguity, reinterpreted to support a more acceptable theory of the state and view of American democracy. Let us anticipate what that interpretation might be in order to suggest counterevidence. As Tufte (1978) did more than a decade ago, one might interpret the findings in cross-national studies of strong partisan differences between conservative and left governments as indicating that the citizenry of these countries simply had different preferences. In good pluralist fashion, one might assume that party competition will result in parties attempting to compete for the support of the median voter, and thus that differences in public opinion will translate into policy differences. While our view of power is more complex, citizens' preferences are part of the process and the hegemonic struggle to shape public consciousness is an essential part of the determination of state policy. As Lukes (1975) has pointed out, the pluralists are not only reluctant to enter the argument about the formation of preferences, but are even likely to declare it fundamentally unscientific, contending that the analyst is likely to project an "objective" or "real" interest on groups based on his/her ideological preferences. By contrast, Lukes contends that the formation of preferences is an essential element of the operation of power, but declares that, precisely because social scientists differ in what they believe the real interest of groups to be, power will always be an "essentially contested concept." Though Lukes holds out some promise of bringing empirical evidence to bear on the question, he is skeptical that debates on the question of power in capitalist society are resolvable through appeals to empirical evidence because of differing ideologies in the social scientific community.

We find the pluralist view to be untenable and Lukes's view to be too pessimistic. To argue that power in democracies does operate in part through successful attempts to influence public opinion is not only a commonplace view in the mass public and among journalists, most pluralist social scientists admit that this is the case also. We agree with Lukes that empirical research will not eliminate paradigmatic diversity in the study of power in social science because divisions of interests in capitalist societies will always be represented in social science theory, though not in a one-to-one fashion and unevenly across social science disciplines. However, that does not mean that empirical evidence cannot be brought to bear to adjudicate disputes about the theory of the state in capitalist society. For example, two decades ago it was a widely held view, not just among Marxist scholars, that the welfare state did not redistribute income, and this was presented as evidence that even social democratic governance could not alter policy outcomes in capitalist societies (e.g., see Westergaard and Resler 1975; Parkin 1971). The evidence from the LIS surveys has made this view completely untenable and thus has changed the terms of the debate.

In the case at hand, the central problem is to account for the differences in preferences across capitalist democracies and for changes in preferences through time. This is a gigantic research project in itself, and we can do no more than outline what we think the positions in the debate are and why we think that the evidence presented in this book supports our point of view. As one saw in our elaboration of long-term change in chapter 2, in our view, the specific policy preferences and even more so the broader ideology of mass publics are historical creations in which social movements, above all the labor movement, but more recently the new social movements, transformed social consciousness. We contend that the differences in social consciousness across countries before the development of modern labor movements (meaning the unions and the related parties and auxiliary organizations), say 130 years ago, would be poor predictors of variation in the policy preference of mass publics today. As these labor movements reached more people with their organizing activity, they gradually transformed social consciousness. As they grew as electoral forces, they began to influence the terms of public debate and policy outcomes. Decisive turns, as our quantitative analysis and comparative case studies indicate, came at the points at which they could influence government formation and, even more, form governments themselves or in coalitions with other parties. The passage of policy initiated what we termed the ratchet effect; once the policy was instituted, its constituency expanded as its benefits became apparent to the citizenry. In countries such as the Nordic ones, this initiated a path-dependent interactive process in which the policy ratchet effect, labor movement counterhegemony, transformation of social consciousness, policy transformation, left governance, and consequent policies facilitating organization fed each other. As our analyses of the development of women's movements and gender-egalitarian legislation showed, an exactly parallel path-dependent process developed later between women's organization, policy developments, and consciousness transformation. At the other extreme, the process, at least in regard to the labor movement and class-egalitarian policies, barely got off the blocks in the United States. Our other cases are arrayed in between these polar types.

In fact, there is a pluralist alternative to our view. It is an extension of the American exceptionalism thesis, so ably defended by Lipset (e.g., 1963, 1977). That thesis links the weakness of American socialism and collectivist social policy (the welfare state) to long-standing, historically rooted American individualism, which in turn can be linked to the opportunity the frontier offered to the destitute in search of betterment. To extend this to explain the full array of our cross-national differences, one must argue that differences in current preferences are products of long-standing differences in (political) culture that predated the development of modern labor movements and in fact explain the differential growth of those movements across these countries.

From the point of view of the outcomes we observed, this argument has some merit in explaining the development of the Christian democratic welfare state. There were long-standing cultural differences between Catholic, Protestant, and mixed countries, which were promoted by powerful institutional actors—the churches themselves and their allies—and go far in explaining the development of modern political Christian democracy. Where the Catholic Church was strong, the development of a strong Christian democratic movement with a multiclass base and a project of mediation of class interests, and thus the development of a Christian democratic welfare state, was much more likely. However, in truth, the existence of a strong Catholic culture and the subsequent development of Christian democracy was a double-edged sword for the development of generous welfare states. On the one hand, it arguably reconciled middle- and upper-class Catholics to the welfare state who, in a Protestant society, would have been opposed to such policies and would have supported secular conservative parties. On the other hand, by attracting working-class support, it stunted the growth of social democracy and thus of a yet more egalitarian thrust of social policy. We remind the reader that while we found Christian democracy to be strongly related to welfare state generosity, it was social democracy, including social democracy in Christian democratic welfare states, that was primarily responsible for the egalitarian thrust of policy, which is the central concern of the power resources theory of the state.

Moreover, other than the observation that a strong Catholic culture weakened the social democratic thrust, there is little in the historical materials to support the view that current policy configurations and the underlying policy preferences can be linked to long-standing cultural differences, and there is much to contradict it. Among the Nordic welfare states, at the one end, Sweden was authoritarian and hierarchical 130 years ago while Norway was egalitarian and near democratic. Yet the welfare states in the two countries are now very similar. More telling is the contrast between the paths of Australia and New Zealand on the one hand and the Nordic countries on the other hand in just the last fifty years. By all accounts, Australia and New Zealand were radically egalitarian in their cultures, as early as only a few decades after their initial colonization, and as of 1950 they were among the most advanced welfare states, in the case of New Zealand the most advanced, in the world. While comparable survey data do not exist, one would be hard pressed to make the case that the Nordic countries, with the possible exception of Norway, were more egalitarian or more supportive of social policy innovation at that time. Moreover, Australia and New Zealand ranked high in the entire post–World War II period on indicators of left and labor strength, such as union density and votes for left parties. Nevertheless, as we saw in chapter 5, the trajectory over the second half of the twentieth century took the two sets of countries in quite different directions. Relatively continuous social democratic government in the Nordic countries was accompanied by the path-dependent pro–welfare state feedback process referred to above, while relatively continuous conservative government led the Antipodes to maintenance of the status quo.

A similar argument can be made about women's movements and the spread of gender-egalitarian values. Here the Nordic countries display the most remarkable transformation. What survey evidence there is indicates that the Nordic publics were more conservative than those in the liberal countries, particularly the United States, in their views on gender roles in the early postwar period. While there has been a movement toward gender egalitarianism in almost all industrial societies, the transformation in the Nordic countries, initiated by the path-dependent feedback process between women's labor force participation, feminist consciousness, women's organization, alliances with social democracy, and gender-egalitarian social policy described in chapter 5, is most remarkable.

Distributive outcomes of state policy, then, are not caused by a distribution of preferences that is somehow rooted in deep and rather immutable cultural traditions, but rather they are caused by historical processes of organization and struggle that created different power distributions and thus different distributions of preferences. We don't mean to suggest a voluntaristic picture of history and politics; rather, these historical processes of organization and struggle were profoundly influenced by economic and social structures. However, we do want to stress that the distribution of preferences, or public opinion, is shaped by underlying power distributions, and that these power distributions can be modified through purposeful political organizing on the part of subordinate groups and through the exercise of governmental power. Thus, ultimately political action by organizers and political choice by governments matter for the distributive outcomes of state policy, albeit within the constraints set by national and international social and economic structures.

# APPENDIX

**Table A.1** Total Government Revenue (Percentage GDP)

| | Levels | | | | | Annual Change | | | |
|---|---|---|---|---|---|---|---|---|---|
| | 1958 | 1973 | 1980 | 1991 | 1996 | 1958–72 | 1973–79 | 1980–90 | 1991–96 |
| *Social democratic welfare states* | | | | | | | | | |
| Sweden | 31 | 48 | 56 | 60 | 62 | 1.36 | 1.45 | .67 | -.25 |
| Norway | 31 | 50 | 53 | 55 | 52 | 1.26 | .20 | .31 | -.10 |
| Denmark | 27 | 47 | 52 | 56 | 58* | 1.33 | .67 | .40 | .38 |
| Finland | 32 | 36 | 42 | 52 | 54 | .28 | .90 | .90 | .60 |
| Mean | 30 | 45.0 | 50.9 | 56.0 | 56.5 | 1.06 | .81 | .57 | .16 |
| *Christian democratic welfare states* | | | | | | | | | |
| Austria | 31 | 42 | 46 | 47 | 48 | .70 | .65 | .01 | .28 |
| Belgium | 25 | 42 | 50 | 50 | 50 | 1.09 | 1.42 | -.04 | .18 |
| Netherlands | 35 | 46 | 53 | 54 | 49 | .69 | .92 | -.12 | -.42 |
| Germany | 36 | 42 | 45 | 44 | 46 | .31 | .37 | -.17 | .42 |
| France | 35 | 38 | 45 | 47 | 48 | .24 | .82 | .20 | .27 |
| Italy | 28 | 30 | 33 | 43 | 46 | .24 | .88 | .93 | .55 |
| Switzerland | 21 | 29 | 33 | 34 | 34 | .40 | .72 | .13 | -.05 |
| Mean | 30.0 | 38.4 | 43.4 | 45.5 | 45.9 | .52 | .83 | .13 | .18 |

**Table A.1**   *(continued)*

|  | Levels | | | | | Annual Change | | | |
|---|---|---|---|---|---|---|---|---|---|
|  | 1958 | 1973 | 1980 | 1991 | 1996 | 1958–72 | 1973–79 | 1980–90 | 1991–96 |
| *Liberal welfare states* | | | | | | | | | |
| Canada | 24 | 35 | 36 | 43 | 43 | .78 | .10 | .61 | .17 |
| Ireland | 26 | 35 | 39 | 40 | 36* | .66 | .23 | −.03 | −.46 |
| U.K. | 31 | 36 | 40 | 39 | 38 | .39 | .40 | −.03 | −.27 |
| U.S.A. | 26 | 30 | 31 | 32 | 32 | .24 | .13 | .13 | .07 |
| Mean | 26.7 | 33.7 | 36.4 | 38.6 | 37.3 | .52 | .22 | .17 | −.12 |
| *Wage earner welfare states* | | | | | | | | | |
| Australia | 27 | 27 | 31 | 34 | 35 | −.14 | .52 | .46 | .03 |
| New Zealand | 21 | 23 | 18 | 34 | 32 | .10 | −.80 | | |
| Japan | 19 | 23 | 28 | 34 | 32 | .17 | .63 | .70 | −.42 |

*Figure for 1995.

**Table A.2** Total Government Expenditure (Percentage GDP)

| | 1958 | 1973 | 1980 | 1991 | 1997 | 1958–72 | 1973–79 | 1980–90 | 1991–97 |
|---|---|---|---|---|---|---|---|---|---|
| *Social democratic welfare states* | | | | | | | | | |
| Sweden | 31 | 45 | 66 | 63 | 63 | 1.09 | 3.37 | -.49 | .27 |
| Norway | 27 | 45 | 49 | 57 | 45 | 1.26 | 1.13 | .55 | -.88 |
| Denmark | 25 | 40 | 56 | 59 | 52 | 1.21 | 2.17 | .24 | -.94 |
| Finland | 28 | 31 | 39 | 56 | 53 | .35 | 1.48 | .74 | .88 |
| Mean | 27.6 | 40.2 | 52.7 | 58.5 | 53.3 | .98 | 2.04 | .26 | -.17 |
| *Christian democratic welfare states* | | | | | | | | | |
| Austria | 33 | 41 | 49 | 51 | 51 | .48 | 1.25 | .09 | .17 |
| Belgium | 27 | 46 | 59 | 57 | 51 | 1.29 | 2.00 | -.34 | -.68 |
| Netherlands | 35 | 49 | 63 | 58 | 49 | .95 | 1.80 | -.50 | -1.23 |
| Germany | 34 | 41 | 47 | 48 | 49 | .41 | .98 | -.12 | .48 |
| France | 35 | 39 | 46 | 51 | 54 | .25 | 1.15 | .37 | .57 |
| Italy | 29 | 38 | 46 | 54 | 51 | .71 | 1.28 | .80 | -.44 |
| Switzerland | 17 | 24 | 30 | 33 | 37* | .34 | 1.00 | .12 | 1.16 |
| Mean | 30.0 | 39.5 | 48.3 | 50.0 | 48.9 | .63 | 1.35 | .06 | .00 |

**Table A.2**  *(continued)*

| | 1958 | 1973 | 1980 | 1991 | 1997 | 1958–72 | 1973–79 | 1980–90 | 1991–97 |
|---|---|---|---|---|---|---|---|---|---|
| *Liberal welfare states* | | | | | | | | | |
| Canada | 27 | 36 | 41 | 51 | 42 | .71 | .55 | .71 | –.85 |
| Ireland | 28 | 39 | 51 | 43 | 32 | .76 | 1.30 | –.94 | –1.28 |
| U.K. | 32 | 41 | 45 | 43 | 40 | .59 | .40 | –.23 | –.38 |
| U.S.A. | 30 | 30 | 34 | 38 | 32 | .12 | .20 | .30 | –.67 |
| Mean | 29.2 | 36.6 | 42.4 | 43.6 | 36.5 | .55 | .61 | –.04 | –.80 |
| *Wage earner welfare states* | | | | | | | | | |
| Australia | 22 | 27 | 34 | 40 | 35 | .30 | 1.07 | .36 | –.39 |
| New Zealand | | | | 55 | 46 | | 1.58 | | –1.62 |
| Japan | 18 | 22 | 33 | 32 | 35 | .25 | 1.58 | –.04 | .42 |

*Figure for 1995.

**Table A.3** Social Security Transfer Expenditure (Percentage GDP)

| | Levels | | | | | Annual Change | | | |
|---|---|---|---|---|---|---|---|---|---|
| | 1958 | 1973 | 1980 | 1991 | 1996 | 1958–72 | 1973–79 | 1980–90 | 1991–96 |
| *Social democratic welfare states* | | | | | | | | | |
| Sweden | 7 | 12 | 18 | 21 | 23 | .38 | .90 | .18 | .51 |
| Norway | 7 | 14 | 14 | 21 | 15*** | .47 | .27 | .51 | –.16 |
| Denmark | 7 | 11 | 17 | 19 | 22** | .28 | .72 | .18 | .62 |
| Finland | 6 | 8 | 9 | 20 | 23 | .16 | .30 | .67 | 1.17 |
| Mean | 6.9 | 11.2 | 14.5 | 20.1 | 20.8 | .32 | .55 | .39 | .54 |
| *Christian democratic welfare states* | | | | | | | | | |
| Austria | 10 | 15 | 19 | 20 | 22 | .40 | .67 | .08 | .34 |
| Belgium | 9 | 15 | 21 | 24 | 21*** | .39 | .90 | .22 | –.19 |
| Netherlands | 10 | 20 | 26 | 26 | 24 | .69 | .85 | –.01 | –.32 |
| Germany | 14 | 14 | 17 | 15 | 19 | –.04 | .50 | –.13 | .56 |
| France | 13 | 17 | 19 | 22 | 23 | .32 | .22 | .20 | .37 |
| Italy | 10 | 14 | 14 | 18 | 19 | .29 | .32 | .41 | .18 |
| Switzerland | 6 | 10 | 13 | 15 | 18** | .17 | .48 | .09 | .80 |
| Mean | 10.2 | 15.1 | 18.3 | 19.9 | 20.8 | .32 | .56 | .12 | .25 |

**Table A.3** *(continued)*

| | Levels | | | | | Annual Change | | | |
|---|---|---|---|---|---|---|---|---|---|
| | 1958 | 1973 | 1980 | 1991 | 1996 | 1958–72 | 1973–79 | 1980–90 | 1991–96 |
| *Liberal welfare states* | | | | | | | | | |
| Canada | 7 | 9 | 10 | 15 | 12*** | .16 | .10 | .30 | –.14 |
| Ireland | 6 | 10 | 13 | 15 | 14** | .22 | .18 | .15 | –.08 |
| U.K. | 6 | 9 | 12 | 13 | 15* | .23 | .37 | .01 | .95 |
| U.S.A. | 5 | 9 | 11 | 12 | 13 | .23 | .20 | .03 | .30 |
| Mean | 6.2 | 9.2 | 11.2 | 13.7 | 13.7 | .21 | .21 | .12 | .26 |
| *Wage earner welfare states* | | | | | | | | | |
| Australia | 6 | 6 | 8 | 11 | 11 | .06 | .33 | .16 | .26 |
| New Zealand | 9 | 11 | 15 | 15 | | .04 | .83 | –.04 | |
| Japan | 5 | 5 | 10 | 11 | 14 | .05 | .78 | .14 | .36 |

*Figure for 1994.
**Figure for 1995.
***Figure for 1997.

**Table A.4**    Social Security Benefit Expenditure (ILO) (Percentage GDP)

| | Levels | | | | Annual Change | | |
|---|---|---|---|---|---|---|---|
| | 1958 | 1973 | 1980 | 1989 | 1958–72 | 1973–79 | 1980–89 |
| *Social democratic welfare states* | | | | | | | |
| Sweden | 11 | 20 | 31 | 33 | .65 | 1.50 | .24 |
| Norway | 8 | 17 | 20 | 19 | .65 | .52 | −.07 |
| Denmark | 11 | 17 | 26 | 28 | .44 | 1.26 | .14 |
| Finland | 9 | 13 | 17 | 21 | .33 | .70 | .37 |
| Mean | 9.6 | 17.1 | 23.6 | 25.3 | .52 | 1.00 | .17 |
| *Christian democratic welfare states* | | | | | | | |
| Austria | 14 | 17 | 21 | 24 | .26 | .76 | .24 |
| Belgium | 13 | 19 | 24 | 24* | .34 | .87 | .03 |
| Netherlands | 11 | 21 | 27 | 27 | .71 | .96 | −.02 |
| Germany | 17 | 18 | 23 | 22 | .06 | .82 | −.10 |
| France | 13 | 18 | 25 | 26 | .35 | .99 | .09 |
| Italy | 11 | 15 | 17 | 22 | .35 | −.55 | .53 |
| Switzerland | 7 | 12 | 13 | 13 | .23 | .21 | .03 |
| Mean | 12.1 | 17.0 | 21.6 | 22.7 | .33 | .58 | .11 |
| *Liberal welfare states* | | | | | | | |
| Canada | 8 | 13 | 13 | 17 | .34 | .00 | .39 |
| Ireland | 9 | 10 | 19 | 17 | .10 | 1.04 | −.18 |
| U.K. | 10 | 13 | 17 | 16 | .27 | .55 | −.11 |
| U.S.A. | 6 | 10 | 12 | 11 | .32 | .19 | −.04 |
| Mean | 8.4 | 11.6 | 15.4 | 15.5 | .26 | .45 | .02 |
| *Wage earner welfare states* | | | | | | | |
| Australia | 4 | 8 | 11 | 8 | .30 | .59 | −.34 |
| New Zealand | 6 | 12 | 17 | 19 | .39 | .95 | .19 |
| *Japan* | 4 | 5 | 10 | 11 | .06 | .70 | .11 |

*Figure for 1986.

**Table A.5**    Public Pension Expenditure (Percentage GDP per Aged Person)

| | Levels | | | | Annual Change | | |
|---|---|---|---|---|---|---|---|
| | 1958 | 1973 | 1980 | 1989 | 1958–72 | 1973–79 | 1980–89 |
| *Social democratic welfare states* | | | | | | | |
| Sweden | 23 | 44 | 59 | 78 | 1.43 | 2.06 | 1.86 |
| Norway | 14 | 54 | 50 | 51 | 2.75 | −.03 | .08 |
| Denmark | 26 | 43 | 54 | 53 | 1.28 | 1.39 | −.14 |
| Finland | 23 | 45 | 50 | 73 | 1.59 | 1.14 | 2.24 |
| Mean | 21.3 | 46.2 | 53.6 | 63.6 | 1.76 | 1.14 | 1.01 |
| *Christian democratic welfare states* | | | | | | | |
| Austria | 36 | 49 | 57 | 71 | 1.10 | 1.17 | 1.38 |
| Belgium | 24 | 36 | 45 | 48* | .68 | 1.49 | .29 |
| Netherlands | 40 | 74 | 98 | 85 | 2.27 | 3.67 | −1.25 |
| Germany | 62 | 52 | 62 | 60 | −.68 | 1.75 | −.17 |
| France | 24 | 43 | 54 | 71 | 1.29 | 1.66 | 1.66 |
| Italy | 33 | 54 | 43 | 80 | 1.64 | −2.06 | 3.70 |
| Switzerland | 14 | 50 | 53 | 50 | 1.88 | .95 | −.34 |
| Mean | 33.1 | 51.3 | 58.9 | 66.5 | 1.17 | 1.23 | .75 |
| *Liberal welfare states* | | | | | | | |
| Canada | 19 | 32 | 34 | 40 | .86 | .28 | .54 |
| Ireland | 16 | 25 | 45 | 42 | .74 | 2.40 | −.29 |
| U.K. | 17 | 33 | 37 | 31 | 1.30 | .64 | −.59 |
| U.S.A. | 19 | 37 | 33 | 36 | 1.07 | −.53 | .25 |
| Mean | 17.7 | 31.7 | 37.5 | 37.2 | .99 | .70 | −.02 |
| *Wage earner welfare states* | | | | | | | |
| Australia | 11 | 28 | 39 | 29 | 1.04 | 2.14 | −.97 |
| New Zealand | 16 | 46 | 85 | 82 | 1.99 | 6.58 | −.31 |
| *Japan* | 1 | 7 | 28 | 33 | .34 | 3.09 | .51 |

*Figure for 1986.

**Table A.6** Civilian Nontransfer Expenditure (Percentage GDP)

| | Levels | | | | | Annual Change | | | |
|---|---|---|---|---|---|---|---|---|---|
| | 1958 | 1973 | 1980 | 1991 | 1996 | 1958–72 | 1973–79 | 1980–90 | 1991–96 |
| *Social democratic welfare states* | | | | | | | | | |
| Sweden | 19* | 29 | 45 | 39 | 48 | .79 | 2.58 | −.64 | 1.46 |
| Norway | 16 | 28 | 32 | 33 | 28 | .80 | .87 | .01 | −.71 |
| Denmark | 15 | 27 | 37 | 38 | 37** | .98 | 1.42 | .09 | −.34 |
| Finland | 20 | 22 | 28 | 34 | 34 | .19 | 1.12 | .10 | .83 |
| Mean | 17.5 | 26.4 | 35.7 | 36.0 | 36.8 | .69 | 1.50 | −.11 | .31 |
| *Christian democratic welfare states* | | | | | | | | | |
| Austria | 22 | 25 | 28 | 30 | 29 | .11 | .53 | .03 | .08 |
| Belgium | 14 | 28 | 35 | 30 | 28 | .96 | 1.02 | −.47 | −.34 |
| Netherlands | 20 | 25 | 34 | 30 | 27 | .36 | .97 | −.44 | −.37 |
| Germany | 17 | 24 | 27 | 31 | 30 | .41 | .52 | .06 | .38 |
| France | 15 | 17 | 23 | 25 | 30 | .13 | .92 | .21 | .79 |
| Italy | 15 | 21 | 29 | 34 | 32 | .45 | 1.05 | .39 | −.29 |
| Switzerland | 9* | 12 | 15 | 16 | 18** | .18 | .53 | .03 | .42 |
| Mean | 16.1 | 21.7 | 27.3 | 27.9 | 27.7 | .37 | .79 | −.03 | .10 |

Table A.6  (continued)

| | Levels | | | | | Annual Change | | | |
|---|---|---|---|---|---|---|---|---|---|
| | 1958 | 1973 | 1980 | 1991 | 1996 | 1958–72 | 1973–79 | 1980–90 | 1991–96 |
| *Liberal welfare states* | | | | | | | | | |
| Canada | 15 | 25 | 29 | 35 | 30 | .78 | .48 | .39 | –.50 |
| Ireland | 20 | 27 | 36 | 26 | 23** | .55 | 1.05 | –1.03 | –.68 |
| U.K. | 19 | 27 | 28 | 26 | 26*** | .49 | .08 | –.15 | –.13 |
| U.S.A. | 14 | 16 | 17 | 21 | 16 | .13 | .15 | .26 | –.65 |
| Mean | 17.0 | 23.9 | 27.7 | 26.8 | 23.9 | .49 | .44 | –.13 | –.49 |
| *Wage earner welfare states* | | | | | | | | | |
| Australia | 14* | 18 | 23 | 27 | 22 | .21 | .82 | .24 | –.67 |
| New Zealand | | | | | | | | | |
| *Japan* | 13* | 16 | 22 | 20 | 22 | .16 | .78 | –.19 | .22 |

*Figure starts in 1960.
**Figure for 1995.
***Figure for 1994.

**Table A.7** Civilian Government Employment (Percentage of the Working-Age Population)

| | Levels | | | | | Annual Change | | | |
|---|---|---|---|---|---|---|---|---|---|
| | 1960 | 1973 | 1980 | 1991 | 1995 | 1958–72 | 1973–79 | 1980–90 | 1991–95 |
| *Social democratic welfare states* | | | | | | | | | |
| Sweden | 8 | 16 | 23 | 25 | 22 | .57 | .99 | .18 | −.67 |
| Norway | 7 | 11 | 16 | 20 | 22 | .26 | .68 | .33 | .45 |
| Denmark | 6 | 14 | 20 | 21 | 21 | .52 | .77 | .18 | −.17 |
| Finland | 5 | 8 | 11 | 14 | 13 | .23 | .45 | .33 | −.21 |
| Mean | 6.5 | 12.6 | 17.6 | 20.2 | 18.7 | .40 | .72 | .26 | −.15 |
| *Christian democratic welfare states* | | | | | | | | | |
| Austria | 7 | 9 | 11 | 12 | 13** | .17 | .38 | .08 | .23 |
| Belgium | 5 | 7 | 9 | 10 | 10** | .15 | .33 | .03 | −.07 |
| Netherlands | 5 | 6 | 6 | 6 | 6 | .04 | .08 | −.03 | .00 |
| Germany | 5 | 7 | 8 | 8 | 8* | .17 | .18 | .03 | .00 |
| France | 8 | 11 | 13 | 14 | 14 | .19 | .22 | .13 | .19 |
| Italy | 5 | 6 | 8 | 8 | 8** | .11 | .19 | .05 | .06 |
| Switzerland | 4 | 6 | 8 | 8 | 9** | .12 | .20 | .00 | .17 |
| Mean | 5.5 | 7.6 | 9.0 | 9.7 | 9.7 | .14 | .23 | .04 | .07 |

**Table A.7** (continued)

| | Levels | | | | | Annual Change | | | |
|---|---|---|---|---|---|---|---|---|---|
| | 1960 | 1973 | 1980 | 1991 | 1995 | 1958–72 | 1973–79 | 1980–90 | 1991–95 |
| *Liberal welfare states* | | | | | | | | | |
| Canada | 9 | 12 | 13 | 15 | 14 | .19 | .10 | .16 | –.14 |
| Ireland | 5 | 7 | 9 | 8 | 9 | .15 | .21 | –.03 | .05 |
| U.K. | 10 | 13 | 14 | 13 | 9 | .19 | .19 | –.07 | –.83 |
| U.S.A. | 7 | 8 | 9 | 9 | 10 | .12 | .03 | .04 | .10 |
| Mean | 8.6 | 11.1 | 11.8 | 12.2 | 11.0 | .17 | .11 | .04 | –.29 |
| *Wage earner welfare states* | | | | | | | | | |
| Australia | 6 | 7 | 10 | 11 | 10 | .14 | .42 | .06 | –.14 |
| New Zealand | | 11 | 12 | | | | .19 | | |
| Japan | 5 | 5 | 6 | 6 | 6 | –.01 | .07 | –.03 | .08 |

*Figure for 1991.
**Figure for 1994.

**Table A.8**  Public Share of Total Health Expenditure

| | Levels | | | | | Annual Change | | | |
|---|---|---|---|---|---|---|---|---|---|
| | 1960 | 1973 | 1980 | 1991 | 1997 | 1960–72 | 1973–79 | 1980–90 | 1991–97 |
| *Social democratic welfare states* | | | | | | | | | |
| Sweden | 73 | 86 | 93 | 88 | 83 | 1.00 | .93 | –.29 | –.93 |
| Norway | 78 | 95 | 98 | 94 | 82 | 1.25 | 1.14 | –.38 | –.15 |
| Denmark | 89 | 81 | 85 | 83 | 84 | –.17 | .66 | –.30 | .02 |
| Finland | 54 | 76 | 79 | 81 | 76 | 1.39 | .36 | .19 | –.70 |
| Mean | 73.3 | 84.5 | 88.8 | 86.5 | 81.3 | .87 | .77 | –.20 | –.44 |
| *Christian democratic welfare states* | | | | | | | | | |
| Austria | 69 | 64 | 69 | 66 | 73 | –.44 | .75 | –.27 | –.08 |
| Belgium | 62 | 83 | 83 | 88 | 88 | 1.77 | –.05 | .55 | –.19 |
| Netherlands | 33 | 71 | 75 | 73 | 73 | 2.65 | 1.00 | –.33 | –.01 |
| Germany | 66 | 75 | 75 | 71 | 77 | .48 | –.05 | –.33 | .12 |
| France | 58 | 75 | 79 | 75 | 74 | 1.27 | .48 | –.43 | –.04 |
| Italy | 83 | 89 | 81 | 78 | 70 | .41 | –.05 | –.31 | –1.17 |
| Switzerland | 61 | 66 | 68 | 69 | 70 | .35 | .20 | .09 | .21 |
| Mean | 61.8 | 74.8 | 75.6 | 74.3 | 75.0 | .93 | .33 | –.15 | –.17 |

**Table A.8**  (continued)

| | Levels | | | | | Annual Change | | | |
| --- | --- | --- | --- | --- | --- | --- | --- | --- | --- |
| | 1960 | 1973 | 1980 | 1991 | 1997 | 1960–72 | 1973–79 | 1980–90 | 1991–97 |
| *Liberal welfare states* | | | | | | | | | |
| Canada | 43 | 74 | 75 | 73 | 70 | 2.25 | .28 | −.16 | −.69 |
| Ireland | 76 | 79 | 82 | 76 | 77 | −.01 | .57 | −.75 | .54 |
| U.K. | 85 | 88 | 89 | 84 | 85 | .18 | .33 | −.52 | .07 |
| U.S.A. | 25 | 38 | 42 | 43 | 46 | .97 | .50 | −.08 | .85 |
| Mean | 57.1 | 69.8 | 72.0 | 68.9 | 69.5 | .85 | .42 | −.38 | .19 |
| *Wage earner welfare states* | | | | | | | | | |
| Australia | 48 | 61 | 63 | 68 | 67 | .77 | .17 | .53 | −.08 |
| New Zealand | 81 | 83 | 84 | 79 | 77 | .45 | .80 | −.13 | −.73 |
| Japan | 60 | 69 | 71 | 72 | 80 | .52 | .91 | .00 | .33 |

**Table A.9** Unemployment Replacement Rates (Person with Average Wages)

| | Levels | | | | | Annual Change | | | |
|---|---|---|---|---|---|---|---|---|---|
| | 1961 | 1973 | 1979 | 1991 | 1995 | 1961–73 | 1973–79 | 1979–91 | 1991–95 |
| *Social democratic welfare states* | | | | | | | | | |
| Sweden | 21 | 25 | 74 | 87 | 74 | .38 | 8.08 | 1.13 | −3.25 |
| Norway | 11 | 14 | 32 | 62 | 62 | .23 | 2.93 | 2.48 | .00 |
| Denmark | 29 | 64 | 72 | 61 | 57 | 2.88 | 1.33 | −.92 | −1.00 |
| Finland | 13 | 31 | 29 | 57 | 65 | 1.49 | −.38 | 2.34 | 1.95 |
| Mean | 18.7 | 33.6 | 51.6 | 66.6 | 64.3 | 1.25 | 2.99 | 1.26 | −.57 |
| *Christian democratic welfare states* | | | | | | | | | |
| Austria | 16 | 15 | 34 | 36 | 30 | −.08 | 3.32 | .13 | −1.48 |
| Belgium | 34 | 48 | 49 | 41 | 41 | 1.17 | .17 | −.67 | .00 |
| Netherlands | 28 | 65 | 65 | 70 | 70 | 3.06 | .00 | .42 | .00 |
| Germany | 45 | 38 | 39 | 37 | 35 | −.52 | .12 | −.14 | −.57 |
| France | 41 | 47 | 89 | 57 | 56 | .43 | 7.13 | −2.69 | −.38 |
| Italy | 10 | 3 | 3 | 7 | 17 | −.53 | −.10 | .41 | 2.50 |
| Switzerland | 16 | 7 | 39 | 66 | 70 | −.73 | 5.30 | 2.27 | .93 |
| Mean | 26.9 | 31.7 | 45.4 | 44.9 | 45.4 | .40 | 2.28 | −.04 | .14 |
| w/o Italy and France | 27.5 | 34.5 | 45.2 | 49.9 | 49.0 | .58 | 1.78 | .40 | −.23 |

**Table A.9**  (*continued*)

| | Levels | | | | | Annual Change | | | |
|---|---|---|---|---|---|---|---|---|---|
| | 1961 | 1973 | 1979 | 1991 | 1995 | 1961–73 | 1973–79 | 1979–91 | 1991–95 |
| *Liberal welfare states* | | | | | | | | | |
| Canada | 39 | 65 | 52 | 58 | 54 | 2.18 | −2.13 | .48 | −1.01 |
| Ireland | 11 | 16 | 48 | 37 | 25 | .38 | 5.37 | −.93 | −2.98 |
| U.K. | 21 | 29 | 29 | 18 | 17 | .64 | .02 | −.88 | −.23 |
| U.S.A. | 18 | 20 | 22 | 19 | 27 | .19 | .33 | −.28 | 1.93 |
| Mean | 22.2 | 32.4 | 37.8 | 33.0 | 30.7 | .85 | .90 | −.40 | −.57 |
| *Wage earner welfare states* | | | | | | | | | |
| Australia | 14 | 13 | 20 | 21 | 22 | −.06 | 1.08 | .11 | .18 |
| New Zealand | 33 | 22 | 21 | 24 | 23 | −.95 | −.10 | .20 | −.15 |
| Japan | 36 | 41 | 25 | 29 | 29 | .42 | −2.58 | .33 | .00 |

**Table A.10**  Unemployment Replacement Rates (Person with Two-Thirds Average Wages)

| | Level | | | | | Average Annual Change | | | |
|---|---|---|---|---|---|---|---|---|---|
| | 1961 | 1973 | 1979 | 1991 | 1995 | 1961–73 | 1973–79 | 1979–91 | 1991–95 |
| *Social democratic welfare states* | | | | | | | | | |
| Sweden | 30 | 38 | 90 | 90 | 90 | .63 | 8.75 | –.02 | .00 |
| Norway | 14 | 15 | 34 | 62 | 62 | .06 | 3.24 | 2.26 | .00 |
| Denmark | 44 | 90 | 90 | 90 | 86 | 3.82 | .00 | .00 | –1.00 |
| Finland | 18 | 46 | 43 | 64 | 70 | 2.35 | –.54 | 1.73 | 1.50 |
| Mean | 26.7 | 47.2 | 64.4 | 76.3 | 76.8 | 1.71 | 2.86 | .99 | .13 |
| *Christian democratic welfare states* | | | | | | | | | |
| Austria | 19 | 22 | 36 | 39 | 32 | .25 | 2.38 | .22 | –1.65 |
| Belgium | 51 | 60 | 60 | 58 | 58 | .75 | .00 | –.12 | .00 |
| Netherlands | 28 | 65 | 65 | 70 | 70 | 3.06 | .00 | .42 | .00 |
| Germany | 44 | 41 | 42 | 39 | 37 | –.27 | .17 | –.19 | –.58 |
| France | 47 | 52 | 89 | 60 | 60 | .40 | 6.29 | –2.48 | .19 |
| Italy | 15 | 5 | 4 | 7 | 17 | –.82 | –.19 | .32 | 2.50 |
| Switzerland | 20 | 10 | 39 | 66 | 70 | –.81 | 4.82 | 2.22 | .94 |
| Mean | 31.8 | 36.2 | 47.8 | 48.4 | 49.2 | .37 | 1.92 | .06 | .20 |
| w/o Italy and France | 32.3 | 39.5 | 48.3 | 54.4 | 53.4 | .60 | 1.47 | .51 | –.26 |

**Table A.10**  (*continued*)

| | Levels | | | | | Annual Change | | | |
|---|---|---|---|---|---|---|---|---|---|
| | 1961 | 1973 | 1979 | 1991 | 1995 | 1961–73 | 1973–79 | 1979–91 | 1991–95 |
| *Liberal welfare states* | | | | | | | | | |
| Canada | 43 | 66 | 58 | 58 | 54 | 1.92 | −1.35 | .00 | −1.00 |
| Ireland | 17 | 24 | 56 | 48 | 38 | .57 | 5.31 | −.60 | −2.65 |
| U.K. | 32 | 39 | 39 | 28 | 26 | .60 | .01 | −.97 | −.40 |
| U.S.A. | 25 | 28 | 28 | 28 | 27 | .22 | .03 | .00 | −.13 |
| Mean | 29.2 | 39.1 | 45.1 | 40.4 | 36.3 | .83 | 1.00 | −.39 | −1.04 |
| *Wage earner welfare states* | | | | | | | | | |
| Australia | 21 | 19 | 30 | 31 | 32 | −.10 | 1.69 | .15 | .27 |
| New Zealand | 50 | 33 | 32 | 36 | 35 | −1.42 | −.17 | .30 | −.15 |
| *Japan* | 35 | 40 | 27 | 31 | 31 | .40 | −2.25 | .33 | .00 |

**Table A.11** Unemployment, Growth, and Inflation

| | Unemployment* | | | | | Growth** | | | | | Inflation | | | | |
|---|---|---|---|---|---|---|---|---|---|---|---|---|---|---|---|
| | 1960–73 | 1974–79 | 1980–89 | 1990–94 | 1995–98 | 1960–73 | 1973–79 | 1979–89 | 1990–94 | 1995–97 | 1960–73 | 1974–79 | 1980–89 | 1990–94 | 1995–98 |
| *Social democratic welfare states* | | | | | | | | | | | | | | | |
| Sweden | 1.9 | 1.9 | 2.4 | 5.2 | 7.6 | 3.4 | 1.5 | 1.8 | −1.6 | 2.2 | 4.7 | 9.8 | 7.9 | 6.0 | 1.3 |
| Norway | 1.0 | 1.8 | 2.7 | 5.6 | 4.3 | 3.5 | 4.4 | 2.3 | 2.0 | 3.8 | 5.1 | 8.7 | 8.3 | 2.7 | 2.2 |
| Denmark | 1.4 | 6.0 | 8.1 | 10.9 | 6.3 | 3.6 | 1.6 | 1.8 | 1.0 | 2.7 | 6.2 | 10.8 | 6.9 | 2.1 | 2.1 |
| Finland | 2.0 | 4.6 | 5.1 | 12.3 | 14.2 | 4.5 | 1.8 | 3.2 | −3.6 | 4.5 | 5.7 | 12.8 | 7.3 | 3.3 | 1.0 |
| Mean | 1.6 | 3.6 | 4.6 | 8.5 | 8.1 | 3.8 | 2.3 | 2.3 | −.6 | 3.3 | 5.4 | 10.5 | 7.6 | 3.5 | 1.7 |
| *Christian democratic welfare states* | | | | | | | | | | | | | | | |
| Austria | 1.7 | 1.6 | 3.3 | 3.9 | 4.1 | 4.3 | 3.0 | 1.9 | 1.0 | 1.9 | 4.2 | 6.3 | 3.8 | 3.4 | 1.5 |
| Belgium | 2.2 | 5.7 | 11.3 | 10.7 | 12.5 | 4.4 | 2.1 | 1.9 | 1.2 | 2.0 | 3.6 | 8.4 | 4.8 | 2.9 | 1.6 |
| Netherlands | 1.3 | 5.0 | 9.7 | 6.2 | 5.8 | 3.6 | 1.9 | 1.1 | 1.2 | 3.3 | 4.9 | 7.2 | 2.8 | 2.9 | 2.0 |
| Germany | .8 | 3.4 | 6.7 | 7.8 | 9.0 | 3.7 | 2.5 | 1.7 | 2.1 | 1.3 | 3.4 | 4.7 | 2.9 | 3.7 | 1.5 |
| France | 2.0 | 4.6 | 9.1 | 10.6 | 12.0 | 4.3 | 2.3 | 1.6 | .2 | 1.5 | 4.6 | 10.7 | 7.3 | 2.6 | 1.5 |
| Italy | 5.3 | 6.3 | 9.3 | 10.6 | 12.1 | 4.6 | 3.2 | 2.4 | .7 | 1.5 | 3.9 | 16.7 | 11.2 | 5.2 | 3.2 |
| Switzerland | .0 | .4 | .6 | 2.7 | 3.9 | 3.0 | −.1 | 1.8 | −.8 | .4 | 4.2 | 4.0 | 3.3 | 3.9 | .8 |
| Mean | 1.9 | 3.9 | 7.1 | 7.5 | 8.5 | 4.0 | 2.1 | 1.8 | .8 | 1.7 | 4.1 | 8.3 | 5.2 | 3.5 | 1.7 |

**Table A.11**  (*continued*)

| | Unemployment* | | | | | Growth** | | | | | Inflation | | | | |
|---|---|---|---|---|---|---|---|---|---|---|---|---|---|---|---|
| | 1960–73 | 1974–79 | 1980–89 | 1990–94 | 1995–98 | 1960–73 | 1973–79 | 1979–89 | 1990–94 | 1995–97 | 1960–73 | 1974–79 | 1980–89 | 1990–94 | 1995–98 |
| *Liberal welfare states* | | | | | | | | | | | | | | | |
| Canada | 5.0 | 7.2 | 9.3 | 10.3 | 9.2 | 3.6 | 2.9 | 1.8 | −1.0 | 1.2 | 3.3 | 9.2 | 6.5 | 2.8 | 1.6 |
| Ireland | 5.2 | 7.6 | 14.3 | 14.9 | 10.5 | 3.7 | 3.3 | 2.7 | 4.8 | 9.4 | 5.9 | 15.0 | 9.2 | 2.7 | 2.0 |
| U.K. | 1.9 | 4.2 | 9.5 | 8.4 | 7.4 | 2.6 | 1.5 | 2.2 | −.3 | 2.5 | 5.1 | 15.6 | 7.4 | 4.6 | 3.1 |
| U.S.A. | 5.0 | 7.0 | 7.6 | 6.6 | 5.1 | 2.6 | 1.4 | 1.5 | .8 | 3.3 | 3.2 | 8.5 | 5.5 | 3.6 | 2.4 |
| Mean | 4.3 | 6.5 | 10.2 | 10.1 | 8.1 | 3.1 | 2.3 | 2.1 | 1.1 | 4.1 | 4.4 | 12.1 | 7.2 | 3.4 | 2.3 |
| *Wage earner welfare states* | | | | | | | | | | | | | | | |
| Australia | 2.0 | 5.1 | 7.5 | 9.6 | 8.4 | 3.2 | 1.5 | 1.8 | .3 | 2.2 | 3.5 | 12.1 | 8.4 | 3.0 | 2.1 |
| New Zealand | .2 | .8 | 4.4 | 9.2 | 6.6 | 2.2 | −.2 | 1.4 | .6 | .7 | 4.8 | 13.8 | 11.8 | 2.6 | 2.2 |
| *Japan* | 1.3 | 1.8 | 2.4 | 2.3 | 3.5 | 8.3 | 2.5 | 3.4 | 2.2 | 1.7 | 6.2 | 9.9 | 2.5 | 2.0 | .6 |
| Grand mean | 2.2 | 4.2 | 6.9 | 8.2 | 7.9 | 3.8 | 2.1 | 2.0 | .6 | 2.6 | 4.6 | 10.2 | 6.5 | 3.3 | 1.8 |

*Figures are percentage of the labor force unemployed.
**Figures are percentage annual increase in GDP per capita. *Source:* OECD

# NOTES

◆

## Chapter One

1. This theory is most explicitly presented in the 1992 book, but has deep roots in our earlier work on the politics of reform (Stephens 1979b; Stephens 1980; Stephens and Stephens 1982, 1986).

2. We adopt the terminology "power resources theory" rather than alternatives denoting the same theoretical position, such as the working class power approach (Weir and Skocpol 1985) or the social democratic model (Shalev 1983) because arguably Korpi's formulation has become the most influential. See O'Connor and Olsen 1998 for a critical appraisal.

3. See our example at the end of the next paragraph.

## Chapter Two

1. Baldwin (1990) presents another line of argument, primarily a critique of the power resources approach, contending that actuarial categories, not social classes, are the real collective actors responsible for influencing welfare state formation. Social groups sharing the same risk situations (i.e., actuarial categories) have the same interests with regards to contributions and benefits from different programs of social protection, and since risk situations frequently cut across social classes, actuarial categories are more likely collective actors. In direct contradiction to the power resources view, Baldwin contends that the middle classes (or risk categories) were the main agents of expansion of generous welfare states. We see no compelling theoretical reasons why one should expect actuarial categories to perceive themselves as members of a collectivity and form organizations to pursue collective interests, such as close social interaction, shared work experiences, etc., nor do we see any empirical evidence that risk categories have been the basis for social identification and mobilization. We present evidence against this view in chapter 5.

2. Orloff (1993b, 1996) and O'Connor (1996) offer excellent analytic reviews of this literature.

3. In our previous work on the politics of reform in Peru (Stephens 1980) and Jamaica (Stephens and Stephens 1986) and in *Capitalist Development and Democracy* we took state autonomy and capacity into account as very important factors, but not in the present study. In other words, we do not categorically reject these variables as causal factors, but rather because they are not important for the patterns of long-term change of welfare state regimes in advanced industrial democracies examined here.

4. For a more thorough discussion of these issues see Rueschemeyer, Stephens, and Stephens 1992: 51–63.

5.  For two modern classic statements of the "price of business confidence" argument from very different theoretical frames, see Lindblom 1977 for a "neopluralist" view and Block 1977 for a neo-Marxist view.

6.  The United States with a presidential system and very weak parties is the one case where this statement might be challenged. There it has been possible for women's organizations to influence policy, particularly antidiscrimination and civil rights policy, largely autonomously from political parties (O'Connor, Orloff, and Shaver 1999).

7.  In countries where civil society and the party system are weaker and political institutions less well consolidated than in the OECD countries that are the subjects of our investigation here, high officials in state bureaucracies may have more leeway to influence legislation. Weyland (1996) makes the case that progressive bureaucrats heavily influenced legislation on health reform in Brazil in the 1980s. However, their influence remained confined to formal legislation; the programs remained empty shells as the balance of power in the society and the structure of the political institutions simply kept them from being funded.

8.  Pierson (1994) makes the plausible argument that power concentration also concentrates blame and thus makes governments reluctant to cut welfare state programs. We address the contending views on this issue in Chapter 7.

9.  Though we are adopting Soskice's terminology, we are not using the same conceptualization of production regimes that he does. He focuses primarily on coordination among enterprises and between enterprises and financial institutions in the areas of training, research, production, financing, etc., whereas we focus on relations between enterprises, banks, labor, and the government in the areas of wage setting, investment, and employment promotion. Thus, our focus has more of a macro orientation than his.

10.  See Western 1991 for a statistical analysis confirming this view.

11.  We are grateful to Paul Pierson for suggesting to us the distinction between changing preferences, a changing universe of actors, and changing expectations.

12.  Thus, we have to recognize that theoretically the ratchet effect could go in a conservative direction. It is possible to create resistance against universalistic and redistributive policies by creating fragmented programs that privilege certain groups over others, or by giving incentives to foster private alternatives. Nevertheless, in practice the ratchet effect on public social policy expenditures has clearly tended upward.

13.  For example, see our discussion of the consequences of the Swedish Social Democratic victory in the 1960 election in chapter 5.

14.  We are particularly indebted to Peter Hall and Gøsta Esping-Andersen for pushing us to clarify our view on this.

15.  See Pierson (1999) on increasing returns and path dependence.

16.  Theories of the causes of retrenchment are reviewed at the beginning of chapter 7.

17.  Clearly, this choice holds level of development and position in the world economy to a large extent constant. We are keenly aware of the fact that developing countries simply do not have the same options in shaping social policy and constructing production regimes as the countries we are studying. In fact, our next project will address precisely the question of options in these areas open to countries in Latin America and the Caribbean. However, the availability of the options to build generous welfare states does not mean that these options are exercised; in other words, a high level of development is a

necessary but by no means sufficient condition for the construction of generous and redistributive welfare states, as our analysis will show.

18. John Stephens acted as a discussant at the initial meeting of the Max Planck group in March 1998 and in the presentation of the draft chapters in February 1999.

19. We say "the single most important determinant," not "the only determinant" or even "the determinant more important than all other factors combined." Moreover, since we know that partisan dominance itself had social and historical determinants, the U.K. with Christian democratic hegemony or the U.S. with social democratic hegemony are difficult scenarios to imagine. Nonetheless we will argue in the conclusion of chapter 5 that other scenarios, such as Germany with social democratic dominance or Norway with bourgeois dominance, are more plausible and that such mental experiments, buttressed with the data contained in chapters 3, 4, and 5, are necessary to assess the causal claims put forward in this book.

20. Here we partly follow Fearon (1996). Fearon adds that one can cite theory (presumably otherwise empirically validated) to support one's counterfactual. This would appear to us to be illegitimate given the aims of our counterfactual analysis. Fearon's goal is to ask if the historical trajectory of a particular case would have been different had an event been different. He assumes uncontested theory. In our case, the theory is contested and we want to ask also what the particular case says about the competing theories. Citing our favored theory to support our favored counterfactual would be circular.

21. See our discussion of these and other related points touched on here (Rueschemeyer, Stephens, and Stephens 1992: 27–39).

22. This passage overstates the pro–social policy reform posture of the Conservatives and even more so the employers since both opposed the tax increases necessary to pay for the reforms.

### Chapter Three

1. The pooled time series of social rights data assembled by the Social Citizenship Indicators Project at the Institute for Social Research at the University of Stockholm is not yet in the public domain. See Korpi 1989, Palme 1990, Kangas 1991, Wennemo 1994, and Carroll 1999 for analyses of these data.

2. This assessment is not universally accepted. For instance, Leira (1992: 170) argues that "the Norwegian welfare state policies towards mothers in employment display a mixture of measures, a passive partnership at best, with more than a tinge of patriarchal overtones." However, it is a fact that the Scandinavian social democratic parties were the first ones to adopt quotas for women's representation in leadership positions and as candidates for election, and their governments made conscious efforts to increase the representation of women in the corporate bodies that are so important in the policy-making process (Hernes 1987: 95).

3. The health employment data are from the WEEP data set (Cusack 1991) and the health expenditure are from Huber, Ragin, and Stephens (1997), originally from the OECD.

4. Both of these studies were available to us in manuscript form when we developed the index of constitutional structure for Huber, Ragin, and Stephens 1993.

5. Besides providing for compulsory referenda on certain legislation, the Swiss constitution also provides the option for any interested parties to collect signatures and force

a popular vote on other legislation. Most of these referenda have resulted in defeat of the proposed legislation. For the function of referenda and their conservatizing impact, see Neidhart 1970.

6. Tsebelis (1995) provides a later development of this idea. See note 10 in this chapter for a further explanation of our index of constitutional structure.

7. The Huber, Ragin, and Stephens (1997) data set can be downloaded at http://www.lis.ceps.lu/compwsp.htm.

8. These data were kindly provided to us directly by Thomas Cusack.

9. Calculations by David Bradley. We use the same adjustments for household size favored by Mitchell (1991) and Atkinson, Rainwater, and Smeeding (1995). Updated data for the overall Gini are available at the LIS web site (http://www.lis.ceps .lu/compwsp.htm). We use the definition of poverty as less than half the median income, adjusted for household size, the same definition favored by Atkinson, Rainwater, and Smeeding (1995) and used for the data available at the LIS website (http://www.lis.ceps .lu/compwsp.htm).

10. In our previous analyses we included single-member districts as an indicator of power dispersion in our index of constitutional structure. Our logic was that proportional representation encourages party discipline and thus concentration of power whereas single-member districts reduce central party control over candidates and thus disperse power. We were criticized on the grounds that single-member district systems greatly exaggerate electoral majorities and thus can contribute to a concentration of power. Based on our comparative historical work, we think that this is true but only where single-member districts coexist with disciplined parties and centralized government, as in Britain and New Zealand. Rather than construct a more complex interactive measure, we have settled for the simpler, and more defensible, measure that eliminates this item from the index. We also constructed an index that included judicial review as an additional indicator of power dispersion; the results differed little from those with the index used and presented here.

11. While we agree with King, Keohane, and Verba (1994: 173) that one should not control for an explanatory variable that is in part a consequence of one's key causal variable, it is worth exploring the link between women's labor force participation and women's mobilization. In cross-sectional data on women's union membership for sixteen countries in the mid 1980s (Lovenduski 1986: 170; ILO 1987: 117; EUTI 1987), we found correlations between female labor force participation and female union membership as a proportion of the female working-age population (in our view, the best measure of mobilization) of .72, female union membership as a proportion of the female labor force of .57, and female share of total union membership of .66. We also looked at the left gender gap in voting for nine countries in the early 1990s; the correlation to female labor force participation was .51. (Leonard Ray provided the gender voting gap data for eight countries from Eurobarometer 38, 1992. We added the data for Sweden.) This evidence does support our contention that female labor force participation was strongly associated with the hypothesized intervening variables.

12. For example, with Leonard Ray we attempted to replicate a finding on change in expenditure reported in a conference paper using OECD data (also the authors' source) on the same expenditure variable and arrived at different results (insignificant instead of significant) from the authors. We then asked the authors for their data, which they generously provided us. As it turns out, the two OECD series were very strongly correlated,

well above .9, but hardly identical as might be assumed by the researcher who has not worked with these data closely. In any case, if the level of expenditure were the dependent variable, it would be unlikely that the two series would yield different results. However, when we calculated annual change in expenditure from the level of expenditure data, the correlation between the two series fell to around .7, which accounted for the difference in the results of the two analyses. We would emphasize that this was not due to the authors' sloppiness. As every researcher who has worked with these data knows, the OECD and the ILO, the two main sources of these data, provide series with discrepancies with no mention of many of the discrepancies and *no criteria for judging which series is more accurate.*

13. Achen (2000) shows mathematically that the lagged dependent variable suppresses the explanatory power of other independent variables in trending data, such as social expenditure. Achen's conference paper appeared while this book was in the copyediting stage, so we were unable to fully integrate his argument in the text here.

14. The inflated coefficient for the lagged dependent variable is a specific example of a more general drawback of regression: a spurious independent variable that is caused by a number of antecedent variables that also combine to cause the dependent variable will appear in the regression as the dominant or even sole cause of the dependent variable. See Rueschemeyer and Stephens (1997: 60 ff.) for a more detailed discussion and demonstration of this.

15. The reason we calculated these variables as cumulative averages rather than cumulations as in the case of the cabinet variables is that they are much larger numbers (in most cases percentages) and the cumulative number would have increased in almost exponential fashion through time, thus lowering the correlation to the dependent variable. It would have been necessary to take the log of the resulting variable. It appeared to us the metric coefficient of cumulative average was easier to interpret, so we opted for this measure.

16. See table 4.2 for the values of the countries on this index.

17. This procedure was added to Shazam 8.0 after the manual (White 1997) was printed. It is described at Shazam's web site (http://shazam.econ.ubc.ca).

18. See the contributions to Engle and Granger 1991 and Durr 1992 and the responses to the latter in the 1992 issue of *Political Analysis.*

19. The inability to do this in cases such as those mentioned in the text is probably one reason why these economists and political scientists (see the previous footnote for references) do not end their analyses with the estimation of long-term effects on levels of the dependent variables. For them, this is only a step, because they want to estimate long-term and short-term effects on short-term change. One way to proceed from the estimation we have done is to regress the residuals of the levels equation and the short-term changes in the independent variables on the short-term change in the dependent variable. This, of course, is not what we want to do. We are interested in the determinants of the levels, not the change in levels.

20. The alternative specifications for the other seven dependent variables are available at our web site, http://www.unc.edu/~jdsteph/Huber_Stephens.html.

21. As we explained in the text, we have dealt with the problem of endogeneity of women's labor force participation by using the cumulative average for the independent variable; this greatly reduces the probability of reverse causality. Moreover, we did the analysis with a ten-year lag on data available in five-year intervals only, and with a two-

year lag on annual data, and the results were similar (Huber and Stephens 2000a). For those still skeptical, we also ran the regression without the women's labor force variable and the interaction term. Not surprisingly, as noted in the text, this resulted in an increased coefficient for left government, in some cases quite substantially, in every regression.

22.   This is a finding that we expected but, given that at least some of the welfare states that we classify as Christian democratic are associated with comparatively quite low degrees of poverty and inequality, this finding becomes a little puzzling. The answer to the puzzle probably lies in part in the influence of social democracy on these welfare states, as competition between the dominant Christian democratic parties and social democratic parties has been intense in these countries, and in part it lies in the nature of the production regime in which these welfare states are embedded.

23.   In all but one of our countries, women make up the overwhelming majority (from 59% to 82%) of public health, education, and welfare employment; the exception is the Netherlands with 49% (WEEP data set).

24.   One might object that growth of the aged increases the cost of providing a given level of benefits per elderly person and that therefore a constant level of benefits per person indicates greater political influence of the elderly. We would counter this argument by pointing out that continuation of the same benefit levels is automatic; it does not require positive action through new legislation and thus power mobilization. What we call the ratchet effect, the fact that levels of universal benefits once achieved are accepted as the norm for that society, helps maintain benefits per elderly constant.

25.   Note that Cameron (1978: 1256) does not predict that these subsequent studies should find openness directly to be related to expenditure as he argues that the effects are indirect through left government and strong labor confederations, the latter of which does not appear in his regression.

## Chapter Four

1.   Japan does not fit into any type and is being treated as a case apart. The economy is a group-coordinated market economy (Soskice 1999) and the welfare state comes closest to a residual model, with very low benefits through the public programs in pensions and health care. The pillars of the system of social provision are private programs in the large corporations, from which only a minority of the labor force benefits, and the family (Pempel forthcoming).

2.   Olli Kangas, personal communication, 1996.

3.   Until separation, Irish policy was made in London and thereafter social policy innovations in Ireland tended to follow the British lead. Thus, the policy patterns in the two countries are much more similar than one would predict given their social and political characteristics.

4.   The Canadian figures for public employment and public share of health employment are subject to some dispute. Our figures are Statistics Canada figures supplied to us by John Myles, then a consultant at Statistics Canada. The WEEP figures for Canada are much lower. The discrepancy is that Statistics Canada included as public not only institutions owned by the state but also "non-profit institutions . . . financed and controlled by . . . government institutions" (Myles e-mail message, March 18, 1999, quoting a Statistics Canada document). Under Statistics Canada's definition, if over 50 percent of the

funding is government funding then the operation of the institution is effectively under government control. Thus, all hospital employees are classified as public employees in the Canadian data, which accounts for the high public share of health employment. This appears to us to be a correct classification decision. Government authorities in Canada can decide what kind of services a publicly funded nonprofit hospital can offer. This is very different from the situation in most Continental European countries, in which public sickness funds simply foot the bill without exercising control of actual delivery of services.

5. Theses figures underestimate the differences between the social democratic and Christian democratic welfare states because they include spending on early pensions and disability pensions, which were employed as means of labor force reduction in a number of the Christian democratic welfare states at this time.

6. The measure of inequality referred to in the text is the LIS posttax, posttransfer Gini index for the early to midnineties, the same data as in table 4.4, column 1, but for a decade later, roughly at the time of the literacy surveys.

7. For a discussion of Austria's outlier status in this regard, see Pontusson 1996.

8. Italy does have a low-wage sector in the black market and Spain and Portugal have yet larger black and informal sectors.

9. Denmark must be partially excepted from this characterization. See below in this chapter and chapter 5.

10. This characterization leans heavily on Mjøset (1986, 1987) and Andersson, Kosonen, and Vartiainen (1993).

11. This is not meant to imply that any of the historical actors necessarily had to have an accurate picture of how the total regime fit together.

12. Gøsta Esping-Andersen (personal communication, 1994) points out that Mitchell's (1991) figures overestimate redistribution because many retired people, particularly in countries in which public pension systems are generous, will have little or no pretransfer income thus exaggerating the degree of pretransfer income inequality. Note that though this would raise the level of pretransfer income inequality, it would not affect posttax and -transfer inequality. Thus, the figures in column 1 of the table are accurate and, given the methodology of the LIS surveys, comparable measures of inequality in disposable income.

13. This begs the question of why targeted welfare states (and targeted welfare policies within welfare states) are so ungenerous. The answer generally given in the comparative welfare states literature is that precisely because they are targeted, they have a narrow support base and thus few supporters and many opponents (e.g., see Korpi 1980).

14. Aside from the data in tables 4.1 through 4.4, the following data sources were consulted for the generalizations made in the next two paragraphs: Kilkey and Bradshaw 1999 (labor force participation among single mothers); Gough et al. 1997 (social assistance); Wennemo 1994 (family allowances); the OECD data in tables A.9 and A.10, Carroll 1999, Esping-Andersen 1990 (unemployment compensation).

15. The German figure would appear to be unexplainably low given the modest levels of all three transfers. This seems to be a result of sampling error in the German data; lone mothers are a small group and thus sampling error can be quite large. The German LIS data for 1983 and 1984 show much higher levels of single mothers in poverty, 18 percent and 20 percent respectively.

16.   Agell (1996) claims that micro disincentives were a serious problem in Sweden, while Korpi (1996) and Dowrick (1996) argue that the aggregate growth figures do not sustain the view that the welfare state is a drag on growth. What we are pointing out is that both could be true. In fact, a recent comprehensive review of the empirical literature on the work disincentives of taxes and social benefits reveals that the studies to date yield very contradictory findings (Atkinson and Mogensen 1993).

17.   We should note that while fragmentation continues to exist with, for instance, different occupational groups being covered by different legislation and programs, there has been a definite historical trend toward equalization of entitlements across programs and groups.

### Chapter Five

1.   This is not to suggest that such attitudes were absent among employers in Norway and Finland. They were simply less able to resist state initiative. Perhaps more important, it was much more difficult for them to claim that they could mobilize the capital necessary for rapid industrialization without state assistance or even direction.

2.   On early social policy development in Sweden, see Olsson 1993, Berge 1995, Elmér 1969, and Baldwin 1990.

3.   The following briefly summarizes the argument in Stephens 1995.

4.   The basic citizenship pension was an exception here. SAF genuinely supported it, as the organization hoped that it would be the definitive solution to retirement pensions for LO-affiliated workers.

5.   Since one could choose two responses it is a good guess that less than 18 percent of conservative voters mentioned any of the reforms. There were a number of other possible responses, such as "world peace" mentioned by 47 percent of all respondents and "more freedom for the individual" and "more freedom for industry," which attracted broad support from bourgeois voters, especially Conservatives. We thank Karin Busch and Hans Zetterberg for making these data available to us.            .

6.   The employers' position on state funds should not be seen as simply antisocialist. By this time, supplementary pensions were common in some sectors, especially large enterprises in the export industry, and the pension funds were an important source of risk capital for these enterprises.

7.   Other things being equal (deduction rules, etc.), joint taxation reduces the attractiveness of entering the labor market for women. Among the Nordic countries, only Norway has a joint taxation system, but couples may opt for separate taxation if this is more favorable for them (Sainsbury 1996). The difference between separate and joint taxation is particularly great where marginal tax rates are highly progressive, as they were in Sweden in this period.

8.   The data presented by Hagen (1992: table 5.9) on maternity cash benefits clearly illustrate this and document the leading role of Sweden in these innovations.

9.   Our discussion below relies heavily on Mjøset 1986, Erixon 1997, Benner 1997, and Pontusson 1992b. See these sources for a more detailed treatment of the development of the Swedish production regime.

10.   The causes of the development of Swedish corporatism are disputed in the literature: Korpi (1983) and Stephens (1979b) emphasize the shifting power balance between labor and capital; Swenson (1991) the interests of employers and a cross-class alliance

with labor; Klausen (n.d.) and Rothstein (1992) the red-green coalition; and Katzenstein (1985) the divided right, proportional representation, and economic openness. All of these made some contribution: proportional representation led to a divided right, which was a precondition for the red-green coalition; the red-green coalition allowed social democracy to come to power, which caused a shift in the balance of power between capital and labor; openness and social democracy in power shaped the interests of employers; and openness and a strong employers' organization shape the interests of labor.

11.   At least in theory. In fact, profits in the export sector could not be controlled by tight fiscal policy. This points to a weakness in Pontusson's (1992a) analysis of the 1980s, which emphasizes the importance of the high-profits policy as a deviation from the past. While it is true that the high profits as Social Democratic policy was new, profits were not in fact higher in the 1980s than in the Golden Age.

12.   The operating surplus data is from the OECD National Accounts. It is a cost component of GDP and a component (along with compensation of employees) of national income. It includes corporate profits (including state enterprises) and profits of unincorporated businesses (including earnings of self employed persons). Though the indicator in table 5.1 is not a conventional measure of corporate profitability, it is the only comparable indicator available for a large group of countries over a long period of time and it covaries strongly with more conventional measures.

13.   Gross fixed capital formation includes public as well as private sector investment. Therefore, our reinvestment ratio is not a measure of the percentage of the profits of private firms that are being reinvested, but rather a measure of the capacity of a country to generate investment at any given level of profits.

14.   On the historical development of Norwegian social policy, see Kuhnle 1983, 1986; Seip 1994; Salminen 1993; West Pedersen 1990; and Esping-Andersen 1985.

15.   On the development of the Norwegian production regime, see Mjøset 1986 and Moses 2000.

16.   Other sources consulted for this overview are Kangas 1988, 1990; Salminen 1993; Mjøset 1986.

17.   As Esping-Andersen (1985) shows, this resulted in a vicious circle: due to Social Democratic weakness and the diversity of its base, it pursued policies that undermined its own electoral support.

18.   Denmark and Britain share characteristics that underpin this policy orientation: strong, decentralized unions, low concentration in industry, few links between banks and industry, and strong international integration of financial interests.

19.   Baldwin uses the opposition of unions and the SPD to the Allied plan as evidence in support of his attacks on class-analytic views of welfare state development. He claims that this opposition instead supports his preferred view of welfare state development as driven by social actors constituting themselves on the basis of actuarial categories. He acknowledges that the left "briefly" favored a Beveridge-type approach but goes on to claim that uniform benefits were not in the interest of the German labor movement (1990: 159–61). This is partly a semantic problem; if uniform benefits are uniform, low, flat rate, then this statement is accurate, but if uniform means a combination of flat-rate with earnings-related benefits under uniform rules, then it is incorrect. Moreover, these statements are flatly contradicted by the historical record of the DGB's and the SPD's consistent and persistent pressures for a unification and standardization of social

policy schemes. Only after the financial unification of the pension schemes of workers and employees under the Grand Coalition (1966–69) and under the impact of the economic problems of the 1970s did the SPD abandon efforts at fundamental reform of the welfare state and concentrated exclusively on improvements within the existing institutional framework. Nevertheless, the question of income limits for compulsory coverage (i.e., the inclusive, solidaristic, and redistributive dimension of the welfare state) remained a subject of intense debate in the 1970s (Alber 1986).

20. The pension reform of 1957 then began gradually to transform the funded system into a pay-as-you-go system.

21. This discussion is based on the very detailed research and fascinating historical account by Hockerts (1980: 174–425).

22. This example, as well as many others, demonstrates that one would arrive at the mistaken interpretation that social security reform was a rather consensual affair if one's research methodology was based on parliamentary votes only. As Alber (1986) points out, 57 percent of the core laws of the German welfare state were passed with the support of the major opposition party, and 85 percent of major welfare state extensions were based on broad political consensus. However, the real political battles took place before the final vote on most social policy bills.

23. In the debate about this legislation, the CDU/CSU opposition argued for child care allowances for all mothers, not for employed mothers only (Kolbe 1999: 155).

24. This minister resigned and the KPÖ withdrew from government in 1947.

25. Unemployment insurance was not integrated into the major sets of social insurance legislation and the Federation of Austrian Social Insurance Institutes that represents all social insurance funds. Instead, it forms part of the Federal Ministry of Social Administration.

26. This discussion is heavily based on Talos and Kittel 1996: 108–13.

27. This universalism excluded married women insofar as their right to a benefit was tied not to their reaching the age of sixty-five but rather to the retirement of their husband. Also, their benefit was paid to the husband (van Kersbergen 1995: 131).

28. In another parallel to Germany, the social democratic forces lacked agrarian allies to push for a universalistic welfare state. Agrarian interests were articulated through the confessional parties and thus weighed in on the side of fragmentation.

29. The small Catholic-based Democratic Labor Party, an anticommunist break off of the Labor Party, did play an important role in the fifties and sixties as it deprived the Labor Party of votes for the lower house, arguably the margin of victory in at least one case, and allied with Labor's opponents in the Senate. So, to the extent that the Catholic political forces affected social welfare development in Australia, it was to make social policy less generous, in contrast to European Christian democracy.

30. Voters may express second, third, etc. preferences and if no candidate receives a majority, the candidate with least first preferences is eliminated and his/her ballots transferred to other candidates listed as second preferences by the voters of the candidate with the fewest first preferences. This procedure continues until one candidate has a majority.

31. See Rueschemeyer, Stephens, and Stephens (1992: 135–40) on the effect of agrarian structures on the development of democracy in New Zealand and South Australia. Both colonies were settled according to Wakefieldian colonization principles, which accounts for the similarity in their landholding patterns.

32. Note that the divisor here is the total labor force not wage and salary workers (the most common divisor for union density figures) much less the nonagricultural wage and salary workers.

33. The notion that industry capacity to pay could be ignored was abandoned during the Depression without, however, abandoning the concept of the basic wage being determined by the needs of an unskilled worker.

34. Pointing to the economic motivations underlying Labor's policy is not meant to imply that it was not racist. The racist element became blatant when the post–World War II Labor government abandoned its previous position and vigorously implemented a scheme for assisted immigration of Europeans. The Labor minister of immigration, Calwell, made the racist element of the policy quite clear in a 1948 public statement that "two Wongs do not make a White" (quoted in Clarke 1992: 269).

35. The OECD figures in tables A.9 and A.10 show a decline in the sixties in contrast to the data in Carroll 1999 from the SCIP project, which show increases in the fifties and stability in the sixties. The SCIP figures are net replacement rates and thus are higher than gross replacement rates in the OECD data for Australia because Australian unemployment (and sickness) benefits were not taxable until 1976, but this should not affect the trend. What may affect the trend is that the OECD figures are a composite of three different family types for a one-year spell of unemployment and Carroll's figures are for two different family types averaged over two different durations of unemployment, one week and six months. In any case, it should be noted that the modest improvement indicated in the text is the best-case scenario.

36. Note that this is not "comparable worth" as defined in the United States debates. U.S.-style comparable worth was explicitly rejected by the Arbitration Commission in 1986 as being incompatible with the Australian system of wage setting (O'Connor, Orloff, and Shaver 1999: 89).

37. The terms "basic security" and "income security" are employed by Palme 1990 to indicate the two types of benefits included in the fully developed "institutional" or "encompassing" welfare state.

38. See the discussions of unemployment replacement rates in chapters 3 and 6.

39. E.g., see Baldwin 1990 and Kuhnle 1983.

40. We should mention the dearth of evidence on the policy preferences of the Antipodean unions as opposed to the labor parties. The available historical materials support the statement in the text, but in many cases the policy preferences of the unions are not mentioned.

41. In earlier periods, maternalist women's movements helped shape policies in ways that were highly consequential for social policies, above all family policies, some of which (unintentionally) turned out to be supportive of the feminist agenda in the later period. E.g., see Jenson 1986.

## Chapter Six

1. Following Garrett and Lange 1991, indices of leftist political power were constructed, as well as comparable indices to measure Christian democracy (see Stephens, Huber, and Ray 1994). Since the results with the cumulative and current cabinet indices generally displayed the greatest dissimilarities, we report these in the text.

2. In an earlier version of this chapter (Stephens, Huber, and Ray 1994), we included

a measure of demographic burden on welfare state programs, which we operationalized as the percent of the population over sixty-five plus the percent of the labor force unemployed. This variable proved to be insignificant in all regressions, so it was dropped from the analysis.

3. In the case of both our figures for pension benefits and Palme's (1990) replacement rates from the SCIP data, the increases are sufficiently large that we feel certain that they would hold even if the factors we discuss below for the case of pension benefits in the eighties were taken into account.

4. There are additional data for the early 1990s available at the ILO web site. However, there appear to be significant discontinuities in the data series, so we decided not to use them.

5. Had we had data for New Zealand for the 1990s, they almost certainly would have indicated deep cuts for that country also.

### Chapter Seven

1. The cuts in New Zealand are too recent to show up in our data analysis, but our case study material will show that these cuts were very significant as well.

2. An earlier version of the chapter (Stephens, Huber, and Ray 1999) contained sketches of developments in the United Kingdom and France. We have also done more limited research on Switzerland, Italy, Canada, and the United States.

3. For an extensive review of the impact of changes in the international and domestic economy on social policy see Swank 1993.

4. This mode of presentation represents a reversal of our research process since our arguments on the causes of retrenchment arose from our examination of case materials on our focus cases and were then generalized on the basis of the cross-national evidence and supplementary evidence on other advanced industrial democracies. We present the argument in this fashion because it is complex and this mode of presentation makes our explanation of developments most transparent. Of course, at the beginning of the research process, we did begin with hypotheses on the causes of retrenchment, but they were hardly the nuanced views presented in the text here.

5. Hicks (1999: 214–17, 225–29) finds in an event history analysis of retrenchment that unemployment was a highly significant factor.

6. The exceptions to this rule are countries enjoying a substantial current account surplus or those whose currencies serve as reserve currencies (e.g., the United States).

7. Many also argue that growth leads to higher investment levels rather than vice versa.

8. Rowthorn (1995) emphasizes the decline in the rate of profit and the real cost of borrowing. Blanchard and Wolfers (1999) agree that the increase in real interest rates had an adverse effect on capital accumulation and thus on unemployment in Europe. In addition, they identify the decline in total factor productivity growth and a decrease in labor demand as shocks responsible for the secular increase in unemployment. They suggest that differences in levels of employment across countries can be explained by the interaction of labor market institutions and these shocks. However, data problems regarding time variant measures of labor market institutions weaken these claims, in view of the fact that one of their most important institutional variables, benefits in unemployment insurance schemes, underwent major changes in the 1980s and 1990s.

9. Our calculations, based on OECD 1995b: 73.

10. According to Glyn's figures for all OECD countries, it was actually higher after 1973 (1.2 vs. 1.1 percent per annum). For the eighteen countries examined here it was slightly lower in the period after 1973.

11. See Czada 1998 for a discussion of the enormous impact of unification on the German production regime and welfare state.

12. See Huber and Stephens 1998 for a more detailed analysis.

13. Even in the United States, broad-based entitlement programs enjoy wide popularity (Marmor, Mashaw, and Harvey 1990: 134).

14. For an analysis of policy in this period, see Martin 1984, 1985.

15. For an illuminating discussion of the "marketization" (our term, not his) of the state in Sweden as well as in Denmark, New Zealand, and Australia, see Schwartz 1994a, 1994b.

16. Along with lowering marginal tax rates, the reform eliminated many deductions (and thus tax loopholes) and child allowances were increased at the same time. An independent simulation study (Schwarz and Gustafsson 1991) confirmed government simulations that the reform as a whole was distributionally neutral. The public perception though, particularly among the Social Democrats' supporters, was otherwise.

17. Interview with Villy Bergström, June 1993.

18. For more details on these reforms, see Huber and Stephens 1993b, which is based on research in Sweden in June and November 1992 including interviews with politicians and interest group experts working on social policy questions.

19. For further discussion and contrasting evaluations of the new Swedish system, see Anderson 1998, Cichon 1999, and Huber and Stephens 2000b.

20. For further discussion of this issue and its contribution to the Social Democrats' defeat in 1991, see Rothstein 1992.

21. The figures on education and health care were provided to us by Bo Rothstein based on his ongoing research and refer to the situation in 1995.

22. The changes mentioned here as well as a number of other changes of lesser import are outlined in Palme 1994 and Palme and Wennemo 1997.

23. For the following discussion of the Swedish case, we draw on Pontusson 1992a, Erixon 1985, Pestoff 1991, Pontusson and Swenson 1996, Feldt 1991, and thirty-one interviews with politicians, academic economists, and economists for unions and employers conducted in Stockholm in May 1992, November 1992, June 1993, and June 1999. We also draw on two excellent comparative analyses of parallel developments in Norway and Sweden, Moene and Wallerstein 1993 and Moses 1994.

24. Interview with a senior labor union economist, June 1999.

25. On the role of the decline of trust between SAF and LO in the decline of Swedish corporatism, see Rothstein 1998.

26. Personal communications.

27. Thanks are due to Joakim Palme and Bo Rothstein for informing us of the exchange of views at this conference. For further elaboration of these issues and more detailed presentation of the evidence mentioned here, see Stephens 2000.

28. We are indebted to Michael Wallerstein for drawing our attention to the importance of the international flow of loans in this context.

29. Two sets of figures from Erixon 1987 for the period 1953–82 support this statement His figures for profit share in the manufacturing sector are somewhat lower than those for operating surplus for the whole economy shown in table 5.1, but the two series move in tandem through time. His preferred figures for "profitability," operating surplus as a percentage of fixed productive capital, for the manufacturing sector move in exact tandem with profit shares for the manufacturing sector (1987: 46).

30. For a general discussion of the problems of macroeconomic management in small open economies in the current period, see Glyn 1995. It is worth noting that the impact of internationalization on countercyclical policy is asymmetric: measures to cool an overheated economy are still effective.

31. For a more in-depth analysis of the recent development of the Norwegian political economy, see Moene and Wallerstein 1993, Moses 1994, and Mjøset et al. 1994.

32. Olli Kangas, personal communication.

33. The sources for these social policy changes are Alestalo 1994 and Olli Kangas, personal communication.

34. Olli Kangas, personal communication.

35. Our source for the 2000 bargaining round is articles from the European Industrial Relations Observatory web site http://www.eiro.eurofound.ie/, articles 1999/12/features/FI9910124N.html, 2000/01/features/FI0001133F.html, and FI0002135N.html.

36. The figures on replacement rates in the text are from the OECD data in tables A.9 and A.10. Hagen (1992: 145) shows a much steeper drop from 80.5 percent in 1975 to 59.2 percent in 1985, compared to a decrease from 70 percent to 64 percent for the same period in the OECD data. Carroll's (1999) data from the SCIP project, which like Hagen's are net (and not gross, as are the OECD data), show a decline on the same order of magnitude as the OECD data, approximately 7 percent.

37. Our source for recent developments in Danish wage bargaining is articles from the European Industrial Relations Observatory web site http://www.eiro.eurofound.ie/, articles 1998/04/features/DK9804163F.html, 2000/02/features/DK0002166N.html, 2000/02/features/DK0002167F.html, and 2000/02/features/DK0002168F.html.

38. For instance, the requirement that recipients of cash sickness benefits contribute to pension and unemployment insurance meant a reduction of these cash benefits by 11.5 percent (Alber 1986: 268), a rather substantial reduction.

39. By 1994, half of the parliamentary delegation of the Green Party and of the East German Party of Democratic Socialism (PDS), and 30 percent of the SPD delegation were women.

40. The following information is taken from Ploug and Kvist 1994.

41. Traxler (1993) mentions the absence of efforts at wage equalization as one of the factors that explain the differences between Austria and Sweden in terms of survival versus decline of corporatist arrangements. Other factors are the higher concentration and centralization of both labor unions and business associations in Austria; the absence of company- and plant-level collective agreements in Austria; the structure of business in terms of the dominance of large enterprises, many of them multinationals, in Sweden, versus the dominance of small and medium enterprises in the private sector and large ones in the public sector in Austria; and the violation of the practice of decisions by consent in Sweden with the codetermination legislation in 1975 and the wage earner funds in 1983, in contrast to the continued observation of this rule in Austria.

42.   Kunkel and Pontusson (1998) explain the decline in electoral support for the SPÖ compared to the greater stability of electoral support for the Swedish Social Democrats with differences in the situation of political competition and differences in labor market developments. In the former arena, the ÖVP and Austrian employers did not take on a neoliberal position to the same extent as the bourgeois parties and employers in Sweden and thus did not offer the SPÖ the chance to present itself as the more socially concerned alternative; the presence of a party to the left of the Swedish Social Democrats provided a vehicle for protest voting and greatly reduced the loss of votes to right-wing populism; and the lack of alternation in office deprived the SPÖ of the chance to blame its competitors for economic difficulties. In the latter arena, the key factor is the stability or even increase in union membership in Sweden compared to the decline in Austria, which Kunkel and Pontusson in turn relate to the smaller size of the public sector in Austria, lower wage solidarity, and lower women's labor force participation and female union membership, as public-sector employees are more likely to belong to unions and both public-sector employment and union membership correlate strongly with left voting.

43.   Kunkel and Pontusson (1998: 7) cite slightly different figures; 56 percent of the employed labor force being employed union members in 1980 and 43 percent in 1992–93.

44.   Data from Penn World Tables (http://pwt.econ.upenn.edu/) for the eighteen countries listed in the tables in chapter 4.

45.   The following discussion of Australia draws on Carney and Hanks 1994; Castles 1996; Castles, Gerritsen, and Vowles 1996; Clarke 1992; Kewley 1980; OECD 1995a, 1996a; Saunders 1994; Schwartz 1994a, 1994b, 2000; and Shaver 1991.

46.   The following discussion of New Zealand draws on Castles 1996; Castles, Gerritsen, and Vowles 1996; Dahlziel and Lattimore 1996; Easton 1981, 1996; Hawke 1992; Johnston and Vowles 1997; Kelsey 1993, 1995; Massey 1995; OECD 1996d; and Schwartz 1994a, 1994b, 2000.

47.   The changes in the U.S. were not as dramatic as in the U.K. and much of the Reagan agenda went unfulfilled (King and Wood 1999). By contrast, the system shift in New Zealand was even more radical than the shift in Britain.

48.   The Swedish Gini for 1975 was 0.22, so despite the move toward greater inequality in the 1980s and 1990s, income distribution is now almost as egalitarian as it was at the close of the Golden Age.

49.   See Stephens, Huber, and Ray 1999 for our analysis of the United Kingdom.

50.   Personal conversation, June 1998.

51.   We are aware that this assertion is contested by neoclassical economists. See our discussion in the second section of this chapter.

52.   It bears repeating here that we are talking about a decline, not disappearance. See our discussion on pp. 305–7.

### Chapter Eight

1.   Note that in the Nordic countries highly skilled labor was not paid a lot more than less skilled labor because of the unions' policy of wage compression. However, the average skill and wage levels were high because of the educational and training systems and because of the absence of a low-wage sector.

2.   This is a skeleton summary of the argument we developed in chapters 2 and 5; see pp. 28–32, 196–201.

3. By recommending increased funding of pension schemes, we are by no means advocating the transformation of pension schemes into fully funded, private, individual account systems, as in the temporarily widely applauded Chilean system. The shortcomings of this system and the errors of the 1994 World Bank report on pension systems have become obvious (see Orszag and Stiglitz 1999). What we are advocating is simply increasing funding and investments of collective, public pension funds. For a further discussion of these issues, see Huber and Stephens 2000b.

4. As King (1995) documents, these countries have a long tradition in which the main aim of training programs and unemployment assistance was to enforce work requirements on the poor. The new workfare programs are consistent with this tradition. For an analysis of the training programs promoted by the Blair government in the United Kingdom, see King and Wickham-Jones 1998.

5. In the Alliance for Growth discussion in 1998, the Swedish LO suggested a system patterned after the Danish with a strong role for a state mediator, but this was rejected by the other parties to the discussion. See Stephens 2000 for a more detailed analysis of these negotiations.

6. In the Netherlands this was true only initially; later reforms were indeed arrived at through tripartite agreements (Ebbinghaus and Hassel 1999).

7. This is not all that surprising, given that the theory was originally conceived to explain what happens in the course of industrialization; Wilensky himself (1975) recognized that it was unlikely to account for variation among the rich countries. Later extensions of the theory (Pampel and Williamson 1988, 1989) came to interpret demographic changes as causal variables via pressure group politics.

8. When Pampel and Williamson (1989: 71) standardize the dependent variable for size of the aged group, they find no effect of the aged on health care and a modest one on pensions. They fail to control for Christian democratic party rule, the most important variable in our equation, which probably accounts for the difference in the findings.

# REFERENCES

$\blacklozenge$

Achen, Christopher. 2000. "Why Lagged Dependent Variables Can Suppress the Explanatory Power of Other Independent Variables." Paper delivered at the Annual Meeting of the Political Methodology Section of the American Political Science Association, University of California, Los Angeles, July 20–22.

Alber, Jens. 1998. "Recent Developments in Continental European Welfare States: Do Austria, Germany, and the Netherlands Prove to Be Birds of a Feather?" Paper presented at the Fourteenth World Congress of Sociology, Montreal, July 27–31.

———. 1996. "Toward a Comparison of Recent Welfare State Developments in Germany and the United States." Paper presented at the Health Policy Seminar of the Institution for Policy Studies, Yale University, February 5.

———. 1986. "Germany." In Flora 1986, 4:250–320.

Albert, Michel. 1991. *Capitalisme contre capitalisme.* Paris: Seuil.

Alestalo, Matti. 1994. "Finland: The Welfare State at the Crossroads." In Ploug and Kvist 1994, 73–84.

———. 1986. *Structural Change, Classes and the State: Finland in an Historical and Comparative Perspective.* Research Reports, no. 33. Research Group for Comparative Sociology, University of Helsinki.

Alestalo, Matti, and Hannu Uusitalo. 1986. "Finland." In Flora 1986, 1:198–292.

Allen, Christopher S. 1989. "The Underdevelopment of Keynesianism in the Federal Republic of Germany." In *The Political Power of Economic Ideas: Keynesianism across Nations.* Ed. Peter A. Hall, 263–89. Princeton: Princeton University Press.

Åmark, Klas. 1998. "Choosing the Encompassing Model: Swedish and Norwegian Labour Movements and Income Maintenance in the Social Security Systems, 1932–1967." Paper presented at the Aronsborg Conference on Welfare States at the Crossroads, June 12–14.

Anderson, Karen M. 1998. "Organized Labor, Policy Feedback, and Retrenchment in Swedish Pension and Unemployment Insurance." Paper presented at the Eleventh International Conference of Europeanists, Baltimore, February 26–28.

Andersson, Jan Otto, Pekka Kosonen, and Juhana Vartiainen. 1993. *The Finnish Model of Economic and Social Policy: From Emulation to Crash.* Åbo: Nationalekonomiska Institutionen, Åbo Akademi.

Atkinson, Anthony B., Lee Rainwater, and Timothy M. Smeeding. 1995. *Income Distribution in OECD Countries: Evidence from the Luxembourg Income Study.* Paris: Organization for Economic Co-operation and Development.

Atkinson, Anthony B., and Gunnar Viby Mogensen. 1993. *Welfare and Work Incentives: A North European Perspective.* Oxford: Clarendon Press.

Baldwin, Peter. 1990. *The Politics of Social Solidarity: Class Bases of the European Welfare State, 1875–1975.* Cambridge: Cambridge University Press.

Beck, Nathaniel, and Jonathan N. Katz. 1996. "Nuisance vs. Substance: Specifying and Estimating Time-Series-Cross-Section Models." *Political Analysis* 6:1–36.

———. 1995. "What to Do (and Not to Do) with Time-Series-Cross-Section Data in Comparative Politics." *American Political Science Review* 89:634–47.

Benner, Mats. 1997. *The Politics of Growth: Economic Regulation in Sweden 1930–1994.* Lund: Arkiv.

Benner, Mats, and Torben B. Vad. 2000. "Sweden and Denmark." In Scharpf and Schmidt 2000b.

Berge, Anders. 1995. *Medborgarrätt och egenansvar: De sociala försäkringarna i Sverige 1901–1935.* Lund: Arkiv.

Bergqvist, Christina. 1998. "Still a Woman-Friendly Welfare State? The Case of Parental Leave and Child Care Policies in Sweden." Paper delivered at the Eleventh International Conference of Europeanists, Baltimore, February 26–March 1.

Blanchard, Olivier, and Justin Wolfers. 1999. "The Role of Shocks and Institutions in the Rise of European Unemployment: The Aggregate Evidence." Harry Johnson Lecture, Massachusetts Institute of Technology.

Block, Fred. 1977. "The Ruling Class Does Not Rule: Notes on the Marxist Theory of the State." *Socialist Revolution* 7:6–28.

Boix, Charles. 1998. *Political Parties, Growth, and Equality: Conservative and Social Democratic Economic Strategies in the World Economy.* New York: Cambridge University Press.

Bonoli, Giuliano. 1997. "Switzerland: The Politics of Consensual Retrenchment." In *Social Insurance in Europe.* Ed. Jochen Clasen, 107–29. Bristol: Policy Press.

Bonoli, Giuliano, and André Mach. 2000. "Switzerland: Adjustment Politics with Institutional Constraints." In Scharpf and Schmidt 2000b.

Borchorst, Anette. 1995. "A Political Niche: Denmark's Equal Status Council." In Stetson and Mazur 1995, 59–75.

———. 1994. "Welfare State Regimes, Women's Interests, and the EC." In Sainsbury 1994a, 26–44.

Braun, Dietmar. 1987. "Political Immobilism and Labor Market Performance: The Dutch Road to Mass Unemployment." *Journal of Public Policy* 7:307–35.

Bray, Mark, and David Nelson. 1996. "Industrial Relations Reform and the Relative Autonomy of the State." In Castles, Gerritsen, and Vowles 1996, 68–81.

Bussemaker, Jet, and Kees van Kersbergen. 1999. "Contemporary Social-Capitalist Welfare States and Gender Inequality." In Sainsbury 1999a, 15–46.

Cameron, David. 1978. "The Expansion of the Public Economy." *American Political Science Review* 72:1243–61.

Carlin, Wendy, and David Soskice. 1997. "Shocks to the System: The German Political Economy under Stress." *National Institute Economic Review* 1 (159): 57–76.

Carroll, Eero. 1999. *Emergence and Structuring of Social Insurance Institutions: Compara-*

*tive Studies on Social Policy and Unemployment Insurance.* Stockholm: Swedish Institute for Social Research.

Castles, Francis G. 1996. "Needs-Based Strategies of Social Protection in Australia and New Zealand." In Esping-Andersen, 1996b, 88–115.

———. 1992. "On Sickness Days and Social Policy." *Australian and New Zealand Journal of Sociology* 28:29–44.

———. 1985. *The Working Class and Welfare.* Sydney: Allen and Unwin.

———, ed. 1982. *The Impact of Parties.* Beverly Hills: Sage.

———. 1978. *The Social Democratic Image of Society.* London: Routledge and Kegan Paul.

Castles, Francis G., Rolf Gerritsen, and Jack Vowles, eds. 1996. *The Great Experiment.* Sydney: Allen and Unwin.

Castles, Francis, and Peter Mair. 1984. "Left-Right Political Scales: Some 'Expert' Judgments." *European Journal of Political Research* 12:73–88.

Castles, Francis, and Deborah Mitchell. 1993. "Worlds of Welfare and Families of Nations." In *Families of Nations: Public Policy in Western Democracies.* Ed. Francis G. Castles, 93–129. Brookfield, Vt.: Dartmouth.

Castles, Francis C., and Ian Shirley. 1996. "Labour and Social Policy." In Castles, Gerritsen, and Vowles 1996, 88–106.

Chapman, Robert. 1992. "From Labour to National." In Rice 1992, 351–84.

Cichon, Michael. 1999. "Notional Defined-Contribution Schemes: Old Wine in New Bottles?" *International Social Security Review* 52:87–105.

Clarke, F. G. 1992. *Australia: A Concise Political and Social History.* Sydney: Harcourt, Brace, Jovanovich.

Classon, Sigvard. 1986. *Vägen till ATP.* Karlskrona: Försäkringskasseförbundetsförlag.

Collier, Ruth Berins, and David Collier. 1992. *Shaping the Political Arena.* Princeton: Princeton University Press.

Cox, Robert H. 1994. "Social Entitlement and the Limits of Retrenchment: Welfare Cutbacks in Denmark and the Netherlands." Paper delivered at the Conference of Europeanists, Chicago, March 31–April 2.

———. 1993. *The Development of the Dutch Welfare State.* Pittsburgh: University of Pittsburgh Press.

Crawford, Aaron, Raymond Harbridge, and Kevin Hince. 1998. "Unions and Union Membership in New Zealand: Annual Review for 1997." *New Zealand Journal of Industrial Relations* 23:191–98.

Crepaz, Markus M. L. 1994. "From Semisovereignty to Sovereignty: The Decline of Corporatism and Rise of Parliament in Austria." *Comparative Politics* 27:45–65.

Cronin, James E. 1991. *The Politics of State Expansion: War, State, and Society in 20th Century Britain.* New York: Routledge.

Crouch, Colin. 1993. *Industrial Relations and European State Traditions.* Oxford: Clarendon Press.

Crowley, F. K. 1974. "1901–14." In *A New History of Australia.* Ed. F. K. Crowley, 260–311. New York: Holmes and Meier.

Cukierman, Alex, Steven B. Webb, and Bilin Neyapti. 1992. "Measuring the Independence of Central Banks." The World Bank Economic Review 6: 353–98.

388                                                      REFERENCES

Curtin, Jennifer, and Marian Sawer. 1996. "Gender Equity in the Shrinking State: Women and the Great Experiment." In Castles, Gerritsen, and Vowles 1996, 149–69.

Cusack, Thomas R. 1991. "The Changing Contours of Government." PIB Paper 91–304. Wissenschaftszentrum Berlin.

Cusack, Thomas R., and Geoffrey Garrett. 1994. "International Economic Change and the Politics of Government Spending, 1962–1988." Unpublished manuscript, Stanford University, Department of Political Science.

Cusack, Thomas R., Tom Notermans, and Martin Rein. 1989. "Political-Economic Aspects of Public Employment." *European Journal of Political Research* 17:471–500.

Cusack, Thomas R., and Martin Rein. 1991. "Social Policy and Service Employment." Unpublished paper, Wissenschaftszentrum, Berlin.

Cyba, Eva. 1996. "Modernisierung im Patriarchat? Zur Situation der Frauen in Arbeit, Bildung und privater Sphäre, 1945 bis 1995." In Sieder, Steinert, and Talos 1996, 435–57.

Czada, Roland. 1998. "Vereinigungskrise und Standortdebatte: Der Beitrag der Wiedervereinigung zur Krise des westdeutschen Modells." *Leviathan* 26, no. 1.

———. 1988. "Bestimmungsfaktoren und Genese politischer Gewerkschaftseinbindung." In *Staatstätigkeit: International und historisch vergleichende Analysen.* Ed. Manfred G. Schmidt, 24–59. Opladen: Westdeutscher Verlag.

Dachs, Herbert. 1996. "Von der 'Sanierungspartnerschaft' zur konfliktgeladenen Unübersichtlichkeit: Über politische Entwicklungen und Verschiebungen während der Grossen Koalition 1986 bis 1994." In Sieder, Steinert, and Talos 1996, 290–303.

Dahlström, Edmund. 1967. *The Changing Roles of Men and Women.* London: Gerald Duckworth.

Dahlziel, Paul, and Ralph Lattimore. 1996. *The New Zealand Macroeconomy: A Briefing on the Reforms.* Melbourne: Oxford University Press.

de Garis, B. K. 1974. "1890–1900." In *A New History of Australia.* Ed. F. K. Crowley, 216–59. New York: Holmes and Meier.

de Geer, Hans. 1989. *I Vänsterwind och Högervåg: SAF under 1970-Talet.* Stockholm: Allmänna Förlaget.

Dowrick, Stephen. 1996. "Swedish Economic Performance and Swedish Economic Debate: A View from Outside." *Economic Journal* 106:1772–99.

Durr, Robert H. 1992. "An Essay on Cointegration and Error Correction Models." In *Political Analysis.* Ed. John R. Freeman, 4:185–228. University of Michigan Press.

Easton, Brian. 1996. "Income Distribution." In *A Study in Economic Reform: The Case of New Zealand.* Ed. Brian Silverstone, Alan Bullard, and Ralph Lattimore, 101–38. Amsterdam: Elsevier.

———. 1981. *Pragmatism and Progress: Social Security in the Seventies.* Christchurch: University of Canterbury Publications.

———. 1980. *Social Policy and the Welfare State in New Zealand.* Sydney: Allen and Unwin.

Easton, Brian, and Rolf Gerritsen. 1996. "Economic Reform: Parallels and Divergences." In Castles, Gerritsen, and Vowles 1996, 22–47.

Ebbinghaus, Bernhard, and Anke Hassel. 1999. "The Role of Tripartite Concertation in the Reform of the Welfare State." *Transfer* 1–2: 64–81.

Ebbinghaus, Bernhard, and Philip Manow. 1998. "Studying Welfare State Regimes and Varieties of Capitalism: An Introduction." Paper presented at the Conference on Varieties of Welfare Capitalism. Max Planck Institute for the Study of Societies, Cologne, June 11–13.

Ebbinghaus, Bernhard, and Jelle Visser. 1992. "European Trade Unions in Figures." Unpublished manuscript, University of Amsterdam, Department of Sociology.

Eder, Hans. 1996. "Die Politik in der Ära Kreisky." In Sieder, Steinert, and Talos 1996, 186–99.

Elmér, Åke. 1969. *Från Fattigsverige till välfärdsstaten.* Stockholm: Bokförlaget Aldus/ Bonniers.

———. 1960. *Folkspensioneringen i Sverige.* Lund: Gleerups.

Elster, Jon. 1985. *Making Sense of Marx.* Cambridge: Cambridge University Press.

Enderle-Burcel, Gertrude. 1996. "Die österreichischen Parteien 1945 bis 1955." In Sieder, Steinert, and Talos 1996, 80–93.

Engle, Robert F., and C. W. J. Granger, eds. 1991. *Long Run Relationships: Readings in Cointegration.* New York: Oxford University Press.

Erixon, Lennart. 1997. *The Golden Age of the Swedish Model.* Oslo: Institute for Social Research.

———. 1996. "The Swedish Model." Unpublished paper, Arbetslivscentrum, Stockholm.

———. 1987. *Profitability in Swedish Manufacturing.* Stockholm: Swedish Institute for Social Research.

———. 1985. *What's Wrong with the Swedish Model?* Stockholm: Institutet för Social Forskning, Meddelande 12.

Esping-Andersen, Gøsta. 1999. *Social Foundations of Postindustrial Economies.* Oxford: Oxford University Press.

———. 1996a. "Welfare States at the End of the Century: The Impact of Labor Market, Family, and Demographic Change." Paper presented at the OECD conference Toward 2000: The New Social Policy Agenda.

———, ed. 1996b. *Welfare States in Transition.* London: Sage.

———. 1996c. "Welfare States without Work: The Impasse of Labour Shedding and Familialism in Continental European Social Poicy." In Esping-Andersen 1996b, 66–87.

———. 1990. *The Three Worlds of Welfare Capitalism.* Princeton: Princeton University Press.

———. 1985. *Politics against Markets.* Princeton: Princeton University Press.

Esping-Andersen, Gøsta, and Jon Eivind Kolberg. 1992. "Welfare States and Employment Regimes." In *The Study of Welfare State Regimes.* Ed. Jon Eivind Kolberg, 3–36. Armonk, N.Y.: M. E. Sharpe.

EUTI. 1987. *Women and Trade Unions in Western Europe.* Brussels: European Trade Union Institute.

Fearon, James D. 1996. "Causes and Counterfactuals in Social Science: Exploring an Analogy between Cellular Automata and Historical Processes." In *Counterfactual Thought Experiments in World Politics: Logical, Methodological, and Psychological Perspectives.* Ed. Philip E. Tetlock and Aaron Belkin, 39–67. Princeton: Princeton University Press.

Feldt, Kjell-Olof. 1991. *Alla Dessa Dagar . . . I Regeringen 1982–1990*. Stockholm: Norstedts.

Ferner, Anthony, and Richard Hyman, eds. 1992. *Industrial Relations in the New Europe*. Oxford: Basil Blackwell.

Ferree, Myra Marx. 1995. "Making Equality: The Women's Affairs Offices in the Federal Republic of Germany." In Stetson and Mazur 1995, 95–113.

Flanagan, Robert J., David. W. Soskice, and Lloyd Ulman. 1983. *Unionism, Economic Stabilization, and Incomes Policies: European Experience*. Washington: Brookings Institution.

Flora, Peter, ed. 1986. *Growth to Limits: The Western European Welfare States since World War II*. Berlin: Walter de Gruyter.

Flora, Peter, and Jens Alber. 1981. "Modernization, Democratization, and the Development of Welfare States in Western Europe." In Flora and Heidenheimer 1981, 37–80.

Flora, Peter, and Arnold J. Heidenheimer, eds. 1981. *The Development of Welfare States in Europe and America*. New Brunswick, N.J.: Transaction Books.

Freeman, Richard. 1995. "The Limits of Wage Flexibility to Curing Unemployment." *Oxford Review of Economic Policy* 11:63–72.

Furåker, Bengt, Leif Johansson, and Jens Lind. 1990. "Unemployment and Labour Market Policies in the Scandinavian Countries." *Acta Sociologica* 33:141–64.

Galant, Henry. 1955. *Histoire politique de la Sécurité Sociale Française, 1945–1952*. Cahiers de la Fondation Nationale des Sciences Politiques. Paris: Librairie Armand Colin.

Ganghof, Steffen. 2000. "Adjusting National Tax Policy to Economic Internationalization: Strategies and Outcomes." In Scharpf and Schmidt 2000b.

Garrett, Geoffrey. 1998. *Partisan Politics in the Global Economy*. New York: Cambridge University Press.

Garrett, Geoffrey, and Peter Lange. 1991. "Political Responses to Interdependence." *International Organization* 45:539–564.

Gauthier, Anne Helene. 1996. *The State and the Family: A Comparative Analysis of Family Policies in Industrialized Countries*. Oxford: Clarendon Press.

Gerlich, P. 1989. "Deregulation in Austria." *European Journal of Political Research* 17: 209–22.

Giddens, Anthony. 1973. *The Class Structure of Advanced Societies*. London: Hutchinson; New York: Harper and Row.

Glyn, Andrew. 1995. "The Assessment: Unemployment and Inequality." *Oxford Review of Economic Policy* 11:1–25.

Golden, Miriam, Peter Lange, and Michael Wallerstein. 1999. *Dataset on Unions, Employers, Collective Bargaining, and Industrial Relations for 16 OECD Countries*. http://www.shelley.polisci.ucla.edu/data.

Golden, Miriam, Michael Wallerstein, and Peter Lange. 1999. "Postwar Trade-Union Organization and Industrial Relations in Twelve Countries." In Kitschelt et al. 1999a, 194–230.

Gornick, Janet. 1999. "Gender Equality in the Labour Market." In Sainsbury 1999a, 210–42.

Gornick, Janet, Marcia K. Meyers, and Katherin E. Ross. 1998. "Public Policies and the Employment of Mothers: A Cross-National Study." *Social Science Quarterly* 79:35–54.

———. 1997. "Supporting the Employment of Mothers: Policy Variation across Fourteen Welfare States." *Journal of European Social Policy* 7:45–70.

Gough, Ian, Jonathan Bradshaw, J. Ditch, Tony Eardley, and Peter Whiteford. 1997. "Social Asistance in OECD Countries." *Journal of European Social Policy* 7:17–43.

Green-Pedersen, Christoffer. 1999. "Welfare State Retrenchment in Denmark and the Netherlands 1982–1998." Paper presented at the Eleventh SASE Conference, Madison, Wis., July 8–11.

Grünwald, Oskar. 1982. "Austrian Industrial Structure and Industrial Policy." In *The Political Economy of Austria*. Ed. Sven W. Arndt, 130–49. Washington: American Enterprise Institute for Public Policy Research.

Guger, Alois, and Wolfgang Polt. 1994. "Corporatism and Incomes Policy in Austria: Experiences and Perspectives." In *The Return to Incomes Policy*. Ed. Ronald Dore, Robert Boyer, and Zoe Mars, 141–60. London: Pinter Pusblishers.

Gustafsson, Siv. 1994. "Childcare and Types of Welfare States." In Sainsbury 1994a, 45–61.

Hadenius, Stig, Hans Wieslander, and Björn Molin. 1991. *Sverige efter 1900*. Stockholm: Bonniers.

Hagen, Kåre. 1992. "The Interaction of Welfare States and Labor Markets." In *The Study of Welfare State Regimes*. Ed. Jon Eivind Kolberg, 124–68. Armonk, N.Y.: M. E. Sharpe.

Hall, Peter. 1999. "The Political Economy of Europe in an Era of Interdependence." In Kitschelt et al. 1999a, 135–63.

———. 1998. "Organized Market Economies and Unemployment in Europe: Is It Finally Time to Accept the Liberal Orthodoxy?" Paper delivered at the Eleventh International Conference of Europeanists, Baltimore, February 26–28.

———. 1986. *Governing the Economy: The Politics of State Intervention in Britain and France*. New York: Oxford University Press.

Hall, Peter, and Robert J. Franzese. 1998. "Mixed Signals: Central Bank Independence, Coordinated Wage Bargaining, and European Monetary Union." *International Organization* 52:505–35.

Hancke, Bob, and David Soskice. 1996. "Coordination and Restructuring in Large French Firms." Discussion paper, Wissenschaftszentrum, Berlin.

Haschek, Helmut H. 1982. "Trade, Trade Finance, and Capital Movements." *The Political Economy of Austria*. Ed. Sven W. Arndt, 176–98. Washington: American Enterprise Institute for Public Policy Research.

Hawke, Gary. 1992. "Economic Trends and Economic Policy, 1938–1992." In Rice 1992, 412–50.

Headey, Bruce. 1970. "Trade Unions and National Wages Policy." *Journal of Politics* 32:407–39.

Heclo, Hugh. 1974. *Modern Social Politics in Britain and Sweden*. New Haven: Yale University Press.

Hemerijck, Anton C., and Robert C. Kloosterman. 1994. "The Postindustrial Transition of Welfare Corporatism." Paper delivered at the Conference of Europeanists, Chicago, March 31–April 2.

Hemerijck, Anton C., and Kees van Kersbergen. 1997. "A Miraculous Model? Explaining the New Politics of the Welfare State in the Netherlands." Unpublished manuscript, Free University, Amsterdam.

Hernes, Gudmund. 1991. "The Dilemmas of Social Democracies." *Acta Sociologica* 34:239–60.

Hernes, Helga Maria. 1987. *Welfare State and Woman Power: Essays in State Feminism.* Oslo: Norwegian University Press.

Hicks, Alexander. 1999. *Social Democracy and Welfare Capitalism: A Century of Income Security Policies.* Ithaca: Cornell University Press.

———. 1994. "Introduction to Pooling." In Janoski and Hicks 1994, 169–88.

Hicks, Alexander, and Lane Kenworthy. 1998. "Cooperation and Political Economic Performance in Affluent Democratic Capitalism." *American Journal of Sociology* 103:1631–72.

Hicks, Alexander, and Joya Misra. 1993. "Political Resources and the Growth of Welfare in Affluent Capitalist Democracies, 1960–82." *American Journal of Sociology* 99:668–710.

Hicks, Alexander, and Duane Swank. 1992. "Politics, Institutions, and Welfare Spending in Industrialized Democracies, 1960–1982." *American Political Science Review* 86:658–74.

———. 1984. "On the Political Economy of Welfare Expansion: A Comparative Analysis of 18 Advanced Capitalist Democracies, 1960–1971." *Comparative Political Studies* 17:81–118.

Hill, Dana Carol Davis, and Lean M. Tigges. 1995. "Gendering the Welfare State: A Cross-National Study of Women's Public Pension Quality." *Gender and Society* 9:99–119.

Hinnfors, Jonas. 1999. "Stability through Change: Swedish Parties and Family Policies, 1960–1980." In Torstendahl 1999, 105–32.

———. 1992. *Familjepolitik: Samhällsförändringar och partistrategier 1960–1990.* Stockholm: Almqvist och Wiksell.

Hinrichs, Karl. 1998. "Reforming the Public Pension Scheme in Germany: The End of the Traditional Consensus?" Paper presented at the Fourteenth World Congress of Sociology, Montreal, July 26–August 1.

———. 1991. "Public Pensions and Demographic Change." *Society* 28:32–37.

Hobson, Barbara. 1998. "Recognition and Redistribution: The Interplay between Identities and Institutions." Paper presented at the Annual Meetings of the American Sociological Association, San Francisco, August 21–24.

———. 1994. "Welfare Policy Regimes, Solo Mothers, and the Logics of Gender." In Sainsbury 1994a, 170–87.

———. 1990. "No Exit, No Voice: Women's Economic Dependency and the Welfare State." *Acta Sociologica* 33:235–50.

Hobson, Barbara, and Marika Lindholm. 1997. "Collective Identities, Women's Power Resources, and the Construction of Citizenship Rights in Welfare States." *Theory and Society* 26:475–508.

Hockerts, Hans Günter. 1992. "Vom Nutzen und Nachteil parlamentarischer Parteienkonkurrenz: Die Rentenreform 1972—ein Lehrstück." In *Staat und Parteien: Festschrift für Rudolf Morsey zum 65. Geburtstag.* Ed. Karl Dietrich Bracher, 903–34. Berlin: Duncker und Humblot.

———. 1980. *Sozialpolitische Entscheidungen im Nachkriegsdeutschland: Alliierte und deutsche Sozialversicherungspolitik 1945 bis 1957.* Stuttgart: Klett-Cotta.

Hofmeister, Herbert. 1981. "Landesbericht Österreich." In *Ein Jahrhundert Sozialversicherung in der Bundesrepublik Deutschland, Frankreich, Grossbritannien, Österreich und der Schweiz.* Ed. Peter A. Köhler and Hans F. Zacher, 445–730. Berlin: Duncker und Humblot.

Hollingsworth, Rogers, Philippe Schmitter, and Wolfgang Streeck, eds. 1994. *Governing Capitalist Economies.* New York: Oxford University Press.

Huber, Evelyne, Charles Ragin, and John D. Stephens. 1997. Comparative Welfare States Data Set, Northwestern University and University of North Carolina. http://www.lis .ceps.lu/compwsp.htm.

———. 1993. "Social Democracy, Christian Democracy, Constitutional Structure, and the Welfare State." *American Journal of Sociology* 99:711–49.

Huber, Evelyne, Dietrich Rueschemeyer, and John D. Stephens. 1997. "The Paradoxes of Contemporary Democracy: Formal, Participatory, and Social Dimensions." *Comparative Politics* 29:323–42.

Huber, Evelyne, and John D. Stephens. 2000a. "Partisan Governance, Women's Employment, and the Social Democratic Service State." *American Sociological Review* 45: 323–42.

———. 2000b. "The Political Economy of Pension Reform: Latin America in Comparative Perspective." Geneva: United Nations Research Institute for Social Development.

———. 1998. "Internationalization and the Social Democratic Model." *Comparative Political Studies* 31:353–97.

———. 1993a. "Political Parties and Public Pensions: A Quantitative Analysis." *Acta Sociologica* 36:309–25.

———. 1993b. "The Swedish Welfare State at the Crossroads." *Current Sweden,* no. 394, January, 1–8.

ILO. 1987. *World Labor Report.* Oxford: Oxford University Press.

Immergut, Ellen. 1992. *The Political Construction of Interests: National Health Insurance Politics in Switzerland, France, and Sweden, 1930–1970.* New York: Cambridge University Press.

———. 1986. "Between State and Market: Sickness Benefits and Social Control." In *Public/Private Interplay in Social Protection.* Ed. Martin Rein and Lee Rainwater, 57–148. Armonk, N.Y.: M. E. Sharpe.

Ingham, Geoffrey K. 1974. *Strikes and Industrial Conflict.* London: Macmillan.

Iversen, Torben. 2000. "The Dynamics of Welfare State Expansion: Trade Openness, Deindustrialization, and Partisan Politics." In Pierson 2000a.

———. 1999. *Contested Economic Institutions: The Politics of Macroeconomics and Wage Bargaining in Advanced Democracies.* New York: Cambridge University Press.

———. 1998. "Wage Bargaining, Central Bank Independence, and the Real Effects of Money." *International Organization* 52:469–504.

———. 1996. "Power, Flexibility, and the Breakdown of Centralized Wage Bargaining: The Cases of Denmark and Sweden in Comparative Perspective." *Comparative Politics* 28:399–436.

Iversen, Torben, Jonas Pontusson, and David Soskice, eds. 2000. *Unions, Employers, and Central Banks: Macroeconomic Coordination and Institutional Change in Social Market Economies.* New York: Cambridge University Press.

Jacobi, Otto, Berndt Keller, and Walther Mueller-Jentsch. 1992. "Germany: Codetermining the Future?" In Ferner and Hyman 1992, 218–73.

Janoski, Thomas. 1990. *The Political Economy of Unemployment: Active Labor Market Policy in West Germany and the United States.* Berkeley and Los Angeles: University of California Press.

Janoski, Thomas, and Antonio Alas. Forthcoming. "Work, Training, or the Dole? Active and Passive Labor Market Policies in Western Europe." In *Models of Capitalism: Lessons for Latin America.* Ed. Evelyne Huber. University Park: Pennsylvania State University Press

Janoski, Thomas, and Alexander Hicks, eds. 1994. *The Comparative Political Economy of the Welfare State.* New York: Cambridge University Press.

Jenson, Jane. 1986. "Gender and Reproduction: Or, Babies and the State." *Studies in Political Economy* 20:9–46.

Jenson, Jane, and Rianne Mahon. 1993. "Representing Solidarity: Class, Gender, and the Crisis in Social-Democratic Sweden." *New Left Review* 201:76–100.

Johnston, Richard, and Jack Vowles. 1997. "The New Rules and the New Game in New Zealand Elections." Paper delivered at the Meetings of the American Political Science Association, Washington, August 28–31.

Kangas, Olli. 1991. *The Politics of Social Rights.* Stockholm: Swedish Institute for Social Research.

———. 1990. *The Politics of Universalism: The Case of Finnish Sickness Insurance.* Publication D-129. Helsinki: School of Economics.

———. 1988. "Politik och ekonomi i pensionsfösäkringen." Stockholm: Institutet för Social Forskning, Meddelande 5.

Kangas, Olli, and Joakim Palme. 1993. "Statism Eroded? Labor-Market Benefits and Challenges to the Scandinavian Welfare States." In *Welfare Trends in the Scandinavian Countries.* Ed. Erik Jørgen Hansen, Robert Erikson, Stein Ringen, and Hannu Uusitalo, 3–24. Armonk, N.Y.: M. E. Sharpe.

Katzenstein, Peter. 1987. *Politics and Policy in West Germany: The Growth of a Semisovereign State.* Philadelphia: Temple University Press.

———. 1985. *Small States in World Markets: Industrial Policy in Europe.* Ithaca: Cornell University Press.

———. 1984. *Corporatism and Change: Austria, Switzerland, and the Politics of Industry.* Ithaca: Cornell University Press.

———. 1982. "Commentary." In *The Political Economy of Austria.* Ed. Sven W. Arndt, 151–55. Washington: American Enterprise Institute for Public Policy Research.

Kelsey, Jane. 1995. *Economic Fundamentalism*. London: Pluto Press.

———. 1993. *Rolling Back the State: Privatization of Power in Aotearoa/New Zealand*. Wellington: Bridget Williams Books.

Kewley, T. H. 1980. *Australian Social Security Today: Major Developments from 1900 to 1978*. Sydney: Sydney University Press.

———. 1973. *Social Security in Australia 1900–72*. Sydney: Sydney University Press.

Kilkey, Majella, and Jonathan Bradshaw. 1999. "Lone Mothers, Economic Well-Being, and Policies." In Sainsbury 1999a, 147–84.

King, Desmond. 1995. *Actively Seeking Work? The Politics of Unemployment and Welfare Policy in the United States and Great Britain*. Chicago: University of Chicago Press.

King, Desmond, and Mark Wickham-Jones. 1998. "Training without the State? New Labour and Labour Markets." *Policy and Politics* 26:439–55.

King, Desmond, and Stewart Wood. 1999. "The Political Economy of Neo-liberalism." In Kitschelt et al. 1999a, 371–97.

King, Gary, Robert Keohane, and Sidney Verba. 1994. *Designing Social Inquiry: Scientific Inference in Qualitative Research*. Princeton: Princeton University Press.

Kitschelt, Herbert, Peter Lange, Gary Marks, and John D. Stephens, eds. 1999a. *Continuity and Change in Contemporary Capitalism*. New York: Cambridge University Press.

———. 1999b. "Convergence and Divergence in Advanced Capitalist Democracies." In Kitschelt et al. 1999a, 427–60.

Kjellberg, Anders. 1992. "Sweden: Can the Model Survive?" In Ferner and Hyman 1992, 88–142.

Klausen, Jytte. N.d. "Political Institutions and Economic Interests: Comparative Theory and the Origins of Swedish and British Wage Policy." Unpublished paper, Brandeis University, Department of Politics.

Kohl, Jürgen. 1981. "Trends and Problems in Postwar Public Expenditure Development in Western Europe and North America." In Flora and Heidenheimer 1981, 307–44.

Kolbe, Wiebke. 1999. "Gender and Parenthood in West German Family Politics from the 1960s to the 1980s." In Torstendahl 1999, 133–68.

Korpi, Walter. 1996. "Eurosclerosis and the Sclerosis of Objectivity: On the Role of Values among Economic Policy Experts." *Economic Journal* 106:1727–46.

———. 1989. "Power, Politics, and State Autonomy in the Development of Social Citizenship: Social Rights during Sickness in Eighteen OECD Countries since 1930." *American Sociological Review* 54:309–29.

———. 1983. *The Democratic Class Struggle*. London: Routledge and Kegan Paul.

———. 1980. "Approaches to the Study of Poverty in the United States: Critical Notes from a European Perspective." Working Paper no. 64. Stockholm: Swedish Institute for Social Research.

———. 1978. *The Working Class in Welfare Capitalism*. London: Routledge and Kegan Paul.

Korpi, Walter, and Joakim Palme. 1998. "The Strategy of Equality and the Paradox of Redistribution." *American Sociological Review* 63:661–87.

Koven, Seth, and Sonia Michel, eds. 1993. *Mothers of the New World: Maternalist Politics and the Origins of the Welfare State*. New York: Routledge.

Kriesi, Hanspeter. 1980. *Entscheidungsstrukturen und Entscheidungsprozesse in der Schweizer Politik.* Frankfurt: Campus Verlag.

Kuhnle, Stein. 1986. "Norway." In Flora 1986, 1:117–96.

————. 1983. Velferedsstatens utvikling: Norge i komparativt perspektiv. Oslo: Universitetsforlaget.

Kunkel, Christoph, and Jonas Pontusson. 1998. "Corporatism versus Social Democracy: Divergent Fortunes of the Austrian and Swedish Labour Movements. *West European Politics* 21, no. 2 (April): 1–31.

Kurzer, Paulette. 1993. *Business and Banking.* Ithaca: Cornell University Press.

Laugesen, Miriam. 2000. "Hidden Institutions: New Zealand Health Care Reform 1935–1995." Ph.D. thesis, Department of Political Science, University of Melbourne.

Lehmbruch, Gerhard. 1984. "Concertation and the Structure of Corporatist Networks." In *Order and Conflict in Contemporary Capitalism.* Ed. John H. Goldthorpe, 60–80. Oxford: Clarendon.

Leichter, Howard M. 1979. *A Comparative Approach to Policy Analysis: Health Care Policy in Four Nations.* New York: Cambridge University Press.

Leira, Arnlaug. 1993. "Mothers, Markets, and the State: A Scandinavian 'Model'?" *Journal of Social Policy* 22:329–47.

————. 1992. *Welfare States and Working Mothers: The Scandinavian Experience.* Cambridge: Cambridge University Press.

Lewis, Jane. 1994. "Gender, the Family, and Women's Agency in the Building of 'Welfare States': The British Case." *Social History* 19:37–55.

————. 1992. "Gender and the Development of Welfare Regimes." *Journal of European Social Policy* 2:159–73.

Lewis, Jane, and Gertrude Åström. 1992. "Equality, Difference, and State Welfare: Labor Market and Family Policies in Sweden." *Feminist Studies* 18:59–87.

Lijphart, Arend. 1984. *Democracies: Patterns of Majoritarian and Consensus Government in Twenty-One Countries.* New Haven: Yale University Press.

Lindblom, Charles. 1977. *Politics and Markets: The World's Political-Economic Systems.* New York: Basic Books.

Lipset, Seymour Martin. 1977. "Why No Socialism in the United States?" In *Sources of Contemporary Radicalism.* Ed. Seweryn Bialer and Sophia Sluzar. Boulder, Colo.: Westview Press.

————. 1963. *The First New Nation: The United States in Historical and Comparative Perspective.* New York: Basic Books.

Lipset, Seymour Martin, and Stein Rokkan, eds. 1967. *Party Systems and Voter Alignments.* New York: Free Press.

LO-SAP 1969. *Jämlikhet.* Stockholm: Bokförlaget Prisma.

Lovenduski, Joni. 1986. *Women and European Politics: Contemporary Feminism and Public Policy.* Amherst: University of Massachusetts Press.

Lubbers, R. F. M., and C. Lemckert. 1980. "The Influence of Natural Gas on the Dutch Economy." In *The Economy and Politics of the Netherlands since 1945.* Ed. Richard T. Griffiths, 87–114. The Hague: Martinus Nijhoff.

Lukes, Stephen. 1975. *Power: A Radical View.* London: Macmillan.

Maier, Charles. 1985. "Inflation and Stagnation as Politics and History." In *The Politics of Inflation and Economic Stagnation*. Ed. Leon Lindberg and Charles Maier, 3–24. Washington: Brookings Institution.

Maioni, Antonia. 1998. *Explaining Differences in Welfare State Development: A Comparative Study of Health Insurance in Canada and the United States*. Princeton: Princeton University Press.

Mann, Michael. 1973. *Consciousness and Action among the Western Working Class*. London: Macmillan.

Manow, Philip, and Eric Seils. 1999. "'Adjusting Badly': The German Welfare State, Structural Change, and the Open Economy." Paper delivered at the conference on the Adjustment of National Employment and Social Policy to Economic Internationalization, Ringberg Castle, Germany, February 17–20.

Marklund, Steffan. 1988. *Paradise Lost?* Lund: Arkiv.

Marmor, Theodore R., Jerry Mashaw, and Philip L. Harvey. 1990. *America's Misunderstood Welfare State*. New York: Basic Books.

Martin, Andrew. 2000. "The Politics of Macroeconomic Policy and Wage Negotiations in Sweden." In Iversen, Pontusson, and Soskice 2000, 232–64.

———. 1996. "Macroeconomic Policy, Politics, and the Demise of Central Wage Negotiations in Sweden." Working Paper no. 63. Cambridge: Harvard University Center for European Studies.

———. 1991. *Wage Bargaining and Swedish Politics: The Implications of the End of Central Negotiations*. Stockholm: FIEF.

———. 1985. "Distributive Conflict, Inflation, and Investment: The Swedish Case." In *The Politics of Inflation and Stagnation*. Ed. Leon Lindberg and Charles Maier, 403–66. Washington: Brooking Institution.

———. 1984. "Trade Unions in Sweden: Strategic Responses to Change and Crisis." In *Unions and Economic Crisis: Britain, West Germany, and Sweden*. Ed. Peter Gourevitch et al. 189–359. London: Allen and Unwin.

Massey, Patrick. 1995. *New Zealand: Market Liberalization in a Developed Economy*. New York: St. Martin's Press.

McRobie, Alan. 1992. "The Politics of Volatility." In Rice 1992, 385–411.

Meidner, Rudolf, and Berndt Öhman. 1972. *Fifteen Years of Wage-Policy*. Stockholm: Swedish Trade Union Confederation.

Mitchell, Deborah. 1991. *Income Transfers in Ten Welfare States*. Brookfield: Avebury.

Mjøset, Lars. 1987. "Nordic Economic Policies in the 1970s and 1980s." *International Organization* 41:403–56.

———, ed. 1986. *Norden Dagen Derpå*. Oslo: Universitetsforlaget.

Mjøset, Lars, Ådne Cappelen, Jan Fagerberg, and Brent Sofus Tranøy. 1994. "Norway." In *The Contours of the West European Left*. Ed. Perry Andersen and Patrick Camiller, 55–76. London: Verso.

Moene, Karl Ove, and Michael Wallerstein. 1993. "The Decline of Social Democracy." In *The Economic Development of Denmark and Norway since 1879*. Ed. Karl Gunnar Persson. Gloschester, U.K.: Edward Elgar.

Moses, Jonathon W. 2000. *Open States in the Global Economy: The Political Economy of Small State Macroeconomic Management*. London: Macmillan.

———. 1994. "Abdication from National Policy Autonomy." *Politics and Society* 22:125–148.

Mosley, Layna. 1998. "Strong but Narrow: International Financial Market Pressures and Welfare State Policies." Paper presented at the Eleventh Annual Conference of Europeanists, Baltimore, February 26–28.

Müller, Wolfgang C. 1998. "Privatising in a Corporatist Economy: The Politics of Privatisation in Austria." *West European Politics* 11, no. 4 (October): 101–16.

Myles, John. 1997. "How to Design a 'Liberal' Welfare State: A Comparison of Canada and the United States." Paper presented at the Conference on Models of Capitalism and Latin American Development, University of North Carolina, Chapel Hill, May 23–24.

———. 1984. *Old Age and the Welfare State*. Boston: Little Brown.

Myles, John, and Paul Pierson. 2000. "The Political Economy of Pension Reform." In Pierson 2000a.

Neidhart, Leonard. 1970. *Plebiszit und pluralitäre Demokratie*. Bern: Francke Verlag.

Nickell, Stephen. 1997. "Unemployment and Labor Market Rigidities: Europe versus North America." *Journal of Economic Perspectives* 11:55–74.

Nørby Johansen, Lars. 1986. "Denmark." In Flora 1986, 1:293–381.

Norris, Pippa. 1987. *Politics and Sexual Equality: The Comparative Position of Women in Western Democracies*. Boulder, Colo.: Lynne Rienner.

O'Connor, Julia. 1996. "From Women in the Welfare State to Gendering Welfare State Regimes." *Current Sociology* 44:1–124.

O'Connor, Julia, and Gregg M. Olsen, eds. 1998. *Power Resource Theory and the Welfare State: A Critical Approach*. Toronto: University of Toronto Press.

O'Connor, Julia S., Ann Shola Orloff, and Sheila Shaver. 1999. *States, Markets, Families: Gender, Liberalism, and Social Policy in Australia, Canada, Great Britain, and the United States*. Cambridge: Cambridge University Press.

OECD. 1999a. *OECD Economic Survey: Austria 1999*. Paris: Organization for Economic Co-operation and Development.

———. 1999b. *OECD Economic Survey: Denmark 1999*. Paris: Organization for Economic Co-operation and Development.

———. 1999c. *OECD Economic Survey: Finland 1999*. Paris: Organization for Economic Co-operation and Development.

———. 1999d. *OECD Economic Survey: Norway 1999*. Paris: Organization for Economic Co-operation and Development.

———. 1999e. *OECD Economic Survey: Australia 1999*. Paris: Organization for Economic Co-operation and Development.

———. 1998a. *OECD Economic Survey: Austria 1998*. Paris: Organization for Economic Co-operation and Development.

———. 1998b. *OECD Economic Survey: Germany 1998*. Paris: Organization for Economic Co-operation and Development.

———. 1998c. *OECD Economic Survey: Netherlands 1998*. Paris: Organization for Economic Co-operation and Development.

———. 1997a. *OECD Economic Survey: Austria 1997*. Paris: Organization for Economic Co-operation and Development.

———. 1997b. *OECD Economic Survey: Netherlands 1997*. Paris: Organization for Economic Co-operation and Development.

———. 1996a. *OECD Economic Survey: Australia 1996*. Paris: Organization for Economic Co-operation and Development.

———. 1996b. *OECD Economic Survey: Germany 1996*. Paris: Organization for Economic Co-operation and Development.

———. 1996c. *OECD Economic Survey: Netherlands 1996*. Paris: Organization for Economic Co-operation and Development.

———. 1996d. *OECD Economic Survey: New Zealand 1996*. Paris: Organization for Economic Co-operation and Development.

———. 1995a. *OECD Economic Survey: Australia 1995*. Paris: Organization for Economic Co-operation and Development.

———. 1995b. *Historical Statistics 1960–1993*. Paris: Organization for Economic Co-operation and Development.

———. 1994a. *New Orientations for Social Policy*. Paris: Organization for Economic Co-operation and Development.

———. 1994b. *OECD Economic Survey: Sweden 1994*. Paris: Organization for Economic Co-operation and Development.

———. 1993a. *OECD Economic Survey: Austria 1993*. Paris: Organization for Economic Co-operation and Development.

———. 1993b. *OECD Economic Survey: Finland 1993*. Paris: Organization for Economic Co-operation and Development.

———. 1990. *Health Care Systems in Transition*. Paris: Organization for Economic Co-operation and Development.

OECD/HRDC. 2000. *Literacy in the Information Age: Final Report of the International Adult Literacy Survey*. Paris: Organization for Economic Co-operation and Development; [Ottawa]: Human Resources Development Canada.

Olivecrona, Gustaf. 1991. *Samtal med Ulf Laurin*. Stockholm: Fischer.

Olson, Mancur. 1982. *The Rise and Decline of Nations: Economic Growth, Stagflation and Social Rigidities*. New Haven: Yale University Press.

Olsson, Sven E. 1993. *Social Policy and Welfare State in Sweden*. 2d ed. Lund: Arkiv.

———. 1990. *Social Policy and Welfare State in Sweden*. Lund: Arkiv.

Orloff, Ann. 1997. "Motherhood, Work, and Welfare in the United States, Britain, Canada, and Australia." Paper presented at the conference Welfare States at the Crossroads, Sigtuna, Sweden, January 9–11.

———. 1996. "Gender in the Welfare State." *Annual Review of Sociology* 22:51–78.

———. 1993a. *The Politics of Pensions: A Comparative Analysis of Britain, Canada, and the United States, 1880–1940*. Madison: University of Wisconsin Press.

———. 1993b. "Gender and the Social Rights of Citizenship: The Comparative Analysis of Gender Relations and Welfare States." *American Sociological Review* 58:303–28.

Orszag, Peter R., and Joseph E. Stiglitz. 1999. "Rethinking Pension Reform: Ten Myths about Social Security Systems." Paper presented at the conference on New Ideas about Old Age Security, World Bank, Washington, September 14–15.

Osberg, Lars. 1995. "The Equity/Efficiency Trade-off in Retrospect." *Canadian Business Economics* 3:5–19.

Oskarson, Maria. 1992. "Sweden." In *Electoral Change.* Ed. Mark N. Franklin, Thomas T. Mackie, and Henry Valen with Clive Bean, 339–61. New York: Cambridge University Press.

Outshoorn, Joyce. 1995. "Administrative Accommodation in the Netherlands: The Department for the Coordination of Equality Policy." In Stetson and Mazur 1995, 168–85.

Palme, Joakim. 1994. "Recent Developments in Income Transfer Systems in Sweden." In Ploug and Kvist 1994, 39–60.

———. 1990. *Pension Rights in Welfare Capitalism.* Stockholm: Swedish Institute for Social Research.

Palme, Joakim, and Irene Wennemo. 1997. "Swedish Social Security in the 1990s: Reform and Retrenchment." CWR Working Paper 9,Centre for Welfare State Research, Copenhagen.

Pampel, Fred, and John Williamson. 1989. *Age, Class, Politics, and the Welfare State.* New York: Cambridge University Press.

———. 1988. "Welfare Spending in Advanced Industrial Democracies, 1950–1980." *American Journal of Sociology* 50:1424–56.

Parkin, Frank. 1971. *Class Inequality and Political Order.* New York: Praeger.

Pedersen, Susan. 1993. *Family, Dependence, and the Origins of the Welfare State: Britain and France, 1914–1945.* Cambridge: Cambridge University Press.

Pempel, T. J. Forthcoming. "Labor Exclusion and Privatized Welfare: Two Keys to Asian Capitalist Development." In *Models of Capitalism: Lessons for Latin America.* Ed. Evelyne Huber. University Park: Pennsylvania State University Press.

Pestoff, Victor. 1999. "The Disappearance of Social Partnership in Sweden during the 1990s and Its Sudden Reappearance in late 1998." Paper presented at the European Consortium for Political Research Joint Sessions, Mannheim, March 29–31.

———. 1998. *Beyond the Market and State: Social Enterprises and Civil Democracy in a Welfare State.* Brookfield, Vt.: Ashgate.

———. 1991. "The Demise of the Swedish Model and the Resurgence of Organized Business as a Major Political Actor." Working Paper, School of Business Administration, University of Stockholm.

Petersen, Klaus. 1998. *Legitimität und Krise: Die politische Geschichte des dänischen Wohlfahrtsstaates 1945–1973.* Berlin: Berlin Verlag.

Pierson, Paul, ed. 2000a. *The New Politics of the Welfare State.* New York: Oxford University Press.

———. 2000b. "Post-industrial Pressures on Mature Welfare States." In Pierson 2000a.

———. 1999. "Increasing Returns, Path Dependence an the Study of Politics." Unpublished paper, Harvard University, Center for European Studies.

———. 1996. "The New Politics of the Welfare State." *World Politics* 48:143–79.

———. 1994. *Dismantling the Welfare State?* New York: Cambridge University Press.

Piven, Frances Fox, and Richard Cloward. 1972. *Regulating the Poor.* New York: Vintage Books.

Ploug, Neils, and Jon Kvist, eds. 1994. *Recent Trends in Cash Benefits in Europe.* Copenhagen: Danish National Institute of Social Research.

Pontusson, Jonas. 1996. "Wage Distribution and Labor Market Institutions in Sweden, Austria, and Other OECD Countries." Working Paper no. 96.4. Ithaca: Cornell University, Institute for European Studies.

———. 1992a. "At the End of the Third Road." *Politics and Society* 20:305–332.

———. 1992b. *The Limits of Social Democracy: Investment Politics in Sweden.* Ithaca: Cornell University Press.

Pontusson, Jonas, and Peter Swenson. 1996. "Labor Markets, Production Strategies, and Wage Bargaining Institutions: The Swedish Employer Offensive in Comparative Perspective." *Comparative Political Studies* 29:223–50.

Przeworski, Adam, and Henry Teune. 1970. *The Logic of Comparative Social Inquiry.* New York: Wiley-Interscience.

Quinn, Dennis, and Carla Inclan. 1997. "The Origins of Financial Openness: A 21 Country Study of Its Determinants, 1950–1988." *American Journal of Political Science* 41:771–813.

Ragin, Charles. 1994. "A Qualitative Comparative Analysis of Pension Systems." In Janoski and Hicks 1994, 320–45.

———. 1987. *The Comparative Method: Moving beyond Qualitative and Quantitative Strategies.* Berkeley and Los Angeles: University of California Press.

Rice, Geoffrey, ed. 1992. *The Oxford History of New Zealand.* 2d ed. Auckland: Oxford University Press.

Richardson, Len. 1992. "Parties and Political Change." In Rice 1992, 201–29.

Roebroek, Joop, and Göran Therborn. N.d. "The Netherlands." Unpublished paper, University of Tilburg, Department for Social Security Science.

Rokkan, Stein. 1970. *Citizens, Elections, Parties.* New York: McKay.

———. 1967. "Geography, Religion, and Social Class: Crosscutting Cleavages in Norwegian Politics." In Lipset and Rokkan 1967, 367–444.

Rosenberger, Sieglinde. 1996. "Lieber gleich-berechtigt als später." In Sieder, Steinert, and Talos 1996, 354–69.

Rothstein, Bo. 1998. "Breakdown of Trust and the Fall of the Swedish Model." Paper delivered the 1998 Annual Meetings of the American Political Science Association, Boston, September 3–6.

———. 1992. "The Crisis of the Swedish Social Democrats and the Future of the Universal Welfare State." Paper delivered at the Eighth International Conference of Europeanists, Chicago, March 27–29.

Rowthorn, Robert. 1995. "Capital Formation and Unemployment." *Oxford Review of Economic Policy* 11:29–39.

Rueschemeyer, Dietrich, Evelyne Huber Stephens, and John D. Stephens. 1992. *Capitalist Development and Democracy.* Chicago: University of Chicago Press.

Rueschemeyer, Dietrich, and John D. Stephens. 1997. "Comparing Historical Sequences: A Powerful Tool for Causal Analysis." *Comparative Social Research* 16:55–72.

Ruggie, Mary. 1984. "Gender, Work, and Social Progress." In *Feminization of the Labor Force.* Ed. Jane Jenson, E. Hagen, and C. Reddy, 173–89. New York: Oxford University Press.

Russet, Bruce. 1970. *What Price Vigilance?* New Haven: Yale University Press.

Sainsbury, Diane, ed. 1999a. *Gender and Welfare State Regimes*. Oxford: Oxford University Press.

———. 1999b. "Taxation, Family Responsibilities, and Employment." In Sainsbury 1999a, 185–209.

———. 1996. *Gender, Equality, and Welfare States*. Cambridge: Cambridge University Press

———, ed. 1994a. *Gendering Welfare States*. London: Sage.

———. 1994b. "Women's and Men's Social Rights: Gendering Dimensions of Welfare States." In Sainsbury 1994a, 150–69.

———. 1992. "Welfare State Retrenchment and Restructuring." Paper delivered at the meetings of the American Political Science Association, Chicago, September 3–6.

Salminen, Kari. 1993. *Pension Schemes in the Making*. Helsinki: Central Pension Security Institute.

Saunders, Peter. 1994. *Welfare and Inequality: National and International Perspectives on the Australian Welfare State*. Melbourne: Cambridge University Press.

———. 1991. "Noncash Income and Relative Poverty in Comparative Perspective: Evidence from the Luxembourg Income Study." Paper delivered at the conference on Comparative Studies of Welfare State Development, Helsinki, August 29–September 1.

Scharpf, Fritz W. 2000. "Economic Changes, Vulnerabilities, and Institutional Capabilities." In Scharpf and Schmidt 2000a, 21–124.

———. 1997. "Balancing Sustainability and Security in Social Policy." In *Family, Market, and Community: Equity and Efficiency in Social Policy,* Social Policy Studies no. 21. Ed. OECD, 211–22. Paris: Organization for Economic Co-operation and Development.

———. 1991. *Crisis and Choice in European Social Democracy*. Ithaca: Cornell University Press.

Scharpf, Fritz W., and Vivien A. Schmidt, eds. 2000a. *Welfare and Work in the Open Economy*. Vol. 1. *From Vulnerability to Competitiveness*. Oxford: Oxford University Press.

———, eds. 2000b. *Welfare and Work in the Open Economy*. Vol. 2. *Diverse Responses to Common Challenges*. Oxford: Oxford University Press.

Schmidt, Manfred G. 1998. *Sozialpolitik in Deutschland: Historische Entwicklung und Internationaler Vergleich*. 2d ed. Opladen: Leske + Budrich.

———. 1992. *Wohlfahrtsstaatliche Politik unter bürgerlichen und sozialdemokratischen Regierungen: Ein internationaler Vergleich*. Frankfurt: Campus.

Schwartz, Herman. 2000. "Internationalization and Two Liberal Welfare States: Australia and New Zealand." In Scharpf and Schmidt 2000b.

———. 1998. Social Democracy Going Down or Down Under: Institutions, Internationalized Capital, and Indebted States." *Comparative Politics* 30:253–72.

———. 1994a. "Public Choice Theory and Public Choices: Bureaucrats and State Reorganization in Australia, Denmark, New Zealand, Sweden in the 1980s." *Administration and Society* 26:48–77.

———. 1994b. "Small States in Big Trouble: The Politics of State Organization in Australia, Denmark, New Zealand, and Sweden." *World Politics* 46:527–55.

Schwarz, B., and Björn Gustafsson. 1991. "Income Redistribution Effects of Tax Reforms in Sweden." *Journal of Policy Modeling* 13:551–70.

Seils, Eric, and Philip Manow. 2000. "Adjusting Badly: The German Welfare State, Structural Change, and the Open Economy." In Scharpf and Schmidt 2000b.

Seip, Anne-Lise. 1994. *Veiene til velferdstaten: Norsk Sosialpolitikk 1920–1975.* Oslo: Gyldendal.

Shalev, Michael. 1983. "The Social Democratic Model and Beyond: Two Generations of Comparative Research on the Welfare State." *Comparative Social Research* 6:315–51.

Shaver, Sheila. 1991. "'Considerations of Mere Logic': The Australian Age Pension and the Politics of Means Testing." In *States, Labor Markets, and the Future of Old Age Policy.* Ed. John Myles and Jill Quadagno, 105–26. Philadelphia: Temple University Press.

Sieder, Reinhard, Heinz Steinert, and Emmerich Talos, eds. 1996. *Österreich 1945–1995: Gesellschaft, Politik, Kultur.* Vienna: Verlag für Gesellschaftskritik.

Skocpol, Theda. 1992. *Protecting Mothers and Soldiers.* Cambridge: Harvard University Press.

———. 1988. "The Limits of the New Deal System and the Roots of Contemporary Welfare Dilemmas." In *The Politics of Social Policy in the United States.* Ed. Margaret Weir, Ann Shola Orloff, and Theda Skocpol, 293–312. Princeton: Princeton University Press.

Söderpalm, Sven Anders. 1980. *Arbetsgivarna och Saltsjöbadspolitiken.* Stockholm.

Sörensen, Kerstin. 1999. "Gender and the Social Democratic Regime Type." M.A. thesis, University of North Carolina, Department of Political Science.

Soskice, David. 2000. "Macroeconomic Analysis and the Political Economy of Unemployment." In Iversen, Pontusson, and Soskice 2000, 38–74.

———. 1999. "Divergent Production Regimes: Coordinated and Uncoordinated Market Economies in the 1980s and 1990s." In Kitschelt et al. 1999a, 101–34.

———. 1994. "Advanced Economies in Open World Markets and Comparative Institutional Advantages; Patterns of Business Coordination, National Institutional Frameworks and Company Product Market Innovation Strategies." Unpublished paper, Wissenschaftszentrum Berlin.

———. 1991. "The Institutional Infrastructure for International Competitiveness: A Comparative Analysis of the UK and Germany." In *Economics for the New Europe.* Ed. Anthony B. Atkinson and Renato Brunetta, 45–66. New York: New York University Press.

———. 1990. "Wage Determination: The Changing Role of Institutions in Advanced Industrial Countries." *Oxford Review of Economic Policy* 6:36–61.

Soskice, David, and Torben Iversen. 1998. "Multiple Wage Bargaining Systems in the Single European Currency Area." *Oxford Review of Economic Policy* 14:110–24.

Ståhlberg, Ann-Charlotte. 1990. "ATP-systemet från Fördelningspolitisk Synpunkt." In *Allmän Pension: Expertrapporter,* 97–188. Huvudbetänkande av Pensionberedningen, SOU 990.

Stallings, Barbara. 1995. *Global Change, Regional Response: The New International Context of Development.* New York: Cambridge University Press.

Stephens, Evelyne Huber. 1980. *The Politics of Workers' Participation: The Peruvian Approach in Comparative Perspective.* New York: Academic Press.

Stephens, Evelyne Huber, and John D. Stephens. 1986. *Democratic Socialism in Jamaica: The Political Movement and Social Transformation in Dependent Capitalism.* Princeton: Princeton University Press.

———. 1982. "The Labor Movement, Political Power, and Workers' Participation in Western Europe." *Political Power and Social Theory* 3:215–49.

Stephens, John. D. 2000. "Is Swedish Corporatism Dead? Thoughts on Its Supposed Demise in the Light of the Abortive 'Alliance for Growth' in 1998." Paper delivered at the Twelfth International Conference of Europeanists, Council of European Studies, Chicago, March 30–April 1.

———. 1996. "The Scandinavian Welfare States." In Esping-Andersen 1996b, 32–65.

———. 1995. "Preserving the Social Democratic Welfare State." *Nordic Journal of Political Economy* 22:143–61.

———. 1991. "Explaining Crossnational Differences in Union Organization: Why Are Small Countries More Organized than Large Ones?" *American Political Science Review* 85:941–49.

———. 1979a. "Class Formation and Class Consciousness." *British Journal of Sociology* 30:389–414.

———. 1979b. *The Transition from Capitalism to Socialism.* London: Macmillan.

———. 1976. "The Consequences of Social Structural Change for the Development of Socialism in Sweden." Ph.D. diss., Yale University.

Stephens, John D., Evelyne Huber, and Leonard Ray. 1999. "The Welfare State in Hard Times." In Kitschelt et al. 1999a, 164–93.

———. 1994. " The Welfare State in Hard Times." Paper presented at the conference on the Politics and Political Economy of Contemporary Capitalism. University of North Carolina, September 9–11.

Stetson, Dorothy McBride, and Amy G. Mazur, eds. 1995. *Comparative State Feminism.* Thousand Oaks: Sage.

Stinchcombe, Arthur. 1968. *Constructing Social Theories.* New York: Harcourt, Brace and World.

Streeck, Wolfgang. 1997. "German Capitalism: Does It exist? Can It Survive?" In *The Political Economy of Modern Capitalisms.* Ed. Colin Crouch and Wolfgang Streeck, 33–54. London: Sage.

———. 1994. "Pay Restraint without Incomes Policy: Institutionalized Monetarism and Industrial Unionism in Germany." In *The Return to Incomes Policy.* Ed. Ronald Dore, Robert Boyer, and Zoe Mars, 118–40. London: Pinter Publishers.

Stryker, Robin. 1989. "Limits on Technocratization of the Law: The Elimination of the National Labor Relations Board's Division of Economic Research." *American Sociological Review* 54:341–58.

Svallfors, Stefan. 1992. "Den Stabila Välfärdsopinionen: Attyder till Svensk Välfärdspolitik 1986–92." Unpublished paper, Umeå Universitet, Sociologsika Institutionen.

———. 1991. "The Politics of Welfare Policy in Sweden: Structural Determinants and Attitudinal Cleavages." *British Journal of Sociology* 42:609–34.

Swank, Duane. Forthcoming. *Diminished Democracy: Global Capital, Political Institu-*

*tions, the Welfare State in Advanced Economies.* Cambridge: Cambridge University Press.

———. 1999. "Global Markets, National Institutions, and the Public Economy in Developed Democracies." Paper presented at the Eleventh Annual Meeting of the Society for the Advancement of Socio-economics, Madison, July 8–11.

———. 1998. "Globalization, Democracy, and the Welfare State: Why Institutions Are So Significant in Shaping the Domestic Response to Internationalization." Political Economy of European Integration Working Paper, University of California Center for German and European Studies.

———. 1993. "Social Democracy, Equity, and Efficiency in an Interdependent World." Paper delivered at the Meetings of the American Political Science Association, Washington, September 2–5.

Swenson, Peter. Forthcoming. *Labor Markets and Welfare States: Employers in the Making of the American and Swedish Systems.*

———. 1999. "Varieties of Capitalist Interests and Illusions of Labor Power: Employers in the Making of the Swedish and American Welfare States." Paper presented at the Conference on Distribution and Democracy, Department of Political Science, Yale University, November 12–14.

———. 1991. "Bringing Capital Back In, or Social Democracy Reconsidered." *World Politics* 43:513–44.

Talos, Emmerich. 1996. "Der Sozialstaat: Vom 'goldenen Zeitalter' zur Krise." In Sieder, Steinert, and Talos 1996, 537–51.

———. 1981. *Staatliche Sozialpolitik in Österreich: Rekonstruktion und Analyse.* Vienna: Verlag für Gesellschaftskritik.

Talos, Emmerich, and Bernhard Kittel. 1996. "Sozialpartnerschaft: Zur Konstituierung einer Grundsäule der Zweiten Republik." In Sieder, Steinert, and Talos 1996, 107–21.

Thelen, Kathleen. 2000. "Why German Employers Cannot Bring Themselves to Dismantle the German Model." In Iversen, Pontusson, and Soskice 2000, 138–72.

Tichy, Gunther. 1996. "Austrokeynesianismus: Ein Konzept erfolgreicher Wirtschaftspolitik?" In Sieder, Steinert, and Talos 1996, 213–22.

Traxler, Franz. 1998. "Austria: Still the Country of Corporatism?" In *Changing Industrial Relations in Europe.* Ed. Anthony Ferner and Richard Hyman, 239–61. Oxford: Blackwell Publishers.

———. 1994. "Collective Bargaining: Levels and Coverage." *OECD Employment Outlook,* July, 167–94.

———. 1993. "European Transformation and Institution-Building in East and West: Preconditions and Performance of Neo-corporatism." Paper presented at the Conference on the End of the Cold War and Small European States. Minneapolis, October 29–31.

———. 1992. "Austria: Still the Country of Corporatism?" In Ferner and Hyman 1992, 270–97.

Torstendahl, Rolf, ed. 1999. *State Policy and Gender System in the Two German States and Sweden 1945–1989.* Sweden: University of Uppsala, Department of History.

Tsebelis, George. 1995. "Decision Making in Political Systems: Veto Players in Presidentialism, Parliamentarism, Multicameralism, and Multipartyism." *British Journal of Political Science* 25:289–325.

Tufte, Edward. 1978. *Political Control of the Economy*. Princeton: Princeton University Press.

UN. 1996. *World Populations Prospects: The 1996 Revision*. New York: Population Division, Department of Economic and Social Affairs of the United Nations Secretariat.

Urwin, Derek W. 1980. *From Ploughshare to Ballot Box: The Politics of Agrarian Defence in Europe*. New York: Columbia University Press.

Valen, Henry. 1992. "Norway." In *Electoral Change*. Ed. Mark N. Franklin, Thomas T. Mackie, and Henry Valen with Clive Bean, 307–26. New York: Cambridge University Press.

Van der Knaap, G. A. 1980. "Sectoral and Regional Imbalances in the Dutch Economy. In *The Economy and Politics of the Netherlands since 1945*. Ed. Richard T. Griffiths, 115–34. The Hague: Martinus Nijhoff.

van Kersbergen, Kees. 1995. *Social Capitalism*. London: Routledge.

Vartiainen, Juhana. 1997. "Understanding State-Led Late Industrialization. In *Government and Growth*. Ed. Villy Bergström, 203–40. Oxford: Oxford University Press.

Visser, Jelle. 1992. "The Netherlands: The End of an Era and the End of a System." In Ferner and Hyman 1992, 323–56.

———. 1991. "Trends in Trade Union Membership." *Employment Outlook: July 1991*. Ed. OECD, 97–134. Paris: Organization for Economic Co-operation and Development.

Visser, Jelle, and Anton Hemerijck. 1997. *A Dutch Miracle: Job Growth, Welfare Reform, and Corporatism in the Netherlands*. Amsterdam: Amsterdam University Press.

Von Nordheim Nielsen, Fritz. 1991. "The Long Shadows of the Past: Scandinavian Pension Politics in the 1980s." In *States, Labor Markets, and the Future of Old Age Policy*. Ed. John Myles and Jill Quadagno, 127–74. Philadelphia: Temple University Press.

———. 1989. "The Scandinavian Model: Reformist Road to Socialism or Dead End Street?" EUI Working Paper no. 89/415, European University Institute, Florence.

Von Oertzen, Christine. 1999. "Women, Work, and the State: Lobbying for Part-Time Work and 'Practical Equality' in the West German Civil Service, 1958–1969." In Torstendahl 1999, 79–104.

von Wahl, Angelika. 1999. *Gleichstellungsregime: Berufliche Gleichstellung von Frauen in den USA und in der Budesrepublik Deutschland*. Opladen: Leske und Budrich.

Wallerstein, Michael. 1991. "Industrial Concentration, Country Size, and Union Membership: Response to Stephens." *American Political Science Review* 85:949–53.

———. 1989. "Union Organization in Advanced Industrial Democracies." *American Political Science Review* 83:481–501.

———. n.d. "Union Centralization and Trade Dependence." Unpublished manuscript, University of California at Los Angeles, Department of Political Science.

Wallerstein, Michael, and Miriam Golden. 1997. "The Fragmentation of the Bargaining Society: Wage Setting in the Nordic Countries, 1950–1992." *Comparative Political Studies* 30:699–731.

Weber, Max. [1922] 1968. *Economy and Society*. 2 vols. New York: Bedminster Press. 2d printing, Berkeley and Los Angeles: University of California Press. Translated from the German (4th ed. of *Wirtschaft und Gesellschaft*) by Ephraim Fischoff et al.

Weir, Margaret, Ann Shola Orloff, and Theda Skocpol. 1988. "Introduction: Understanding American Social Politics." In *The Politics of Social Policy in the United States*. Ed.

Margaret Weir, Ann Shola Orloff, and Theda Skocpol, 1–37. Princeton: Princeton University Press.

Weir, Margaret, and Theda Skocpol. 1985. "State Structures and the Possibilities for Keynesian Responses to the Great Depression in Sweden, Britain, and the United States." In *Bringing the State Back In.* Ed. Peter Evans, Dietrich Rueschemeyer, and Theda Skocpol, 106–63. New York: Cambridge University Press.

Wennemo, Irene. 1994. *Sharing the Costs of Children.* Stockholm: Swedish Institute for Social Research.

West Pedersen, Axel. 1990. *Fagbevegelsen og folketrygden: LO's målsetninger, strategi og innflytelse I pensjonspolitkken 1945–1966.* Oslo: FAFO.

Westergaard, John, and Henrietta Resler. 1975. *Class in a Capitalist Society.* New York: Basic Books.

Western, Bruce. 1997. *Between Class and Market: Postwar Unionization in the Capitalist Democracies.* Princeton: Princeton University Press.

———. 1991. "A Comparative Study of Corporatist Development." *American Sociological Review* 56:283–94.

Western, Bruce, and Katherine Beckett. 1999. "How Unregulated Is the U.S. Labor Market? The Penal System as a Labor Market Institution." *American Journal of Sociology* 104:1030–60.

Weyland, Kurt. 1996. *Democracy without Equity: Failures of Reform in Brazil.* Pittsburgh: University of Pittsburgh Press.

White, Kenneth. 1997. *Shazam: The Econometrics Computer Program, Version 8.0.* New York: McGraw-Hill.

Wierink, Marie. 1997. "Pays-Bas: Pensions de retraite." *Chronique Internationale de l'IRES,* no. 48 (September).

Wilensky, Harold. Forthcoming. *Rich Democracies: Political Economy, Public Policy, and Performance.* Berkeley and Los Angeles: University of California Press.

———. 1990. "Common Problems, Divergent Patterns: An 18-Nation Study of Family Policy." *Public Affairs Report* 31 (3): 1–3.

———. 1981. "Leftism, Catholicism, and Democratic Corporatism." In Flora and Heidenheimer 1981, 314–78.

———. 1975. *The Welfare State and Equality.* Berkeley and Los Angeles: University of California Press

Zimmerman, Erwin. 1986. *Neokorporative Politikformen in den Niederlanden: Industriepolitik, kollektive Arbeitsbeziehungen und hegemoniale Strukturen seit 1918.* Frankfurt am Main: Campus.

Zysman, John. 1983. *Governments, Markets, and Growth: Financial Systems and the Politics of Industrial Change.* Ithaca: Cornell University Press.

# INDEX

◆